# Points of View
Readings in American Government and Politics

# Points of View
## Readings in American Government and Politics
FIFTH EDITION

Edited by

Robert E. DiClerico
Allan S. Hammock
West Virginia University

**McGraw-Hill, Inc.**
New York  St. Louis  San Francisco  Auckland  Bogotá
Caracas  Lisbon  London  Madrid  Mexico  Milan
Montreal  New Delhi  Paris  San Juan  Singapore
Sydney  Tokyo  Toronto

**POINTS OF VIEW**
Readings in American Government and Politics

Copyright © 1992, 1989, 1986, 1983, 1980 by McGraw-Hill, Inc. All rights
reserved. Printed in the United States of America. Except as permitted under the
United States Copyright Act of 1976, no part of this publication may be
reproduced or distributed in any form or by any means, or stored in a data
base or retrieval system, without the prior written permission of the
publisher.

1 2 3 4 5 6 7 8 9 0 HAL HAL 9 0 9 8 7 6 5 4 3 2 1

ISBN 0-07-016849-0

This book was set in Times Roman by Better Graphics, Inc.
The editors were Bertrand W. Lummus and Fred H. Burns;
the production supervisor was Richard A. Ausburn.
The cover was designed by Fern Logan.
Arcata Graphics/Halliday was printer and binder.

Library of Congress Cataloging-in-Publication Data

Points of view: readings in American government and politics/edited
  by Robert DiClerico and Allan S. Hammock.—5th ed.
     p.      cm.
  ISBN 0-07-016849-0;
    1. United States—Politics and government.      I. DiClerico, Robert
E.     II. Hammock, Allan S., (date).
JK21.P59      1992
320.973—dc20

# About the Authors

ROBERT E. DICLERICO is a Professor of Political Science at West Virginia University. An Indiana University (Bloomington, Ind.) Ph.D. and a Danforth fellow, he is author of *The American President* (1983); co-author, *Few Are Chosen: Problems In Presidential Selection* (1984); and editor, *Analyzing the Presidency* (1985).

ALLAN S. HAMMOCK is an Associate Professor and Chairman of the Department of Political Science at West Virginia University. He received his Ph.D. from the University of Virginia and is the author of numerous professional papers and university publications.

# Contents

# CHAPTER 11

## Presidential Power   201

# CHAPTER 12

## President and Congress   215

# CHAPTER 13

## Bureaucracy   237

# CHAPTER 14

## The Supreme Court   259

# Preface

Reflecting the press of events, we have made numerous changes in this, the fifth edition of *Points of View*. One or more of the selections that fall under the topics of "Federalism," "Interest Groups," "Congress," "Bureaucracy," "The Supreme Court," "Civil Liberties" (Free Speech, Pornography), and "Civil Rights" (Abortion) have been changed.

The basic goals of the book remain the same—namely, to provide students with a manageable number of selections that present readable, thoughtful, and diverse perspectives across a broad range of issues related to American government.

We would like to take this opportunity to thank Bert Lummus, Political Science Editor at McGraw-Hill for his encouragement and assistance with this book over a period of several years. In addition, a very special debt of gratitude is owed to Fred H. Burns, who had primary editorial responsibility for this latest edition of *Points of View*. His keen eye for detail was instrumental in helping us to improve both the style and content of the final manuscript.

The authors are also grateful for the suggestions made by the following academicians who reviewed the current edition of the text: Manley Elliot Banks, Virginia Commonwealth University; Ken Collier, University of Kansas; Julia Flaherty, Midland College; John Gilbert, North Carolina State University—Raleigh; Carl Liberman, University of Akron; John F. Sitton, Indiana University of Pennsylvania; A. Jay Stephens, California State University—Long Beach; and David Weaver, Saginaw Valley State University.

Morgantown, West Virginia
December, 1990

R.E.D.
A.S.H.

# A Note to the Instructor

For some years now, both of us have jointly taught the introductory course to American government. Each year we perused the crop of existing readers, and while we adopted several different readers over this period, we were not wholly satisfied with any of them. It is our feeling that many of the readers currently on the market suffer from one or more of the following deficiencies: (1) Some contain selections which are difficult for students to comprehend because of the sophistication of the argument, the manner of expression, or both. (2) In many instances, readers do not cover all of the topics typically treated in an introductory American government course. (3) In choosing selections for a given topic, editors do not always show sufficient concern for how—or whether—one article under a topic relates to other articles under the same topic. (4) Most readers contain too many selections for each topic—indeed, in several cases the number of selections for some topics exceeds ten. Readers are nearly always used in conjunction with a textbook. Thus, to ask a student to read a lengthy chapter—jammed with facts—from a textbook and then to read anywhere from five to ten selections on the same topic from a reader is to demand that students read more than they can reasonably absorb in a meaningful way. Of course, an instructor need not assign all the selections under a given topic. At the same time, however, this approach justifiably disgruntles students who, after purchasing a reader, discover that they may only be asked to read one-half or two-thirds of it.

Instead of continuing to complain about what we considered to be the limitations of existing American government readers, we decided to try our own hand at putting one together. In doing so, we were guided by the following considerations:

## Readability

Quite obviously, students will not read dull, difficult articles. As well as having something important to say, we feel that each of the articles in *Points of View* is clearly written, well organized, and free of needless jargon.

## Comprehensiveness

The sixteen topics included in *Points of View* constitute all the major areas of concern that are typically treated in the standard introductory course to American government.

## Economy of Selections

We decided, in most instances, to limit the number of selections to two per topic, although we did include four selections for some topics that we deemed especially important. The limitation on selections will maximize the possibility that students will read them. It has been our experience that when students are assigned four, five, or more selections under a given topic, they simply do not read them all. In addition, by limiting the selections for each topic, there is a greater likelihood that students will be able to associate an argument with the author who made it.

## Juxtaposition

The two selections for each topic will take *opposing* or *different* points of view on some aspect of a given topic. This approach was chosen for three reasons. First, we believe that student interest will be enhanced by playing one article off against the other. Thus, the "interest" quality of a given article will derive not only from its own content, but also from its juxtaposition with the other article. Second, we think it is important to sensitize students to the fact that one's perspective on an issue will depend upon the values that he or she brings to it. Third, by having both selections focus on a particular issue related to a given topic, the student will have a greater depth of understanding about that issue. We think this is preferable to having five or six selections under a topic, with each selection focusing on a different aspect, and with the result that the student ultimately is exposed to "a little of this and a little of that"—that is, if the student even bothers to read all five or six selections.

While the readers currently available take into account one or, in some instances, several of the considerations identified above, we believe that the uniqueness of *Points of View* lies in the fact that it has sought to incorporate *all* of them.

*Robert E. DiClerico*
*Allan S. Hammock*

# Points of View
Readings in American Government and Politics

# 1

# Democracy

*Any assessment of a society's democratic character will be fundamentally determined by what the observer chooses to use as a definition of democracy. While the concept of democracy has commanded the attention of political thinkers for centuries, the following selections by Howard Zinn and Sidney Hook serve to demonstrate that there continues to be considerable disagreement over its meaning. Each of them has scanned the American scene and reached different conclusions regarding the democratic character of our society. This difference of opinion is explained primarily by the fact that each approaches his evaluation with a different conception of what democracy is.*

*For Zinn, the definition of democracy includes not only criteria which bear upon how decisions get made, but also upon what results from such decisions. Specifically, he argues that such results must lead to a certain level of human welfare within a society. In applying these criteria of human welfare to the United States, he concludes that we fall short of the mark in several areas.*

*Although Sidney Hook is willing to acknowledge that democracy may indeed function more smoothly in societies where the conditions of human welfare are high, he insists that these conditions do not themselves constitute the definition of democracy. Rather, he maintains that democracy is a process—a way of making decisions. Whether such decisions lead to the conditions of human welfare that Zinn prescribes is irrelevant. The crucial test, according to Hook, is whether or not the people have the right, by majority rule, to make choices about the quality of their lives—whatever those choices may be.*

# How Democratic Is America?

## Howard Zinn

To give a sensible answer to the question "How democratic is America?" I find it necessary to make three clarifying preliminary statements. First, I want to define "democracy," not conclusively, but operationally, so we can know what we are arguing about, or at least what I am talking about. Second, I want to state what my criteria are for measuring the "how" in the question. And third, I think it necessary to issue a warning about how a certain source of bias (although not the only source) is likely to distort our judgments.

Our definition is crucial. This becomes clear if we note how relatively easy is the answer to our question when we define democracy as a set of formal institutions and let it go at that. If we describe as "democratic" a country that has a representative system of government, with universal suffrage, a bill of rights, and party competition for office, it becomes easy to answer the question "how" with the enthusiastic reply, "Very!" . . .

I propose a set of criteria for the description "democratic" which goes beyond formal political institutions, to the quality of life in the society (economic, social, psychological), beyond majority rule to a concern for minorities, and beyond national boundaries to a global view of what is meant by "the people," in that rough, but essentially correct view of democracy as "government of, by, and for the people."

Let me list these criteria quickly, because I will go on to discuss them in some detail later:

1. To what extent can various people in the society participate in those decisions which affect their lives: decisions in the political process and decisions in the economic structure?
2. As a corollary of the above: do people have equal access to the information which they need to make important decisions?
3. Are the members of the society equally protected on matters of life and death—in the most literal sense of that phrase?
4. Is there equality before the law: police, courts, the judicial process—as well as equality *with* the law-enforcing institutions, so as to safeguard equally everyone's person, and his freedom from interference by others, and by the government?
5. Is there equality in the distribution of available resources: those economic goods necessary for health, life, recreation, leisure, growth?

Howard Zinn is a professor of political science at Boston University. This essay was originally published in Robert A. Goldwin, ed., *How Democratic Is America?* pp. 39–60 (Chicago: Rand McNally, 1971). The author revised and updated the original for *Points of View* in 1985.

6. Is there equal access to education, to knowledge and training, so as to enable persons in the society to live their lives as fully as possible, to enlarge their range of possibilities?
7. Is there freedom of expression on all matters, and equally for all, to communicate with other members of the society?
8. Is there freedom for individuality in private life, in sexual relations, family relations, the right of privacy?
9. To minimize regulation: do education and the culture in general foster a spirit of cooperation and amity to sustain the above conditions?
10. As a final safety feature: is there opportunity to protest, to disobey the laws, when the foregoing objectives are being lost—as a way of restoring them? . . .

Two historical facts support my enlarged definition of democracy. One is that the industrialized Western societies have outgrown the original notions which accompanied their early development: that constitutional and procedural tests sufficed for the "democracy" that overthrew the old order; that democracy was quite adequately fulfilled by the Bill of Rights in England at the time of the Glorious Revolution, the Constitution of the United States, and the declaration of the Rights of Man in France. It came to be acknowledged that the rhetoric of these revolutions was not matched by their real achievements. In other words, the limitations of that "democracy" led to the reformist and radical movements that grew up in the West in the middle and late nineteenth century. The other historical note is that the new revolutions in our century, in Africa, Asia, Latin America, while rejecting either in whole or in part the earlier revolutions, profess a similar democratic aim, but with an even broader rhetoric. . . .

My second preliminary point is on standards. By this I mean that we can judge in several ways the fulfillment of these ten criteria I have listed. We can measure the present against the past, so that if we find that in [1991] we are doing better in these matters than we were doing in 1860 or 1910, the society will get a good grade for its "democracy." I would adjure such an approach because it supports complacency. With such a standard, Russians in 1910 could point with pride to how much progress they had made toward parliamentary democracy; as Russians in [1985] could point to their post-Stalin progress away from the gulag; as Americans could point in 1939 to how far they had come toward solving the problem of economic equality; as Americans in the South could point in 1950 to the progress of the southern Negro. Indeed, the American government gives military aid to brutal regimes in Latin America on the ground that a decrease in the murders by semiofficial death squads is a sign of progress.

Or, we could measure our democracy against other places in the world. Given the high incidence of tyranny in the world, polarization of wealth, and lack of freedom of expression, the United States, even with very serious defects, could declare itself successful. Again, the result is to let us all off easily; some of our most enthusiastic self-congratulation is based on such a standard.

On the other hand, we could measure our democracy against an ideal (even if admittedly unachievable) standard. I would argue for such an approach, because, in what may seem to some a paradox, the ideal standard is the pragmatic one; it affects what we *do*. To grade a student on the basis of an improvement over past performance is justifiable if the intention is to encourage someone discouraged about his ability. But if he is rather pompous about his superiority in relation to other students (and I suggest this is frequently true of Americans evaluating American "democracy"), and if in addition he is a medical student about to graduate into a world ridden with disease, it would be best to judge him by an ideal standard. That might spur him to an improvement fast enough to save lives. . . .

My third preliminary point is a caution based on the obvious fact that we make our appraisals through the prism of our own status in society. This is particularly important in assessing democracy, because if "democracy" refers to the condition of masses of people, and if we as the assessors belong to a number of elites, we will tend (and I am not declaring an inevitability, just warning of a tendency) to see the present situation in America more benignly than it deserves. To be more specific, if democracy requires a keen awareness of the condition of black people, of poor people, of young people, of that majority of the world who are not American—and we are white, prosperous, beyond draft age, and American—then we have a number of pressures tending to dull our sense of inequity. We are, if not doomed to err, likely to err on the side of complacency—and we should try to take this into account in making our judgments.

## 1. PARTICIPATION IN DECISIONS

We need to recognize first, that whatever decisions are made politically are made by representatives of one sort or another: state legislators, congressmen, senators, and other elected officials, governors and presidents; also by those appointed by elected officials, like Supreme Court justices. These are important decisions, affecting our lives, liberties, and ability to pursue happiness. Congress and the president decide on the tax structure, which affects the distribution of resources. They decide how to spend the monies received, whether or not we go to war; who serves in the armed forces; what behavior is considered a crime; which crimes are prosecuted and which are not. They decide what limitations there should be on our travel, or on our right to speak freely. They decide on the availability of education and health services.

If representation by its very nature is undemocratic, as I would argue, this is an important fact for our evaluation. Representative government is *closer* to democracy than monarchy, and for this reason it has been hailed as one of the great political advances of modern times; yet, it is only a step in the direction of democracy, at its best. It has certain inherent flaws—pointed out by Rousseau in the eighteenth century, Victor Considerant in the nineteenth century, Robert Michels in the beginning of the twentieth century, Hannah Arendt in our own time. No representative can adequately represent another's needs; the representative tends to become a member of a special elite; he has privileges which weaken his sense of concern at others' grievances; the passions of the troubled lose force (as Madison noted in *The Federalist 10*) as they are filtered through the representative system; the elected official develops an expertise which tends toward its own perpetuation. Leaders develop what Michels called "a mutual insurance contract" against the rest of society. . . .

If only radicals pointed to the inadequacy of the political processes in the United States, we might be suspicious. But established political scientists of a moderate bent talk quite bluntly of the limitations of the voting system in the United States. Robert Dahl, in *A Preface to Democratic Theory,* drawing on the voting studies of American political scientists, concludes that "political activity, at least in the United States, is positively associated to a significant extent with such variables as income, socio-economic status, and education." He says:

> By their propensity for political passivity the poor and uneducated disfranchise themselves. . . . Since they also have less access than the wealthy to the organizational, financial, and propaganda resources that weigh so heavily in campaigns, elections, legislative, and executive decisions, anything like equal control over government policy is triply barred to the members of Madison's unpropertied masses. They are barred by their relatively greater inactivity, by their relatively limited access to resources, and by Madison's nicely contrived system of constitutional checks.[1]

Dahl thinks that our society is essentially democratic, but this is because he expects very little. (His book was written in the 1950s, when lack of commotion in the society might well have persuaded him that no one else expected much more than he did.) Even if democracy were to be superficially defined as "majority rule," the United States would not fulfill that, according to Dahl, who says that "on matters of specific policy, the majority rarely rules."[2] After noting that "the election is the critical technique for insuring that governmental leaders will be relatively responsive to nonleaders," he goes on to say that "it is important to notice how little a national election tells us about the preferences of majorities. Strictly speaking, all an election reveals is the first preferences of some citizens among the candidates standing for office."[3] About 45 percent of the potential voters in national elections, and about 60 percent of the voters in local elections do not vote, and this cannot be attributed, Dahl says, simply to indifference. And if, as Dahl points out, "in no large nation state can elections tell us much about the preferences of majorities and minorities," this is "even more true of the interelection period." . . .

Dahl goes on to assert that the election process and interelection activity "are crucial processes for insuring that political leaders will be *somewhat* responsive to the preferences of *some* ordinary citizens.''[4] I submit (the emphasized words are mine) that if an admirer of democracy in America can say no more than this, democracy is not doing very well.

Dahl tells us the election process is one of "two fundamental methods of social control which, operating together, make governmental leaders so responsive to nonleaders that the distinction between democracy and dictatorship still makes sense." Since his description of the election process leaves that dubious, let's look at his second requirement for distinguishing democracy: "The other method of social control is continuous political competition among individuals, parties, or both." What it comes down to is "not minority rule but minorities rule."[5]

If it turns out that this—like the election process—also has little democratic content, we will not be left with very much difference—by Dahl's own admission—between "dictatorship" and the "democracy" practiced in the United States. Indeed, there is much evidence on this: the lack of democracy within the major political parties, the vastly disproportionate influence of wealthy groups over poorer ones (what consumers' group in 1983 could match the $1 million spent by the Natural Gas Supply Association to lobby, in fifteen key congressional districts, for full control of natural gas prices?);[6] the unrepresentative nature of the major lobbies (the wealthy doctors speaking for all through the AMA, the wealthy farmers speaking for the poorer ones through the American Farm Bureau Federation, the most affluent trade unions speaking for all workers). All of this, and more, supports the idea of a "decline of American pluralism" that Henry Kariel has written about. What Dahl's democracy comes down to is "the steady appeasement of relatively small groups."[7] If these relatively small groups turn out to be the aircraft industry far more than the aged, the space industry far more than the poor, the Pentagon far more than the college youth—what is left of democracy?

Sometimes the elitism of decision-making is defended (by Dahl and by others) on the ground that the elite is enacting decisions passively supported by the mass, whose tolerance is proof of an underlying consensus in society. But Murray Levin's studies in *The Alienated Voter* indicate how much nonparticipation in elections is a result of hopelessness rather than approval. And Robert Wiebe, a historian at Northwestern University, talks of "consensus" becoming a "new stereotype." He approaches the question historically.

> Industrialization arrived so peacefully not because all Americans secretly shared the same values or implicitly willed its success but because its millions of bitter enemies lacked the mentality and the means to organize an effective counterattack.[8]

Wiebe's point is that the passivity of most Americans in the face of elitist decision-making has not been due to acquiescence but to the lack of resources for effective combat, as well as a gulf so wide between the haves and have-nots that there was no ground on which to dispute. Americans neither revolted violently nor reacted at the polls; instead they were subservient, or else worked out their hostilities in personal ways. . . .

Presidential nominations and elections are more democratic than monarchical rule or the procedures of totalitarian states, but they are far from some reasonable expectation of democracy. The two major parties have a monopoly of presidential power, taking turns in the White House. The candidates of minority parties don't have a chance. They do not have access to the financial backing of the major parties, and there is not the semblance of equal attention in the mass media; it is only the two major candidates who have free access to prime time on national television.

More important, both parties almost always agree on the fundamentals of domestic and foreign policy, despite the election-year rhetoric which attempts to find important differences. Both parties arranged for United States intervention in Vietnam in the 1950s and 1960s, and both, when public opinion changed, promised to get out (note the Humphrey–Nixon contest of 1968). In 1984, Democratic candidate Walter Mondale agreed with Republican candidate Ronald Reagan that the United States (which had ten thousand thermonuclear warheads) needed to continue increasing its arms budget, although he asked for a smaller increase than the Republicans. Such a position left Mondale unable to promise representatives of the black community (where unemployment was over 20 percent) that he would spend even a few billion dollars for a jobs program. Meanwhile, Democrats and Republicans in Congress were agreeing on a $297 billion arms bill for the 1985 fiscal year.[9]

With all the inadequacies of the representative system, it does not even operate in the field of foreign policy. In exactly those decisions which are the most vital—matters of war and peace, life and death—power rests in the hands of the president and a small group of advisers. We don't notice this when wars seem to have a large degree of justification (as World War II); we begin to notice it when we find ourselves in the midst of a particularly pointless war.

I have been talking so far about democracy in the political process. But there is another serious weakness that I will only mention here, although it is of enormous importance: the powerlessness of the American to participate in economic decision-making, which affects his life at every moment. As a consumer, that is, as the person whom the economy is presumably intended to serve, he has virtually nothing to say about what is produced for him. The corporations make what is profitable; the advertising industry persuades him to buy what the corporations produce. He becomes the passive victim of the misallocation of resources, the production of dangerous commodities, the spoiling of his air, water, forests, beaches, cities.

## 2. ACCESS TO INFORMATION

Adequate information for the electorate is a precondition for any kind of action (whether electoral or demonstrative) to affect national policy. As for the voting process, Berelson, Lazarsfeld, and McPhee tell us (in their book, *Voting*) after extensive empirical research: "One persistent conclusion is that the public is not particularly well informed about the specific issues of the day." . . .

Furthermore, . . . there are certain issues which never even reach the public because they are decided behind the scenes. . . .

Consider the information available to voters on two major kinds of issues. One of them is the tax structure, so bewilderingly complex that the corporation, with its corps of accountants and financial experts, can prime itself for lobbying activities, while the average voter, hardly able to comprehend his own income tax, stands by helplessly as the president, the Office of Management and Budget, and the Congress decide the tax laws. The dominant influences are those of big business, which has the resources both to understand and to act.

Then there is foreign policy. The government leads the citizenry to believe it has special expertise which, if it could only be revealed, would support its position against critics. At the same time, it hides the very information which would reveal its position to be indefensible. The mendacity of the government on the Bay of Pigs operation, the secret operations of the CIA in Iran, Indonesia, Guatemala, and other places, the withholding of vital information about the Tonkin Gulf events are only a few examples of the way the average person becomes a victim of government deception.

When the United States invaded the tiny island of Grenada in the fall of 1983, no reporters were allowed to observe the invasion, and the American public had little opportunity to get independent verification of the reasons given by the government for the invasion. As a result, President Reagan could glibly tell the nation what even one of his own supporters, journalist George Will, admitted was a lie: that he was invading Grenada to protect the lives of American medical students on the island. He could also claim that documents found on the island indicated plans for a Cuban-Soviet takeover of Grenada; the documents showed no such thing.[10]

Furthermore, the distribution of information to the public is a function of power and wealth. The government itself can color the citizens' understanding of events by its control of news at the source: the presidential press conference, the "leak to the press," the White Papers, the teams of "truth experts" going around the country at the taxpayers' expense. As for private media, the large networks and mass-circulation magazines have the greatest access to the public mind. There is no "equal time" for critics of public policy. . . .

## 3. EQUAL PROTECTION

Let us go now from the procedural to the substantive, indeed to the *most* substantive of questions: the right of all the people to life itself. Here we find democracy in America tragically inadequate. The draft, which has been a part of American law since 1940 (when it passed by one vote) decides, in wartime, who lives and who dies. Not only Locke, one of the leading theorists of the democratic tradition, declared the ultimate right of any person to safeguard his own life when threatened by the government; Hobbes, often looked on as the foe of democratic thought, agreed. The draft violates this principle, because it compels young people to sacrifice their lives for any cause which the leaders of government deem just; further it discriminates against the poor, the uneducated, the young.

It is in connection with this most basic of rights—life itself, the first and most important of those substantive ends which democratic participation is designed to safeguard—that I would assert the need for a global view of democracy. One can at least conceive of a democratic decision for martial sacrifice by those ready to make the sacrifice; a "democratic" war is thus a theoretical possibility. But that presumption of democracy becomes obviously false at the first shot because then *others* are affected who did not decide. . . . Nations making decisions to slaughter their own sons are at least theoretically subject to internal check. The victims on the other side fall without any such chance. For the United States today, this failure of democracy is total; we have the capacity to destroy the world without giving it a chance to murmur a dissent; we did, in fact, destroy a part of southeast Asia on the basis of a unilateral decision made in Washington. There is no more pernicious manifestation of the lack of democracy in America than this single fact.

## 4. EQUALITY BEFORE THE LAW

Is there equality before the law? At every stage of the judicial process—facing the policeman, appearing in court, being freed on bond, being sentenced by the judge—the poor person is treated worse than the rich, the black treated worse than the white, the politically or personally odd character is treated worse than the orthodox. The details are given in the 1963 report of the Attorney General's Committee on Poverty and the Administration of Federal Criminal Justice. There a defendant's poverty is shown to affect his preliminary hearing, his right to bail, the quality of his counsel. The evidence is plentiful in the daily newspapers, which inform us that a Negro boy fleeing the scene of a two-dollar theft may be shot and killed by a pursuing policeman, while a wealthy man who goes to South America after a million-dollar swindle, even if apprehended, need never fear a scratch. The wealthy price-fixer for General Motors, who costs consumers millions, will get ninety days in jail, the burglar of a liquor store will get five years. A Negro youth, or a bearded white youth poorly dressed, has much more chance of being clubbed by a policeman on the street than a well-dressed white man, given the fact that both respond with equal tartness to a question. . . .

Aside from inequality among citizens, there is inequality between the citizen and his government, when they face one another in a court of law. Take the matter of counsel: the well-trained government prosecutor faces the indigent's court-appointed counsel. Four of my students did a study of the City Court of Boston several years ago. They sat in the court for weeks, taking notes, and found that the average time spent by court-appointed counsel with his client, before arguing the case at the bench, was seven minutes.

# 5. DISTRIBUTION OF RESOURCES

Democracy is devoid of meaning if it does not include equal access to the available resources of the society. In India, democracy might still mean poverty; in the United States, with a Gross National Product of [more than] $3 trillion a year, democracy should mean that every American, working a short work-week, has adequate food, clothing, shelter, health care, education for himself and his family—in short, the material resources necessary to enjoy life and freedom. Even if only 20 percent of the American population is desperately poor . . . in a country so rich, that is an inexcusable breach of the democratic principle. Even if there is a large, prosperous middle class, there is something grossly unfair in the wealthiest fifth of the population getting 40 percent of the nation's income, and the poorest fifth getting 5 percent (a ratio virtually unchanged from 1947 to [1990]). . . .[11]

   Whether you are poor or rich determines the most fundamental facts about your life: whether you are cold in the winter while trying to sleep, whether you suffocate in the summer; whether you live among vermin or rats; whether the smells around you all day are sweet or foul; whether you have adequate medical care; whether you have good teeth; whether you can send your children to college; whether you can go on vacation or have to take an extra job at night; whether you can afford a divorce, or an abortion, or a wife, or another child. . . .

# 6. ACCESS TO EDUCATION

In a highly industrialized society, education is a crucial determinant of wealth, political power, social status, leisure, and the ability to work in one's chosen field. Educational resources in our society are not equitably distributed. Among high-school graduates of the same IQ levels, a far higher percentage of the well-to-do go on to college than the poor.[12] A mediocre student with money can always go to college. A mediocre student without money may not be able to go, even to a state college, because he may have to work to support his family. Furthermore, the educational resources in the schools—equipment, teachers, etc.—are far superior in the wealthy suburbs than in the poor sections of the city, whether white or black.

# 7. FREEDOM OF EXPRESSION

Like money, freedom of expression is available to all in America, but in widely varying quantities. The First Amendment formally guarantees freedom of speech, press, assembly, and petition to all—but certain realities of wealth, power, and status stand in the way of the equal distribution of these rights. Anyone can stand on a street corner and talk to ten or a hundred people. But someone with the resources to buy loudspeaker equipment, go through the necessary red tape, and post a bond with the city may hold a meeting downtown and reach a thousand or five thousand people. A person or a corporation with $100,000 can buy time on television and reach 10 million people. A rich person simply has much more freedom of speech than a poor person. The government has much more freedom of expression than a private individual, because the president can command the airwaves when he wishes, and reach 60 million people in one night.

Freedom of the press also is guaranteed to all. But the student selling an underground newspaper on the street with a nude woman on the cover may be arrested by a policeman, while the airport newsstand selling *Playboy* and ten magazines like it will remain safe. Anyone with $10,000 can put out a newspaper to reach a few thousand people. Anyone with $10 million can buy a few newspapers that will reach a few million people. Anyone who is penniless had better have a loud voice; and then he might be arrested for disturbing the peace.

## 8. FREEDOM FOR INDIVIDUALITY

The right to live one's life, in privacy and freedom, in whatever way one wants, so long as others are not harmed, should be a sacred principle in a democracy. But there are hundreds of laws, varying from state to state, and sometimes joined by federal laws, which regulate the personal lives of people in this country: their marriages, their divorces, their sexual relations. Furthermore, both laws and court decisions protect policemen and the FBI in their use of secret devices which listen in on private conversations, or peer in on private conduct.

## 9. THE SPIRIT OF COOPERATION

The maintenance of those substantive elements of democracy which I have just sketched, if dependent on a pervasive network of coercion, would cancel out much of the benefit of that democracy. Democracy needs rather to be sustained by a spirit in society, the tone and the values of the culture. I am speaking of something as elusive as a mood, alongside something as hard as law, both of which would have to substitute cooperation tinged with friendly competition for the fierce combat of our business culture. I am speaking of the underlying drive that keeps people going in the society. So long as that drive is for money and power, with no ceiling on either, so long as ruthlessness is built into the rules of the game, democracy does not have a chance. If there is one crucial cause in the failure of American democracy—not the only one, of course, but a fundamental one—it is the drive for corporate profit, and the overwhelming influence of money in every aspect of our daily lives. That is the uncontrolled libido of our society from which the rape of democratic values necessarily follows.

The manifestations are diverse and endless: the Kefauver hearings on the drug industry in 1961 disclosed that the drive for profit in that industry had led to incredible overpricing of drugs for consumers (700 percent markup, for instance, for tablets to arthritic patients) as well as bodily harm resulting from "the fact that they market so many of their failures."

It was disclosed in 1979 that Johns-Manville, the nation's largest asbestos manufacturer, had deliberately withheld from its workers X-ray results which showed they were developing cancer.[13] The careless disposition of toxic wastes throughout the country and the repeated accidents at nuclear plants were testimony to the concern for corporate profit over human life.

If these were isolated cases, reported and then eliminated, they could be dismissed as unfortunate blemishes on an otherwise healthy social body. But the major allocations of resources in our society are made on the basis of money profit rather than social use. . . .

. . . [N]ews items buttress what I have said. The oil that polluted California's beautiful beaches in the 1960s . . . was produced by a system in which the oil companies' hunger for profit has far more weight than the ordinary person's need to swim in clean water. This is not to be attributed to Republicanism overriding the concern for the little fellow of the Democratic Party. Profit is master whichever party is in power; it was the liberal Secretary of the Interior Stewart Udall who allowed the dangerous drilling to go on. . . .

In 1984, the suit of several thousand veterans against the Dow Chemical Company, claiming that they and their families had suffered terrible illnesses as a result of exposure in Vietnam to the poisonous chemical Agent Orange, was settled. The Dow corporation avoided the disclosures of thousands of documents in open court by agreeing to pay $180 million to the veterans. One thing seemed clear: the company had known that the defoliant used in Vietnam might be dangerous, but it held back the news, and blamed the government for ordering use of the chemical. The government itself, apparently wanting to shift blame to the corporation, declared publicly that Dow Chemical had been motivated in its actions by greed for profit.

## 10. OPPORTUNITY TO PROTEST

The first two elements in my list for democracy—decision-making and information to help make them—are procedural. The next six are substantive, dealing with the consequences of such procedures on life, liberty, and the pursuit of happiness. My ninth point, the one I have just discussed, shows how the money motive of our society corrupts both procedures and their consequences by its existence and suggests we need a different motive as a fundamental requisite of a democratic society. The point I am about to discuss is an ultimate requisite for democracy, a safety feature if nothing else—neither procedures nor consequences nor motivation—works. It is the right of citizens to break through the impasse of a legal and cultural structure, which sustains inequality, greed, and murder, to initiate processes for change. I am speaking of civil disobedience, which is an essential safeguard even in a successful society, and which is an absolute necessity in a society which is not going well.

If the institutional structure itself bars any change but the most picayune and grievances are serious, it is silly to insist that change must be mediated through the processes of that legal structure. In such a situation, dramatic expressions of protest and challenge are necessary to help change ways of thinking, to build up political power for drastic change. A society that calls itself democratic (whether accurately or not) must, as its ultimate safeguard, allow such acts of disobedience. If the government prohibits them (as we must expect from a government committed to the existent) then the members of a society concerned with democracy must not only defend such acts, but encourage them. Somewhere near the root of democratic thought is the theory of popular sovereignty, declaring that government and laws are instruments for certain ends, and are not to be deified with absolute obedience; they must constantly be checked by the citizenry, and challenged, opposed, even overthrown, if they become threats to fundamental rights.

Any abstract assessment of *when* disobedience is justified is pointless. Proper conclusions depend on empirical evidence about how bad things are at the moment, and how adequate are the institutional mechanisms for correcting them. . . .

One of these is the matter of race. The intolerable position of the black person, in both North and South, has traditionally been handled with a few muttered apologies and tokens of reform. Then the civil disobedience of militants in the South forced our attention on the most dramatic (southern) manifestations of racism in America. The massive black urban uprisings of 1967 and 1968 showed that nothing less than civil disobedience (for riots and uprisings go beyond that) could make the nation see that the race problem is an American—not a southern—problem and that it needs bold, revolutionary action.

As for poverty: it seems clear that the normal mechanisms of congressional pretense and presidential rhetoric are not going to change things very much. Acts of civil disobedience by the poor will be required, at the least, to make middle-class America take notice, to bring national decisions that begin to reallocate wealth.

The war in Vietnam showed that we could not depend on the normal processes of "law and order," of the election process, of letters to *The Times,* to stop a series of especially brutal acts against the Vietnamese and against our own sons. It took a nationwide storm of protest, including thousands of acts of civil disobedience (14,000 people were arrested in one day in 1971 in Washington, D.C.), to help bring the war to an end. The role of draft resistance in affecting Lyndon Johnson's 1968 decision not to escalate the war further is told in the Defense Department secret documents of that period. In the 1980s civil disobedience [continued,] with religious pacifists and others risking prison in order to protest the arms race and the plans for nuclear war.

The great danger for American democracy is not from the protesters. That democracy is too poorly realized for us to consider critics—even rebels—as the chief problem. Its fulfillment requires us all, living in an ossified system which sustains too much killing and too much selfishness, to join the protest.

## NOTES

1 Robert A. Dahl, *A Preface to Democratic Theory* (Chicago: University of Chicago Press, 1963), p. 81.
2 *Ibid.*, p. 124.
3 *Ibid.*, p. 125.
4 *Ibid.*, p. 131.
5 *Ibid.*, pp. 131–32.
6 Thomas B. Edsall, *The New Politics of Inequality* (New York: Norton, 1984), p. 112.
7 Dahl, *A Preface to Democratic Theory*, p. 146.
8 Robert Wiebe, "The Confinements of Consensus," *TriQuarterly*, 1966, Copyright by TriQuarterly 1966. All rights reserved.
9 *New York Times*, September 25, 1984.
10 The *New York Times*, reported, November 5, 1983: "There is nothing in the documents, however, that specifically indicates that Cuba and the Soviet Union were on the verge of taking over Grenada, as Administration officials have suggested."
11 Edsall, *The New Politics of Inequality*, p. 221.
12 See the Carnegie Council on Children study, *Small Futures*, by Richard deLore, 1979.
13 *Los Angeles Times*, May 3, 1979.

# How Democratic Is America?
## A Response to Howard Zinn

**Sidney Hook**

Charles Peirce, the great American philosopher, once observed that there was such a thing as the "ethics of words." The "ethics of words" are violated whenever ordinary terms are used in an unusual context or arbitrarily identified with another concept for which other terms are in common use. Mr. Zinn is guilty of a systematic violation of the "ethics of words." In consequence, his discussion of "democracy" results in a great many methodological errors as well as inconsistencies. To conserve space, I shall focus on three.

## I

First of all, he confuses democracy as a political *process* with democracy as a political *product* or state of welfare; democracy as a *"free* society" with democracy as a *"good* society," where good is defined in terms of equality or justice (or both) or some other constellation of values. One of the reasons for choosing to live under a democratic political system rather than a non-democratic system is our belief that it makes possible a better society. That is something that must be empirically established, something denied by critics of democracy from Plato to Santayana. The equality which is relevant to democracy as a *political process* is, in the first instance, political equality with respect to the rights of citizenship. Theoretically, a politically democratic community could vote, wisely or unwisely, to abolish, retain, or establish certain economic inequalities. Theoretically, a benevolent despotism could institute certain kinds of social and even juridical equalities. Historically, the Bismarckian political dictatorship introduced social welfare legislation for the masses at a time when such legislation would have been repudiated by the existing British and American political democracies. Some of Mr. Zinn's proposed reforms could be introduced under a dictatorship or benevolent despotism. Therefore, they are not logically or organically related to democracy.

The second error in Mr. Zinn's approach to democracy is "to measure our democracy against an ideal (even if inadvertently unachievable) standard . . . even if utopian . . ." without *defining* the standard. His criteria admittedly are neither necessary nor sufficient for determining the presence of

Sidney Hook (1902–1989) was head of the department of philosophy at New York University from 1934 to 1969, and from 1973 to 1989 a senior research fellow at the Hoover Institution on War, Revolution, and Peace at Stanford University. This essay was originally published in *How Democratic Is America?* ed. Robert A. Goldwin, pp. 62–75 (Chicago: Rand McNally, 1971). The author revised and updated the original for *Points of View* in 1985.

democracy since he himself admits that they are applicable to societies that are not democratic. Further, even if we were to take his criteria as severally defining the presence of democracy—as we might take certain physical and mental traits as constituting a definition of health—he gives no operational test for determining whether or not they have been fulfilled. For example, among the criteria he lists for determining whether a society is democratic is this: "Are the members of the society equally protected on matters of life and death—in the most literal sense of that phrase?" A moment's reflection will show that here—as well as in other cases where Zinn speaks of equality—it is impossible for all members to be equally protected on matters of life and death—certainly not in a world in which men do the fighting and women give birth to children, where children need *more* protection than adults, and where some risk-seeking adults require and deserve less protection (since resources are not infinite) than others. As Karl Marx realized, "in the most literal sense of that phrase," there cannot be absolute equality even in a classless society. . . .

The only sensible procedure in determining the absence or presence of equality from a democratic perspective is comparative. We must ask whether a culture is more or less democratic in comparison to the past with respect to some *desirable* feature of equality (Zinn ignores the fact that not all equalities are desirable). It is better for some people to be more intelligent and more knowledgeable than others than for all to be unintelligent and ignorant. There never is literally equal access to education, to knowledge and training in any society. The question is: Is there more access today for more people than yesterday, and how can we increase the access tomorrow?

Mr. Zinn refuses to take this approach because, he asserts, "it supports complacency." It does nothing of the sort! On the contrary, it shows that progress is possible, and encourages us to exert our efforts in the same direction if we regard the direction as desirable.

It will be instructive to look at the passage in which Mr. Zinn objects to this sensible comparative approach because it reveals the bias in his approach:

"With such a standard," he writes, "Russia in 1910 could point with pride to how much progress they had made toward parliamentary democracy; as Russians in 1985 could point to their post-Stalin progress away from the gulag; as Americans could point in 1939 to how far they had come in solving the problem of economic equality; as Americans in the South could point in 1950 to the progress of the southern Negro."

**a.** In 1910 the Russians were indeed moving toward greater progress in local parliamentary institutions. Far from making them complacent, they moved towards more inclusive representative institutions which culminated in elections to the Constituent Assembly in 1918, which was bayoneted out of existence by Lenin and the Communist Party, with a minority party dictatorship established.

**b.** Only Mr. Zinn would regard the slight diminution in terror from the days of Stalin to the regime of Chernenko as progress toward democracy. Those who observe the ethics of words would normally say that the screws of repression had been slightly relaxed. Mr. Zinn seems unaware that as bad as the terror was under Lenin, it was not as pervasive as it is today.* But no one with any respect for the ethics of words would speak of "the progress of democracy" in the Soviet Union from Lenin to Stalin to Khrushchev to Chernenko. Their regimes were varying degrees of dictatorship and terror.

**c.** Americans could justifiably say that in 1939 progress had been made in giving workers a greater role, not as Mr. Zinn says in "solving the problem of economic equality" (a meaningless phrase), but in determining the conditions and rewards of work that prevailed in 1929 or previously because the existence of the Wagner Labor Relations Act made collective bargaining the law of the land. They could say this *not* to rest in complacency, but to use the organized force of their trade unions to influence further the political life of the country. And indeed, it was the organized labor movement in 1984 which in effect chose the candidate of the Democratic Party.

**d.** Americans in the South in 1950 could rightfully speak of the progress of the southern Negro over the days of unrestricted Jim Crow and lynching bees of the past, *not* to rest in complacency, but to agitate for further progress through the Supreme Court decision of *Brown* v. *Board of Education in Topeka* and through the Civil Rights Act of Congress. This has not made them complacent, but more resolved to press further to eliminate remaining practices of invidious discrimination.

Even Mr. Zinn should admit that with respect to some of his other criteria this is the only sensible approach. Otherwise we get unhistorical answers, the hallmark of the doctrinaire. He asks—criterion 1—"To what extent can various people in the society participate in those decisions which affect their lives?" and—criterion 7—"Is there freedom of expression on all matters, and equally for all, to communicate with other members of the society?" Why doesn't Mr. Zinn adopt this sensible comparative approach? Because it would lead him to inqure into the extent to which people are free to participate in decisions that affect their lives *today,* free to express themselves, free to organize, free to protest and dissent today, *in comparison with the past.* It would lead him to the judgment *which he wishes to avoid at all costs,* to wit, that despite the grave problems, gaps, and tasks before us, the United States is *more* democratic today than it was a hundred years ago, fifty years ago, twenty years ago, five years ago with respect to every one of the criteria he has listed. To recognize this is *not* an invitation to complacency. On the contrary, it indicates the possibility of broadening, deepening, and using the democratic political process to improve the quality of human life, to modify and redirect social institutions in order to realize on a wider scale the moral commitment of

* These words and subsequent references to the Soviet Union preceded the reforms initiated under Mikhail Gorbachev—*Editors*.

democracy to an equality of concern for all its citizens to achieve their fullest growth as persons. This commitment is to a process, not to a transcendent goal or a fixed, ideal standard.

In a halting, imperfect manner, set back by periods of violence, vigilantism, and xenophobia, the political democratic process in the United States has been used to modify the operation of the economic system. The improvements and reforms won from time to time make the still-existing problems and evils more acute in that people become more aware of them. The more the democratic process extends human freedoms, and the more it introduces justice in social relations and the distribution of wealth, the greater grows the desire for *more* freedom and justice. Historically and psychologically, it is false to assume that reforms breed a spirit of complacency. . . .

The third and perhaps most serious weakness in Mr. Zinn's view is his conception of the nature of the formal political democratic process. It suffers from several related defects. First, it overlooks the central importance of majority rule in the democratic process. Second, it denies in effect that majority rule is possible by defining democracy in such a way that it becomes impossible. . . .

"Representation by its very nature," claims Mr. Zinn, "is undemocratic." This is Rousseauistic nonsense. For it would mean that no democracy— including all societies that Mr. Zinn ever claimed at any time to be democratic—could possibly exist, not even the direct democracies or assemblies of Athens or the New England town meetings. For all such assemblies must elect officials to carry out their will. If no representative (and an official is a representative, too) can adequately represent another's needs, there is no assurance that in the actual details of governance, the selectmen, road commissioners, or other town or assembly officials will, in fact, carry out their directives. No assembly or meeting can sit in continuous session or collectively carry out the common decision. In the nature of the case, officials, like representatives, constitute an elite and their actions *may* reflect their interests more than the interests of the governed. This makes crucial the questions whether and how an elite can be removed, whether the consent on which the rule of the officials or representatives rests is free or coerced, whether a minority can peacefully use these mechanisms, by which freely given consent is registered, to win over or become a majority. The existence of representative assemblies makes democracy difficult, not impossible.

Since Mr. Zinn believes that a majority never has any authority to bind a minority as well as itself by decisions taken after free discussion and debate, he is logically committed to anarchy. Failing to see this, he confuses two fundamentally different things—the meaning or definition of democracy, and its justification.

**1.** A democratic government is one in which the general direction of policy rests directly or indirectly upon the freely given consent of a majority of the adults governed. Ambiguities and niceties aside, that is what democracy means. It is not anarchy. The absence of a unanimous consensus does not entail the absence of democracy.

**2.** One may reject on moral or religious or personal grounds a democratic society. Plato, as well as modern totalitarians, contends that a majority of mankind is either too stupid or vicious to be entrusted with self-government, or to be given the power to accept or reject their ruling elites, and that the only viable alternative to democracy is the self-selecting and self-perpetuating elite of "the wise," or "the efficient," or "the holy," or "the strong," depending upon the particular ideology of the totalitarian apologist. The only thing they have in common with democrats is their rejection of anarchy.

**3.** No intelligent and moral person can make an *absolute* of democracy in the sense that he believes it is always, everywhere, under any conditions, and no matter what its consequences, ethically legitimate. Democracy is obviously not desirable in a head-hunting or cannibalistic society or in an institution of the feeble-minded. But wherever and whenever a principled democrat accepts the political system of democracy, he must accept the binding authority of legislative decisions, reached after the free give-and-take of debate and discussion, as binding upon him whether he is a member of the majority or minority. Otherwise the consequence is incipient or overt anarchy or civil war, the usual preface to despotism or tyranny. Accepting the decision of the majority as binding does not mean that it is final or irreversible. The processes of freely given consent must make it possible for a minority to urge amendment or repeal of any decision of the majority. Under carefully guarded provisions, a democrat may resort to civil disobedience of a properly enacted law in order to bear witness to the depths of his commitment in an effort *to reeducate* his fellow citizens. But in that case he must voluntarily accept punishment for his civil disobedience, and so long as he remains a democrat, voluntarily abandon his violation or noncompliance with law at the point where its consequences threaten to destroy the democratic process and open the floodgates either to the violent disorders of anarchy or to the dictatorship of a despot or a minority political party.

**4.** That Mr. Zinn is not a democrat but an anarchist in his views is apparent in his contention that not only must a democracy allow or tolerate civil disobedience within limits, but that "members of a society concerned with democracy must not only defend such acts, but encourage them." On this view, if southern segregationists resort to civil disobedience to negate the long-delayed but eminently just measures adopted by the government to implement the amendments that outlaw slavery, they should be encouraged to do so. On this view, any group that defies any law that violates its conscience—with respect to marriage, taxation, vaccination, abortion, education—should be encouraged to do so. Mr. Zinn, like most anarchists, refuses to generalize the principles behind his action. He fails to see that if all fanatics of causes deemed by them to be morally just were encouraged to resort to civil disobedience, even our imperfect existing political democracy would dissolve in chaos, and that civil disobedience would soon become quite uncivil. He fails to see that *in a democracy the processes of intelligence, not individual conscience, must be supreme.*

# II

I turn now to some of the issues that Mr. Zinn declares are substantive. Before doing so I wish to make clear my belief that the most substantive issue of all is the procedural one by which the inescapable differences of interests among men, once a certain moral level of civilization has been reached, are to be negotiated. The belief in the validity of democratic procedures rests upon the conviction that where adult human beings have freedom of access to relevant information, they are, by and large, better judges of their own interests than are those who set themselves up as their betters and rulers, that, to use the homely maxim, those who wear the shoes know best where they pinch and therefore have the right to change their political shoes in the light of their experience. . . .

Looking at the question "How democratic is America?" with respect to the problems of poverty, race, education, etc., we must say "Not democratic enough!", but not for the reasons Mr. Zinn gives. For he seems to believe that the failure to adopt *his* solutions and proposals with respect to foreign policy, slum clearance, pollution, etc., is evidence of the failure of the democratic process itself. He overlooks the crucial difference between the procedural process and the substantive issues. When he writes that democracy is devoid of meaning if it does not include "equal access to the available resources of the society," he is simply abusing language. Assuming such equal access is desirable (which some might question who believe that access to *some* of society's resources—for example, to specialized training or to scarce supplies—should go not equally to all but to the most needful or sometimes to the most qualified), a democracy may or may not legislate such equal access. The crucial question is whether the electorate has the power to make the choice, or to elect those who would carry out the mandate chosen. . . .

When Mr. Zinn goes on to say that "in the United States . . . democracy should mean that every American, working a short work-week, has adequate food, clothing, shelter, health care, . . ." he is not only abusing language, he is revealing the fact that the procedural processes that are essential to the meaning of democracy, in ordinary usage, are not essential to his conception. He is violating the basic ethics of discourse. If democracy "should mean" what Zinn says it should, then were Huey Long or any other dictator to seize power and introduce a "short work-week" and distribute "adequate food, clothing, shelter, health care" to the masses, Mr. Zinn would have to regard his regime as democratic.

After all, when Hitler came to power and abolished free elections in

Germany, he at the same time reduced unemployment, increased the real wages of the German worker, and provided more adequate food, clothing, shelter, and health care than was available under the Weimar Republic. On Zinn's view of what democracy "should mean," this made Hitler's rule more democratic than that of Weimar. . . .

Not surprisingly, Mr. Zinn is a very unreliable guide even in his account of the procedural features of the American political system. In one breath he maintains that not enough information is available to voters to make intelligent choices on major political issues like tax laws. (The voter, of course, does not vote on such laws but for representatives who have taken stands on a number of complex issues.) "The dominant influences are those of big business, which has the resources both to understand and to act." In another breath, he complains that the electorate is at the mercy of the propagandist. "The propagandist does not need to lie; he overwhelms the public with so much information as to lead it to believe that it is all too complicated for anyone but the experts."

Mr. Zinn is certainly hard to please! The American political process is not democratic because the electorate hasn't got enough information. It is also undemocratic because it receives too much information. What would Zinn have us do so that the public gets just the right amount of information and propaganda? Have the government control the press? Restrict freedom of propaganda? But these are precisely the devices of totalitarian societies. The evils of the press, even when it is free of government control, are many indeed. The great problem is to keep the press free and responsible. And as defective as the press and other public media are today, surely it is an exaggeration to say that with respect to tax laws "the dominant influences are those of big business." If they were, how can we account for the existence of the income tax laws? If the influence of big business on the press is so dominant and the press is so biased, how can we account for the fact that although 92 percent of the press opposed Truman's candidacy in 1948, he was reelected? How can we account for the profound dissatisfaction of Vice President Agnew with the press and other mass media? And since Mr. Zinn believes that big business dominates our educational system, especially our universities, how can we account for the fact that the universities are the centers of the strongest dissent in the nation to public and national policy, that the National Association of Manufacturers bitterly complained a few years ago that the economics of the free enterprise system was derided, and often not even taught, in most Departments of Economics in the colleges and universities of the nation?

Mr. Zinn's exaggerations are really caricatures of complex realities. Far from being controlled by the monolithic American corporate economy, American public opinion is today marked by a greater scope and depth of dissent than at any time in its history, except for the days preceding the Civil War. The voice and the votes of Main Street still count for more in a democratic polity than those of Wall Street. Congress has limited, and can still further limit, the influence of money on the electoral process by federal subsidy and regulations.

There are always abuses needing reforms. By failing to take a comparative approach and instead focusing on some absolute utopian standard of perfection, Mr. Zinn gives an exaggerated, tendentious, and fundamentally false picture of the United States. There is hardly a sentence in his essay that is free of some serious flaw in perspective, accuracy, or emphasis. Sometimes they have a comic effect, as when Mr. Zinn talks about the lack of "equal distribution of the right of freedom of expression." What kind of "equal distribution" is he talking about? Of course, a person with more money can talk to more people than one with less, although this does not mean that more persons will listen to him, agree with him, or be influenced by him. But a person with a more eloquent voice or a better brain can reach more people than you or I. What shall we therefore do to insure equal distribution of the right of freedom of expression? Insist on equality of voice volume or pattern, and equality of brain power? More money gives not only greater opportunity to talk to people than less money but the ability to do thousands of things barred to those who have less money. Shall we then decree that all people have the same amount of money all the time and forbid anyone from depriving anyone else of any of his money even by fair means? "The government," writes Mr. Zinn, "has much more freedom of expression than a private individual because the president can command the airwaves when he wishes, and reach 60 million people in one night."

Alas! Mr. Zinn is not joking. Either he wants to bar the president or any public official from using the airwaves or he wants all of us to take turns. One wonders what country Mr. Zinn is living in. Nixon spoke to 60 million people several times, and so did Jimmy Carter. What was the result? More significant than the fact that 60 million people hear the president is that 60 million or more can hear his critics, sometimes right after he speaks, and that no one is compelled to listen.

Mr. Zinn does not understand the basic meaning of equality in a free, open democratic society. Its philosophy does not presuppose that all citizens are physically or intellectually equal or that all are equally gifted in every or any respect. It holds that all enjoy a *moral* equality, and that therefore, as far as is practicable, given finite resources, the institutions of a democratic society should seek to provide an equal opportunity to all its citizens to develop themselves to their full desirable potential.

Of course, we cannot ever provide complete equal opportunity. More and more is enough. For one thing, so long as children have different parents and home environments, they cannot enjoy the same or equal opportunities. Nonetheless, the family has compensating advantages for all that. Let us hope that Mr. Zinn does not wish to wipe out the family to avoid differences in opportunity. Plato believed that the family, as we know it, should be abolished because it did not provide equality of opportunity, and that all children should be brought up by the state.

Belief in the moral equality of men and women does not require that all individuals be treated identically or that equal treatment must be measured or determined by equality of outcome or result. Every citizen should have an equal right to an education, but that does not mean that, regardless of capacity and interest, he or she should have the same amount of schooling beyond the adolescent years, and at the same schools, and take the same course of study. With the increase in national wealth, a good case can be made for an equal right of all citizens to health care or medical treatment. But only a quack or ideological fanatic would insist that therefore all individuals should have the same medical regimen no matter what ails them. This would truly be putting all human beings in the bed of Procrustes.

This conception of moral equality as distinct from Mr. Zinn's notions of equality is perfectly compatible with intelligent recognition of human inequalities and relevant ways of treating their inequalities to further both the individual and common good. Intelligent and loving parents are equally concerned with the welfare of all their children. But precisely because they are, they may provide different specific strategies in health care, education, psychological motivation, and intellectual stimulation to develop the best in all of them. The logic of Mr. Zinn's position—although he seems blissfully unaware of it—leads to the most degrading kind of egalitarian socialism, the kind which Marx and Engels in their early years denounced as "barracks socialism."

It is demonstrable that democracy is healthier and more effective where human beings do not suffer from poverty, unemployment, and disease. It is also demonstrable that to the extent that property gives power, private property in the means of social production gives power over the lives of those who must live by its use, and, therefore, that such property, whether public or private, should be responsible to those who are affected by its operation. Consequently one can argue that political democracy depends not only on the extension of the franchise to all adults, not only on its active exercise, but on programs of social welfare that provide for collective bargaining by free trade unions of workers and employees, unemployment insurance, minimum wages, guaranteed health care, and other social services that are integral to the welfare state. It is demonstrable that although the existing American welfare state provides far more welfare than was ever provided in the past—my own lifetime furnishes graphic evidence of the vast changes—it is still very far from being a genuine welfare state. Political democracy can exist without a welfare state, but it is stronger and better with it.

The basic issue that divides Mr. Zinn from others no less concerned about human welfare, but less fanatical than he, is how a genuine welfare state is to be brought about. My contention is that this can be achieved by the vigorous exercise of the existing democratic process, and that by the same coalition politics through which great gains have been achieved in the past, even greater gains can be won in the future.

For purposes of economy, I focus on the problem of poverty, or since this is a relative term, hunger. If the presence of hunger entails the absence of the democratic political process, then democracy has never existed in the past—which would be an arbitrary use of words. Nonetheless, the existence of hunger is always a *threat* to the continued existence of the democratic process because of the standing temptation of those who hunger to exchange freedom for the promise of bread. This, of course, is an additional ground to the even weightier moral reasons for gratifying basic human needs.

That fewer people go hungry today in the United States than ever before may show that our democracy is better than it used to be but not that it is as good as it can be. Even the existence of one hungry person is one too many. How then can hunger or the extremes of poverty be abolished? Certainly not by the method Mr. Zinn advises: "Acts of civil disobedience by the poor will be required, at the least, to make middle-class America take notice, to bring national decisions that begin to reallocate wealth."

This is not only a piece of foolish advice, it is dangerously foolish advice. Many national decisions to reallocate wealth have been made through the political process—what else is the system of taxation if not a method of reallocating wealth?—without resort to civil disobedience. Indeed, resort to civil disobedience on this issue is very likely to produce a backlash among those active and influential political groups in the community who are aware that normal political means are available for social and economic reform. The refusal to engage in such normal political processes could easily be exploited by demagogues to portray the movement towards the abolition of hunger and extreme poverty as a movement towards the confiscation and equalization of all wealth.

The simplest and most effective way of abolishing hunger is to act on the truly revolutionary principle, enunciated by the federal government, that it is responsible for maintaining a standard of relief as a minimum beneath which a family will not be permitted to sink. . . .

For reasons that need no elaboration here, the greatest of the problems faced by American democracy today is the race problem. Although tied to the problems of poverty and urban reconstruction, it has independent aspects exacerbated by the legacy of the Civil War and the Reconstruction period.

Next to the American Indians, the American Negroes have suffered most from the failure of the democratic political process to extend the rights and privileges of citizenship to those whose labor and suffering have contributed so much to the conquest of the continent. The remarkable gains that have been made by the Negroes in the last twenty years have been made primarily through the political process. If the same rate of improvement continues, the year 2000 may see a rough equality established. The growth of Negro suffrage, especially in the South, the increasing sense of responsibility by the white community, despite periodic setbacks resulting from outbursts of violence, opens up a perspective of continuous and cumulative reform. The man and the organization he headed, chiefly responsible for the great gains made by the Negroes, Roy Wilkins and the NAACP, were convinced that the democratic political process can be more effectively used to further the integration of Negroes into our national life than by reliance on any other method. . . .

The only statement in Mr. Zinn's essay that I can wholeheartedly endorse is his assertion that the great danger to American democracy does not come from the phenomena of protest as such. Dissent and protest are integral to the democratic process. The danger comes from certain modes of dissent, from the substitution of violence and threats of violence for the mechanisms of the political process, from the escalation of that violence as the best hope of those who still have grievances against our imperfect American democracy, and from views such as those expressed by Mr. Zinn which downgrade the possibility of peaceful social reform and encourage rebellion. It is safe to predict that large-scale violence by impatient minorities will fail. It is almost as certain that attempts at violence will backfire, that they will create a climate of repression that may reverse the course of social progress and expanded civil liberties of the last generation. . . .

It is when Mr. Zinn is discussing racial problems that his writing ceases to be comic and silly and becomes irresponsible and mischievous. He writes:

> The massive black urban uprisings of 1967 and 1968 showed that nothing less than civil disobedience (for riots and uprisings go beyond that) could make the nation see that the race problem is an American—not a southern—problem and that it needs bold, revolutionary action.

First of all, every literate person knows that the race problem is an American problem, not exclusively a southern one. It needs no civil disobedience or "black uprisings" to remind us of that. Second, the massive uprisings of 1967 and 1968 were violent and uncivil, and resulted in needless loss of life and suffering. The Civil Rights Acts, according to Roy Wilkins, then head of the NAACP, were imperiled by them. They were adopted despite, not because, of them. Third, what kind of "revolutionary" action is Mr. Zinn calling for? And by whom? He seems to lack the courage of his confusions. Massive civil disobedience when sustained becomes a form of civil war.

Despite Mr. Zinn and others, violence is more likely to produce reaction than reform. In 1827 a resolution to manumit slaves by purchase (later, Lincoln's preferred solution) was defeated by three votes in the House of Burgesses of the State of Virginia. It was slated to be reintroduced in a subsequent session with excellent prospects of being adopted. Had Virginia adopted it, North Carolina would shortly have followed suit. But before it could be reintroduced, Nat Turner's rebellion broke out. Its violent excesses frightened the South into a complete rejection of a possibility that might have prevented the American Civil War—the fiercest and bloodiest war in human history up to that time, from whose consequences American society is still suffering. Mr. Zinn's intentions are as innocent as those of a child playing with matches.

# III

One final word about "the global" dimension of democracy of which Mr. Zinn speaks. Here, too, he speaks sympathetically of actions that would undermine the willingness and capacity of a free society to resist totalitarian aggression.

The principles that should guide a free democratic society in a world where dictatorial regimes seek to impose their rule on other nations were formulated by John Stuart Mill, the great defender of liberty and representative government, more than a century ago:

> To go to war for an idea, if the war is aggressive not defensive, is as criminal as to go to war for territory or revenue, for it is as little justifiable to force our ideas on other people, as to compel them to submit to our will in any other aspect. . . . *The doctrine of non-intervention, to be a legitimate principle of morality, must be accepted by all governments.* The despots must consent to be bound by it as well as the free states. Unless they do, the profession of it by free countries comes but to this miserable issue, that the wrong side may help the wrong side but the right may not help the right side. Intervention to enforce non-intervention is always right, always moral *if not always prudent.* Though it may be a mistake to give freedom (or independence—S. H.) to a people who do not value the boon, it cannot but be right to insist that if they do value it, they shall not be hindered from the pursuit of it by foreign coercion (*Fraser's Magazine,* 1859, emphasis mine).

Unfortunately, these principles were disregarded by the United States in 1936 when Hitler and Mussolini sent troops into Spain to help Franco overthrow the legally elected democratic Loyalist regime. The U.S. Congress, at the behest of the administration, adopted a Neutrality Resolution which prevented the democratic government of Spain from purchasing arms here. This compelled the Spanish government to make a deal with Stalin, who not only demanded its entire gold supply but the acceptance of the dread Soviet secret police, the NKVD, to supervise the operations. The main operation of the NKVD in Spain was to engage in a murderous purge of the democratic ranks of anti-Communists which led to the victory of Franco. The story is told in George Orwell's *Homage to Catalonia.* He was on the scene.

The prudence of American intervention in Vietnam may be debatable but there is little doubt that Adlai Stevenson, sometimes referred to as the liberal conscience of the nation, correctly stated the American motivation when he said at the UN on the very day of his death: "My hope in Vietnam is that resistance there may establish the fact that changes in Asia are not to be precipitated by outside force. This was the point of the Korean War. This is the point of the conflict in Vietnam."

Today the Soviet Union and Communist Cuba are engaged in extensive operations to help indigenous elements overthrow regimes in Central America. Mr. Zinn's remarks about Grenada show he is opposed to the liberal principles expressed by J. S. Mill in the passage cited above. His report of the facts about Grenada is as distorted as his account of present-day American democracy. On tiny Grenada, whose government was seized by Communist terrorists, were representatives of every Communist regime in the Kremlin's orbit, Cuban troops, and a Soviet general. I have read the documents captured by the American troops. They conclusively establish that the Communists were preparing the island as part of the Communist strategy of expansion.[1]

It is sad but significant that Mr. Zinn, whose heart bleeds for the poor

Asians who suffered in the struggle to prevent the Communist takeover in Southeast Asia, has not a word of protest, not a tear of compassion for the hundreds of thousands of tortured, imprisoned, and drowned in flight after the victory of the North Vietnamese "liberators," not to mention the even greater number of victims of the Cambodian and Cuban Communists.

One summary question may be asked whose answer bears on the issue of how democratic America is. Suppose all the iron and bamboo and passport curtains of the world were lifted today, in what direction would freedom loving and democratic people move? Anyone is free to leave the United States today, except someone fleeing from the law, but in the countries arrayed against the United States people are penned in like animals and cannot cross a boundary without risking death. Has this no significance for the "global" aspect of our question?

## NOTES

1. *THE GRENADA PAPERS: The Inside Story of the Grenadian Revolution—and the Making of a Totalitarian State as Told in Captured Documents* (San Francisco: Institute of Contemporary Studies, 1984).

# Rebuttal to Sidney Hook

**Howard Zinn**

Mr. Hook *does* have the courage of his confusions. I have space to point out only a few.

**1.** He chooses to define democracy as a "process," thus omitting its substance. Lincoln's definition was quite good—"government of, by, and for the people." Mr. Hook pooh-poohs the last part as something that could be done by a despot. My definition, like Lincoln's, requires "of" and "by" as well as "for," process as well as content. Mr. Hook is wild about voting, which can also be allowed by despots. Voting is an improvement over autocracy, but insufficient to make any society democratic. Voting, as Emma Goldman said (true, she was an anarchist), and as Helen Keller agreed (true, she was a socialist), is "our modern fetish." It is Mr. Hook's fetish.

Mr. Hook's "democracy" is easily satisfied by hypocrisy, by forms and procedures which look good on paper, and behind which the same old injustices go on. Concealed behind the haughty pedant's charge of "methodological errors" is a definition of democracy which is empty of human meaning, a lifeless set of structures and procedures, which our elementary school teachers tried to pawn off on us as democracy—elections, checks and balances, how a bill becomes a law. Of course, we can't have perfect democracy, and can't avoid representation, but we get closer to democracy when representation is supplemented by the direct action of citizens.

The missing heart, the flowing blood, the life-giving element in democracy is the constant struggle of people inside, around, outside, and despite the ordinary political processes. That means protest, strikes, boycotts, demonstrations, petitions, agitation, education, sometimes the slow buildup of public opinion, sometimes civil disobedience.

**2.** Mr. Hook seems oblivious of historical experience in the United States. His infatuation with "political process" comes out of ancient textbooks in which presidents and congresses act in the nick of time to save us when we're in trouble. In fact, that political process has never been sufficient to solve any crucial problem of human rights in our country: slavery, corporate despotism, war—all required popular movements to oppose them, movements outside those channels into which Mr. Hook and other apologists for the status quo constantly invite us, so we can get lost. Only when popular movements go into action do the channels themselves suddenly come to life.

The test is in history. When Mr. Hook says blacks got their gains "primarily through the political process" he simply does not know what he is

Howard Zinn's rebuttal was written specifically for this volume.

talking about. The new consciousness of the rights of blacks, the gains made in the past twenty years—were they initiated by the "political process"? That process was dead for one hundred years while five thousand blacks were lynched, segregation flourished, and presidents, Congress, and the Supreme Court turned the other cheek. Only when blacks took to the streets by the tens of thousands, sat-in, demonstrated, even broke the law, did the "political process" awaken from its long lethargy. Only then did Congress rush to pass civil rights laws, just in time for Mr. Hook to say, cheerily, "You see, the process works."

Another test. Mr. Hook talks about the progress made "because the existence of the Wagner Labor Relations Act made collective bargaining the law of the land." He seems unaware of the wave of strikes in 1933–34 throughout the nation that brought a dead labor relations act to life. Peter Irons, in his prize-winning study, *The New Deal Lawyers,* carefully examines the chronology of 1934, and concludes: "It is likely that the existing National Labor Relations Board would have limped along, unable to enforce its orders, had not the industrial workforce erupted in late April, engulfing the country in virtual class war. . . . Roosevelt and the Congress were suddenly jolted into action." Even after the act was passed in 1935, employers resisted it, and it took the sit-down strikes of 1936–37—yes, civil disobedience—to get contracts with General Motors and U.S. Steel.

A third test. The political process was pitifully inept as a handful of decision-makers, telling lies, propelled this country into the ugly war in Vietnam. (Mr. Hook joins them, when he quotes Adlai Stevenson that we were in Vietnam to act against "outside force"; the overwhelming "outside force" in Vietnam was the United States, with 525,000 troops, dropping 7 million tons of bombs on Southeast Asia.) A president elected in 1964 on his promises to keep the peace took us into war; Congress, like sheep, voted the money; the Supreme Court enveloped itself in its black robes and refused to discuss the constitutionality of the war. It took an unprecedented movement of protest to arouse the nation, to send a surge of energy moving through those clogged processes, and finally bring the war to an end.

**3.** Mr. Hook doesn't understand civil disobedience. He makes the common error of thinking that a supporter of Martin Luther King's civil disobedience must also support that of the Ku Klux Klan. He seems to think that if you believe civil disobedience is sometimes justified, for some causes, you must support civil disobedience done any time, by any group, for any reason. He does not grasp that the principle is not one of absolute civil disobedience; it simply denies absolute obedience. It says we should not be fanatics about "law and order" because sometimes the law supports the disorder of poverty, or racism, or war.

We can certainly distinguish between civil disobedience for good causes and for bad causes. That's what our intelligence is for. Will this lead to "chaos," as Mr. Hook warns? Again, historical experience is instructive: Did the civil disobedience of blacks in the sixties lead to chaos? Or the civil disobedience of antiwar protesters in the Vietnam years? Yes, they involved some disorder, as all social change does; they upset the false tranquility of segregation, they demanded an end to the chaos of war.

**4.** Mr. Hook thinks he is telling us something new when he says we can't, and sometimes should not, have perfect equality. Of course. But the point of having ideals is not that they can be perfectly achieved, but that they do not let us rest content, as Mr. Hook is, with being somewhat better off today than yesterday. By his standard, we can give just enough more to the poor to appease anger, while keeping the basic injustice of a wealthy society. In a country where some people live in mansions and others in slums, should we congratulate ourselves because the slums now have TV antennas sticking out of the leaky roofs? His prescription for equality would have us clean out the Augean stables with a spoon, and boast of our progress, while comparing us to all the terrible places in the world where they don't even have spoons. Mr. Hook tries to avoid this issue of inequality by confusing inequality in intellect and physique, which obviously can't be helped much, with inequality of wealth, which is intolerably crass in a country as wealthy as ours.

Mr. Hook becomes ludicrous when he tries to deny the crucial importance of wealth in elections and in control of the media. When he says, "The voice and votes of Main Street still count for more in a democratic polity than those of Wall Street," I wonder where he has been. If Main Street counts more than Wall Street, how come congressional cutbacks in social programs in 1981–82 brought the number of people officially defined as poor to its highest level since 1965—25.3 million—while at the same time eight thousand millionaires saved a billion dollars in lowered taxes? And how can we account for this news item of October 16, 1984, in the *New York Times:* "Five of the nation's top dozen military contractors earned profits in the years 1981, 1982, and 1983, but paid no Federal income taxes." Can you name five schoolteachers or five social workers who paid no federal income taxes?

What of the system of justice—has it not always favored Wall Street over Main Street? Compare the punishment given to corporation executives found guilty of robbing billions from consumers by price-fixing with the punishment given to auto thieves and house burglars.

Money talks loudly in this "democratic polity." But, Mr. Hook says, in an absurd defense of the control of the media, you don't have to listen! No, the mother needing medical aid doesn't have to listen, but whether her children live or die may result from the fact that the rich dominate the media, control the elections, and get legislation passed which hurts the poor. A *Boston Globe* dispatch, May 24, 1984:

> Infant mortality, which had been declining steadily in Boston and other cities in the 1970s, shot up suddenly after the Reagan Administration reduced grants for health care for mothers and children and cut back sharply on Medicaid eligibility among poor women and children in 1981, according to new research.

**5.** As for "the global dimension of democracy," Mr. Hook's simple view of the world as divided between "free society" and "totalitarian aggression" suggests he is still living back in the heroic battles of World War II. We are now in the nuclear age, and that neat division into "free" and "totalitarian" is both factually wrong and dangerous. Yes, the United States is a relatively free society, and the Soviet Union is a shameful corruption of Marx's dreams of freedom. But the United States has established or supported some of the most brutal totalitarian states in the world: Chile, South Africa, El Salvador, Guatemala, South Korea, the Philippines. Yes, the Soviet Union has committed cruel acts of aggression in Hungary, Czechoslovakia, and especially Afghanistan. But the United States has also, whether by the military or the CIA, committed aggression in Iran, Guatemala, Cuba, and the Dominican Republic, and especially in Vietnam, Laos, and Cambodia.

You cannot draw a line across the globe, as Mr. Hook does, to find good on one side and evil on the other. We get a sense of Mr. Hook's refusal to face the complexities of evil when he passes off the horror of the American invasion of Southeast Asia, which left a million dead, with: "The prudence of American intervention in Vietnam may be debatable." One can hear Mr. Hook's intellectual counterparts in the Soviet Union saying about the invasion of Afghanistan: "Our prudence . . . may be debatable." Such moral blindness will have to be overcome if there is to be movement toward real democracy in the United States, and toward real socialism in the Soviet Union. It is the fanaticism on both sides, justifying war "to defend freedom," or "to defend socialism," or simply, vaguely, "national security," that may yet kill us all. That will leave the issue of "how democratic we are" for archeologists of a future era.

# Rejoinder to Howard Zinn

**Sidney Hook**

I may have been mistaken about Mr. Zinn's courage. I am not mistaken about his confusion—his persistent confusion of a free or democratic society with a good society as he defines a good society. Zinn has not understood my criticism and therefore not replied to it. Perhaps on rereading it he will grasp the point.

**1.** Of course, there is no guarantee that the democratic process will yield a good society regardless of how Zinn or anyone else defines it. Democracies, like majorities, may sometimes be wrong or unwise. But if the decision is a result of a free and fair discussion and vote, it is still democratic. If those who lose in the electoral process resort to civil disobedience, democratic government ultimately breaks down. Even though the processes of democracy are slow and cumbersome and sometimes result in unwise action, its functioning Bill of Rights makes it possible to set them right. That is why Churchill observed, "Democracy is the worst of all forms of government except all the others that have been tried," including, we should add, anarchism.

Zinn dismisses our democratic processes as "a lifeless set of structures and procedures." But it is these very structures and procedures which have enabled us to transform our society from one in which only white men with property voted to one in which all white men voted, then all men, then all men and women. It is these structures and procedures which have extended and protected the right to dissent, even for all sorts of foolishness like Zinn's. They currently protect Mr. Zinn in his academic freedom and post, in his right to utter any criticism of the democratic system under which he lives—a right he would never enjoy in any so-called socialist society in the world today.

Mr. Zinn gives his case away when he refers to the democratic process, which requires voting in *free* elections, as a "fetish." A fetish is an object of irrational and superstitious devotion which enlightened persons reject. Like Marx, Zinn rejects "the fetishism of commodities." Is he prepared to reject the democratic process, too, if its results do not jibe with *his* conception of the good society?

How, one wonders, does Zinn know that his conception is inherently more desirable than that of his fellow citizens? The democrat says: *Let us leave this choice to the arbitrament of the democratic process.* Zinn has a shorter way. He labels any conception other than his own as undemocratic; and if it prevails, he urges the masses to take to the streets.

**2.** The space allotted to me does not permit adequate discussion of the international aspects of the struggle for a free society. (I refer students to my *Philosophy and Public Policy* and *Marxism and Beyond*.) Suffice it to say here that

Sidney Hook's rejoinder was written specifically for this volume.

sometimes when the feasible alternatives are limited, the wisest choice between evils is the lesser one. This is the same principle, supported by Zinn, that justified military aid to the Soviet Union when Nazi Germany invaded, although Stalin's regime at the time oppressed many more millions than Hitler's. From the standpoint of the free society, Stalin was the lesser evil then. Today Nazism is destroyed and globally expanding communism has taken its place. If, and only if, we are anywhere confronted by a choice of support between an authoritarian regime and a totalitarian one, the first is the lesser evil. This is not only because the second is far more oppressive of human rights (compare Batista to Castro, Thieu to Hanoi, Syngman Rhee to North Korea, Lon Nol to Pol Pot) but because authoritarian regimes sometimes develop peacefully into democracies (Spain, Portugal, Greece, Argentina) whereas no Communist regime allied to the Kremlin so far has.

**3.** Within narrowly prescribed limits, a democracy may tolerate civil disobedience of those who on grounds of conscience violate its laws and willingly accept their punishment. (Cf. the chapter in my *Revolution, Reform and Social Justice*.) But Zinn does not advocate civil disobedience in this sense. He urges what is clearly *uncivil* disobedience like the riotous actions that preceded the Civil Rights Acts from which the blacks, not white racists, suffered most, and the extensive destruction of property from factory sit-ins. Roy Wilkins, who should know, is my authority for asserting that the Civil Rights Acts were adopted by Congress not because of, but despite of, these disorders. The most significant racial progress since 1865 was achieved by *Brown* v. *Topeka Board of Education* without "the disorders" Zinn recommends—a sly term that covers broken heads, loss of property, and sometimes loss of life, which are no part of civil disobedience.

Until now, the most charitable thing one could say of Zinn's position is what Cicero once said of another loose thinker: there is no absurdity to which a person will not resort to defend another absurdity. But when Zinn with calculated ambiguity includes "disorders" in the connotation of civil disobedience, *without denouncing violence as no part of it as Gandhi and Martin Luther King did,* he is verging on moral irresponsibility. From the safety of his white suburbs, he is playing with fire.

Law and order are possible without justice; but Mr. Zinn does not seem to understand that justice is impossible without law and order.

# 2

# The Constitution
## *Founding Fathers: The Question of Motive*

*Of the many books that have been written about the circumstances surrounding the creation of our Constitution, none generated more controversy than Charles Beard's* An Economic Interpretation of the Constitution of the United States *(1913). A historian by profession, Beard challenged the belief that our Constitution was fashioned by men of democratic spirit. On the contrary, in what appeared to be a systematic marshaling of evidence, Beard sought to demonstrate: (1) that the impetus for a new constitution came from individuals who saw their own economic interests threatened by a growing trend in the population toward greater democracy; (2) that the Founding Fathers themselves were men of considerable "personalty" (i.e., holdings other than real estate), who were concerned not so much with fashioning a democratic constitution as they were with protecting their own financial interests against the more democratically oriented farming and debtor interests within the society; and, finally, (3) that the individuals charged with ratifying the new Constitution also represented primarily the larger economic interests within the society. While space limitations prevent a full development of Beard's argument, the portions of his book that follow should provide some feel for both the substance of his argument and his method of investigation.*

*Beard's analysis has been subject to repeated scrutiny over the years. The most systematic effort in this regard came in 1956 with the publication of Robert Brown's* Charles Beard and the Constitution: A Critical Analysis of "An Economic Interpretation of the Constitution." *Arguing that the rigor of Beard's examination was more apparent than real, Brown accuses him of citing only the facts that supported his case while ignoring those that did not. Moreover, he contends that even the evidence Beard provided did not warrant the interpretation he gave to it. Brown concludes that the best evidence now available does not support the view that "the Constitution was put over undemocratically in an undemocratic society by personal property."*

# An Economic Interpretation of the Constitution of the United States

## Charles A. Beard

Suppose it could be shown from the classification of the men who supported and opposed the Constitution that there was no line of property division at all; that is, that men owning substantially the same amounts of the same kinds of property were equally divided on the matter of adoption or rejection—it would then become apparent that the Constitution had no ascertainable relation to economic groups or classes, but was the product of some abstract causes remote from the chief business of life—gaining a livelihood.

Suppose, on the other hand, that substantially all of the merchants, money lenders, security holders, manufacturers, shippers, capitalists, and financiers and their professional associates are to be found on one side in support of the Constitution and that substantially all or the major portion of the opposition came from the nonslaveholding farmers and the debtors—would it not be pretty conclusively demonstrated that our fundamental law was not the product of an abstraction known as "the whole people," but of a group of economic interests which must have expected beneficial results from its adoption? Obviously all the facts here desired cannot be discovered, but the data presented in the following chapters bear out the latter hypothesis, and thus a reasonable presumption in favor of the theory is created.

Of course, it may be shown (and perhaps can be shown) that the farmers and debtors who opposed the Constitution were, in fact, benefited by the general improvement which resulted from its adoption. It may likewise be shown, to take an extreme case, that the English nation derived immense advantages from the Norman Conquest and the orderly administrative processes which were introduced, as it undoubtedly did; nevertheless, it does not follow that the vague thing known as "the advancement of general welfare" or some abstraction known as "justice" was the immediate, guiding purpose of the leaders in either of these great historic changes. The point is, that the direct, impelling motive in both cases was the economic advantages which the beneficiaries expected would accrue to themselves first, from their action. Further than this, economic interpretation cannot go. It may be that some larger world process is working through each series of historical events: but ultimate causes lie beyond our horizon. . . .

Charles A. Beard (1874–1948) was professor of history and political science at Columbia University and former president of the American Political Science Association. This selection is reprinted with permission of Macmillan Publishing Co., Inc., from *An Economic Interpretation of the Constitution of the United States* by Charles A. Beard, pp. 16–18, 149–151, 268–270, 288–289, 324–325. Copyright 1913, 1935, by Macmillan Publishing Co., Inc., renewed 1941 by Charles A. Beard; renewed 1963 by William Beard and Miriam Beard Vagts.

## THE FOUNDING FATHERS: AN ECONOMIC PROFILE

A survey of the economic interests of the members of the Convention presents certain conclusions:

A majority of the members were lawyers by profession.

Most of the members came from towns, on or near the coast, that is, from the regions in which personalty was largely concentrated.

Not one member represented in his immediate personal economic interests the small farming or mechanic classes.

The overwhelming majority of members, at least five-sixths, were immediately, directly, and personally interested in the outcome of their labors at Philadelphia, and were to a greater or less extent economic beneficiaries from the adoption of the Constitution.

1. Public security interests were extensively represented in the Convention. Of the fifty-five members who attended no less than forty appear on the Records of the Treasury Department for sums varying from a few dollars up to more than one hundred thousand dollars. . . .

    It is interesting to note that, with the exception of New York, and possibly Delaware, each state had one or more prominent representatives in the Convention who held more than a negligible amount of securities, and who could therefore speak with feeling and authority on the question of providing in the new Constitution for the full discharge of the public debt. . . .
2. Personalty invested in lands for speculation was represented by at least fourteen members. . . .
3. Personalty in the form of money loaned at interest was represented by at least twenty-four members. . . .
4. Personalty in mercantile, manufacturing, and shipping lines was represented by at least eleven members. . . .
5. Personalty in slaves was represented by at least fifteen members. . . .

    It cannot be said, therefore, that the members of the Convention were "disinterested." On the contrary, we are forced to accept the profoundly significant conclusion that they knew through their personal experiences in economic affairs the precise results which the new government that they were setting up was designed to attain. As a group of doctrinaires, like the Frankfort assembly of 1848, they would have failed miserably; but as practical men they were able to build the new government upon the only foundations which could be stable: fundamental economic interests.[1] . . .

## RATIFICATION

### New York

There can be no question about the predominance of personalty in the contest over the ratification in New York. That state, says Libby, "presents the problem in its simplest form. The entire mass of interior counties . . . were solidly Anti-federal, comprising the agricultural portion of the state, the last settled and the most thinly populated. There were however in this region two Federal cities (not represented in the convention [as such]), Albany in Albany county and Hudson in Columbia county. . . . The Federal area centred about New York city and county: to the southwest lay Richmond county (Staten Island); to the southeast Kings county, and the northeast Westchester county; while still further extending this area, at the northeast lay the divided county of Dutchess, with a vote in the convention of 4 to 2 in favor of the Constitution, and at the southeast were the divided counties of Queens and Suffolk. . . . These radiating strips of territory with New York city as a centre form a unit, in general favorable to the new Constitution; and it is significant of this unity that Dutchess, Queens, and Suffolk counties broke away from the anti-Federal phalanx and joined the Federalists, securing thereby the adoption of the Constitution."[2]

Unfortunately the exact distribution of personalty in New York and particularly in the wavering districts which went over to the Federalist party cannot be ascertained, for the system of taxation in vogue in New York at the period of the adoption of the Constitution did not require a state record of property.[3] The data which proved so fruitful in Massachusetts are not forthcoming, therefore, in the case of New York; but it seems hardly necessary to demonstrate the fact that New York City was the centre of personalty for the state and stood next to Philadelphia as the great centre of operations in public stock.

This somewhat obvious conclusion is reinforced by the evidence relative to the vote on the legal tender bill which the paper money party pushed through in 1786. Libby's analysis of this vote shows that "no vote was cast against the bill by members of counties north of the county of New York. In the city and county of New York and in Long Island and Staten Island, the combined vote was 9 to 5 against the measure. Comparing this vote with the vote on the ratification in 1788, it will be seen that of the Federal counties 3 voted against paper money and 1 for it; of the divided counties 1 (Suffolk) voted against paper money and 2 (Queens and Dutchess) voted for it. Of the anti-Federal counties none had members voting against paper money. The merchants as a body were opposed to the issue of paper money and the Chamber of Commerce adopted a memorial against the issue."[4]

Public security interests were identified with the sound money party. There were thirty members of the New York constitutional convention who voted in favor of the ratification of the Constitution and of these no less than sixteen were holders of public securities. . . .

## South Carolina

South Carolina presents the economic elements in the ratification with the utmost simplicity. There we find two rather sharply marked districts in antagonism over the Constitution. "The rival sections," says Libby, "were the coast or lower district and the upper, or more properly, the middle and upper country. The coast region was the first settled and contained a larger portion of the wealth of the state; its mercantile and commercial interests were important; its church was the Episcopal, supported by the state." This region, it is scarcely necessary to remark, was overwhelmingly in favor of the Constitution. The upper area, against the Constitution, "was a frontier section, the last to receive settlement; its lands were fertile and its mixed population was largely small farmers. . . . There was no established church, each community supported its own church and there was a great variety in the district."[5]

A contemporary writer, R. G. Harper, calls attention to the fact that the lower country, Charleston, Beaufort, and Georgetown, which had 28,694 white inhabitants, and about seven-twelfths of the representation in the state convention, paid £28,081:5:10 taxes in 1794, while the upper country, with 120,902 inhabitants, and five-twelfths of the representation in the convention, paid only £8390:13:3 taxes.[6] The lower districts in favor of the Constitution therefore possessed the wealth of the state and a disproportionate share in the convention—on the basis of the popular distribution of representation.

These divisions of economic interest are indicated by the abstracts of the tax returns for the state in 1794 which show that of £127,337 worth of stock in trade, faculties, etc. listed for taxation in the state, £109,800 worth was in Charleston, city and county—the stronghold of Federalism. Of the valuation of lots in towns and villages to the amount of £656,272 in the state, £549,909 was located in that city and county.[7]

The records of the South Carolina loan office preserved in the Treasury Department at Washington show that the public securities of that state were more largely in the hands of inhabitants than was the case in North Carolina. They also show a heavy concentration in the Charleston district.

At least fourteen of the thirty-one members of the state-ratifying convention from the parishes of St. Philip and Saint Michael, Charleston (all of whom favored ratification) held over $75,000 worth of public securities. . . .

## Conclusions

At the close of this long and arid survey—partaking of the nature of catalogue—it seems worthwhile to bring together the important conclusions for political science which the data presented appear to warrant.

The movement for the Constitution of the United States was originated and carried through principally by four groups of personalty interests which had been adversely affected under the Articles of Confederation: money, public securities, manufactures, and trade and shipping.

The first firm steps toward the formation of the Constitution were taken by a small and active group of men immediately interested through their personal possessions in the outcome of their labors.

No popular vote was taken directly or indirectly on the proposition to call the Convention which drafted the Constitution.

A large propertyless mass was, under the prevailing suffrage qualifications, excluded at the outset from participation (through representatives) in the work of framing the Constitution.

The members of the Philadelphia Convention which drafted the Constitution were, with a few exceptions, immediately, directly, and personally interested in, and derived economic advantages from, the establishment of the new system.

The Constitution was essentially an economic document based upon the concept that the fundamental private rights of property are anterior to government and morally beyond the reach of popular majorities.

The major portion of the members of the Convention are on record as recognizing the claim of property to a special and defensive position in the Constitution.

In the ratification of the Constitution, about three-fourths of the adult males failed to vote on the question, having abstained from the elections at which delegates to the state conventions were chosen, either on account of their indifference or their disfranchisement by property qualifications.

The Constitution was ratified by a vote of probably not more than one-sixth of the adult males.

It is questionable whether a majority of the voters participating in the elections for the state conventions in New York, Massachusetts, New Hampshire, Virginia, and South Carolina, actually approved the ratification of the Constitution.

The leaders who supported the Constitution in the ratifying conventions represented the same economic groups as the members of the Philadelphia Convention; and in a large number of instances they were also directly and personally interested in the outcome of their efforts.

In the ratification, it became manifest that the line of cleavage for and against the Constitution was between substantial personalty interests on the one hand and the small farming and debtor interests on the other.

The Constitution was not created by "the whole people" as the jurists have said; neither was it created by "the states" as Southern nullifiers long contended; but it was the work of a consolidated group whose interests knew no state boundaries and were truly national in their scope.

## NOTES

1 The fact that a few members of the Convention, who had considerable economic interests at stake, refused to support the Constitution does not invalidate the general conclusions here presented. In the cases of Yates, Lansing, Luther Martin, and Mason, definite economic reasons for their action are forthcoming; but this is a minor detail.

2 O. G. Libby, *Geographical Distribution of the Vote of the Thirteen States on the Federal Constitution,* p. 18. Libby here takes the vote in the New York convention, but that did not precisely represent the popular vote.

3 *State Papers: Finance,* vol. 1, p. 425.

4 Libby, *Geographical Distribution,* p. 59.

5 *Ibid.,* pp. 42–43.

6 "Appius," *To the Citizens of South Carolina* (1794), Library of Congress, Duane Pamphlets, vol. 83.

7 *State Papers: Finance,* vol. 1, p. 462. In 1783 an attempt to establish a bank with $100,000 capital was made in Charleston, S.C., but it failed. "Soon after the adoption of the funding system, three banks were established in Charleston whose capitals in the whole amounted to twenty times the sum proposed in 1783." D. Ramsey, *History of South Carolina* (1858 ed.), vol. 2, p. 106.

# Charles Beard and the Constitution:
## A Critical Analysis

**Robert E. Brown**

At the end of Chapter XI [of *An Economic Interpretation of the Constitution of the United States*], Beard summarized his findings in fourteen paragraphs under the heading of "Conclusions." Actually, these fourteen conclusions merely add up to the two halves of the Beard thesis. One half, that the Constitution originated with and was carried through by personalty interests— money, public securities, manufactures, and commerce—is to be found in paragraphs two, three, six, seven, eight, twelve, thirteen, and fourteen. The other half—that the Constitution was put over undemocratically in an un-democratic society—is expressed in paragraphs four, five, nine, ten, eleven, and fourteen. The lumping of these conclusions under two general headings makes it easier for the reader to see the broad outlines of the Beard thesis.

Before we examine these two major divisions of the thesis, however, some comment is relevant on the implications contained in the first paragraph. In it Beard characterized his book as a long and arid survey, something in the nature of a catalogue. Whether this characterization was designed to give his book the appearance of a coldly objective study based on the facts we do not know. If so, nothing could be further from reality. As reviewers pointed out in 1913, and as subsequent developments have demonstrated, the book is any-thing but an arid catalogue of facts. Its pages are replete with interpretation, sometimes stated, sometimes implied. Our task has been to examine Beard's evidence to see whether it justifies the interpretation which Beard gave it. We have tried to discover whether he used the historical method properly in arriving at his thesis.

If historical method means the gathering of data from primary sources, the critical evaluation of the evidence thus gathered, and the drawing of conclusions consistent with this evidence, then we must conclude that Beard has done great violation to such method in this book. He admitted that the evidence had not been collected which, given the proper use of historical method, should have precluded the writing of the book. Yet he nevertheless proceeded on the assumption that a valid interpretation could be built on secondary writings whose authors had likewise failed to collect the evidence. If we accept Beard's own maxim, "no evidence, no history," and his own admission that the data had never been collected, the answer to whether he used historical method properly is self-evident.

Robert E. Brown is professor emeritus of history at Michigan State University. This selection is from Robert E. Brown, *Charles Beard and the Constitution: A Critical Analysis of "An Economic Interpretation of the Constitution."* Copyright © 1956, renewed 1984 by Princeton University Press. "Conclusion," pp. 194–200, reprinted by permission of Princeton University Press.

Neither was Beard critical of the evidence which he did use. He was accused in 1913, and one might still suspect him, of using only that evidence which appeared to support his thesis. The amount of realty in the country compared with the personalty, the vote in New York, and the omission of the part of *The Federalist,* No. 10, which did not fit his thesis are only a few examples of the uncritical use of evidence to be found in the book. Sometimes he accepted secondary accounts at face value without checking them with the sources; at other times he allowed unfounded rumors and traditions to color his work.

Finally, the conclusions which he drew were not justified even by the kind of evidence which he used. If we accepted his evidence strictly at face value, it would still not add up to the fact that the Constitution was put over undemocratically in an undemocratic society by personalty. The citing of property qualifications does not prove that a mass of men were disfranchised. And if we accept his figures on property holdings, either we do not know what most of the delegates had in realty and personalty, or we know that realty outnumbered personalty three to one (eighteen to six). Simply showing that a man held public securities is not sufficient to prove that he acted only in terms of his public securities. If we ignore Beard's own generalizations and accept only his evidence, we have to conclude that most of the country, and that even the men who were directly concerned with the Constitution, and especially Washington, were large holders of realty.

Perhaps we can never be completely objective in history, but certainly we can be more objective than Beard was in this book. Naturally, the historian must always be aware of the biases, the subjectivity, the pitfalls that confront him, but this does not mean that he should not make an effort to overcome these obstacles. Whether Beard had his thesis before he had his evidence, as some have said, is a question that each reader must answer for himself. Certain it is that the evidence does not justify the thesis.

So instead of the Beard interpretation that the Constitution was put over undemocratically in an undemocratic society by personal property, the following fourteen paragraphs are offered as a possible interpretation of the Constitution and as suggestions for future research on that document.

**1.** The movement for the Constitution was originated and carried through by men who had long been important in both economic and political affairs in their respective states. Some of them owned personalty, more of them owned realty, and if their property was adversely affected by conditions under the Articles of Confederation, so also was the property of the bulk of the people in the country, middle-class farmers as well as town artisans.

**2.** The movement for the Constitution, like most important movements, was undoubtedly started by a small group of men. They were probably interested personally in the outcome of their labors, but the benefits which they expected were not confined to personal property or, for that matter, strictly to things economic. And if their own interests would be enhanced by a new government, similar interests of other men, whether agricultural or commercial, would also be enhanced.

**3.** Naturally there was no popular vote on the calling of the convention which drafted the Constitution. Election of delegates by state legislatures was the constitutional method under the Articles of Confederation, and had been the method long established in this country. Delegates to the Albany Congress, the Stamp Act Congress, the First Continental Congress, the Second Continental Congress, and subsequent congresses under the Articles were all elected by state legislatures, not by the people. Even the Articles of Confederation had been sanctioned by state legislatures, not by popular vote. This is not to say that the Constitutional Convention should not have been elected directly by the people, but only that such a procedure would have been unusual at the time. Some of the opponents of the Constitution later stressed, without avail, the fact that the Convention had not been directly elected. But at the time the Convention met, the people in general seemed to be about as much concerned over the fact that they had not elected the delegates as the people of this country are now concerned over the fact that they do not elect our delegates to the United Nations.

**4.** Present evidence seems to indicate that there were no ''propertyless masses'' who were excluded from the suffrage at the time. Most men were middle-class farmers who owned realty and were qualified voters, and, as the men in the Convention said, mechanics had always voted in the cities. Until credible evidence proves otherwise, we can assume that state legislatures were fairly representative at the time. We cannot condone the fact that a few men were probably disfranchised by prevailing property qualifications, but it makes a great deal of difference to an interpretation of the Constitution whether the disfranchised comprised 95 percent of the adult men or only 5 percent. Figures which give percentages of voters in terms of the entire population are misleading, since less than 20 percent of the people were adult men. And finally, the voting qualifications favored realty, not personalty.

**5.** If the members of the Convention were directly interested in the outcome of their work and expected to derive benefits from the establishment of the new system, so also did most of the people of the country. We have many statements to the effect that the people in general expected substantial benefits from the labors of the Convention.

**6.** The Constitution was not just an economic document, although economic factors were undoubtedly important. Since most of the people were middle class and had private property, practically everybody was interested in the protection of property. A constitution which did not protect property would have been rejected without any question, for the American people had fought the Revolution for the preservation of life, liberty, and property. Many people believed that the Constitution did not go far enough to protect property, and they wrote these views into the amendments to the Constitution. But property was not the only concern of those who wrote and ratified the Constitution, and we would be doing a grave injustice to the political sagacity of the Founding Fathers if we assumed that property or personal gain was their only motive.

**7.** Naturally the delegates recognized that protection of property was important under government, but they also recognized that personal rights were equally important. In fact, persons and property were usually bracketed together as the chief objects of government protection.

**8.** If three-fourths of the adult males failed to vote on the election of delegates to ratifying conventions, this fact signified indifference, not disfranchisement. We must not confuse those who could *not* vote with those who *could* vote but failed to exercise their right. Many men at the time bewailed the fact that only a small portion of the voters ever exercised their prerogative. But this in itself should stand as evidence that the conflict over the Constitution was not very bitter, for if these people had felt strongly one way or the other, more of them would have voted.

    Even if we deny the evidence which I have presented and insist that American society was undemocratic in 1787, we must still accept the fact that the men who wrote the Constitution believed that they were writing it for a democratic society. They did not hide behind an iron curtain of secrecy and devise the kind of conservative government that they wanted without regard to the views and interests of "the people." More than anything else, they were aware that "the people" would have to ratify what they proposed, and that therefore any government which would be acceptable to the people must of necessity incorporate much of what was customary at the time. The men at Philadelphia were practical politicians, not political theorists. They recognized the multitude of different ideas and interests that had to be reconciled and compromised before a constitution would be acceptable. They were far too practical, and represented far too many clashing interests themselves, to fashion a government weighted in favor of personalty or to believe that the people would adopt such a government.

**9.** If the Constitution was ratified by a vote of only one-sixth of the adult men, that again demonstrates indifference and not disfranchisement. Of the one-fourth of the adult males who voted, nearly two-thirds favored the Constitution. Present evidence does not permit us to say what the popular vote was except as it was measured by the votes of the ratifying conventions.

**10.** Until we know what the popular vote was, we cannot say that it is questionable whether a majority of the voters in several states favored the Constitution. Too many delegates were sent uninstructed. Neither can we count the towns which did not send delegates on the side of those opposed to the Constitution. Both items would signify indifference rather than sharp conflict over ratification.

**11.** The ratifying conventions were elected for the specific purpose of adopting or rejecting the Constitution. The people in general had anywhere from several weeks to several months to decide the question. If they did not like the new government, or if they did not know whether they liked it, they could have voted *no* and there would have been no Constitution. Naturally the leaders in the ratifying conventions represented the same interests as the members of the Constitutional Convention—mainly realty and some personalty. But they also represented their constituents in these same interests, especially realty.

**12.** If the conflict over ratification had been between substantial personalty interests on the one hand and small farmers and debtors on the other, there would not have been a constitution. The small farmers comprised such an overwhelming percentage of the voters that they could have rejected the new government without any trouble. Farmers and debtors are not synonymous terms and should not be confused as such. A town-by-town or county-by-county record of the vote would show clearly how the farmers voted.

**13.** The Constitution was created about as much by the whole people as any government could be which embraced a large area and depended on representation rather than on direct participation. It was also created in part by the states, for as the *Records* show, there was strong state sentiment at the time which had to be appeased by compromise. And it was created by compromising a whole host of interests throughout the country, without which compromises it could never have been adopted.

**14.** If the intellectual historians are correct, we cannot explain the Constitution without considering the psychological factors also. Men are motivated by what they believe as well as by what they have. Sometimes their actions can be explained on the basis of what they hope to have or hope that their children will have. Madison understood this fact when he said that the universal hope of acquiring property tended to dispose people to look favorably upon property. It is even possible that some men support a given economic system when they themselves have nothing to gain by it. So we would want to know what the people in 1787 thought of their class status. Did workers and small farmers believe that they were lower class, or did they, as many workers do now, consider themselves middle class? Were the common people trying to eliminate the Washingtons, Adamses, Hamiltons, and Pinckneys, or were they trying to join them?

As did Beard's fourteen conclusions, these fourteen suggestions really add up to two major propositions: the Constitution was adopted in a society which was fundamentally democratic, not undemocratic; and it was adopted by a people who were primarily middle-class property owners, especially farmers who owned realty, not just by the owners of personalty. At present these points seem to be justified by the evidence, but if better evidence in the future disproves or modifies them, we must accept that evidence and change our interpretation accordingly.

After this critical analysis, we should at least not begin future research on this period of American history with the illusion that the Beard thesis of the

Constitution is valid. If historians insist on accepting the Beard thesis in spite of this analysis, however, they must do so with the full knowledge that their acceptance is founded on "an act of faith," not an analysis of historical method, and that they were indulging in a "noble dream," not history.

# A New Constitutional Convention?

*When the Founding Fathers wrote our Constitution, they provided that amendments to it could be* proposed *in either of two ways: (1) by a two-thirds vote of both houses of Congress; or (2) by a constitutional convention called at the request of two-thirds of the state legislatures. Not since the Founding Fathers convened in 1787, however, has our nation held a constitutional convention. Rather, all amendments to our Constitution have been proposed by Congress.*

*In the last several years, the growing federal deficit has become a matter of national concern in this country. As a solution to this critical problem, some have advocated a constitutional amendment which would require the federal government to balance its budget each year. That this solution commands considerable support within the population is indicated by the fact that thirty-two state legislatures—just two short of the necessary two-thirds—have already passed resolutions calling for a constitutional convention for the purpose of formally proposing this amendment.*

*Not only has the wisdom of the balanced budget proposal been questioned by some, but so has the call for a constitutional convention to propose it. In the first selection which follows, Melvin Laird gives voice to these concerns, arguing that a convention could lead to fundamental and undesirable changes in our political system and have damaging international consequences as well. Griffin Bell, on the other hand, feels that Laird and others are creating a tempest in a teapot. He believes there is little likelihood that a convention will actually be called, but even if it is, that we have little to fear. In his judgment, the option of a convention provides the population with a needed check over a potentially unresponsive Congress. Moreover, given the history of constitutional conventions at the* state *level, there is every reason to believe that a* national *constitutional convention would act prudently and responsibly.*

# James Madison Wouldn't Approve

## Melvin R. Laird

> . . . The prospect of a second [constitutional] convention would be viewed by all Europe as a dark and threatening Cloud hanging over the Constitution.

These are the words of James Madison, the father of the U.S. Constitution; they were written in 1787, upon the adjournment of the only federal constitutional convention held in our nation's history. Although Madison, as it turned out, worried needlessly over the possible disruptive impact on our foreign relations of a constitutional convention in the 1700s, he along with "all Europe"—certainly the free nations of Europe—would have cause to worry. . . . And so should America. In fact, most Americans may be surprised to learn that we may be on the verge of convening the Second Constitutional Convention.

As a former member of both the legislative and executive branches, I am concerned . . . about the drastic and divisive consequences of action that would lead to the call for a constitutional convention.

Under Article V, there are two procedures for amending the U.S Constitution. Under the only procedure used in our history, Congress considers, passes, and submits a proposed amendment to the states for ratification. If ratified by three-quarters of the states, the amendment becomes a part of the Constitution. That has proved to be a responsive and orderly procedure.

The second procedure requires the convening of a full constitutional convention whose scope and authority are not defined or limited by our Constitution. If thirty-four states submit valid petitions to Congress for a convention, it must be convened. Any and all amendments that are considered and passed by such a convention are then forwarded to the states for ratification.

Our citizens understandably have been wary of a constitutional convention, and there is little or no historical or constitutional guidance as to its proper powers and scope. The Constitution does not spell out, for example, how delegates would be chosen or time limits for the convention or payment of costs.

The only precedent we have for a constitutional convention took place in Philadelphia in 1787. That convention, it must be remembered, broke every legal restraint designed to limit its power and agenda. It violated specific instructions from Congress to confine itself to amending the Articles of Confederation and instead discarded the Articles and wrote our present Constitution. Moreover, that convention acted in violation of the existing Articles of

Melvin R. Laird was U.S. Secretary of Defense under President Richard Nixon and a former Republican member of the U.S. House of Representatives from Wisconsin. This article is reprinted from the *Washington Post*. From Melvin R. Laird, "James Madison Wouldn't Approve," *Washington Post*, February 13, 1984, © *The Washington Post*.

Confederation by devising a new method for ratifying the proposed Constitution, specifically prohibited by the Articles of Confederation.

Reputable scholars have recently grappled with these complexities, but the realistic fact remains that two hundred years later there is no certainty that our nation would survive a modern-day convention with its basic structures intact and its citizens' traditional rights retained. The convening of a federal constitutional convention would be an act of the greatest magnitude for our nation. I believe it would be an act fraught with danger and recklessness.

Today, thirty-two of the required thirty-four states have petitioned Congress for a convention to draft an amendment requiring the federal government to maintain a balanced budget. Well-meaning and learned people differ on the desirability of mandating a balanced federal budget. I favor the adoption of an amendment through the traditional congressional procedure that would require the federal government to live within its means. Nevertheless, I cannot support and will oppose any attempt to force this issue upon Congress through petitions for a convention.

Ironically, while a constitutional convention could totally alter our way of life, the petitions for a convention regrettably have often been acted upon hastily at the state legislature level in a cavalier manner. Over one-half of the states calling for a convention have done so without the benefit of public hearings, debate, or recorded vote. This momentous decision, in other words, is being made surreptitiously, as if it cannot withstand the scrutiny and discussion of a concerned and intelligent citizenry.

In addition to its perils for the internal workings of our nation, a constitutional convention would have serious, frequently overlooked, international repercussions. The United States is the oldest, largest, and most stable republic in the world. It is also the cornerstone of the entire economic life of the Western world and a significant factor in the economy of almost every country on the globe.

If Madison were justifiably concerned over the foreign policy implications of a U.S. constitutional convention in the eighteenth century, our concern should be multiplied by the infinitely more prominent world role our country plays in the twentieth century. The potential disruptions to our vital foreign policy interests—NATO is an example—are disturbing to contemplate.

If a convention were called, our allies and foes alike would soon realize the new pressures imposed upon our republic. The mere act of convening a constitutional convention would send tremors throughout all those economies that depend on the dollar; would undermine our neighbors' confidence in our constitutional integrity; and would weaken not only our economic stability but the stability of the free world. That is a price we cannot afford.

The domestic and international instability engendered by a convention cannot be justified by the prospect of a balanced federal budget. Even if the convention passed a balanced budget amendment in short order and then disbanded, the ratification process would take years. In addition, it is unlikely that an amendment would require a balanced budget in its first effective year:

each of the drafts historically considered to date has allowed a multiyear phasing in of the limitations.

So even in the best case, a convention would not cure our budget deficit problems quickly. And the price for a long-term solution achieved through a convention would be incalculable domestic and international confusion.

The concept that a constitutional convention would be harmless is not conservative, moderate, or liberal philosophy. That concept is profoundly radical, born either of naiveté or the opportunistic thought that the end justifies the means. Our duty, as citizens of this nation, is to guard and protect our Constitution, to uphold its integrity, and to weigh the impact not only of proposed revisions but also of the means proposed to adopt them. We must work together to preserve all that is good in our system and to resolve problems by rational means. This nation certainly does not need a constitutional crisis; it should not take the first steps toward a possible wholesale revision of its Constitution; it must not, by moving closer to a constitutional convention, engender crippling domestic and international uncertainty.

Especially now, when international relations are precarious and global economies are struggling to regain the momentum of growth, a convention would divert our domestic attentions from pressing national problems and legislative and executive branch responsibilities, while focusing global attention on what would certainly appear, to friends and enemies alike, as a profound weakness in our national fabric. To say a constitutional convention should be called to balance the federal budget is a deception. A convention cannot perform magic; at best, it could offer an over-the-horizon possibility of a balanced budget amendment, while creating the certainty of profound mischief.

# Constitutional Convention:
## Oh, Stop the Hand-Wringing

**Griffin B. Bell**

Like most Americans, I am deeply concerned by the federal government's continuing failure to control the budget deficits. The interest payments on the debt now amount to 12 percent of the current budget [15 percent in 1990—Editors]. Basic to this failure is that no counterforce exists against the special interest groups that are the driving force behind excessive government spending.

Because Congress has failed to control runaway government deficits, the people have acted through their state legislatures, 32 of which have called for a constitutional convention to draft a balanced federal budget amendment. When 34 states have so acted, Congress, under Article V of the Constitution, must call a convention.

We are now hearing predictions of doom and gloom that have not been heard since the passage of the Seventeenth Amendment seventy-two years ago. . . . In our original Constitution, senators were appointed by the state legislatures rather than elected by the people. By 1912, the people had concluded by a wide margin that the Senate should be elected, not appointed. The House of Representatives agreed, five times passing a proposed constitutional amendment to make the Senate elective.

But five times the Senate killed the amendment in committee, thereby forcing the people to take action. State legislatures began passing conditional calls for a convention, if Congress did not approve the amendment.

At that time, the two-thirds required was 32 state legislatures. When 31 states had acted, the Senate read the handwriting on the wall and passed the amendment. Without the use of the alternative route in Article V of our Constitution, the Seventeenth Amendment would not have been passed and senators would still be appointed.

This is precisely what the Founding Fathers had in mind. They provided for amendment through action of the state legislatures to deal with those situations in which Congress was part of the problem and would not act. That situation prevailed in 1912. It prevails equally in 1984 [and in 1990].

Aside from the specious argument that a convention is "alien" to the constitutional process, we also hear other objections. It is argued that our friends abroad would recoil in horror at the prospect of a U.S. constitutional convention that would presumably destabilize America. But the free world has been decimated by our interest rates and the dollar exchange rate, which

Griffin B. Bell was Attorney General of the United States under President Jimmy Carter. This selection is reprinted from the *Washington Post*. From Griffin B. Bell, "Constitutional Convention: Oh, Stop the Hand-Wringing." *Washington Post*, April 14, 1984 © *The Washington Post*.

foreign financial experts attribute to our huge deficits and general fiscal profligacy. A serious effort to install long-term constitutional control over U.S. fiscal practices would be welcomed by our friends abroad.

Also, we are bombarded with ominous stories about a "runaway" constitutional convention that, presumably, would repeal the Bill of Rights, dismantle the Constitution, and install some sort of totalitarian regime. Well, while we have not had a federal convention since 1787, there have been over two hundred conventions held in various states, many of whose constitutions provide for periodic conventions to propose amendments. Such gatherings have brought out the best, not the worst, in people's government.

It is claimed that James Madison said a "new" constitutional convention would be a cloud over the Constitution. He did in fact utter those words, but in response to critics who declared that the Constitution written in Philadelphia in 1787 should be rejected and a new convention be held immediately. Thomas Jefferson, author of the Declaration of Independence, assumed that we would have a new convention about every twenty years.

In fact, fears about a "runaway" convention are groundless. The various state applications to Congress not only exhort Congress to pass the Tax Limitation–Balanced Budget Amendment but limit the scope of a convention to the sole and exclusive purpose of the balanced budget issue.

Those who wring their hands over the prospects of a convention run the risk of exposing their elitism, implying that the average citizen cannot be trusted. At the same time, they are willing to place their full faith in Congress, the very institution that has precipitated the fiscal mess that, in turn, has prompted the Tax Limitation–Balanced Budget movement.

But, suppose that other resolutions were offered at the Balanced Budget Convention. Congress would not be compelled, nor would it have any incentive, to send along to the states for ratification any proposals emanating from the convention that exceeded the scope of the call. And thirty-eight states are not about to ratify any proposal that does violence to or seeks to dismantle fundamental constitutional protections and guarantees.

Finally, it is important to understand that a convention will not necessarily take place upon the application of thirty-four states. The state calls have said: if Congress does not pass the amendment, then a convention for that purpose is called. The calls are conditional, not absolute. I believe there will not be a balanced budget constitutional convention. Congress simply will not abide letting mere citizens decide its taxing and spending power. Congress will act, I predict, as it did on the issue of the direct elections of senators—when overwhelming pressure from the states and the people can no longer be ignored.

# 3

# Federalism

*The Tenth Amendment to the U.S. Constitution states: "The powers not delegated to the United States by the Constitution, nor prohibited by it to the States, are reserved to the States respectively, or to the people." Although this brief amendment, containing just slightly more than 25 words, seems amazingly simple and uncomplicated, it has, in fact, constituted the basis for one of the more protracted debates in U.S. history—namely, the extent of powers of the national government versus those of the states.*

*A contemporary manifestation of this debate is to be found in a recent proposal by the executive director of the U.S. Advisory Commission on Intergovernmental Relations—John Kincaid—who suggests that in order to reduce what he believes to be the current excessive powers of the national government, the U.S. Supreme Court should be required to have all issues bearing on state powers decided by a three-fourths vote rather than the traditional simple majority. Alarmed by the evident encroachment of national power over the states, Director Kincaid argues that such a three-fourths vote proposal would "plug the leak" of increasing national power at the expense of the states. It has the added virtue, he argues, of being only a modest reform, requiring neither constitutional amendment nor radical change in the basic federal system.*

*Responding to the Kincaid proposal is political science professor Richard A. Brisbin, Jr. While Professor Brisbin sees a number of specific problems with the three-fourths vote proposal, not the least of which is that it might endanger the rights of minorities, the main issue for him is the simple fact that the three-fourths proposal assumes that "federalism" is a "fundamental value" that ought to be protected. In Professor Brisbin's view, federalism is a means to an end, not an end in and of itself: federalism is merely the instrument to preserve liberty; and if there is to be any "tinkering" with our federal system, one should be careful that it does not reduce liberty. Professor Brisbin has the suspicion that the three-fourths proposal might, in fact, have such an effect. The reader will see, therefore, that the Kincaid-Brisbin debate is not only a matter of some minor disagreements over the effects of such a reform, but also over the fundamental nature and purposes of federalism itself.*

# A Proposal to Strengthen Federalism: A Three-Fourths Vote of the U.S. Supreme Court to Void State Law

**John Kincaid**

. . . This article calls attention to the role of the U.S. Supreme Court in nationalizing the federal system and advances a modest proposal that the U.S. Supreme Court be constitutionally required to reach a three-fourths vote to void a state law or local ordinance. This rule would apply to state or local acts that are said to violate the U.S. Constitution or a federal statute enacted pursuant to congressional and presidential interpretations of national power under the U.S. Constitution. . . .

The basic premise for the three-fourths vote proposal is that federalism is a fundamental constitutional value. A key problem in protecting this value is that a federal distribution of powers can be stipulated in general terms, and with a few specifics, but not in detailed constitutional terms capable of meeting all future contingencies. Therefore, enduring decision rules and representative structures must be established to protect fundamental values—such as federalism, the separation of powers and individual rights. It is not enough, for example, to stipulate a separation of powers, one must also structure the separation so that, in James Madison's words: "Ambition [can] be made to counteract ambition." . . .

Surprisingly, for a document otherwise attentive to checks and balances, the U.S. Constitution provides no voting rules for the U.S. Supreme Court, nor for that matter does it provide for judicial review, the size of the Court, or written decisions. Yet, state constitutions at least stipulate the size of the state high court or courts. Many state constitutions also require written opinions with "the grounds stated"; many establish a quorum rule; and some require the state high court to sit *in banc* for certain cases. The North Dakota Constitution goes so far as to say that [the] "supreme court shall not declare a legislative enactment unconstitutional unless at least four of the [five] members of the court so decide." For the U.S. Supreme Court, however, judicial review, nine members, written decisions and simple majority voting are all traditions.

The absence of constitutional rules governing these matters is an important reason why the U.S. Supreme Court is so independent and powerful. The Court has had considerable freedom to define its powers. For much of U.S.

John Kincaid is executive director of the U.S. Advisory Commission on Intergovernmental Relations, Washington, D.C., and professor of political science at North Texas State University. The article is reprinted from John Kincaid, "A Proposal to Strengthen Federalism," *The Journal of State Government*, 62 (January/February 1989), pp. 36–45. © 1989 The Council of State Governments. Reprinted with permission from *The Journal of State Government*. The views expressed here are his own.

history, the Court exercised a large measure of restraint. It was not the powerful player that it is today in the political system, although it occasionally tried to be such a player, as in the infamous *Dred Scott* case (1857). Now, however, the Court exerts considerable power and makes policies having far-ranging effects on American society. One key to this power is that it can be wielded by as few as five or even four justices. . . .

## THE LEAST DANGEROUS BRANCH?

Writing in defense of the proposed Constitution in 1788, Alexander Hamilton asserted that the federal "judiciary, from the nature of its functions, will always be the least dangerous to the political rights of the Constitution; because it will be least in a capacity to annoy or injure them" (*Federalist* 78). After all, argued Hamilton, the U.S. Supreme Court would not dispense honors, hold "the sword of the community," command the purse, or prescribe "the rules by which the duties and rights of every citizen are to be regulated." Thus, unless Hamilton was slipping a Trojan horse into the ratification debate, we have to take him at his word; even though the Court would be highly independent and would exercise the power of what we now call judicial review, the Court would not be a major center of power or an independent instrument for the aggrandizement of national power. Sufficient checks had been placed on the federal judiciary to prevent such a development.

Although the judiciary was not a prominent target of critics of the proposed Constitution, Brutus, who was one of the most important and articulate Antifederalist essayists, disagreed with Hamilton. Brutus argued that the judiciary would become the most dangerous branch, at least with respect to the preservation of state powers. "Perhaps nothing could have been better conceived to facilitate the abolition of the state governments than the constitution of the judicial," he wrote in 1788 (Storing 1981). "The judicial power will operate to effect, in the most certain, but yet silent and imperceptible manner . . . an entire subversion of the legislative, executive and judicial powers of the individual states." Brutus was convinced: "That the judicial power of the United States, will lean strongly in favour of the general government, and will give such an explanation to the constitution, as will favour an extension of its jurisdiction." . . .

In retrospect, the U.S. Supreme Court has been neither as tame as predicted by Hamilton nor as dangerous as expected by Brutus. The Court has not sought "to abolish entirely the state governments, and to melt down the states into one entire government," as Brutus thought it would do. Yet the Court has become much more powerful and has had a more corrosive effect on state powers than Hamilton led his readers to believe in 1788. By declaring the 10th Amendment to be a "mere truism" in 1942 (*United States v. Darby*) and by holding in the 1980s that the states must protect their interests through a deficient political process that the 10th Amendment was designed to correct, the Supreme Court has abrogated the ratification agreement of 1788, opened the door to unchecked congressional interpretations of its own powers vis-a-vis the states, and altered even the design of the original Constitution that was to have made the federal judiciary the least dangerous branch.

If state and local governments wish to remedy this situation, they must, as the Court said, turn to the political process. Although the Supreme Court majority had the congressional and presidential arenas in mind when it told the states to protect their interests through the national political process, there is no reason to construe this process so narrowly. The national political process also includes Article V, namely, constitutional amendment. Constitutional politics is high politics and should not be entered into lightly, but it is fully provided for in the U.S. Constitution.

## COURT EROSION OF STATE AUTHORITY

Brutus was perhaps most correct in arguing that the federal judiciary would be partisan. As an agency of the national government, the federal judiciary would naturally favor expansions of national power over state powers. In this, the federal courts also would have a self-interest because any expansion of national power would be an expansion of federal judicial power.

One way of looking at how this observation has been tested by history is to examine U.S. Supreme Court decisions that have held congressional acts, state laws and local ordinances to be unconstitutional. From 1789 through mid-1986, the Supreme Court had declared only 121 acts of Congress to be unconstitutional in whole or in part. During that same period, however, the Court held 1,026 state acts and 113 local ordinances to be unconstitutional in whole or in part (Congressional Research Service 1987). The exercise of this power has grown during 25-year periods (except 1964–1986) since 1789 (Table 1). Clearly, the data in Table 1 indicate that the Court was comparatively restrained for about the first 130 years of U.S. history. Looking at the exercise of judicial review from 1789 until the 1920s, one might well agree with Hamilton that the federal judiciary was the least dangerous branch. Since World War I, however, the Court has become much more interventionist.

During the 73 years from 1914 through mid-1986, the Court overturned more congressional and state-local acts than it did during the first 125 years of U.S. history. Put another way, 72 percent of all congressional acts and 78 percent of all state-local acts voided by the U.S. Supreme Court since 1789 were overturned during a period that accounted for only 37 percent of U.S. history.

It is also apparent, however, that the Court has been comparatively restrained in voiding acts of Congress. This restraint is another reason why the Court has acquired power. The Congress and the president can strike back at

**TABLE 1 Congressional and State-Local Acts Held Unconstitutional
By the U.S Supreme Court 1789-1986**

| Period | Number of Acts Declared Unconstitutional | |
|---|---|---|
|  | Congressional | State-Local |
| 1789–1813 | 1 | 3 |
| 1814–1838 | 0 | 15 |
| 1839–1863 | 1 | 20 |
| 1864–1888 | 15 | 99 |
| 1889–1913 | 17 | 118 |
| 1914–1938 | 31 | 301 |
| 1939–1963 | 8 | 183 |
| 1964–1986 | 48 | 399 |
| **Totals** | **121** | **1,139** |

*SOURCE:* Congressional Research Service, *The Constitution of the United States: Analysis and Interpretation* (Washington, D.C.: Government Printing Office, 1987) and *1986 Supplement.*

the Court. By being restrained in attacking congressional and presidential exercises of power that erode state authority, the Court protects itself from its natural competitors (or predators).

Indeed, when the Court first mounted an historically unusual assault on congressional-presidential legislation in the 1920s and 1930s, it soon found itself under siege. Although President Franklin D. Roosevelt's court-packing plan failed, the "switch in time that saved nine" clearly signaled that the Court got the message. The states, however, do not have the same ability to strike back. As a result, having been tamed and put back into its "least dangerous" place with respect to the other two branches of the national government, the Court has, during the past 50 years, regained power and prestige by turning its attention to state powers—a direction that not only makes the Court king of a new hill, but also mollifies its competitors on Capitol Hill.

Given that the Court voided 48 congressional acts from 1964 through mid-1986, one might think that this apparently bold re-entry into the congressional-presidential thicket would have provoked another counterattack. Yet this has not been the case, in large part because there is a crucial difference today. More than three-quarters of the Court's decisions overturning acts, or usually portions of acts, of Congress during 1964–1986 involved questions of individual civil, criminal, or welfare rights having benefits for persons but only marginally frustrating effects on national policies.

Except for a few decisions, such as *National League of Cities v. Usery*, now overturned by the Court, and *Oregon v. Mitchell* (1970), now overruled by the 26th Amendment (18-year-old voting), the Supreme Court has not been thwarting congressional and presidential policies that expand national power or contract state power. Furthermore, some of those 48 decisions have benefited one or both of the other branches. For example, *INS v. Chadha* (1983), which overturned the legislative veto, benefited the President, while *Buckley v. Valeo*

(1986), which voided certain campaign-spending limits, benefited the electoral interests of members of Congress and numerous aspirants for federal office. No wonder the Court is so powerful. By doing favors for its sister branches, the Court stays well out of harm's way.

Unwilling to meddle with the powers of its strong sister branches in a significant way, the Court meddles with the powers of what are now routinely regarded as the nation's "lower level" governments. This is an astonishing development because it means that the Court is not vigorously policing the borders created by two of the most fundamental features of our national Constitution: the separation of powers and federalism. Hamilton was right. No sibling rivalry here. For Congress and the president, the federal judiciary is the least dangerous branch. For the states, however, Brutus had more than an idle point. . . .

## THE RISE OF SPLIT VOTING

Changing patterns of voting on the Supreme Court add [an] element of unpredictability to the status of state and local governments in the federal system. From 1789 through 1929, some 64 percent of the Court's decisions striking down state laws and local ordinances were made by unanimous votes. Since 1929, however, only about 50 percent of these decisions have been unanimous—a significant decline in Court agreement on questions of federalism and a significant increase in the ability of a small number of nationalist-minded justices to overturn the work of numerous governors and perhaps thousands of state legislators.

Another indicator of dissension is David G. Savage's examination of 38 Supreme Court decisions affecting state and local governments in 1987. States and localities won 21 and lost 17 of those 1987 cases. Strikingly, only seven (18 percent) of those 38 decisions were unanimous. Fully 14 of the decisions (37 percent) were decided by 5-4 votes, while another seven (18 percent) were decided by 6-3 votes (Savage 1988). Such voting behavior hardly lends confidence to the idea that the justices are dispassionately interpreting the same document.

Figure 1 graphically illustrates the historical trends discussed here. The graph shows the dramatic rise in Supreme Court decisions striking down state and local acts as unconstitutional, as well as the trends in dissenting behavior. Since 1789, there have been three periods of sharp increases in Court nullifications of state and local acts: (1) the 1860s through the 1880s, (2) the 1910s and 1920s, and (3) the 1960s through mid-1986.

There have been six decades in which the number of cases having one or more dissenters has equaled or exceeded 50 percent: the 1820s (50 percent), the 1840s (56 percent), the 1850s (86 percent), the 1940s (66 percent), the 1950s (58 percent) and the 1980s (50 percent). Overall, however, all six decades since 1929 have been marked by historically high levels of dissent.

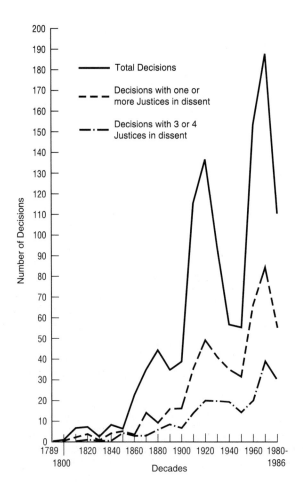

**FIGURE 1** U.S. Supreme Court Decisions and Dissents in Decisions Holding State Acts and Local Ordinances Unconstitutional 1789–1986.

## WHAT MIGHT HAVE BEEN?

If the Supreme Court had been required since 1789 to reach a three-fourths vote (7-2 today) in order to void state laws and local ordinances, what would have been the effects of the rule on state and local governments? We cannot, of course, be certain what behavior would have been like in the past; however, we can get an indication by tallying the numbers of cases in which state and local acts were voided on constitutional grounds by less than three-quarters of the justices. The results of this tally are presented in Table 2.

Except for the 1850s when 71 percent of the voided state acts (5 of 7 cases) would have been upheld, the three-fourths rule would have had modest but useful benefits for state and local governments (Table 2). National supremacy within the domain constitutionally assigned to the national government would not have been severely compromised by the rule, but state and

**TABLE 2 Percent of Voided State-Local Acts That Would Have Been Upheld if Three-Fourths Rule Had Been in Effect, 1789–1986**

| Decade | Percent | Decade | Percent |
|--------|---------|--------|---------|
| 1789–1799 | — | 1890–1899 | 28 |
| 1800–1809 | 0 | 1900–1909 | 20 |
| 1810–1819 | 0 | 1910–1919 | 13 |
| 1820–1829 | 13 | 1920–1929 | 15 |
| 1830–1839 | 33 | 1930–1939 | 25 |
| 1840–1849 | 11 | 1940–1949 | 36 |
| 1850–1859 | 71 | 1950–1959 | 26 |
| 1860–1869 | 13 | 1960–1969 | 15 |
| 1870–1879 | 8 | 1970–1979 | 23 |
| 1880–1889 | 11 | 1980–1986 | 32 |

local governments would have gained varying degrees of relief from expansive national powers. This is why the three-fourths rule is a "modest" reform proposal. It would change the rules of the game so as to give the benefit of the doubt to state and local governments, but it would not upset the constitutional apple cart or paralyze the national government. Thus, so far in the 1980s, the national government would still have won 68 percent of the cases, but 32 percent (or nearly a third) of the state and local acts voided by the Court would not have been vacated if the rule had been in effect—no small measure of relief in this era of nationalization.

One question that comes to mind immediately, though, is: What would have been the effect of the three-fourths rule on historic decisions, especially those involving individual rights? Although any list of historic decisions is a matter of judgment, what follows is a list of what would probably be generally accepted as historic decisions, each of which would have withstood the three-fourths rule.

*Fletcher v. Peck*, 1810 (Georgia law violates contracts clause).

*McCulloch v. Maryland*, 1819 (state tax on U.S. Bank violates supremacy clause).

*Dartmouth College v. Woodward*, 1819 (New Hampshire law altering private charter violates contracts clause).

*Gibbons v. Ogden*, 1824 (New York cannot grant exclusive rights to navigate interstate waters).

*Brown v. Maryland*, 1827 (state cannot regulate foreign commerce or levy import duty).

*DeJonge v. Oregon*, 1937 (state criminal syndicalism law violates First Amendment).

*Hague v. C.I.O.*, 1939 (Jersey City ordinance prohibiting distribution of printed matter and public assembly without permit violates First Amendment).

*Thornhill v. Alabama*, 1940 (state law prohibiting publicizing of facts in a labor dispute violates First Amendment).

*Cantwell v. Connecticut*, 1940 (state law prohibiting solicitation for religion without license and proof of religious cause violates First Amendment).

*Joseph Burstyn, Inc. v. Wilson*, 1952 (New York prohibition of showing of film deemed sacrilegious violates First Amendment).

*Brown v. Board of Education*, 1954 (state laws segregating white and black children in public schools violate 14th Amendment).

*Gomillion v. Lightfoot*, 1960 (Alabama law altering Tuskegee boundary to exclude black voters violates 15th Amendment).

*Torasco v. Watkins*, 1961 (Maryland religious test for public office violates First Amendment).

*Gideon v. Wainwright*, 1963 (Florida law not giving indigent defendant court-appointed counsel violates 14th Amendment).

*Abington School District v. Schempp*, 1963 (Pennsylvania law requiring public-school Bible-reading violates First Amendment).

*Wesberry v. Sanders*, 1964 (Georgia law creating congressional districts of unequal population size violates Article I, Section 2).

*Reynolds v. Sims*, 1964 (Alabama law creating state legislative districts of unequal population size violates 14th Amendment).

*Dombrowski v. Pfister*, 1965 (Louisiana subversive and Communist law violates First Amendment).

*Griswold v. Connecticut*, 1965 (law prohibiting use of contraceptives violates privacy).

*Stanley v. Georgia*, 1969 (law prohibiting private possession of obscenity violates First Amendment).

*Lemon v. Kurtzman*, 1971 (state laws providing certain aid to sectarian schools violate First Amendment).

*Roe v. Wade*, 1973 (Texas law narrowly limiting abortion violates 14th Amendment).

What are some important decisions that would not have withstood the three-fourths voting rule? One decision of continuing concern for state and local governments is *National Bellas Hess* v. *Illinois* (1967) [limiting state taxation of out-of-state mail orders], decided by a 6-3 vote. Another decision is *Kassel v. Consolidated Freightways Corp.* (1981), which voided state laws prohibiting 65-foot double-trailer trucks on state highways where all neighboring states permitted them. *Democratic Party v. Wisconsin ex. rel. La Follette* (1981), a 6-3 decision, further strengthened national political-party powers. In *First National Bank v. Bellotti* (1978), a 5-4 decision, the Court struck down a criminal statute prohibiting banks and business corporations from spending money to influence referendum votes on questions not directly affecting them.

Two major rights decisions that would not have withstood the three-fourths rule are *Near v. Minnesota* (1931), which struck down a newspaper gag law by a 5-4 vote, and *Furman v. Georgia* (1972), which struck down state death-penalty statutes by a 5-4 vote. Other rights decisions that would not have passed three-fourths muster include *Nixon v. Condon* (1932), which struck down a Texas white primary law, and *Shapiro v. Thompson* (1969), which voided one-year residency requirements for welfare assistance.

Looking farther into the past, however, there is a now infamous rights ruling that also would not have passed muster: *Lochner v. New York* (1905), a 5-4 decision. This ruling struck down state efforts to regulate working hours on behalf of employees. Although today we tend to view the Supreme Court as an institution that expands individual rights over against restrictive state and local laws, in the late 19th and early 20th centuries, the Court often struck down rights-expanding state legislation designed to protect workers, farmers and consumers.

Such Court behavior, moreover, may not be a thing of the past. The recent 6-3 ruling in *City of Richmond v. J. A. Croson Co.* (1989), which restricted municipal affirmative action programs intended to benefit minority contractors, suggests that the Court may increasingly overturn state and local policies that can be described as progressive or rights-expanding. In some cases, it will be possible to rescue state and local policies by grounding them in state constitutional law (Kincaid 1987); however, in the absence of a three-fourths voting rule on the U.S. Supreme Court, the much-heralded resurgence of the states, which has involved the institutionalization of many now widely accepted reforms and federally induced policies, may be thwarted by narrow majorities on the Court. A small number of justices deinstitutionalized liberal state and local policies by asserting national supremacy just as readily as they deinstitutionalized conservative state and local policies. The knife cuts both ways.

## RATIONALES FOR A THREE-FOURTHS RULE

The basic reason for proposing that three-fourths of the justices on the U.S. Supreme Court be required to reach an agreement to vacate state laws and local ordinances is that federalism is an important value deserving protection in its own right. This is not the place to make the case for federalism, but suffice to say that there is no evidence that conditions in the modern world require unabated centralization and nationalization. Evidence from around the world suggests that decentralization in both private and public sector organizations has many progressive and adaptive benefits. Of course, there continues to be a vital role for national governments. Blind across-the-board decentralization would be as unwise as blind across-the-board centralization. Hence, we are back to questions of balance in the federal system and to the original challenge faced by the framers of the United States Constitution: How can we have a strong union with strong states?

This question cannot be answered for all time by a comprehensive list of national and state powers. This is why proposals to rewrite the 10th Amendment are futile. Even if we could agree on a revision, there would be no way of knowing how the Supreme Court would interpret the new language 20, 50, 100 or 200 years from now. Even a simple change, such as adding "expressly" to the 10th Amendment, would conflict with other portions of the Constitution and still leave the task of interpretation to a Court that can usually find a way to strengthen national powers when four or five justices have a will to do so. Similarly, proposals to require the Court to enforce the 10th Amendment are, under current Court voting rules, tantamount to inviting the wolf to come back to guard what's left of the flock.

What is needed is a procedural or deliberative rule that can afford a greater measure of protection for state and local authority than has been the case for practically a century, a rule that can also restrain a Congress and, indirectly, an executive branch that now exhibit all the liabilities of bigness and power. The distinct advantage of a procedural rule is that it allows us to adapt to circumstances. It does not freeze a dynamic principle like federalism into a deadweight, and it does not require us to answer in advance questions that cannot be answered in advance. A procedural rule is also a neutral principle; it cuts both ways on the political spectrum. Most important, a procedural rule recognizes that most questions of balance in the federal system are, in the final analysis, matters of judgment. The key issue, then, is who should render this judgment.

One set of proposed procedural reforms would change the way we amend the Constitution. These proposals seek to make it easier for states to initiate constitutional amendments by either resolving or avoiding the problem of a runaway constitutional convention. This fear of a runaway convention is ironic because a constitutional convention is the highest expression of popular sovereignty—the very foundation of our constitutional republic—but the fear exists nonetheless. Hence, changes in the amendment process are worth exploring, but such change would clearly be a major step, the outcome of which is uncertain.

An interim and perhaps sufficient step could be the proposed three-fourths voting rule on the Supreme Court. This procedural rule recognizes that the U.S. Constitution is, in a *de facto* sense, amended by interpretation, mainly by the Court. The Supreme Court is the umpire or gatekeeper of our federal system. Much of the development and change in the federal system can be attributed to the Court. The problem is that the Court has opened the gate too frequently to allow national power to escape from its constitutional corral. Moreover, the Court in *Garcia* and *South Carolina* has removed the 10th Amendment gate, thus compelling the states and their local governments to protect themselves from injury in the political stampede.

It is this *de facto* amendment power of the Supreme Court that highlights the need for an extraordinary vote rule because, where else do we find such a rule already embedded in the Constitution? We find it in Article V. No amendment can go into effect without the consent of the legislatures or popular conventions in three-fourths of the states. The Congress cannot propose amendments unless two-thirds of both Houses deem it necessary. Amendments also can be initiated by two-thirds of the states, in which case the Congress "shall call a Convention." Here, no extraordinary vote rule is provided for the Congress because the call originates from the people of two-thirds of the states. Given that Congress is the servant of the people, it must call a convention. No voting rule is provided for a convention because a convention is an expression of popular sovereignty, and any amendments proposed by it would still require ratification by three-fourths of the states.

"We the people" inserted these extraordinary vote rules in Article V for three basic reasons. First, the Constitution is fundamental law that should not be subjected to the vagaries of simple majority voting. Second, except for conventions, the actors in the amendment process are legislative bodies. The extraordinary vote rules greatly increase the likelihood that legislatively enacted amendments will reflect as much public consensus as is possible in a diverse society without paralyzing the union by a rule of unanimity. Third, the Constitution establishes the fundamental distribution of powers between the nation and the states. This is the basic federal bargain, and the framers knew that to make this bargain vulnerable to simple majority voting would be to jeopardize the whole arrangement. Indeed, in order to go into effect itself, the proposed Constitution needed the consent of conventions in nine of the 13 states—the original extraordinary vote rule that brought the union into being.

In short, to protect the lawful powers of the states and the nation and thereby federalism, the Constitution erects, among other things, extraordinary vote rules. Note too that neither party to the agreement, state or nation, can amend the Constitution unilaterally. It takes two to do the amendment tango. Furthermore, Article V is ultimately more protective of state powers than national powers because the only discretionary authority given to Congress is to propose amendments. If the Congress refuses to propose amendments, then two-thirds of the states can require it to call a constitutional convention. Thus, when two-thirds of the states believe that the national government is being truculent, they can appeal to the ultimate sovereign, the people, to arbitrate the issue. The states, moreover, get to ratify all amendments; whether they originate in the Congress or a convention. Congress, however, can neither approve nor veto amendments proposed by a convention. No wonder the Congress is so fearful of a convention. The principal protection for national powers in Article V is the three-fourths state ratification rule. The Congress needs only a minority of states to side with it to block an unfriendly amendment.

If this is not enough evidence that extraordinary vote rules were intended to be important procedural devices for protecting federalism and especially state powers, then consider another major extraordinary vote rule in the Constitution: Treaties must be ratified by two-thirds of the members of the U.S. Senate who are present. Given that treaties can expand national powers and damage the interests of all or some states, the Constitution gives the states extra protection here. Still another extraordinary vote protection for the states is that a two-thirds vote is needed in the U.S. House to expel a member.

There are still more extraordinary vote rules in the Constitution. A two-thirds vote in both houses of Congress is needed to override a presidential veto of legislation. A conviction in an impeachment trial requires a two-thirds vote of the members of the U.S. Senate who are present.

Two very important patterns underlie these extraordinary vote rules.

First, the Congress is their primary target. They impose procedural restrictions on the Congress because the Congress is the principal repository of the powers delegated to the national government and because the Congress is the principal institutional vehicle for majority rule. Thus, the Constitution's extraordinary vote rules are designed to prevent the Congress, the potentially most dangerous branch, from tyrannizing both its sister branches and the states.

Second, therefore, these extraordinary vote rules are designed to afford a substantial, but not paralyzing, measure of protection for the Constitution's distribution of powers within the national government and between the nation and the states. In other words, when it came to protecting two of the most fundamental features of our national Constitution—federalism and the separation of powers—"we the people" decided that the measure of nationwide consensus required by extraordinary majority voting on fundamental questions is superior to the intrigue, instability and divisiveness that can arise from simple majority voting. Extraordinary vote rules are among what Madison called republican remedies for republican diseases (*Federalist* 10).

This proposed three-fourths voting rule for the U.S. Supreme Court is, therefore, fully consistent with the letter and spirit of the U.S. Constitution. If those who framed and ratified the Constitution had believed that the Court would be as powerful as it is today, they probably would have provided for such a rule. They, however, did not. As Hamilton said, they expected the Court to be the least dangerous branch. Only people like Brutus thought differently, but ratification of the 10th Amendment was to have taken care of the problem. Those who supported the 10th Amendment could not possibly have believed that the Supreme Court would be able to ignore it, to say nothing of ignoring it by a 5-4 vote.

In effect, the constitutional design of our federal system has sprung an enormous leak. The dam constructed by the 10th Amendment and the Constitution's extraordinary vote rules to contain and regulate the flow of national power has been battered by many developments in this century. Although the legal origins of rising national power lie primarily in the Congress and presidency, ultimately it is the Supreme Court that not only legitimizes that power but also adds to it by independently striking down state and local laws and by refusing to stand tall against its sister branches.

A three-fourths voting rule would plug the leak and repair the dam, not for the purpose of stopping the flow of national power, but of regulating its flow in a manner consistent with the design of the Constitution. The rule also would have the advantage of strengthening the separation of powers by giving the Supreme Court the constitutional backbone to perform its interbranch duty of checking and balancing congressional and presidential exercises of powers. . . .

# SOURCES

Congressional Research Service, Library of Congress. 1987. *The Constitution of the United States of America: Analysis and Interpretation.* Washington, D.C.: U.S. Government Printing Office and 1986 Supplement. To ensure comparability of data over time, I have relied entirely on the CRS information and have not sought to update beyond that published information.

Kincaid, John. 1988. "State Court Protections of Individual Rights Under State Constitutions: The New Judicial Federalism," *The Journal of State Government* 61 (September/October): 163–169.

Savage, David G. 1988. "States Win Some, Lose Some Before '87 High Courts," *State Legislatures* 14 (January): 22–25.

Storing, Herbert J. with Murray Dry, eds. 1981. *The Complete Anti- Federalist.* Chicago: University of Chicago Press.

U.S. Advisory Commission on Intergovernmental Relations. 1989. *Hearings on Constitutional Reform on Federalism: Statements by State and Local Government Association Representatives.* Wasington, D.C.: ACIR, January.

# Tinkering with the Machinery of Government:
## Federalism, the Supreme Court, and Liberty

**Richard A. Brisbin, Jr.**

As offered in the preceding article, Professor John Kincaid's proposal to require a 7-2 vote of the Supreme Court of the United States for the justices to invalidate state laws tinkers with the existing practice of American government. It is, I believe, an unwise proposal that could do harm to American liberty. However, before plunging into a rebuttal to Professor Kincaid's argument, let me review the design of American constitutional government with attention to the relationship between liberty and federalism. Only through an understanding of the connections between liberty and federalism as established by the Founders can we evaluate why the 7-2 vote proposal is ill-advised.

## THE AMERICAN POLITICAL ENGINE

Between 1767 and 1770 the American patriot and scientist David Rittenhouse constructed an orrery. The orrery was a machine designed to depict the movement of the planets around the sun and the moons around the planets. When a crank was turned, ivory spheres representing the planets moved around a brass sun while moons moved around Earth and Jupiter. The device astounded Thomas Jefferson and James Madison. Rittenhouse's orrery provided a model of a solar system that obeyed the physics of its day, a physics largely shaped by Sir Isaac Newton's laws of gravity and motion. Rittenhouse's orrery and Newton's laws pointed toward a regular and orderly universe, a universe where humans could create a harmonious existence.[1]

When framers of the United States Constitution, like Madison, set about drafting the document in 1787, they too sought an orderly and harmonious world. To free themselves from dangers from abroad and internal strife like Shays' Rebellion—a taxpayers' revolt in western Massachusetts—the framers sought to create a political order with the same characteristics as a Newtonian universe. It would be a political engine featuring action and reaction among political institutions and governmental leaders. The interaction would move the political machine in an orderly progression around a central sun. The sun was *liberty*.[2]

One problem confronted the framers' construction of a constitution designed to harmonize political behavior. The problem was "corruption." For the framers corruption was more than criminal wrongdoing. Corruption was a

Richard A. Brisbin, Jr., is a professor of political science at West Virginia University. This article was written especially for *Points of View*.

lack of virtue and personal integrity. It was intemperance and sloth. It was pomp, waste, voluptuousness, and luxury. It was a lack of public spiritedness. It was tyrannical rule by the selfish and ignoble.[3] Yet, the idea of liberty seemed to imply that people had the freedom to be corrupt and act in a selfish, greedy, and wasteful manner. Thus, the framers agreed that liberty had to be ordered or controlled for the good of the political community.

According to Madison, reputed Father of the Constitution and its most thoughtful defender, the Constitution would protect liberty from corruption by controlling factions, majority or minority impulses, interests, and "passions" that were "adverse to the rights of other citizens, or to the permanent and aggregate interests of the community."[4] To control faction the Constitution relied on a machinery of institutional constraints. Like the orrery, the Constitution allowed the spheres of interest a free movement; no liberties were to be abolished to eliminate factions by terror (as in Nazi Germany, 1933–1945, or in Stalinist Russia, 1928–1953) or intimidatory civic education campaigns (like the Cultural Revolution in China, 1965–1969). Like the orrery, political interests and leaders were to move in orderly orbits, but these orbits were determined by the gears and cogs of the constitutional machinery. The constitutional machinery insured that the orbiting spheres retained their symmetry and did not corrupt liberty. Through the gravitational tugging and actions and reactions among political institutions,[5] institutional interaction would stifle corruption and keep harmony in the political universe.

According to Madison, the Constitution would protect liberty from corruption through two primary devices. First, the selection of national leaders through complicated processes of direct election, state legislative selection, electoral college selection, and appointment would curb the corruption of political leaders. The complicated design of the selection process was meant to prevent any one faction, including majority factions of the citizenry, from domination of politics. Thus, the mechanics of leadership selection supposedly would result in leaders of virtue, wisdom, and patriotism inclined to act as a gear restraining threats to liberty. Second, Madison delineated the merits of having a "large republic." The establishment of the large republic of many states stretching across half a continent, he argued, would permit many factions to surface. Each faction would act as a gear grating against the interests of other factions, and no single faction could corrupt the machinery of government and threaten liberty.[6]

Also, the machinery was to have "auxiliary" devices to ensure the protection of liberty from corruption. One auxiliary device, separated powers, featured a "checking and balancing" action and reaction among national leaders. Through the countering spins of the competing constitutional and personal interests of the three branches, threats to liberty were to be retarded.[7] The other auxiliary device was federalism. Through a complicated set of countervailing and duplicative responsibilities the institutional authority of the federal government and the governments of the states became gears meshing in such a way as to retard threats to liberty and popular control of the machinery of government.[8]

## THE 7-2 VOTE PROPOSAL

Professor Kincaid's proposal to require a 7-2 vote of the Supreme Court to invalidate state laws is but one of a series of efforts to tinker with the machinery of American government. The Constitution itself sanctions such tinkering and adjustment. Through the Constitution's own amendment process, most notably through the addition of the Bill of Rights and the Fourteenth Amendment, and through constitutional language so general that the branches of government are invited to elaborate on their function in the machine, Americans have redesigned the machinery in innumerable ways over the two centuries of its operation. Thus, the 7–2 vote proposal is legitimate. It is, however, not a wise proposal.

The 7-2 vote proposal, I will argue, is unwise for four reasons. First, the proposal rests on unsound assumptions about the importance and proper role of federalism in the constitutional system. Second, Professor Kincaid selectively presents evidence in support of the proposal. Third, he fails to consider how the proposal might endanger the institutional restraints on corruption and faction already built into the constitutional machinery. Finally, the proposal does not take into account features of contemporary federalism that will cause it to fall short of its objective of protecting and energizing the function of federalism in American politics. Let us consider each of these problems in turn.

## IS FEDERALISM A FUNDAMENTAL VALUE?

The primary problem with the 7-2 vote proposal is the assumption about the importance and role of federalism in American constitutional government. Early in his essay Professor Kincaid states that "federalism is a fundamental constitutional value," and he places it on a par with separated powers and individual rights. Later in the essay he exhibits an almost pathological fear that federalism is under assault by ill-defined forces of centralization. Yet, except for some vague statements about the danger of centralization and allusions to the text of the Constitution, he affords the reader no concrete justifications for the enhancement of state and local power. Thus, he assumes that federalism is a fundamental constitutional value, and he assumes that in its proper role federalism demands hostility between the national government and the states.

What Professor Kincaid has failed to consider is that the framers included federalism in the Constitution not just to have a federal state but to advance personal liberties and prevent corruption. What is missing in the Kincaid conception of federalism is a recognition that federalism is an *instrumental* mechanism. It is not the product of the political engine or the end sought by the Constitution; rather, liberty is the end. Federalism is to help generate liberty.

The text of the Constitution, from Preamble to signatures, details the instrumental nature of federalism. The Constitution provides very little detail on the reasons for federal relations and the powers of state governments. What the constitutional text does, particularly in Article I, sections 8, 9, and 10 and

Article VI, sections 2 and 3, is restrain state authority in very significant ways while securing national supremacy. The tenor of the text even implies a danger in extensive state governmental powers, a danger seen by the authors of the *Federalist Papers*.[9] Even the so-called Federalism Article of the Constitution, Article IV, gives us very little indication that federalism is a fundamental constitutional value.

The dominant stream of American judicial interpretation of the Constitution has also regarded federalism as more of an instrumental mechanism. Although Professor Kincaid seems to reject some of these interpretations, even under the 7-2 vote rule he willingly would accept the substantial impediments on state and local authority legitimated by the United States Supreme Court in many cases.[10] The opinions for the majority in each of these cases defend the extensive authority of the Congress and the Court against restrictions on that authority favorable to states' powers. Federalism clearly emerges from these decisions as less than a fundamental value for the Supreme Court.

The one constitutional provision that might provide comfort to Professor Kincaid is the Tenth Amendment which states that, "The powers not delegated to the United States by the Constitution, nor prohibited by it to the States, are reserved to the States respectively, or to the people."[11] The proponents of states' powers[12] long have used this amendment as source for the defense of a sphere of state authority, especially state "police" or regulatory powers, from the national government. However, the proponents of the Tenth Amendment have not been able to use it as a base for making federalism a fundamental constitutional value. Even in the years between 1837 and 1937 when the Supreme Court sometimes adapted the Tenth Amendment to constrain congressional powers and national supremacy under the rubric of "dual federalism,"[13] it did not consistently indicate that federalism was a fundamental value and that national and state governments were to be locked in an adversarial relationship. Then, Justice Harlan Fiske Stone, speaking for a unanimous Supreme Court in *United States* v. *Darby*,[14] laid most Tenth Amendment claims to rest. Carefully reading the ambiguous text of the Amendment, Stone declared it to be "a truism" devoid of content as a restraint on congressional powers. Consequently, federalism must be placed in its proper slot in the machinery of constitutional government. Federalism is not a device that pits the states and Washington in a hostile adversarial relationship. Constitutional history teaches that federalism is simply a legal mechanism to protect liberty by preventing all powers from accumulating in one set of corrupt or corruptible hands. As long as some powers remain in the states and as long as corruption by either state or national leaders is curtailed, it functions appropriately.

## THE EVIDENCE IN SUPPORT OF THE 7-2 VOTE PROPOSAL

Believing that federalism is endangered, Professor Kincaid introduces the argument that the Supreme Court of the United States has become a special threat to the proper functioning of federalism. There are two problems with this argument. First, he skews the evidence against the Court. Second, he avoids discussing how the Court's defense of liberty against corruption, especially when there is harm to the rights of minorities by corrupt majority factions, forces the justices to restrict states' powers.

Kincaid's evaluation of the data about the Supreme Court's treatment of state powers misstates how judicial review has affected state legislation. From data presented in Table 1 of his article, he concludes that today there is more federal judicial meddling in state affairs. These data are limited in three respects. First, the reader is not informed about the *percentage* of all state statutes held to be unconstitutional by the Court. Since the year 1900 there has been a vast upsurge in the production of statutes by state legislatures as they moved to longer sessions and began to consider more policy matters. Although no source publishes the number of state statutes per year since 1790, we should not regard the leap from 15 statutes held unconstitutional between 1814–1838, to 399 between 1964–1986 as significant when the total number of statutes also increased geometrically. The same problem of no comparison of review actions to total laws also exists with the data presented in his Figure 1.

Second, Professor Kincaid fails to tell us anything about the statutes held unconstitutional. For example, in these statutes did the state harm fundamental liberties, and did the Court act to protect the basic political value of liberty? Or, did the Court meddle in the internal operational procedures of state government? It would seem that judicial review to preserve liberty against arbitrary state action should be applauded and not lumped in and analyzed with cases that he calls meddling. Third, he fails to inform the reader that much state lawmaking prior to the twentieth century occurred when state courts, without reference to legislation, decided private cases and created legal standards. The United States Supreme Court subjected this activity, known as "common law making," to extensive review and revision. He needs to account for Supreme Court intervention in this form of state judicial policymaking if he is to offer a full assessment of historical trends in federal judicial-state government relations.

The argument about the effects of a 7-2 vote rule to void state legislation also skews the data. By including all cases in which the extraordinary majority rule would be in effect in his Table 2, Kincaid avoids telling us anything about what state laws would have been upheld. Even when he moves to provide a list of state statutes that would have been voided or upheld by his 7-2 rule, the list is highly selective. Additionally, not only is the list selective, it assumes that past precedent will be a stable guide to the future of national judiciary-state relationships on critical issues of rights and policy. Yet, if the 7-2 vote rule were adopted, many Americans would find little comfort in knowing that seemingly long-settled doctrines could be overturned if raised again and three instead of five justices decided not to support the precedent.

Professor Kincaid not only skews the data to favor his case, he needs to more fully consider the effect of the 7-2 vote rule on the interpretation of the

Bill of Rights guarantees so essential for American liberty. The logic of his approach is that sometimes in American constitutional government we require extraordinary majorities to restrict some congressional actions (overriding presidential vetoes, impeachments) and constructing significant changes in the national governance (constitutional amendments). To apply the same logic to Supreme Court decisions on federalism misses an important point. The veto and amendment processes were designed to control majority factions in Congress from running roughshod over liberties or other factional interests protected by the other branches or the states.

The Court, however, is not the Congress. The Court is a forum where people can assert claims that their rights have been abused by the national and state governments and by national and state officials. The 7-2 vote rule would make it much harder for minorities to assert claims against state legislation discriminating against their liberties. With the 7-2 proposal the states could censor books and newspapers before they were even published,[15] states could force children to salute a flag despite deeply held religious beliefs in opposition to the practice,[16] and state and local governmental support for various majoritarian religious doctrines and symbols would increase despite the penalties the support might impose on other denominations.[17] Also, rights to privacy related to pregnancy decisions would be even more restricted by states than at present.[18] States could engage in more extensive discrimination on the basis of gender[19] and length of residency in a state.[20] Consequently, the 7-2 vote proposal might not be adequate to defend the constitutional rights of minorities against arbitrary state legislation. Indeed, it might promote the state abuse of minority rights. Given the endemic nature of racism and sexism in the American political culture, it would not serve the goal of liberty for all citizens to permit state legislative majorities to have a greater opportunity to abuse minorities and other groups with unpopular ideas.

## THE DANGERS OF THE 7-2 VOTE PROPOSAL

Although the 7-2 vote proposal contains a threat for minority interests seeking to vindicate their rights, the author at least considers the effect of his proposal on rights. What he fails to discuss, however, are the implications of his proposal for other constitutional mechanisms designed to curtail corruption and faction as threats to liberty. This neglect creates some hidden dangers for the traditional operations of the machinery of American politics.

First, sometimes the 7-2 vote rule would allow state legislation special preference over the views of a national majority. Many of the federalism decisions that Kincaid most strongly objects to required the Court to choose between a state and a federal legislative standard (e.g., *National League of Cities v. Usery*,[21] *Garcia v. SAMTA*,[22] *South Carolina v. Baker*[23]). This means that after all the pulling and hauling among diverse interest groups and factions in the Congress is completed and the president approves the legislation, a mere three justices could find the national law to be unconstitutional because it damages the powers of states generally or the legislative initiatives of one state or locality. The danger with this situation is that it enhances the potential for a faction to refute the policy choices made by representative leaders after factional compromise. Although the small number of justices might act to preserve a valued aspect of our federalism, the potential for abuse and corruption of political processes by a few is increased.

Second, the proposal presents some dangers for the role of the Supreme Court in the system of constitutional government. The proposal is an effort to deny the Supreme Court the authority to establish its own procedural rules, and it marks a change in the historical pattern of deference afforded the Court to manage its own procedures. Although the Congress has changed the Court's jurisdiction over the *kinds* of cases it hears on numerous occasions, the Congress would be altering *how* the Court operates. The danger with such a change is not just a potential separation of powers conflict; it is the potential for more congressional restrictions on the justices in ways that could threaten the notion of judicial independence and neutrality that the framers sought to promote.[24]

Additionally, the 7-2 vote proposal also could lead to calls for 7-2 vote rules on other issues. For example, some might consider the Court's review of state judicial standards and doctrines to be equivalent to the review of legislation. A 7-2 vote rule on review of state judicial standards would call the Court's entire criminal justice jurisprudence into question. Therefore, the proposal might open up a host of policy problems thought settled by Congress or the Court for new debate and perhaps for debilitating conflict. The energy of the machinery of politics would have to be spent to establish a new harmony in multiple policy arenas.

## WHAT THE 7-2 VOTE PROPOSAL CANNOT ACCOMPLISH

The 7-2 vote proposal suffers from a final defect. This tinkering with Supreme Court decision-making would probably fail to enhance the role of the states in the machinery of American government. Specifically, if enacted the proposal would probably be ineffective because it cannot engineer a way past two difficulties.

First, the proposal would affect a small number of cases with limited implications for public policy. As the author's Table 2 notes, only 20 to 40 cases in recent decades would be decided differently under the 7-2 vote rule. Although some of those decisions would harm minority interests, few would achieve Kincaid's goal of energizing state governments. Consider the issues raised by the cases of *National League of Cities v. Usery* and *Garcia v. SAMTA*. These cases questioned the authority of the United States Congress to require state or local governments to abide by provisions of the Fair Labor Standards Act of 1938, including not employing child labor, paying a minimum wage, establishing a forty-hour work week, and paying overtime wages for hours worked beyond the forty a week. The local governments represented in the two cases saw this as an erosion of federalism and an interference with their authority to structure integral operations in areas of traditional state or local governmental functions like the working conditions of state employees. Although the *Usery* decision favored the states, in the nine years it functioned before the *Garcia* decision, which overturned it, and in the years since *Garcia*, nothing much has changed in American federalism. *Usery* did not lead to a wave of great policy change and *Garcia* did not suddenly make the states inferior political entities. These cases only affected the pay of employees of a few very poor states and localities.

Would a 7-2 vote rule on other, often narrow issues of national legislation like the pay and hours of state employees have a significant effect on national-state relations? Not unless the new rule was somehow able to overturn, through case by case adjudication, the vast body of decisions legitimating the dominance of congressional policies since the *Darby* decision of 1941, which rendered the Tenth Amendment a truism. Historically few Supreme Court decisions have had much immediate and direct impact on American life. Also, political leaders have often not complied with the Court decisions. Even thirty-seven years after *Brown v. Board of Education*[25] overturned state Jim Crow laws and required the desegregation of American schools, most minority children go to overwhelmingly minority schools. Thus, will a new rule protecting state legislation before the Supreme Court ultimately have much effect on how effective a role state governments play in American public life? It would seem not. Unless the states are prepared both to find reasons to litigate again all decisions defining their constitutional status and to secure compliance through additional pressure on the federal government with any decisions improving their status, the proposal will not engineer a new federalism in America.

Second, the tinkering nature of the 7-2 vote proposal will not afford solutions to other critical problems or practices at the state level that prevent these governments from effectively restraining *any* exercise of national power. As Madison noted, effective government must have wise and virtuous leaders. It must have leaders and other personnel who can engage in creative policymaking to address the demands of the citizenry of the state or locality.

Throughout the twentieth century the states have not possessed a leadership that made the citizenry want to support active and independent state governments. In many domestic policy arenas it was the recalcitrance or incapacity of state leaders to address public problems that led to citizens demanding and getting federal legislation. Federal legislation was needed because many state leaders did not act to curtail employers' abuses of workers' incomes, safety, and pensions. Federal legislation was needed because state leaders could not provide income for retired persons and a modicum of food and health care for the retired, the poor, the unemployed, and the mentally ill. Federal legislation was needed because state leaders did not act to preserve the purity of the water and air and did not act to protect the environment. Federal legislation was needed because state leaders did not act to build adequate

highways or address the deterioration of the nation's housing. The proposal
will not somehow reconstruct politics to make state leaders more attentive to
future policy problems.[26]

State leaders have even benefited from dependency of states and localities on the federal government. Since 1960 federal financial grants to state
and local governments have risen from $7 billion to over $135 billion.[27] The
vast sums granted to the states in these intergovernmental programs as well as
the assumption of some state duties by the federal government have made
many state and local leaders supporters of a strong national government.
Recently, for example, one city official told this author that he did not mind
going to Washington and asking for federal money. The money would replace
local tax dollars that would be spent on a local program. Although the city
leader would be dependent on national officials for the funding of the program,
breaching the ideal of independence of national and local governments, the
official would win credits for the next election both by satisfying a public
demand for the program and by pleasing voters by not raising local taxes to pay
for the program. The 7-2 vote rule would not eliminate this kind of behavior
from our political machinery.

The proposal will not redesign the judicial role in government, either. The
reason the United States Supreme Court became active in the defense of
personal liberties was the failure of the state judiciaries to protect the rights of
what the justices call "discrete and insular minorities."[28] Throughout much of
the twentieth century state courts denied fundamental rights of free speech,
press, and religious exercise to political and religious minorities. The state
courts also neglected the rights of criminal defendants and let racism mar the
criminal justice process. They rarely supported racial or gender equality.
Despite greater attention by state courts to rights in recent years (what is called
the "new judicial federalism"), most minorities still see value in winning
national protection for their rights. When confronted by a Court hostile to their
claims, as became true in the 1980s, these minorities sought relief through the
passage of Civil Rights Acts and other protective legislation by Congress.
These groups simply find state judicial action either so limited in scope or so
insensitive to their needs that federal action is desired. The 7-2 vote proposal
will not alter these beliefs.

Finally, it appears that the 7-2 vote proposal will not change the general
habit of Americans to prefer federal political machinery to address the nation's
or their personal ills. Even the leaders of the past half-century most distrustful
of the Congress and the federal bureaucracy, Richard Nixon and Ronald
Reagan, did little to invigorate state government. The "New Federalism"
proposals of both men were largely campaign rhetoric. During the Nixon
administration the federal government even accepted far greater responsibility
in the environmental area from the states.[29] The Reagan administration stifled
state regulatory initiatives and reduced fiscal support for creative state policies.[30] If both the people and the states and national leaders operating the
federal machine decline to change its operation, can we expect that one legal
change in the machinery will readjust what it accomplishes?

## NOTES

1 Daniel J. Boorstin, *The Americans: The Colonial Experience* (New York: Vintage Books, 1958), pp. 246–251. For further discussion of the orrery, see Brooke Hindle, *The Pursuit of Science in Revolutionary America 1767–1789* (Chapel Hill: University of North Carolina Press, 1956), pp. 166–172; it is pictured following p. 194. For additional information, see William Barton, *Memoirs of the Life of David Rittenhouse* (Philadelphia: Edward Parker, 1813).

2 Alexander Hamilton, "Federalist No. 9," in Alexander Hamilton, James Madison, and John Jay, *The Federalist*, ed. Jacob E. Cooke (Middletown, CT: Wesleyan University Press, 1961), pp. 50–51.

3 Gordon S. Wood, *The Creation of the American Republic, 1776–1787* (New York: W.W. Norton & Co., 1969), pp. 28–45.

4 James Madison, "Federalist No. 10," *op. cit.*, p. 57.

5 A decidedly Newtonian concept first formulated by the French philosopher Charles Louis de Secondat, Baron de Montesquieu, in his *Spirit of the Laws*, trans. Thomas Nugent (New York: Haeffner, 1949 ed. of 1784).

6 James Madison, "Federalist No. 10," *op. cit.*, pp. 61–65.

7 James Madison, "Federalist No. 51," *op. cit.*, pp. 344–351.

8 James Madison, "Federalist Papers Nos. 39, 45," *op. cit.*, pp. 250–257, 322–323.

9 See, for example, Alexander Hamilton, "Federalist Nos. 21–36," *op. cit.*, pp. 129–230.

10 See for examples, *Fletcher v. Peck*, 6 Cranch 87 (1810); *Martin v. Hunter's Lessee*, 1 Wheaton 304 (1816); *McCulloch v. Maryland*, 4 Wheaton 316 (1819); *Cohens v. Virginia*, 6 Wheaton 264 (1821); *Gibbons v. Ogden*, 9 Wheaton 1 (1824); *Ableman v. Booth*, 21 Howard 506 (1859); *Heart of Atlanta Motel v. United States*, 379 U.S. 241 (1964); *South Carolina v. Katzenbach*, 383 U.S. 301 (1966); *City of Philadelphia v. New Jersey*, 437 U.S. 617 (1978); *Supreme Court of New Hampshire v. Piper*, 470 U.S. 274 (1985); *South Dakota v. Dole*, 483 U.S. 203 (1987); and *South Carolina v. Baker*, 485 U.S. 505 (1988).

11 United States Constitution, Amendment X.

12 Or, what used to be called "states' rights," based on the misconception that institutions as well as people could possess liberty.

13 Edward S. Corwin, *The Twilight of the Supreme Court* (New Haven: Yale University Press, 1934), pp. 1–51, offers the fullest definition of "dual federalism." His critique of the use of dual federalism to curtail congressional policymaking is set forth in Edward S. Corwin, *The Commerce Power versus States Rights* (Princeton: Princeton University Press, 1936).

14 312 U.S. 100 (1941).

15 *Near v. Minnesota*, 283 U.S. 697 (1931).

16 *West Virginia State Board of Education v. Barnette*, 319 U.S. 624 (1942).

17 *Grand Rapids School District v. Ball*, 105 S.Ct. 3216 (1985); *County of Allegheny v. American Civil Liberties Union*, 109 S.Ct. 3086 (1989).

18 *Thornburgh v. American College of Obstetricians*, 106 S.Ct. 2169 (1986); *Hodgson v. Minnesota*, 110 S.Ct. 2729 (1990): *Ohio v. Akron Center for Reproductive Health*, 110 S.Ct. 2972 (1990).

19 *Craig v. Boren*, 429 U.S. 190 (1976); *Mississippi University for Women v. Hogan*, 458 U.S. 718 (1982).

20 *Shapiro v. Thompson*, 394 U.S. 618 (1969).

21 426 U.S. 833 (1976).

22  469 U.S. 528 (1985).
23  485 U.S. 505 (1988).
24  Alexander Hamilton, "Federalist No. 78," *op. cit.*, pp. 525–529.
25  347 U.S. 483 (1954).
26  State governments might be capable of shaking off this malaise. For hopeful signs, see Mavis Mann Reeves, "The States as Polities: Reformed, Reinvigorated, and Resourceful," *Annals of the American Academy of Political and Social Science* 509: 83–93 (1990).
27  Robert Jay Dilger, *National Intergovernmental Programs* (Englewood Cliffs, NJ: Prentice-Hall, Inc., 1989), p. 8.
28  *United States v. Carolene Products Co.*, 304 U.S. 144, n. 4 (1938).
29  Susan Hunter and Victoria Noonan, "Energy, Environment, and the Presidential Agenda," unpublished paper, 1990.
30  Dilger, *op. cit.*, p. 211; Richard P. Nathan and Fred C. Doolittle, *Reagan and the States* (Princeton: Princeton University Press, 1987).

# 4

# Public Opinion

*The process of governing has always been a two-way street between those who rule and those who are ruled. In totalitarian countries, the relationship between the rulers and the ruled is tilted in favor of the rulers because they make decisions without much regard for the wishes of the people. In democratic countries, however, the relationship between the rulers and the ruled is presumed to be more reciprocal—the rulers must at all times be concerned about what the people desire.*

*The United States, of course, is an example of a democratic system in which "representatives" are chosen to make decisions by and with the consent of the people. But how much influence ought the people to have? Should our representatives act merely on the basis of public opinion polls— a kind of national referendum on every issue—or should these officials be free to act on their own beliefs and judgments without having to be responsive to their constituents' views?*

*This issue is addressed in a very unusual and interesting way in the following two articles. The authors have written commentaries on a significant technological development in our society—"teledemocracy."* Teledemocracy *refers to the use of electronic devices for the purpose of instantly recording people's preferences on anything from consumer goods to political issues. In the first article, political scientist Ted Becker describes these new electronic devices, reviews their use in the United States and elsewhere, and presents an argument for their increased use as a way of making our political system even more democratic.*

*Taking issue with Becker is Michael Malbin, who sees a danger in instant electronic polling. To Malbin, the act of governance is more than a simple recording of public opinion, electronically or otherwise; it involves "deliberation," which can come only with the give-and-take of discussion. Pushing a button on a black box in the privacy of a living room, argues Malbin, will hardly lead to enlightened public discussion on the critical issues of the day.*

# Teledemocracy
## Bringing Power Back to the People

**Ted Becker**

These are bad times for democracy. Only half those American citizens eligible to vote did so in the last presidential election, following a trend of declining voter participation in recent years. Many nonvoters in the United States feel powerless and forgotten, ignored by elected representatives and overwhelmed by what they perceive as the power and influence of special and vested interests.

These are good times for democracy. In Europe, there is a trend for national governments to put vital questions directly to the people for them to decide the destiny of their countries:

• England—join the Common Market?
• Spain—adopt a new constitution?
• Italy—allow abortion?

But whether the trend is favorable or not, there is a deep yearning in nations everywhere to increase the democratic essence of their political life.

Fortunately, new technologies and techniques present exciting prospects for involving people directly in governing themselves. Teledemocracy—the term coined for electronically aided, rapid, two-way political communication—could offer the means to help educate voters on issues, to facilitate discussion of important decisions, to register instantaneous polls, and even to allow people to vote directly on public policy.

Experiments in teledemocracy first began in earnest in the 1970s. The first tests were modest in scale, using small groups like apartment complexes and housing communities.

Perhaps the first successful large-scale adventure was Alternatives for Washington (AFW), which ran from 1974 to 1976. The brainchild of Governor Dan Evans, AFW was a state-sponsored project that sought to involve as many of the state's citizens as possible in conceiving and choosing among a number of potential long-range futures for the state.

AFW started with meetings of a wide-based group of citizens in workshops and seminars, then employed several survey methods to involve even more people. To draw the public-at-large into the process, AFW sponsored programs on public television, then published over a million questionnaires in all the state's major newspapers that presented eleven futures and asked people

Ted Becker is professor of political science at Auburn University. This article is from "Teledemocracy: Bringing Power Back to the People," by Ted Becker, *The Futurist*, December 1981, pp. 6–9.

for their views. Random-sample polls were conducted to determine what a representative group of citizens would choose as well.

As an exercise designed to provide broad-based, long-distance future planning, AFW was a huge success. More than 45,000 citizens answered the newspaper surveys and thousands more cooperated in the telephone random surveys. Perhaps hundreds of thousands of others watched some part of the TV programming. And many thousands participated in a multitude of meetings around the state.

AFW proved that people are eager to get involved in politics when they believe their opinions are valued and see how the decisions directly affect their futures. Despite the great response to the program, however, the state legislature proved recalcitrant in moving on the recommendations AFW developed.

## INTERACTIVE TV INVOLVES PUBLIC

Perhaps the most famous teledemocratic experiment is the QUBE interactive cable TV system in Columbus, Ohio. Set up by Warner Communications Corporation in 1977 and still running, it is the most ambitious and glamorous such system in existence.

Each household subscribing to QUBE has a small black box with five buttons connected to its TV set. The viewing public can respond to questions put to it about programs by pushing the buttons as instructed.

The interaction mostly involves various kinds of entertainment (games) or marketing (the viewer as consumer), but QUBE does provide regular public affairs shows. In an interview program called "Columbus Alive" and special affairs programs, the public—the audience—is asked for opinions on selected issues. The results of this flash "polling" register instantaneously on the screen.

QUBE does have its flaws—it is mainly oriented to consumerism, merchandising, and entertainment. The home console, the black box, does cost money: it nearly doubles the cost of the basic service and would, in "real" voting, represent a "poll tax" that poor people might be hard pressed to pay. QUBE was tested in a rather well-to-do suburb that may not be a reliable gauge of how the rest of America would respond.

But look what QUBE proves! Between 80 and 90 percent of the potential pool of users of this system opt to use it. The evidence is clear that these folks truly enjoy using this teledemocratic system: they express avid interest in participating in feedback; they find the use of the system easy and rewarding. And they are willing to pay for the service directly out of their own pockets.

Another future-planning exercise using television considered highly successful by its organizers, and by participating citizens, was conducted in Canada in 1978–79. "Talking Back" was mainly a network television extravaganza of the Canadian Broadcasting Company.

Telephones, television, and computers linked a large number of simultaneous conferences in a series of electronic meetings to generate a nationwide discussion on several topics of national concern.

Although the Canadian Parliament did not crank out relevant policies as a direct result of "Talking Back," the experiment was an enormous success. In large numbers, from coast to coast, people responded with interest, time, energy, and creative thought.

## NEW ZEALANDERS PLAN THEIR FUTURE

New Zealand Televote added some new dimensions to teledemocratic experiments. It was conducted in mid-1981 by a permanent government agency, the Commission for the Future, that was created by New Zealand's parliament for the purpose of involving the public in long-range future studies.

The project used a new kind of public opinion survey—televote—that is two parts telephone survey and one part mail survey. Televote organizers do extensive research for the public, then present the best pro and con argumentation on a subject in easy-to-read formats. People phone in their replies, which gives them time to do the poll at their own convenience. The method is capable of obtaining informed and deliberated opinion from representative samples of citizenry on complicated issues.

Televote originated in Hawaii, where it was used to aid the constitutional convention of 1978 and the state legislature from 1978 to 1980. Hawaii Televote operated out of a university, making the college part of the public government decision-making system. This system has also been less costly than comparable efforts by conventional polling organizations.

To cover the entire country, New Zealand Televote used a three-university network of televote centers.

Although confronted with a complex set of philosophical and policy choices, New Zealanders took to teledemocracy like birds to trees.

Thousands of New Zealanders answered a newspaper televote (with the same information and questions as in the "official televote") that was printed in half of New Zealand's major dailies and promoted by a thirty-station community radio network.

New Zealand Televote showed, too, that all segments of the nation's population—all ages, races, economic, and educational levels—were willing to join in teledemocracy.

## TWO TELEDEMOCRATIC SYSTEMS

These examples are not the only teledemocratic experiments of recent vintage, nor are they necessarily the most important. Taken together, though, they help reveal two models of teledemocracy—and demonstrate the even greater promise of teledemocracy given the new hardware already on line, waiting to be plugged in.

The first of these two types of teledemocratic systems might be called Television Talkback (TT). The other is a blend of groups (workshops, conferences, task forces, meetings); polling (random and newspaper); and electronic media involvement (radio and TV) that might be called the Public Participation (PP) model.

Improved teledemocratic projects in the not-so-distant future must combine both kinds to overcome shortfalls each has alone.

For example, the TT system tends to balkanize the public by isolating individuals and families in their homes in front of the TV. Also, printed material has greater versatility than material displayed on a TV screen—and perhaps greater staying power.

The PP models have lacked the flair of the TT model. The modernity, novelty, and spontaneity of Television Talkback—whether via home console, the new "votaphone" method, or conventional telephone—inspire great public participation.

Recent innovations in technology will entice even greater mass participation. By way of illustration, the dramatic increase in electronic games that plug into TV sets will recondition people to interact with their sets rather than sit passively in front of the tube.

Other advances that will stimulate teledemocracy are the video recording and playback systems and the personal home computer. The home is on the verge of becoming *the* major educational and informational center.

New electronic interactive systems are on line and ready for everyday use in several countries, including Canada (Teledon), France (Intelmatique), and Japan (Hi-Ovia). Cable television is ready to spread through the United States like wildfire. The forecast is nothing but bright for teledemocracy, thanks to modern science.

All systems are go for more and better teledemocratic experiments: the theory and knowledge are there; the enthusiasm and enthusiasts are there; the public is there; the paraphernalia are there. Future experimentation will bring us closer and closer to implementing pure electronic democracy in a real-life situation and allow us to transform public opinion as developed and measured by teledemocratic means into the law of some lands.

What is missing is a commitment by policymakers and planners to promote and respond to teledemocratically derived opinion. Such a commitment might arise in the business sector when it is understood that teledemocratic systems, combining these hard technologies and soft techniques, have enormous profit-making potential. Millions of people are already willing to "play and pay" for electronic town meetings, just as they are already paying to shoot down space invaders and enjoy ballets. A similar commitment from the political sector may be harder to come by.

Sometime in the near future the degree of alienation may be so great, the amount of social turbulence so distressing, and the threat of chaos so imminent that a drastic political realignment will be the only path open.

We could take the radical detour to the right and march down the iron road to totalitarianism, with a government akin to the Big Brotherism foreseen by George Orwell.

But it may be preferable to embrace greater and purer democracy, to let people in, to divest, diffuse, and decentralize power as never before. At that moment, teledemocracy will be ready for its greatest challenge and responsibility. The public will no longer expect those in power to ignore its will, because the real power will rest in the will of the public itself. With the help of teledemocratic processes, public opinion will become the law of the land, as in all places where referendums and initiatives are used.

# Teledemocracy and Its Discontents

## Michael Malbin

Professional survey researchers like to dismiss electronic straw polls as pseudoscientific. They're right, of course, but that only begins to get at what's most troubling about this new phenomenon. The more basic issues have to do with the proper function of issue polling in a representative democracy, and the future possibilities for electronic initiatives and referendums. These issues would have to be addressed even if straw polls could be made every bit as accurate as polls using standard sampling techniques.

Let's consider electronic referendums first. It would be easy to imagine every person in the country, in a few years or decades, having access to a cable or other system that would record his opinions on issues. It also would be easy to imagine that the owners of the various systems, or the Federal Communications Commission, could devise a technology—national identity cards, fingerprint readers, or whatever—that would prevent double voting and limit participation to eligible or registered voters. Of course, there would be political resistance to the central management that would be required, but let's ignore this impediment for the moment. The point is that technologically, the country is on the threshold of an era in which frequent and direct participation of the people in their government will be possible.

Some of the new technology's supporters look forward to the coming era with unfettered enthusiasm. One such person is [Auburn University] political scientist Ted Becker, who refers to the phenomenon as "teledemocracy." In an article in the December [1981] issue of *The Futurist*, Becker eagerly anticipates the day when "with the help of teledemocratic processes, public opinion will become the law of the land, as in all places where referendums and initiatives are used." Becker notes that where QUBE is in place, "folks truly enjoy using this teledemocratic system: they express avid interest in participating in feedback; they find the use of the system rewarding. And they are willing to pay for the service."

Becker surely seems right on one point: as more people experience the joys of electronic political self-expression, the pressure for turning such expressions into law will increase. The way of the future seems clear. At least, the way is clear if no convincing case can be mounted to show that it should not be.

Just such a case was mounted successfully almost two hundred years ago in *The Federalist Papers*. It would be worthwhile to think once again about what *The Federalist* had to say—not because the work is old and venerated,

Michael Malbin is director of the Center for Legislative Studies, Rockefeller Institute of Government, and professor of political science at the State University of New York at Albany. This article is reprinted from *Public Opinion*, June/July 1982, pp. 58–59. Reprinted with permission of American Enterprise Institute for Public Policy Research.

but because its arguments are still alive and can help clarify the problems of today.

## DRAWBACKS OF DIRECT DEMOCRACY

The first, and most important, thing to remember about the Constitution's framers is that democracy was less basic to them than liberty. They wanted to set up a democracy, to be sure, but it had to be one that worked toward securing the inalienable rights enumerated in the Declaration of Independence. Every form of government poses some danger to those rights, they thought, but some government is necessary to secure them. The threat to rights peculiar to democracies, the Founders believed, was that posed by majority tyranny. The Constitution is the framers' attempt to minimize that danger in a manner consistent with democratic principles. Representation was a key part of that solution in at least two different ways.

First, the framers thought majority tyranny is most likely if the majority gets swept up by a single, common special interest or passion. Their solution called for a large, economically complex republic where no one interest would be likely to predominate. But large republics obviously have to be representative. Two hundred million people cannot fit into one room. And if they could, the result would not be democracy but mob rule, in which an oligarchy inevitably would rise to the top and control the proceedings.

What makes electronic initiatives and referendums so attractive is that they seem on the surface to overcome these traditional objections to direct democracy. Through modern technology, people across a large republic can act in concert without taking on the characteristics of a mob. Technology, in other words, would seem to allow the country to enjoy the advantages of a large republic's diversity together with a small republic's direct participation.

## UNREFINED OPINIONS

The problem with this argument is that it fails to deal with the second, and more important, reason for having a system of representation. Representatives were expected to be accountable to public opinion, but they were not simply to reflect it as if they were mere physical surrogates for the people. The need to form majorities out of multiple factions was supposed to force representatives, in the words of *Federalist* No. 10, "to refine and enlarge the public views"— that is, to modify and compromise legislative proposals *before* adopting or rejecting them. The process, in other words, was supposed to force legislators to deliberate and to think of the needs of others.

Modern mass communications cannot overcome these objections to direct democracy for two reasons. First, initiatives, like polls, place unwarranted power in the hands of those who frame the questions. Second, even if direct democracy were limited to referendums on questions drawn up by the legislature, the answers given by citizens isolated in their homes would add nothing worthwhile to the deliberative process. Political deliberation is not a solitary activity. Opinions only become refined through the give-and-take of discussion with people whose backgrounds and opinions differ from one's own. And discussion presupposes reasonably well-informed discussants. A "discussion" between a well- and an ill-informed person is nothing more than an exhortation. This is all one can expect from a referendum campaign, however. Referendums may be useful in small countries, or on statewide constitutional issues, or in local areas in which citizens may know almost as much as their representatives about the issues. But on complicated national and statewide legislative matters, referendums merely give special interest groups an opportunity to use demagogic advertising appeals to frustrate the legislative will.

There is no conceivable way the public could "refine and enlarge" its own views in a manner that would be conducive to sound legislation. The public is, and necessarily will remain, poorly informed on most issues. Even members of Congress, who devote their lives to public affairs, have to depend on committee specialists for most of their information. Think of how much more difficult it would be for the average citizen, for whom politics is only a passing interest. For confirmation, look at the level of public confusion shown by issue polls in which slightly different questions produce contradictory results, or those on which follow-ups yield little but gaps or "don't knows."

This is not meant as a slap at the American people. The question is not so much the people's ability as how people choose to use their time. The purpose of the Republic, after all, is not to make every citizen a public figure. The United States is not and was not meant to be another Switzerland. Rather, the purpose of our government is to use public action to secure the private rights to life, liberty, and the pursuit of happiness.

If referendums and initiatives are dismissed, what about the increased use of issue polls for purely advisory purposes? I have no doubt that both electronic and nonelectronic issue polling will continue their steady rate of growth. The problem with them is that the opinions they solicit are, in *The Federalist*'s terms, unrefined and unenlarged. They are raw pieces of data that deserve to be treated with extreme caution. Increasing the frequency of issue polling, through QUBE or other systems, cannot make their results more refined but it can add to the public pressure for taking unrefined results more seriously. It may become increasingly difficult for legislators to dismiss such polls without becoming labeled "enemies of democracy." Labeling of this sort should be resisted. Legislators who read issue polls with jaundiced eyes may be a democratic republic's best friends.

# 5

# Voting

*Despite the fact that our population is better educated and faces fewer procedural impediments to voting than ever before, a significant portion of the American electorate does not participate in elections. Indeed, from 1960 through 1988 voting turnout declined some thirteen percentage points. The turnout figure of just over 50 percent in 1988 was the lowest in sixty-four years.*

*Is nonvoting in the United States a source of concern? The two selections in this chapter address this question. In the first selection, the director of the Committee for the Study of the American Electorate, Curtis Gans, argues that we should be quite disturbed about both the* causes *and* consequences *of low turnout. While acknowledging that the mechanics of voting have been made easier, Gans insists that the fundamental reason for nonvoting is quite simple—citizens no longer believe that their vote has any importance in the political system. Equally disturbing to him is the fact that a declining pool of voters leaves government vulnerable to the influence of special interests, thereby lessening the capacity to make decisions in the public interest. The author of the second article, political scientist Austin Ranney, argues that we need not fear the fact that many persons choose not to vote. Ranney bases his argument on two main propositions: first, he argues that since voters and nonvoters do not differ significantly in policy and candidate preferences, no great harm is done to our system of representation if a lot of people do not vote; second, nonvoting does not offend any basic democratic principle, for the right not to vote is every bit as precious as the right to vote. The fact that both Gans and Ranney have chosen to write about the issue of nonvoting reveals, of course, the importance of this issue to the student of government and even to the average voting or nonvoting citizen.*

# The Problem of Nonvoting

## Curtis B. Gans

Since 1960, with the exception of 1982 and 1984, voter turnout has declined by 10 percent in both presidential and congressional elections. Fully 20 million eligible Americans who previously voted regularly or sporadically have ceased voting. Even in 1982, 90 million eligible Americans failed to cast their ballots. And in the presidential year of 1984, more than 80 million Americans did not vote. Voting today in America has reached a level so low that of all the world's democracies, only Botswana has a consistently lower voter participation rate than the United States; although Switzerland, which referends all important issues and thus makes office holding meaningless, and India, which tends to have wars in one or more of its provinces at any given point, approach the United States's low participation rate.

This decline in voting affects all ages, races, and classes, with only two exceptions. The South, because of both the Voting Rights Act and the rise of two-party competition, has been increasing its vote, and younger women— between the ages of 25 and 44—are also increasing their share of the vote. Minorities voted more heavily in 1982, but it is too early to tell whether this trend will continue, absent Reagan as a national motivating and polarizing force.

This decline has occurred during precisely the time when the United States has made it easier to vote. We have abolished literacy tests and the poll tax; we have enfranchised our young and effectively enfranchised our minorities; we have adopted liberalized voting procedures, including shortening the time between the close of registration and voting, enacting in a majority of states postcard registration, and establishing in a few states election-day registration. We have provided multilingual ballots in some places and voter outreach programs in others. . . .

In one sense, it would be a wonder had voter participation not declined during the past two decades. For in that period, we have had Watergate and Vietnam, Agnew and Abscam; we have had Johnson, Nixon, Carter, and Reagan and with them images of public leadership not commensurate with the high title of President; we have had early 1960s promises which were not fulfilled by programs or performance; we have had growing complexity in our national life and of our national problems and growing confusion about how to deal with it and them; we have had increasingly larger and larger political, economic, and social institutions and a corresponding feeling of citizen impo-

Curtis B. Gans is director of the Committee for the Study of the American Electorate, Washington, D.C. This article is excerpted from a speech delivered on September 26, 1983, to The Consultation on Citizen Responsibility, Political Participation and Government Accountability: Foundation Responsibility and Opportunity. Permission to use this speech has been granted to these authors only. All further permission must be referred to Curtis Gans.

tence in the face of them; and we have had an increasingly atomized society, increasingly confused about their choices, courtesy of the coaxial cable. Sadly but surely, nonvoting is growing to be an increasingly rational act. . . .

There are some who say that the size of the electorate is not important, that those who don't vote would not vote any differently than those who do. They are flatly and dangerously wrong.

There may well be no optimal level of participation in America, but:

(1) to the extent that fewer and fewer Americans bother to vote, the ability of organized political minorities, special interest and single-issue zealots to polarize American politics and influence the course of public policy will be enhanced;

(2) to the extent that American political participation dwindles and the business of politics is increasingly the province of organized interest groups, the ability of the political system to produce public policy in the interests of the society as a whole decreases correspondingly. (Perhaps an example is in order. If public employees constitute one-sixth of the nation but vote heavily, as they do, then when only a half of the rest of the nation votes, as they do in presidential elections, the force of the public employee vote is equal to one-third. If only one-third of the nation votes, as roughly they do in congressional elections, then public employees constitute one-half of the electorate. It is thus no wonder that it is difficult to modify civil service, abolish agencies, shrink unnecessary bureaucracy or devolve power to other levels of government);

(3) to the extent that interest and involvement with the political process declines and the citizenry is content to abdicate their responsibility to others, the potential for unstable, demagogic, and even authoritarian leadership increases;

(4) to the extent, as it has been shown, that voting is a lowest common denominator act—that people who don't vote tend not to participate in any form of civil, social, or political activity—then any diminution of the voting force is also sapping the voluntary spirit of participation upon which the health and vitality of our institutions depend.

* * *

Democracy is not only the most humane form of government, it is also the most fragile. It depends not only for its legitimacy but also for its health and well-being on the involvement of the governed.

Government may not be, as many people now seem to feel, the answer to all of society's ills, but unless the American people wish to abdicate to oligarchic or authoritarian rule, the resolution of societal problems must come through the democratic political process.

The continuing withdrawal of American people from voting and political participation threatens not only wise governance, but the underlying vitality of the political process and the democratic ideal.

We are simply and bluntly in danger of becoming a nation governed of, for, and by the interested few.

Having said all of this, it might be well to look at who these nonvoters are. For if we are to begin to address both the general problem of nonparticipation or the more particular problem of participation of certain important subgroups, it would be well to know the lay of the land.

In 1976 [the Committee for the Study of the American Electorate] undertook a survey of a scientifically selected sample of nonvoters to attempt to ascertain who they were and why they weren't participating. And while I found that survey less than fully satisfying as a total answer to the problem (although surely more satisfying than anything which has been done before or since), it does provide some clues.

For the purposes of this discussion, I would like to categorize nonvoters in four broad groups. Any such categorizing is, of course, imperfect, but the categories may serve to show at least something of the nature of the problem which confronts us.

By far the largest group are chronic nonvoters, people who have never, or in Gilbert and Sullivan's phrase "hardly ever," voted. They tend to come from families who have never voted. They tend to be poorer, younger, less educated, more unorganized working class, more unemployed, more minority, more southern, more rural, and more urban underclass than the rest of the population. They are also likely to be participants in nothing else. With the exception of a few chronic nonvoters in the South who participate in fundamentalist religion (and who are likely to have been the source of the Reverend Jerry Falwell's additions to the voter rolls . . .), the chronic nonvoter tends to participate in no organized political, social, religious, or civic activities. They are a nation larger than France within our midst, who, if one were to describe them in the terms used by the Bureau of Labor Statistics to describe the elements of the labor force, would be out of the labor and voting force. It is unlikely that any substantial portion of these people will be engaged in the polity unless and until we make much greater strides than we have to address the problem of class in America and to integrate them not only politically, but economically and socially as well, into the mainstream of American society. Until then, politics is likely to appear to the chronic nonvoter as irrelevant.

The second group are those who have dropped out of the political process in the past two decades, some 20 million Americans. They are still more heavily weighted to the poorer and more minority segments of our population. But they also include a 40 percent component who are educated, middle-class, professional, and white-collar workers in the suburbs in the middle Atlantic, northeastern, and western states. These people were in our survey the most alienated and the most motivated by events and by a belief that their vote no longer had any efficacy either in the improvement of their individual lives or the conduct of public policy. They can be returned to the polity only when and if they come to believe that in the political marketplace there are choices that will truly affect their personal and the societal well-being.

The third group is the young. For the lowest participating group in America is the nation's youth. Bluntly, fewer young people are voting than ever before. They are becoming socialized to participate at a slower rate than previous generations and their interest in politics as a group is substantially lower than that of the rest of the nation. If they are to become participants, they need to be engaged early and often, something which is not being done either by our high schools or our extracurricular institutions.

Finally, there are those who are still impeded by procedures governing registration and voting and those for whom the word "apathetic" is an accurate description. For while in our survey, nonvoters by a margin of 4 to 1 gave substantive reasons for their nonparticipation, there were still some who felt intimidated at the polls or impeded from participation, by polling hours, registration procedures, and the like. And, of course, there are some who just don't give a damn.

But for the vast majority of Americans, nonvoting is an intentional act. . . .

If there are solutions to those problems, they must come from a variety of directions.

Having said earlier that the central problem of low and declining voting is not principally a matter of procedure, I would like to suggest that procedure is not altogether irrelevant. For it has been estimated that if the nation would adopt election day registration there would be an immediate 9 percent rise in voter participation. I believe such a claim is somewhat excessive. On the other hand, if we just accept the evidence of our eyes—that when Wisconsin, Minnesota, Oregon, and Maine adopted election day registration, they experienced initial increases of from 2 to 4 percent in the face of national voting declines—we know we could add from 4 to 9 million Americans to the voter rolls. Bluntly speaking, America need not be, as it is today, the only major democracy in the world which puts the principal onus for registration on the citizen rather than the state. We need not necessarily have a system in which we must advertise "Register and Vote," forcing the citizen into not one but two acts in order to participate and knowing that the two are increasingly no longer synonymous. We can explore election day registration in more states, or better still, universal enrollment, as they have in Canada, which offers the prospect of fraud-free elections while lifting the burden of registration from the citizen's back. And in the interim we can explore those things which will bring us closer to this ideal—further shortening the time between the close of registration and election, drivers' license registration, and the like. . . .

We should constructively reduce the length of our ballots. There are no good reasons that the secretaries of state and attorneys general should be elected—they are not policymaking but rather policy implementing positions. Similarly, we could reduce the number of other elected offices and the number of ballot propositions. With ballots a mile long and information about them scarce as hen's teeth, it is no wonder that the public says in public opinion polls that it is confused, and it is no wonder that there are discouragingly long lines at the polling places.

We can and should have, instead of more elections, more polling places and longer hours (although not a twenty-four-hour voting day).

We should be concerned about the information, or rather lack thereof, the average citizen has available to him or her in making voting decisions. If citizens depend on television for the bulk of their information, they may know a little about the candidates who are running for the offices of president, governor, and senator, but they have no means of knowing anything about the other offices and issues at stake in any particular election. If they read most newspapers, they have little prospect for learning much more (the *New York Times,* the *Los Angeles Times,* and a few others being notable exceptions). Only through the continuing work of the League of Women Voters do some people in some places know what is going on. But that information ought to be available to everyone. We need, in short, to see whether the type of voter information pamphlets provided by the counties of Oregon, which provide information about each office and issue at stake in each election, pamphlets which can be carried into the voting booth, ought not to be used in every state in the union.

We should here and now begin the process of establishing a commission to look into and recommend remedies for those last vestiges of discrimination and intimidation which still plague our polls. There is no reason why the registration books of Upper Marlboro, Maryland, should be open for two unadvertised hours every two years. Jesse Jackson is right when he suggests that people should not be asked to register in one place for one election and in another for another. Eddie Williams is right when he decries the discriminatory effects of at-large elections, full slate requirements, and redistricting. We should be concerned about districting that effectively disenfranchises blacks from voting in their place of residence and on the officeholders and issues which will affect their lives. We should be concerned about students who are denied the vote in either their place of education or home because of discriminatory residency requirements in both places. . . .

We could, of course, do all of these things I have so far suggested and still not have a healthy democracy and high level of voter participation. For unless and until the public believes that it is voting for something meaningful and that its vote will make a difference, low voter participation will continue to be the order of the day.

The simple answer to this problem is, of course, to have candidates who speak relevantly to the issues of public concern and who can deliver upon their political promises once in office.

Life and reality are rarely so simple. For this relatively simple answer runs us smack against the five central political problems afflicting our political life—the problems of policy, parties, institutions, media, and governance.

## A. POLICY

We may lament the quality of our candidates. Such laments have been common for the past twenty years. Yet leadership does not spring full blown upon the political scene. The business of a politician is, in its best sense, to move the center of America in creative directions and to preserve the option to move in other directions. It involves very fine antennae about how far one can move to the center without making one's self irrelevant. The problem within America today is that there is no such center of ideas to which the politician can repair. If all our politicians sound like throwbacks to the New Deal (or, as in the case of the President, to the 1920s) it is because they are repairing to the only safe grounds they know. The problem lies not with our leaders but with the state of the art.

For three decades, we had such a consensual center. Out of the two great crises of the 1930s and 1940s, the Great Depression and World War II, there emerged a national consensus. On the domestic side we had Keynesian economics and the New Deal, a programmatic federal response to each perceived problem taken ad seriatim. On the foreign side, we had an increasing American global role in the containment first of fascism and later of communism. We argued about issues but only in degree. Was this domestic program necessary? How much aid should we be sending abroad and should it be military or economic?

The consensus broke down in the 1960s. The war in Vietnam revealed the limits of American power and resources in the world to assume a truly global role. The blight of our cities, the pollution of our environment were but two ways which showed that treating our problems ad seriatim might bring by-products as bad as the disease the original programs were designed to cure. Burgeoning unresponsive bureaucracies showed the limits to the maxim "let the federal government do it." . . .

In retrospect, [President Franklin] Roosevelt had an easier time, because he could accomplish those changes in outlook in an atmosphere of perceived crisis. In many ways the problems confronting us are nearly as great, but the perceived sense of crisis is not there. Thus, it becomes an exercise in leadership, an exercise no less necessary because it is difficult.

## B. PARTIES

If the candidate has difficulty in knowing what to say because of a lack of a central American consensus, then he also has difficulty as an officeholder in delivering upon his promises because there is no organizational force to discipline the individual officeholder and make him part of a collective.

That is the traditional role of the political party, which should serve as the training ground for leadership, the mobilizer of voters, the mediator of contending factions, the sorter of public programs from contending interests, the disciplinarian of individual self-interest, the enactor of programs, and the implementor of legislation.

But political parties are now in disarray. Their patronage functions have been supplanted by government, their informational functions by television, their role in the conduct of the campaigns by money, media, and political consultants.

They are in disarray also for other reasons—in that they either stand for something irrelevant or stand for nothing at all.

## C. INSTITUTIONS

Related to the problem of parties is the problem of our institutions. Part of that problem is simply that the institutional base of our society has atrophied as people have been atomized by television. Part of the problem is that some of our institutions have grown so large as to make them unresponsive.

But perhaps a more critical problem is the degree to which traditional institutions no longer stand for what they once did. Rather than being adversaries, business and labor are in an entente for jobs and production to the detriment of other elements of society. Unions, once the place where the common man could repair, have too often (and not without significant exceptions) become the protector of the long-term employed at the expense of the unemployed or marginally employed. The middle-class liberals, once a reliable source of strength for redistributive policies, are increasingly literally and figuratively cultivating their own gardens. Because of this, it is unlikely that we will ever again have the type of coalition of interests that existed within the New Deal.

But we can and should have interest groups that accurately reflect the interests of their issue or class. We can and should have different coalitions for different societal problems. Too often now the institutional interests of one group tend to resist cooperation with another for the public good. We need to have some general recognition of the role of time in our politics—that it is possible to be on the same side tomorrow with today's enemy. We need, in short, to return civility to the way we conduct our politics and rekindle an outlook that seeks ways to cooperate with others in temporary coalition for the common good.

## D. MEDIA

There is also the problem of media. For if the politician had the consensus through which to lead, the parties through which to implement program, the institutions in floating formation to back some or all of his or her program, there would still be the problem of communications.

. . . If there is one such development which acted to society's detriment, it has been television.

For not only has it served to atomize our society; weaken our institutions; reduce participation by making people spectators and consumers rather than involved participants; decrease reading, comprehension, and conversation; and increase public confusion by giving information in undifferentiated blips and by highlighting the most visually exciting—it has also established unreal expectations for our political system by creating heroes and as quickly destroying them and by offering in its advertising medical panaceas which give the society a belief it can have equally rapid social panaceas.

But perhaps most pertinent of all is the degree to which there is in the television message no sense of history, no sense of the slow pace of progress, no sorting out of the important from the unimportant. In the coverage of a political campaign, it is easier to focus on a politician's gaffe than on his record. . . .

## E. GOVERNANCE

Finally there is the problem of governance. . . . While we may look with some satisfaction at the slight increase in turnout in 1984, we can almost surely look for a decline in turnout in 1988 if a Democrat should be elected and find himself not quite up to government. For at the root of public cynicism about politics is a disillusionment with government. We need to make the politician in office as effective as he is appealing on the stump. And this, in turn, mandates a program of leadership education in the arts of administration, politics, and governance. . . .

# Nonvoting Is Not a Social Disease

## Austin Ranney

In 1980 only 53 percent of the voting-age population in the United States voted for president, and in 1982 only 38 percent voted for members of the House. As the statistics are usually presented, this rate is, on the average, from ten to forty points lower than in the democratic nations of Western Europe, Scandinavia, and the British Commonwealth—although such numbers involve major technical problems of which we should be aware.* We also know that the level of voter participation has been declining steadily since the early 1960s.

All forms of *in*voluntary nonvoting—caused by either legal or extralegal impediments—are violations of the most basic principles of democracy and fairness. Clearly it is a bad thing if citizens who want to vote are prevented from doing so by law or intimidation. But what about *voluntary* nonvoters—the 30 percent or so of our adult citizens who *could* vote if they were willing to make the (usually minimal) effort, but who rarely or never do so? What does it matter if millions of Americans who could vote choose not to?

We should begin by acknowledging that suffrage and voting laws, extralegal force, and intimidation account for almost none of the nonvoting. A number of constitutional amendments, acts of Congress, and court decisions since the 1870s—particularly since the mid-1960s—have outlawed all legal and extralegal denial of the franchise to blacks, women, Hispanics, people over the age of eighteen, and other groups formerly excluded. Moreover, since the mid-1960s most states have changed their registration and voting laws to make casting ballots a good deal easier. Many states, to be sure, still demand a somewhat greater effort to register than is required by other democratic countries. But the best estimates are that even if we made our voting procedures as

* European and American measures of voting and nonvoting differ significantly. In all countries the numerator for the formula is the total number of votes cast in national elections. In most countries the denominator is the total number of persons on the electoral rolls—that is, people we would call "registered voters"—which includes almost all people legally eligible to vote. In the United States, on the other hand, the denominator is the "voting-age population," which is the estimate by the Bureau of the Census of the number of people in the country who are eighteen or older at the time of the election. That figure, unlike its European counterpart, includes aliens and inmates of prisons and mental hospitals as well as persons not registered to vote. One eminent election analyst, Richard M. Scammon, estimates that if voting turnout in the United States were computed by the same formula as that used for European countries, our average figures would rise by eight to ten percentage points, a level that would exceed Switzerland's and closeiy approach those of Canada, Ireland, Japan, and the United Kingdom.

Austin Ranney is professor and chairman of the Department of Political Science at the University of California–Berkeley. This selection was adapted from a paper delivered to the ABC/Harvard Symposium on Voter Participation on October 1, 1983. From *Public Opinion,* October/November 1983, pp. 16–19. Reprinted with permission of American Enterprise Institute for Public Policy Research.

undemanding as those in other democracies, we would raise our average turnouts by only nine or so percentage points. That would still leave our voter participation level well below that of all but a handful of the world's democracies, and far below what many people think is the proper level for a healthy democracy.

Throughout our history, but especially in recent years, many American scholars, public officials, journalists, civic reformers, and other people of good will have pondered our low level of voting participation and have produced a multitude of studies, articles, books, pamphlets, manifestoes, and speeches stating their conclusions. On one point they agree: All start from the premise that voluntary, as well as involuntary, nonvoting is a bad thing for the country and seek ways to discourage it. Yet, despite the critical importance of the question, few ask *why* voluntary nonvoting is a bad thing.

Voluntary nonvoting's bad name stems from one or a combination of three types of arguments or assumptions. Let us consider these arguments in turn.

## WHAT HARM DOES IT DO?

One of the most often-heard charges against nonvoting is that it produces unrepresentative bodies of public officials. After all, the argument runs, if most of the middle-class WASPs vote and most of the blacks, Hispanics, and poor people do not, then there will be significantly lower proportions of blacks, Hispanics, and poor people in public office than in the general population. Why is that bad? For two reasons. First, it makes the public officials, in political theorist Hanna Pitkin's term, "descriptively unrepresentative." And while not everyone would argue that the interests of blacks are best represented by black officials, the interests of women by women officials, and so on, many people believe that the policy preferences of the underrepresented groups will get short shrift from the government. Second, this not only harms the underrepresented groups but weakens the whole polity, for the underrepresented are likely to feel that the government cares nothing for them and they owe no loyalty to it. Hence it contributes greatly to the underclasses' feelings of alienation from the system and to the lawlessness that grows from such alienation.

This argument seems plausible enough, but a number of empirical studies comparing voters with nonvoters do not support it. They find that the distributions of policy preferences among nonvoters are approximately the same as those among voters, and therefore the pressures on public officials by constituents for certain policies and against others are about the same as they would be if everyone, WASPs and minorities, voted at the same rate.

Moreover, other studies have shown that the level of cynicism about the government's honesty, competence, and responsiveness is about the same among nonvoters as among voters, and an increased level of nonvoting does not signify an increased level of alienation or lawlessness. We can carry the argument a step further by asking if levels of civic virtue are clearly higher and levels of lawlessness lower in Venezuela (94 percent average voting turnout), Austria (94 percent), and Italy (93 percent) than in the United States (58 percent), Switzerland (64 percent), and Canada (76 percent). If the answer is no, as surely it is, then at least we have to conclude that there is no clear or strong relationship between high levels of voting turnout and high levels of civic virtue.

Another argument concerns future danger rather than present harm to the Republic. Journalist Arthur Hadley asserts that our great and growing number of "refrainers" (his term for voluntary nonvoters) constitutes a major threat to the future stability of our political system. In his words:

> These growing numbers of refrainers hang over the democratic process like a bomb, ready to explode and change the course of our history as they have twice in our past. . . . Both times in our history when there have been large numbers of refrainers, sudden radical shifts of power have occurred. As long as the present gigantic mass of refrainers sits outside of our political system, neither we nor our allies can be certain of even the normally uncertain future. This is why creating voters, bringing the refrainers to the booth, is important.

Hadley's argument assumes that if millions of the present nonvoters suddenly voted in some future election, they would vote for persons, parties, and policies radically different from those chosen by the regular voters. He asserts that that is what happened in 1828 and again in 1932, and it could happen again any time. Of course, some might feel that a sudden rush to the polls that produces another Andrew Jackson or Franklin Roosevelt is something to be longed for, not feared, but in any case his assumption is highly dubious. We have already noted that the policy preferences of nonvoters do not differ greatly from those of voters, and much the same is true of their candidate preferences. For example, a leading study of the 1980 presidential election found that the five lowest voting groups were blacks, Hispanics, whites with family incomes below $5,000 a year, whites with less than high school educations, and working-class white Catholics. The study concluded that if all five groups had voted at the same rate as the electorate as a whole, they would have added only about one-and-a-half percentage points to Carter's share of the vote, and Reagan would still have been elected with a considerable margin. So Hadley's fear seems, at the least, highly exaggerated.

## WHAT SOCIAL SICKNESS DOES NONVOTING MANIFEST?

Some writers take the position that, while a high level of voluntary nonvoting may not in itself do harm to the nation's well-being, it is certainly a symptom of poor civic health. Perhaps they take their inspiration from Pericles, who, in his great funeral oration on the dead of Marathon, said:

> . . . Our ordinary citizens, though occupied with the pursuits of industry, are still fair judges of public matters; for, unlike any other nation, regarding him who takes no part in these duties not as unambitious but as useless. . . .

One who holds a twentieth-century version of that view is likely to believe that our present level of voluntary nonvoting is a clear sign that millions of Americans are civically useless—that they are too lazy, too obsessed with their own selfish affairs and interests, and too indifferent to the welfare of their country and the quality of their government to make even the minimum effort required to vote. A modern Pericles might ask, How can such a nation hope to defend itself in war and advance the public welfare in peace? Are not the lassitude and indifference manifested by our high level of nonvoting the root cause of our country's declining military strength and economic productivity as well as the growing corruption and bungling of our government?

Perhaps so, perhaps not. Yet the recent studies of nonvoters have shown that they do not differ significantly from voters in the proportions who believe that citizens have a civic duty to vote or in the proportions who believe that ordinary people have a real say in what government does. It may be that nonvoters are significantly less patriotic citizens, poorer soldiers, and less productive workers than voters, but there is no evidence to support such charges. And do we accept the proposition that the much higher turnout rates for the Austrians, the French, and the Irish show that they are significantly better on any or all of these counts than the Americans? If not, then clearly there is no compelling reason to believe that a high level of nonvoting is, by itself, a symptom of sickness in American society.

## WHAT BASIC PRINCIPLES DOES IT OFFEND?

I have asked friends and colleagues whether they think that the high level of voluntary nonvoting in America really matters. Almost all of them believe that it does, and when I ask them why they usually reply not so much in terms of some harm it does or some social illness it manifests but rather in terms of their conviction that the United States of America is or should be a democracy, and that a high level of voluntary nonvoting offends some basic principles of democracy.

Their reasoning goes something like this: The essential principle of democratic government is government by the people, government that derives its "just powers from the consent of the governed." The basic institution for ensuring truly democratic government is the regular holding of free elections at which the legitimate authority of public officials to govern is renewed or terminated by the sovereign people. Accordingly, the right to vote is the basic right of every citizen in a democracy, and the exercise of that right is the most basic duty of every democratic citizen.

Many have made this argument. For example, in 1963 President John F.

Kennedy appointed an eleven-member Commission on Registration and Voting Participation. Its report, delivered after his death, began:

> Voting in the United States is the fundamental act of self-government. It provides the citizen in our free society the right to make a judgment, to state a choice, to participate in the running of his government. . . . The ballot box is the medium for the expression of the consent of the governed.

In the same vein the British political philosopher Sir Isaiah Berlin declares, "Participation in self-government is, like justice, a basic human requirement, *an end in itself.*"

If these views are correct, then any nominal citizen of a democracy who does not exercise this basic right and fulfill this basic duty is not a full citizen, and the larger the proportion of such less-than-full citizens in a polity that aspires to democracy, the greater the gap between the polity's low realities and democracy's high ideals.

Not everyone feels this way, of course. Former Senator Sam Ervin, for example, argues:

> I'm not going to shed any real or political or crocodile tears if people don't care enough to vote. I don't believe in making it easy for apathetic, lazy people. I'd be extremely happy if nobody in the United States voted except for the people who thought about the issues and made up their own minds and wanted to vote. No one else who votes is going to contribute anything but statistics, and I don't care that much for statistics.

The issues between these two positions are posed most starkly when we consider proposals for compulsory voting. After all, if we are truly convinced that voluntary nonvoting is a violation of basic democratic principles, and a major social ill, then why not follow the lead of Australia, Belgium, Italy, and Venezuela and enact laws *requiring* people to vote and penalizing them if they do not?

The logic seems faultless, and yet most people I know, including me, are against compulsory voting laws for the United States. All of us want to eradicate all vestiges of *in*voluntary nonvoting, and many are disturbed by the high level of voluntary nonvoting. Yet many of us also feel that the right to abstain is just as precious as the right to vote, and the idea of legally compelling all citizens to vote whether they want to or not is at least as disturbing as the large numbers of Americans who now and in the future probably will not vote without some compulsion.

## THE BRIGHT SIDE

In the light of the foregoing considerations, then, how much should we worry about the high level of voluntary nonvoting in our country? At the end of his magisterial survey of voting turnout in different democratic nations, Ivor

Crewe asks this question and answers, "There are . . . reasons for *not* worrying—too much."

I agree. While we Americans can and probably should liberalize our registration and voting laws and mount register-and-vote drives sponsored by political parties, civic organizations, schools of government, and broadcasting companies, the most we can realistically hope for from such efforts is a modest increase of ten or so percentage points in our average turnouts. As a college professor and political activist for forty years, I can testify that even the best reasoned and most attractively presented exhortations to people to behave like good democratic citizens can have only limited effects on their behavior, and most get-out-the-vote drives by well-intentioned civic groups in the past have had disappointingly modest results.

An even more powerful reason not to worry, in my judgment, is that we are likely to see a major increase in our voting turnouts to, say, the 70 or 80 percent levels, only if most of the people in our major nonvoting groups—blacks, Hispanics, and poor people—come to believe that voting is a powerful instrument for getting the government to do what they want it to do. The recent register-and-vote drives by the NAACP and other black-mobilization organizations have already had significant success in getting formerly inactive black citizens to the polls. These new black voters played a more important role in the congressional and other local elections in 1982 and 1983 than ever before, and they are likely to be even more significant in the elections of 1984. Organizations like the Southern Voter Registration Education Project have had some success with Hispanic nonvoters in Texas and New Mexico and may have more. Jesse Helms and Jerry Falwell may also have success in their newly launched efforts to urge more conservatives to register and vote. But hard evidence that voting brings real benefits, not exhortations to be good citizens, will be the basis of whatever success any of these groups enjoy.

If we Americans stamp out the last vestiges of institutions and practices that produce *in*voluntary nonvoting, and if we liberalize our registration and voting laws and procedures to make voting here as easy as it is in other democracies, and if the group-mobilization movements succeed, then perhaps our level of voting participation may become much more like that of Canada or Great Britain. (It is unlikely ever to match the levels in the countries with compulsory voting or even those in West Germany or the Scandinavian countries.)

But even if that does not happen, we need not fear that our low voting turnouts are doing any serious harm to our politics or our country, or that they deprive us of the right to call ourselves a democracy.

# 6

# Campaigns
# and the Media

*Probably nothing has so revolutionized American politics as the emergence of television as the principal means of communicating with the voters. What used to be the experience of only a few people—hearing and seeing a candidate at a campaign rally, for example—is now an experience shared by many millions of Americans. Since television enables political candidates literally to be seen and heard in every living room in the country, it is no wonder that politicians devote so much time and resources to producing television advertisements and other political programming.*

*What impact has television had on the voter? Can voters be manipulated into voting blindly for candidates because of clever image making on the television screen? Or are voters more discerning than the political advertising executives would have us believe?*

*While certainly not all the evidence is in on the impact of television on the American voter, two well-known, indeed, classic books have dealt with the question and arrived at very different conclusions. One book,* The Selling of the President 1968 *by Joe McGinniss, excerpts from which are presented here, presents a firsthand account of the 1968 television campaign of former President Richard M. Nixon—a campaign that, according to McGinniss, featured a carefully packaged television image of Nixon. The success of the Nixon campaign in 1968, compared to 1960, convinced McGinniss and many others that all political campaigning was now merely a matter of projecting the right image on the television screen and "selling" the politician to the public.*

*Political scientists Thomas Patterson and Robert McClure, on the other hand, after studying a second campaign involving Richard Nixon (the 1972 campaign between Nixon and George McGovern) concluded that the public, far from being manipulated, was actually better informed and better able to make decisions as a result of exposure to televised political commercials than without that exposure.*

*What accounts for the seemingly contradictory results of these two studies? One hint might be found in the fact that the authors are proceeding from different perspectives and methodologies. McGinniss is writing from the point of view of an insider in the Nixon campaign. Patterson and McClure base their findings on the results of some two thousand interviews conducted during the 1972 campaign.*

# Politics as a Con Game

**Joe McGinniss**

Politics, in a sense, has always been a con game.

The American voter, insisting upon his belief in a higher order, clings to his religion, which promises another, better life; and defends passionately the illusion that the men he chooses to lead him are of a finer nature than he.

It has been traditional that the successful politician honor this illusion. To succeed today, he must embellish it. Particularly if he wants to be President.

"Potential presidents are measured against an ideal that's a combination of leading man, God, father, hero, pope, king, with maybe just a touch of the avenging Furies thrown in," an adviser to Richard Nixon wrote in a memorandum late in 1967. Then, perhaps aware that Nixon qualified only as father, he discussed improvements that would have to be made—not upon Nixon himself, but upon the image of him which was received by the voter. . . .

Advertising, in many ways, is a con game, too. Human beings do not need new automobiles every third year; a color television set brings little enrichment of the human experience; a higher or lower hemline no expansion of consciousness, no increase in the capacity to love.

It is not surprising, then, that politicians and advertising men should have discovered one another. And, once they recognized that the citizen did not so much vote for a candidate as make a psychological purchase of him, not surprising that they began to work together. . . .

Advertising agencies have tried openly to sell presidents since 1952. When Dwight Eisenhower ran for reelection in 1956, the agency of Batton, Barton, Durstine and Osborn, which had been on a retainer throughout his first four years, accepted his campaign as a regular account. Leonard Hall, national Republican chairman, said: "You sell your candidates and your programs the way a business sells its products." . . .

With the coming of television, and the knowledge of how it could be used to seduce voters, the old political values disappeared. Something new, murky, undefined started to rise from the mists. "In all countries," Marshall McLuhan writes, "the party system has folded like the organization chart. Policies and issues are useless for election purposes, since they are too specialized and hot. The shaping of a candidate's integral image has taken the place of discussing conflicting points of view." . . .

The television celebrity is a vessel. An inoffensive container in which someone else's knowledge, insight, compassion, or wit can be presented. And

Joe McGinniss is a New York writer and author of several books on politics. This selection is reprinted from Chapter 2 of *The Selling of the President 1968* by Joe McGinnis, pp. 19–34. Copyright © 1969 by Joemac, Inc. Reprinted by permission of Simon & Schuster, Inc.

we respond like the child on Christmas morning who ignores the gift to play with the wrapping paper.

Television seems particularly useful to the politician who can be charming but lacks ideas. Print is for ideas. Newspapermen write not about people but policies; the paragraphs can be slid around like blocks. Everyone is colored gray. Columnists—and commentators in the more polysyllabic magazines—concentrate on ideology. They do not care what a man sounds like; only how he thinks. For the candidate who does not, such exposure can be embarrassing. He needs another way to reach the people.

On television it matters less that he does not have ideas. His personality is what the viewers want to share. He need be neither statesman nor crusader; he must only show up on time. Success and failure are easily measured: How often is he invited back? Often enough and he reaches his goal—to advance from "politician" to "celebrity," a status jump bestowed by grateful viewers who feel that finally they have been given the basis for making a choice.

The TV candidate, then, is measured not against his predecessors—not against a standard of performance established by two centuries of democracy—but against [TV variety talk-show host] Mike Douglas. How well does he handle himself? Does he mumble, does he twitch, does he make me laugh? Do I feel warm inside?

Style becomes substance. The medium is the message and the masseur gets the votes. . . .

"The success of any TV performer depends on his achieving a low-pressure style of presentation," McLuhan has written. The harder a man tries, the better he must hide it. Television demands gentle wit, irony, understatement. . . . The TV politician cannot make a speech; he must engage in intimate conversation. He must never press. He should suggest, not state; request, not demand. Nonchalance is the key word. Carefully studied nonchalance.

Warmth and sincerity are desirable but must be handled with care. Unfiltered, they can be fatal. Television did great harm to Hubert Humphrey [the Democratic nominee]. His excesses—talking too long and too fervently, which were merely annoying in an auditorium—became lethal in a television studio. The performer must talk to one person at a time. He is brought into the living room. He is a guest. It is improper for him to shout. Humphrey vomited on the rug.

It would be extremely unwise for the TV politician to admit such knowledge of his medium. The necessary nonchalance should carry beyond his appearance while *on* the show; it should rule his attitude *toward* it. He should express distaste for television; suspicion that there is something "phony" about it. This guarantees him good press, because newspaper reporters, bitter over their loss of prestige to the television men, are certain to stress antitelevision remarks. Thus, the sophisticated candidate, while analyzing his own on-the-air technique as carefully as a golf pro studies his swing, will state frequently that there is no place for "public relations gimmicks" or "those show business guys" in his campaign. Most of the television men working for him will be unbothered by such remarks. They are willing to accept anonymity, even scorn, as long as the pay is good.

Into this milieu came Richard Nixon: grumpy, cold, and aloof. He would claim privately that he lost elections because the American voter was an adolescent whom he tried to treat as an adult. Perhaps. But if he treated the voter as an adult, it was as an adult he did not want for a neighbor.

This might have been excused had he been a man of genuine vision. An explorer of the spirit. Martin Luther King, for instance, got by without being one of the boys. But Richard Nixon did not strike people that way. He had, in Richard Rovere's words, "an advertising man's approach to his work," acting as if he believed "policies (were) products to be sold the public—this one today, that one tomorrow, depending on the discounts and the state of the market."

So his enemies had him on two counts: his personality, and the convictions—or lack of such—which lay behind. They worked him over heavily on both. . . .

But Nixon survived, despite his flaws, because he was tough and smart, and—some said—dirty when he had to be. Also, because there was nothing else he knew. A man to whom politics is all there is in life will almost always beat one to whom it is only an occupation.

He nearly became President in 1960, and that year it would not have been by default. He failed because he was too few of the things a President had to be—and because he had no press to lie for him and did not know how to use television to lie about himself.

It was just Nixon and John Kennedy and they sat down together in a television studio and a little red light began to glow and Richard Nixon was finished. Television would be blamed but for all the wrong reasons.

They would say it was makeup and lighting, but Nixon's problem went deeper than that. His problem was himself. Not what he said but the man he was. The camera portrayed him clearly. America took its Richard Nixon straight and did not like the taste.

The content of the programs made little difference. Except for startling lapses, content seldom does. What mattered was the image the viewers received, though few observers at the time caught the point. . . .

What the camera showed was Richard Nixon's hunger. He lost, and bitter, confused, he blamed it on his beard. . . .

He was afraid of television. He knew his soul was hard to find. Beyond that, he considered it a gimmick; its use in politics offended him. It had not been part of the game when he had learned to play, he could see no reason to bring it in now. He half suspected it was an eastern liberal trick: one more way to make him look silly. It offended his sense of dignity, one of the truest senses he had.

So his decision to use it to become President in 1968 was not easy. So much of him argued against it. But in his Wall Street years, Richard Nixon had traveled to the darkest places inside himself and come back numbed. He was, as in the Graham Greene title, a burnt-out case. All feeling was behind him; the machine inside had proved his hardiest part. He would run for President again and if he would have to learn television to run well, then he would learn it.

America still saw him as the 1960 Nixon. If he were to come at the people again, as a candidate, it would have to be as something new; not this scarred, discarded figure from their past.

He spoke to men who thought him mellowed. They detected growth, a new stability, a sense of direction that had been lacking. He would return with fresh perspective, a more unselfish urgency.

His problem was how to let the nation know. He could not do it through the press. He knew what to expect from them, which was the same as he had always gotten. He would have to circumvent them. Distract them with coffee and doughnuts and smiles from his staff and tell his story another way.

Television was the only answer, despite its sins against him in the past. But not just any kind of television. An uncommitted camera could do irreparable harm. His television would have to be controlled. He would need experts. They would have to find the proper settings for him, or if they could not be found, manufacture them. These would have to be men of keen judgment and flawless taste. He was, after all, Richard Nixon, and there were certain things he could not do. Wearing love beads was one. He would need men of dignity. Who believed in him and shared his vision. But more importantly, men who knew television as a weapon: from broadest concept to most technical detail. This would be Richard Nixon, the leader, returning from exile. Perhaps not beloved, but respected. Firm but not harsh; just but compassionate. With flashes of warmth spaced evenly throughout.

Nixon gathered about himself a group of young men attuned to the political uses of television. . . .

Harry Treleaven, hired as creative director of advertising in the fall of 1967, immediately went to work on the more serious of Nixon's personality problems. One was his lack of humor.

"Can be corrected to a degree," Treleaven wrote, "but let's not be too obvious about it. Romney's* cornball attempts have hurt him. If we're going to be witty, let a pro write the words."

Treleaven also worried about Nixon's lack of warmth, but decided that "he can be helped greatly in this respect by how he is handled. . . . Give him words to say that will show his *emotional* involvement in the issues. . . . Buchanan wrote about RFK talking about the starving children in Recife. *That's* what we have to inject. . . .

"He should be presented in some kind of 'situation' rather than cold in a studio. The situation should look unstaged even if it's not."

Some of the most effective ideas belonged to Raymond K. Price, a former editorial writer for the *New York Herald Tribune,* who became Nixon's best

* George Romney was a candidate for the Republican nomination for president in 1968—*Editors.*

and most prominent speech writer in the campaign. Price later composed much of the inaugural address.

In 1967, he began with the assumption that "the natural human use of reason is to support prejudice, not to arrive at opinions." Which led to the conclusion that rational arguments would "only be effective if we can get the people to make the *emotional* leap, or what theologians call (the) 'leap of faith.'"

Price suggested attacking the "personal factors" rather than the "historical factors" which were the basis of the low opinion so many people had of Richard Nixon.

"These tend to be more a gut reaction," Price wrote, "unarticulated, nonanalytical, a product of the particular chemistry between the voter and the *image* of the candidate. *We have to be very clear on this point: that the response is to the image, not to the man.* . . . It's not what's *there* that counts, it's what's projected—and carrying it one step further, its not what *he* projects but rather what the voter receives. It's not the man we have to change, but rather the *received impression.* And this impression often depends more on the medium and its use than it does on the candidate himself."

So there would not have to be a "new Nixon." Simply a new approach to television.

"What, then, does this mean in terms of our uses of time and of media?" Price wrote.

"For one thing, it means investing whatever time RN needs in order to work out firmly in his own mind that vision of the nation's future that he wants to be identified with. This is crucial. . . ."

So, at the age of fifty-four, after twenty years in public life, Richard Nixon was still felt *by his own staff* to be in need of time to "work out firmly in his own mind that vision of the nation's future that he wants to be identified with."

"Secondly," Price wrote, "it suggests that we take the time and the money to experiment, in a controlled manner, with film and television techniques, with particular emphasis on pinpointing those *controlled* uses of the television medium that can *best* convey the *image* we want to get across. . . .

"The TV medium itself introduces an element of distortion, in terms of its effect on the candidate and of the often subliminal ways in which the image is received. And it inevitably is going to convey a partial image—thus ours is the task of finding how to control its use so the part that gets across is the part we want to have gotten across. . . .

"Voters are basically lazy, basically uninterested in making an *effort* to understand what we're talking about . . . ," Price wrote. "Reason requires a high degree of discipline, of concentration; impression is easier. Reason pushes the viewer back, it assaults him, it demands that he agree or disagree; impression can envelop him, invite him in, without making an intellectual demand. . . . When we argue with him we demand that he make the effort of replying. We seek to engage his intellect, and for most people this is the most difficult work of all. The emotions are more easily roused, closer to the surface, more malleable. . . .''

So, for the New Hampshire primary, Price recommended "saturation with a film, in which the candidate can be shown better than he can be shown in person because it can be edited, so only the best moments are shown; then a quick parading of the candidate in the flesh so that the guy they've gotten intimately acquainted with on the screen takes on a living presence—not saying anything, just being seen. . . .

"[Nixon] has to come across as a person larger than life, the stuff of legend. People are stirred by the legend, including the living legend, not by the man himself. It's the aura that surrounds the charismatic figure more than it is the figure itself, that draws the followers. Our task is to build that aura. . . .

"So let's not be afraid of television gimmicks . . . get the voters to like the guy and the battle's two-thirds won."

So this was how they went into it. Trying, with one hand, to build the illusion that Richard Nixon, in addition to his attributes of mind and heart, considered, in the words of Patrick K. Buchanan, a speech writer, "communicating with the people . . . one of the great joys of seeking the Presidency''; while with the other they shielded him, controlled him, and controlled the atmosphere around him. It was as if they were building not a President but an Astrodome, where the wind would never blow, the temperature never rise or fall, and the ball never bounce erratically on the artificial grass.

They could do this, and succeed, because of the special nature of the man. There was, apparently, something in Richard Nixon's character which sought this shelter. Something which craved regulation, which flourished best in the darkness, behind clichés, behind phalanxes of antiseptic advisers. Some part of him that could breathe freely only inside a hotel suite that cost a hundred dollars a day.

And it worked. As he moved serenely through his primary campaign, there was new cadence to Richard Nixon's speech and motion; new confidence in his heart. And, a new image of him on the television screen.

TV both reflected and contributed to his strength. Because he was winning he looked like a winner on the screen. Because he was suddenly projecting well on the medium he had feared, he went about his other tasks with assurance. The one fed upon the other, building to an astonishing peak in August as the Republican convention began and he emerged from his regal isolation, traveling to Miami not so much to be nominated as coronated. On live, but controlled, TV.

# The Impact of Televised Political Commercials

## Thomas E. Patterson and Robert D. McClure

One minute after a product commercial fades from the television screen, most viewers have forgotten what was advertised. They cannot recall whether the ad trumpeted aspirin, shaving cream, or automobiles. A particularly clever or amusing commercial may draw some notice, and linger in their thoughts, but most product ads pass from the mind as quickly as from the screen.[1]

Presidential ads affect viewers differently. On television only a month or two every four years, their novelty attracts attention. Also their subject matter. They picture and discuss men seeking the nation's highest office, and most Americans feel that choosing a President deserves more consideration than selecting a brand of antacid. A clear indication of presidential advertising's attention-getting ability is that most viewers can rather fully recall the message of a presidential spot. When asked to describe a commercial they had seen during the 1972 election, 56 percent of the viewers gave a remarkably full and complete description of one, and only 21 percent were unable to recall anything at all from political ads.[2] In market research, any product whose commercials are recalled with half this accuracy is considered to have had a very successful advertising campaign.[3]

People also evaluate presidential advertising differently than product advertising. A study conducted for the American Association of Advertising Agencies in the 1960s discovered that television viewers judge product commercials more on *how* they communicate their message than on *what* they say about a product.[4] A commercial for a soft drink or a paper towel is regarded as good or bad by the television audience more on whether it is enjoyable to watch than on the truthfulness of its message or the value of the information it contains. People judge presidential ads, on the other hand, primarily on *what* they say, not *how* they say it. Whether the techniques used in presidential spots are visually appealing or unappealing seems to matter little. Viewers seem concerned mainly with whether the advertising message is truthful and worth knowing. Where the American Association of Advertising Agencies' study found that only 46 percent of viewer reactions to product ads related to the information communicated, 74 percent of viewer reactions to presidential commercials shown in 1972 centered on the information contained in the message.[5]

Thomas E. Patterson and Robert D. McClure are professors of political science at Syracuse University. This selection is reprinted by permission of G. P. Putnam's Sons from *The Unseeing Eye: The Myth of Television Power in National Elections* by Thomas E. Patterson and Robert D. McClure, pp. 109–117, 132–138. Copyright © 1976 by Thomas E. Patterson and Robert D. McClure.

**115**

Thus, presidential spots get noticed, and the attention centers on the message. But to what end? Does the viewer learn anything about the candidates? Does he find out anything about the issues?

For years, most political observers have been certain they knew the answers: Advertising builds false political images and robs the American electorate of important issue information. On both counts, this orthodox view is wrong. In a presidential campaign, spot commercials do much more to educate the public about the issues than they do to manipulate the public about the candidates.

## ADVERTISING'S IMAGE IMPACT

In presidential politics, advertising image-making is a wasted effort. All the careful image planning—the coaching, the camera work, the calculated pleas—counts for nothing. Just as with network news appearances, people's feelings about the candidate's politics—his party, past actions, and future policies—far outweigh the influence of televised commercials.

Strong evidence for advertising's ineffectiveness comes from a look at *changes* in voters' images during the 1972 campaign. Just before presidential ads began appearing on television and again when the candidates' ad campaigns were concluding, the same people were asked to judge the images of Nixon and McGovern. They evaluated each candidate on seven traits associated with personality and leadership. Because the same people were questioned each time, an exact measure exists of how their images changed during the time when the candidates' ads were appearing on television.

These changes in voters' images indicate that advertising image-making had no effect. . . . Among people who preferred Nixon, his image showed a 35 percent improvement and McGovern's image a 28 percent decline. This happened among people exposed to many of the candidates' ads and to those seeing few commercials, if any. Among people backing McGovern, however, his image made a 20 percent improvement and Nixon's had an 18 percent decline. And again, no significant difference occurred in the image changes of people heavily and lightly exposed to presidential advertising.

Thus, whether people watched television regularly, and constantly saw the advertised images of Nixon and McGovern, had no influence on their impressions of the two candidates. Whatever people were getting from political spots, it was not their image of the candidates. . . .

By projecting their political biases, people see in candidates' commercials pretty much what they want to see. Ads sponsored by the candidate who shares their politics get a good response. They like what he has to say. And they like him. Ads sponsored by the opposing candidate are viewed negatively. They object to what he says. And they object to him.

A sampling of viewers' reactions to the series of image commercials used by George McGovern throughout the general election campaign illustrates how strongly political bias affects viewers. These spots pictured McGovern among small groups of people in natural settings, discussing their problems and promising to help them if elected. The commercials were intended to project an image of McGovern as a man who cared about people. Whether viewers received this image, however, had little to do with what happened on the television screen. It was all in their minds:[6]

> He really cares what's happened to disabled vets. They told him how badly they've been treated and he listened. He will help them.
> —37-year-old, pro-McGovern viewer

> McGovern was talking with these disabled vets. He doesn't really care about them. He's just using them to get sympathy.
> —33-year-old, pro-Nixon viewer

> It was honest, down-to-earth. People were talking and he was listening.
> —57-year-old, pro-McGovern viewer

> Those commercials are so phoney. He doesn't care.
> —45-year-old, pro-Nixon viewer

> McGovern had his coat off and his tie was hanging down. It was so relaxed, and he seemed to really be concerned with those workers.
> —31-year-old, pro-McGovern viewer

> He is trying hard to look like one of the boys. You know, roll up the shirt sleeves and loosen the tie. It's just too much for me to take.
> —49-year-old, pro-Nixon viewer

> I have seen many ads where McGovern is talking to common people. You know, like workers and the elderly. He means what he says. He'll help them.
> —22-year-old, pro-McGovern viewer

> He's with all these groups of people. Always making promises. He's promising more than can be done. Can't do everything for everyone.
> —41-year-old, pro-Nixon viewer

These people were watching the same George McGovern, listening to the same words, and yet they were receiving vastly different impressions of the Democratic presidential nominee.

Even undecided voters are not influenced by advertising image-making. Just like partisans, the candidate images of undecided voters fluctuate with vote choice, not advertising exposure. In 1972, undecided voters' images changed very little and fit no definite pattern until *after* they had picked their candidate. Among those choosing Nixon, and only *after* they had done so, his image had a 35 percent improvement and McGovern's a 35 percent decline. This pattern of image change was the rule for those seeing many presidential ads and those seeing few or none. Likewise, for those picking McGovern, his image showed a 40 percent improvement and Nixon's a 55 percent decline. Again, there was no difference in this pattern based on the undecided voter's exposure to televised political commercials.

Spot ads do not mold presidential images because voters are not easily

misled. They recognize that advertising imagery is heavily laden with something that is not intrinsically related to personal character at all—how the
candidate looks on camera. This pseudocharacter, to some extent coached,
posed, and created by the best media talent money can buy, is a "look" built
into spots that is totally unreal. And viewers recognize its meaninglessness.
Even the candid portrayals of presidential aspirants that sometimes appear in
image appeals are ineffective. People's guards go up when a spot goes on. So
no matter the style of presentation, when only 60 seconds are used to say that a
candidate is big enough to handle the presidency, voters find the message
skimpy, debatable, and unconvincing. They know that the candidate will display his strengths and mask his weaknesses and that a 60-second glimpse does
not provide much of an insight into a man's fitness for the nation's highest
office.

Symbolic manipulation through televised political advertising simply does
not work. Perhaps the overuse of symbols and stereotypes in product advertising has built up an immunity in the television audience. Perhaps the symbols
and postures used in political advertising are such patently obvious attempts at
manipulation that they appear more ridiculous than reliable. Whatever the
precise reason, television viewers effectively protect themselves from manipulation by staged imagery.

## ADVERTISING'S ISSUE IMPACT

But where image appeals fail, issue appeals work. Through commercials,
presidential candidates actually inform the electorate. In fact, the contribution
of advertising campaigns to voter knowledge is truly impressive.

During the 1972 presidential election, people who were heavily exposed
to political spots became more informed about the candidates' issue positions. . . . On every single issue emphasized in presidential commercials, persons with high exposure to television advertising showed a greater increase in
knowledge than persons with low exposure. And on the typical issue, individuals who happened to see many commercials were nearly half again as likely to
become more knowledgeable as people who saw few, if any, televised spots.
Issue knowledge among people with considerable advertising exposure
achieved a 36 percent increase compared with a 25 percent increase among
those with minimal exposure. Persons heavily exposed to advertising were
particularly aided in their knowledge about Nixon's position on China and
military spending and about McGovern's position on military spending and
taxes.

This information gain represents no small achievement. Televised political advertising has been widely maligned for saying nothing of consequence.
Although the issue material contained in spots is incomplete and over-
simplified, it also is abundant. So abundant in fact, that presidential advertising
contributes to an informed electorate.

Advertising also educates voters because of the powerful way it transmits its issue content. Three basic advertising strategies—simplicity, repetition, and sight-sound coordination—combine to make presidential spots good communicators. Ads contain such simple messages that they leave almost no room for misunderstanding. . . .

## THE EXTENT OF ADVERTISING MANIPULATION

Precise statistics on advertising's manipulative effects are hard to develop, because advertising, like other forms of media persuasion, works among and through a complex web of other influences. Seldom does a voter make his candidate choice for a single reason, whether the reason be political commercials, party loyalty, or a particular issue. Moreover, most people make up their minds about the candidates prior to the general election campaign, the time when presidential advertising saturates television programming. In 1972, as in previous elections where survey data have been gathered, about 80 percent of the electorate stayed with the choice it had decided upon before the general election began. Without doubt, some of these voters were reinforced in their initial vote choice by what they saw through television advertising. But how does one identify—among the people not changing their minds—those who would have changed their minds were it not for advertising? It is a treacherous task to assess whether people might have done something they did not do. So the effects of advertising on a voting decision are not that easily typed.

But some voters do decide their vote choice during a presidential general election and these people offer the best opportunity for understanding advertising's influence. In three interviews conducted with the same people during the 1972 general election, voters were asked which candidate they planned to support. If they changed their mind between one interview and the next, they were asked the reasons for the change and, if information about the candidates played some part in the change, where that information came from. By looking for advertising themes and sources in the reasons people gave for their vote changes, one way of estimating advertising's effects is provided. . . .

For three in every four people who arrived at their final vote choice during the 1972 general election, televised advertising had *no* discernible influence. . . . Some 42 percent cited important events, such as the Paris peace talks, as the reason why they selected their candidate; 11 percent said they decided to follow party allegiance, as did the factory worker who said, "I've always been a Democrat and McGovern is the Democrat"; 12 percent gave an old maxim, such as "not changing horses" or "it's time for a change," as their reason; 7 percent said they made their choice on the advice of their spouse or a friend or a co-worker; and 5 percent, although unable to provide a specific reason for choosing a candidate, did not watch much, if any, television during the 1972 campaign. In all of these decisions, televised advertising may have played some part, but at most, it was only a contributory influence. Additionally, 7 percent of vote changers present the situation of undetermined advertising effect. These people could give no clear reason for their candidate choice, but they were widely exposed to political ads during the campaign. Televised advertising, then, might have been the reason for their choice although other explanations, such as party loyalty or important political events, are also plausible.

So the first fact that must be recognized is that political advertising competes with other influences for the loyalties of indecisive voters. Before televised spots were used, less-informed voters were choosing candidates because they had a vague feeling that it was time for a change, because their father had pulled the same party lever years before, because an event triggered a reaction, because their spouse or union leader told them what to do. Today, most indecisive voters still select their candidate for such reasons.

Clear cases of advertising influence occurred among only 16 percent of those people making their candidate choice during the general election, or roughly 3 percent of the total electorate, since only one in five voters make up their minds during this time. But not even all these people can be labeled the victims of advertising manipulation. Indeed, the second fact about advertising influence is that simply because spot information helps people make up their minds does not mean manipulation occurs. True manipulation through advertising involves more than voters obtaining information that subsequently guides their vote choice. Spots are truly manipulative only when they convince the voter to act in the candidate's best interests and not the voter's. By this definition, of the 16 percent influenced by advertising, about half (9 percent) *were not* manipulated and about half (7 percent) *were* manipulated. To distinguish between these two types of advertising influence, here are the brief, but actual, voting histories of two people who during the 1972 general election made their vote choice from advertising information.

The first voter is a 74-year-old woman, who before she retired worked at an unskilled job. In 1972, she was deeply concerned about having enough income to live on; her social security and small savings forced her to make ends meet on only $3,000 a year. Asked at the beginning of the campaign what one political problem troubled her most, she replied: "The amount of social security. It is not enough for most people to live on." Asked the same question at the end of the campaign, she said that "taxes were too high for older people on fixed incomes."

This woman called herself an Independent, but her past voting behavior had been strongly Democratic. She claimed to have backed Kennedy, Johnson, and Humphrey in the three previous presidential elections. Her choice for the 1972 Democratic nomination was George Wallace, and when McGovern got the nod, she was undecided about whether to vote for him or Nixon. In late October, she made her choice. She selected McGovern and gave this reason:

> I've seen many commercials where George McGovern wants to help older people, to get them more social security and otherwise help them all he could. Nixon has vetoed bills for helping older people and McGovern has shown a

definite interest in doing something for us. If Nixon hasn't done anything in the last four years, he probably won't do it now. He looks after big business, not the worker. Nixon's funds are from big business and they'll try to put him in again. I've no use for him.

The second voter is a 30-year-old hospital worker with two years of college. He is married and has one child. At the start of the general election, he was mainly concerned that the United States maintain a flexible foreign policy. At the campaign's end, he labeled unemployment the nation's major problem.

This man called himself a lukewarm Republican and in 1968 had not bothered to vote. But he registered to vote in 1972, and when the general election campaign began, he intended to support McGovern. By October, he had become undecided about McGovern, and just before the election day he switched to Nixon. He cited one particular commercial as the major reason:

> I saw this ad where it says McGovern keeps changing his mind. It said he had first said this and then that. He did this last year and what about next year. It put a question in my mind whether I wanted to vote for McGovern. He doesn't seem reliable as a person. He seems to be changeable with regard to the issues. So I eliminated him. Actually I guess Nixon has done okay the last four years. I'm not crazy about either one, but I'm voting for Nixon.

Advertising did not manipulate the first voter. It did the second. The woman used the best information available to her to maximize her political values. Although McGovern was making the same arguments about the elderly in his campaign speeches and they were more fully reported and criticized in newspaper reports, the woman did not depend heavily on the news media. But she received from advertising the information she most needed. It informed her about the candidates' social security and other old-age benefits, and she chose the candidate who promised to do her the most good.

The man, on the other hand, was manipulated. He responded to the candidate's interest, not his own. Through commercials, this man's view of his stake in the political system was replaced by the candidate's view. He was concerned about America's role in world affairs and unemployment, and yet he cast his vote on the basis of an idea placed in his head by advertising and seemingly unrelated to his own political concerns. He was used. He had no strong feelings that the nation needed decisive leadership and no firm ground for assuming McGovern would not provide it. His view of politics simply came to mimic the view of a Nixon advertisement.

America can tolerate the effect that advertising has on people like this man. Counting for one or perhaps two voters in every hundred that got to the polls, this man and others like him will select a candidate for trivial reasons with or without advertising. (Before being persuaded by the Nixon commercial, the man indicated his vote for McGovern was premised on the fact that "McGovern had got a raw deal because of all the criticism about Eagleton.") And besides, since their reasons for choosing a candidate seem randomly selected, their votes distribute about equally between the candidates.

The benefits provided other voters by televised political advertising far exceed this kind of cost. Not only do more Americans, like the woman who learned which candidate was best for her, obtain information that helps them determine how their self-interest can be served, but many more people acquire information that helps them to validate a prior decision. And then there are people who simply learn a little more from ads than what they would have otherwise been able to learn. . . .

## NOTES

1 Leo Bogart, *Strategy in Advertising* (New York: Harcourt Brace & World, 1967), p. 139.
2 Respondents were first asked whether they had seen a Nixon or McGovern commercial. If they indicated seeing an ad, they were then asked: "Would you tell me what you can about the Nixon (McGovern) commercial you remember best?" Those remembering nothing about the ad were classified as "unable to recall." Other replies were classified as partial or full recall depending on whether respondents stated the central message of the commercial they had seen.
3 Bogart, *Strategy in Advertising,* p. 139.
4 Raymond A. Bauer and Stephen A. Greyser, *Advertising in America* (Boston: Harvard University Press, 1968), chap. 7.
5 *Ibid.* Percentages based on a reconstruction of data contained in source.
6 Responses come from interviews conducted with potential voters during the 1972 general election. Responses have been edited to improve readability. Ages and occupations have been changed to protect identities of respondents.

# 7

## Nominations and Elections
### Nominations

*The nominating process is the crucial stage in the electoral cycle, determining as it does the choices we are ultimately faced with on election day. This point was not lost on that noted practitioner of politics Boss Tweed, who was fond of telling his compatriots: "I don't care who does the electin, so long as I do the nominatin."*

*It is fair to say that our presidential nominating process has been subject to more sustained criticism in the last fifteen years than any other feature of the American political system. Indeed, from scholars, journalists, and public officials alike have come warnings that much is wrong with this process which, since 1968, has taken the nomination decision out of the hands of party elites and given it to masses of caucus and primary voters. In the first selection, journalist Paul Taylor gives point to these concerns, arguing that the current nominating process demeans the candidates; is excessively long and costly; confers undue influence on the media as well as certain primary and caucus states; and is poorly suited to testing the ability of candidates to govern once in office. These limitations, he further argues, have consequences both for who runs and who wins. Taylor concludes by identifying several proposals which are designed to remedy the deficiencies he sees in the current nominating process.*

*Eric Uslaner, a political scientist, provides further reinforcement to Taylor's criticisms of the nominating process but parts company with him on solutions. In his judgment, the changes proposed by Taylor and others amount to nothing more than tinkering with the nominating process and will do little to address its fundamental weaknesses—weaknesses that were*

*present well before the current president-by-primary process. Uslaner advo-
cates a much bolder solution, insisting that it will give us better nominees
and better government as well.*

# The Way We Choose Presidents Is Crazy and Getting Crazier

## Paul Taylor

This is what running for president has come to. Your name is Dick Gephardt*
and you are cruising through New Hampshire with a small statue of a German
shepherd in your hand. You've just spotted it in a gift shop in Nashua. You're
thrilled.

Tomorrow you'll take it to Cedar Rapids, Iowa, and present it to a local
Democratic activist named Connie Clark, who collects such things. She is vital,
or so you've calculated, to your long march on the White House. You desper-
ately want her on your team. Your plan is to surprise her with this bauble and
then don an apron and spend four hours flipping pancakes and schmoozing with
the guests at a Sunday breakfast she's put together.

You began waging this all-out assault on Connie Clark's affections in mid-
January. Since then, you've contacted her between six and 16 times (the figure
is a matter of some dispute), and yet she's not even close to committing to your
campaign. Maybe, she says, by mid-May.

What does this chilling little courtship—details all true—tell us about the
way we go about nominating our presidents? This: It's wacky.

It's now been 18 years and four elections since Democratic Party reformers set about to transfer power in the nomination processes from the bosses to
the masses. What they wanted was more democracy, small "d".

They got it. The jerry-built system of direct election primaries and caucuses they concocted is unlike anything practiced anywhere else in the world.
It was born of fine intentions, and it still has much to recommend it. It gives
play to an egalitarianism (everybody gets a chance to be president) and an anti-
elitism (in theory, nobody but the people now choose their leaders) that are at
the core of our political culture. It forces the candidates to learn the country
(though they invariably wind up better-versed in the folkways of Des Moines
than Detroit).

But it also contains a set of tail-wags-dog distortions that grow more
baroque with each passing election. It has created a new class of politicians
who demonstrate their good sense by not running for president. And it has

---

*Congressman Richard Gephardt (D-Mo.) was one of several candidates who sought the Demo-
cratic nomination for president in 1988. Others mentioned in this article are U.S. Senator Joseph
Biden (D-Del.) and Bruce Babbitt, former governor of Arizona—*Editors*.

Paul Taylor is a reporter and feature writer for *The Washington Post*. From Paul Taylor, "The Way
We Choose Presidents Is Crazy and Getting Crazier," *The Washington Post,* March 29, 1987,
pp. C1, 2 © *The Washington Post*.

**125**

created its own new set of elites. One is the media. Another is the small cadre of Iowa and New Hampshire activists who keep getting more proficient at gaming the system, at profiteering—psychologically, politically, even monetarily—from the power conferred upon them by accidents of history and timing and process.

The hoary New Hampshire joke—"How can I be sure about him for president, he's only been in my kitchen three times!"—is way out of date, as the Connie Clark courtship demonstrates. "These aren't primaries anymore," Walter F. Mondale says of Iowa and New Hampshire, speaking with the authority of a man who's been there before and isn't heading back, "they're ambushes."

This year, candidates of both parties will spend record-breaking spans of time campaigning in those two states—and they'll do so even though the South, inflamed with regional jealousy at having been bypassed before, tried to force the early action into its backyard by bunching 14 of its primaries right after the Iowa/New Hampshire slingshot. It hasn't worked. The two early states loom larger than ever.

"The system has gone crazy," says Norman Ornstein, an American Enterprise Institute political scientist. So crazy that some believe it's about to break. There's a school of thought that says the old bosses may have to reinvent themselves next year when, for the first time in the media age, the Democrats could be headed for a brokered convention.

How do we know the system is riding for a fall? Exhibit A is the list of presidential first-stringers who have chosen to stay on the sidelines for the 1988 presidential campaign, even though it's the first one in 20 years that doesn't start out with an incumbent seeking reelection.

Count the Democrats who are taking a pass: Mario Cuomo, Bill Bradley, Sam Nunn, Edward M. Kennedy, Dale Bumpers, Charles S. Robb. And the Republicans: Howard H. Baker Jr., James R. Thompson, Lamar Alexander, Thomas Kean, George Deukmejian.

"It is clear that this year, more than ever before, if you polled people knowledgeable about national government, and put together a list of the 10 best candidates, not more than two or three who are actually running would be on it," says Austin Ranney, a political science professor at Berkeley.

"This is striking," says Ornstein. "There have been good people who have backed off before. But when you have a Mario Cuomo, who had an extraordinarily good chance of making it, get out, you ask, 'Is something amiss?' When you have not a single candidate get in from the South in a year when Democrats are all saying they need to appeal in the South, it's worrisome."

What keeps them out? All have personal reasons unconnected to the dysfunctions of the modern nominating system. But for each of them, the bizarre pitfalls, hoops and hurdles of that system served as a deterrent. Consider:

It's way too long. In 1968, the last election for which the old rules were still in force, the winning Democratic nominee declared for the presidency 121 days before his party's convention. In 1984, the winning Democratic nominee announced his candidacy 511 days before. This length of time makes it hard for people with jobs to compete. It also demands a "single-minded obsession that can distort people somewhat," says Mondale. "For four years, that's all I did. I mean, all I did. That's all you think about. That's all you talk about. That's who you're around. That's your schedule. That's your leisure. That's your luxury. That's your reading. I told someone, 'The question is not whether I can get elected. The question is can I be elected and not be nuts when I get there.' It can twist people."

It increasingly demands that candidates do things beneath the dignity of the office they are seeking. "It's more at the level of running for county clerk," says Stuart Eizenstat, former adviser to President Carter, who says he and other reformers in his party ought to "plead guilty to raising exponentially the aggravation level of running for president." Joe Biden has been sending flowers to Iowa activists. Dick Gephardt visits them in the hospital when they take ill. Bruce Babbitt spent 10 days riding a bike across the state.

Then there's the profit motive. "There gets to be a seamy side to this," says Mondale. "When the Manchester [N.H.] Chamber of Commerce asked me to pay $1,500 for the right to speak to them [in 1984]. When the New Hampshire party charges me $1,000 to address their convention, and then they rent space on the convention wall that I have to pay for to put up my signs, something has gone wrong."

This time, it's Iowa that's discovering how to make a buck off the passing parade. In 1986, the political action committees of various Republican and Democratic presidential candidates ponied up at least $147,620 to Iowans running for state and local office, according to a tally by *The Des Moines Register*. "It's new, but we love it," the article quoted Phil Roeder, spokesman for the Iowa Democratic Party, as saying. This year, Don Avenson, speaker of the Iowa House, already made it clear that more "tribute"—the word is from a recent column in *The Des Moines Register*—is expected before he or members of this caucus make any endorsements.

This isn't to argue that Iowans are in it for the buck. To the contrary, the overwhelming majority of activists are decent, civic-spirited citizens who take their privileged role in dead earnest. For example, Connie Clark, head of the Cedar Rapids local of the American Federation of State, County and Municipal Employees, says she is so torn between Biden, Babbitt and Gephardt that she's concocted her own elaborate numerical rating system.

The process rewards skills that have precious little to do with governing. "It puts a premium on sitting in someone's living room and being a pleasant fellow," says Ranney. "But that isn't what a president is supposed to do."

The process all but eliminates peer review as a check against the excesses of small "d" democracy. Mondale again: "In the previous situation you had a community of people—national committeemen and women, state party chairmen, members of Congress—who knew and could discuss the private failings of a candidate. They also had a sense of the political requirements of the jobs. Now, they made mistakes, too, but the old system produced characters like Roosevelt, Truman, and Kennedy."

The process invests too much power in the laps of the media. After the bosses got fired from their job as gatekeepers, the press found itself drafted for the role because politics abhors a vacuum. Now, everyone knows the journalistic profession is populated by saints, prophets and wisemen. But who elected them?

The current crop of candidates, for obvious reasons, won't talk much about any of this. Babbitt comes as close as anyone. "The wire keeps getting stretched tighter and tighter in Iowa and New Hampshire, and sooner or later, it will snap—but not this year," he says. "My job is not to reform the system. My job is to use the system to get elected." Babbitt plans to spend 50 days this year in New Hampshire, 90 in Iowa.

If this is such a manifestly silly way of doing business, two questions beg answers: Who thought it up? And how do we fix it?

The first is easy: Nobody. Like so much else about our institutional life, it just sort of grew. Much of it is not enforced by rules. It is enforced, rather, by political folkways. Jimmy Carter's longshot victory in 1976 was a watershed event in codifying these new folkways into "law." It was born, in part, of a brilliant tactical understanding of the cracks and crevices in the new rules. But its lessons have been overlearned. It is not the only way of winning modern nominations. It's merely the most famous way.

Of course, there *are* rules, and they must be heeded. In the aggregate, they elongate the process. There are two key reasons:

- Money. The $1,000 limit on what individuals can give to a presidential campaign means it takes a candidate a long, long time to raise the $10 to $20 million he or she needs.
- Frontloading. Because a majority of the primaries are now scheduled before March 15, most of the deadlines for filing delegate lists will arrive in January or February. For a campaign to go into a state and find scores of individuals willing to take nominating petitions around to their neighbors "is a backbreaking organizational challenge," says Babbitt's deputy campaign manager, Elaine Kamarck. To compete for delegates, therefore, one must be up and running at the latest by the fall of the year before the election.

How to fix the system? There's no shortage of suggestions, especially among Democrats. Mondale, for one, would like to preserve many features of the current system but reintroduce the role of peer review as a major component. (The party has taken modest steps in this direction in the last two rule changes.) He would keep the small-state start (the theory being that these are places where anybody can compete, because having a big name and big bank account means less). He proposes rotating the small states each cycle.

To shorten the season, perhaps a lottery could be held in the fall of the odd-numbered year before a presidential election to select the two first states. No one could do much meaningful campaigning before then.

These small states would be followed by a series of regional primaries, three weeks apart, with their order rotated from one election to the next.

The point is not to design a perfect system. There are lots of ideas. The bigger question is, who will force the system to change?

A series of court rulings makes it plain that the national parties have the power to set the rules that determine who will be seated at their national conventions.

But having legal power is one thing; having political power is another. From 1981 to 1984, then-Democratic National Committee chairman Charles Manatt struggled mightily to strip Iowa and New Hampshire of their special status. He broke his pick.

But this might happen: The will of the masses will be thwarted. The candidate who gets a plurality of votes cast in the primaries and caucuses won't win the nomination. People will scream. The system will come under attack. Somebody is apt to point a finger at Iowa, New Hampshire, dog statues and four-year marathons. And in the cause of direct democracy, changes will be made.

# Choosing Our Presidents:
## It Hasn't Always Been Crazy

**Eric M. Uslaner**

Paul Taylor is correct. The way we nominate our Presidents is crazy. Americans put Presidential aspirants through a series of tests more typical of a marathon sports event than of the training required of someone who will have to govern the most powerful nation on earth. Since Americans love to root for underdogs, we often shower our affection on candidates who aver their status as outsiders not connected to "the Washington establishment." It is as if East Idaho State University persevered throughout the long college basketball season and became one of the much-touted "Final Four" of the National Collegiate Athletic Association's (NCAA) tournament.

The legendary Mr. Dooley once said that "politics ain't beanbag." He meant that this sport is of greater consequence than other games of skill and chance. Yet, we persevere in a process of selecting our chief executive that formally takes almost a year—from the Iowa caucuses in January through the general election in November—and has many of the characteristics of what former major league baseball player Jim Brosnan called "the long season." Indeed, our system of selecting Presidential nominees is even more tortured than the NCAA tournament. David Broder, Taylor's distinguished colleague at the *Washington Post,* argued that there is more order in the college basketball playoffs. Once a team is eliminated in the early rounds, it cannot attempt to make a comeback. Contenders for the Presidency can and often do bounce back after Iowa (as Vice President George Bush did in 1988). Even more critically, in college basketball, there is a set of "experts" who decide which teams can play. In Presidential primaries, almost anybody can run—and sometimes it seems that almost anybody does.[1]

What, precisely, is wrong with our nominating system? Yes, as Taylor and others argue, it is far too long. The campaign actually lasts much longer than one year. Some think that it takes more than the four-year term to which some aspirant will ultimately be elected. Of course, it permits anyone who wants to throw a hat into the ring to do so, regardless of the candidate's qualifications for the office. Most critically, "the long season" and Americans' love affair with underdogs—and distrust of the power of big government—lead to what Meg Greenfield has called "the cult of the amateur":

> We have developed something new in our politics: the professional amateur. It is by now a trend, a habit, a cult. You succeed in this line of activity by de-

Eric M. Uslaner is professor of political science at the University of Maryland. This article was prepared especially for this volume by Eric M. Uslaner. The author gratefully acknowledges the support of the General Research Board and the College of Behavioral and Social Sciences of the University of Maryland.

**130**

claring your aversion to it and unfitness for it. That will bring you the cheers of the multitude. It will also bring in time . . . the kind of troubles the Carter presidency has sustained and seemed, almost perversely, to compound.[2]

Where are the great leaders of yesteryear, the George Washingtons, the Abraham Lincolns, the Teddy and Franklin Roosevelts? The conventional wisdom, including Taylor, argues that our primary and caucus system is responsible for this "cult of the amateur." If only we could do away with the reforms of the 1970s that led to the multiplication of primaries and caucuses and if only we could restore some power to party leaders, we would get the types of candidates who would lead us through trying times. Such arguments, I maintain, miss the point. *The problem is not with the nominating system. It is with the voters!* Simply tinkering with what we have will not rid us of the most fundamental problem we face: We no longer treat politics as if it were a mere spectator sport, like basketball tournaments. Instead, we have made it a participant sport in which the great American ideal—that anyone can grow up to become President—often seems to come true. There is a fundamental contradiction between the way we nominate our Presidents and what we expect of them once in office. We vote for people who make us feel good—and who make us feel important. We choose people like ourselves but we expect Presidents to solve all of the world's problems and react strongly against them when they fail to live up to these impossible expectations.[3] We rarely wonder whether our future leaders have the experience to govern a diverse nation of 225 million people. Unfortunately, as we shall see, this is hardly a new problem, so that a quick fix, such as going back to the pre-1970s reforms, won't resolve our problems.

## WHO'S IN CHARGE HERE?

The system of primaries and caucuses, covering every state, is biased against "insiders." Leading American politicians who had established records of leadership in the Congress—Senator Edward Muskie (1972), Senator Howard Baker (1980), Senator Robert Dole (1980 and 1988), Representative Morris Udall (1976), and Vice President Hubert Humphrey (1972 and 1976)—each failed to obtain their party's nomination. Instead, Americans in both parties selected candidates who ran against the "mess in Washington." In 1972, the Democrats selected George McGovern, who stood far to the left of most of his party and was known as a Senate powerhouse. Four years later the party nominated a former one-term Governor of Georgia, Jimmy Carter, who ran from the moderate right. In 1980, the Republicans chose former California Governor Ronald Reagan. Not only did he delight in attacking Washington, but he himself had not held public office in more than a half a decade.

In 1976 Reagan tried to deprive a sitting President—Gerald Ford—of his party's nomination, something that had not been done since the Whigs dumped

Millard Fillmore in 1852. He almost succeeded. Four years later Senator Edward M. Kennedy was somewhat less successful in his challenge to President Carter. In 1984 former Vice President Walter Mondale had to come from behind to overtake Colorado Senator Gary Hart, a loner whose only close friend in Congress was a Republican lawmaker, William Cohen of Maine. In 1988 the Reverend Jesse Jackson, who never held any public office, became the newest outsider to rack up a string of primary victories. As Representative Les Aspin (D, Wisc.) said, "Primaries are about sending messages, not about electing Presidents as far as the average voter is concerned."[4] Even when candidates associated with "the Washington establishment" have prevailed and obtained their party's nomination—Humphrey in 1968, Ford in 1976, Carter in 1980, and Mondale in 1984—their parties were so divided over the exhaustive primary and caucus battles that they lost the general election.

This trend toward rewarding amateurs is disturbing because "outsider" Presidents have had difficulties in governing when they come to Washington. Carter and his staff of Georgians disdained learning the whys and wherefores of Washington bargaining. Reagan and his Californians did somewhat better at the beginning, but once his momentum faded, he took on the same kind of adversarial style of dealing with Congress that caused Carter to lose public popularity. Both Presidents ultimately were overcome by international situations they did not know how to control: Carter by the Iranian hostage crisis and Reagan by the Iran-Contra affair.

But before we conclude that the reforms of the 1970s are the culprit, consider the musings of a young political scientist who later entered politics somewhat successfully himself:

> We are too apt to think both the work of legislation and the work of administration easy enough to be done readily, with or without preparation, by any man of discretion and character. No one imagines that the drygoods or hardware trade, or even the cobbler's craft, can be successfully conducted except by those who have worked through a laborious and unremunerative apprenticeship, and who have devoted their lives to perfecting themselves. . . . But . . . administration is regarded as something which . . . a popular politician may be trusted to take to by instinct. No man of tolerable talents need despair of having been born a Presidential candidate.[5]

So wrote Woodrow Wilson in 1885. Thirty years later Lord James Bryce, the great British observer of the American scene, argued that Americans' belief in rewarding talent leads to the expectation that

> . . . the highest place would always be won by a man of brilliant gifts. But from the time that the heroes of the Revolution died out . . . no person except General [Ulysses] Grant had, down till the end of the (nineteenth) century, reached the chair whose name would have been remembered had he not been President.[6]

To be sure, American voters showed a marked preference for "amateurs" prior to the 1972 reforms in the nominating system. But there is precious little evidence that the old system of conventions dominated by party leaders was any better. It was this set of procedures that gave us such distinguished Presidents as Andrew Johnson (who was impeached and almost convicted) and Warren G. Harding (who died before anyone could do anything about impeaching him). Harding's nomination was engineered by some of his Ohio cronies who later secured positions in his administration and were ultimately convicted of malfeasance in the Teapot Dome scandal.

What Taylor (and Broder) seem to want is a shorter nomination season with a greater role for party leaders. We must remember that it was these very leaders—people like Mayor Richard J. Daley of Chicago—whose strong-armed control of party politics led to the demands for a more open nominating system. These were not the party activists whose major concern was finding someone who could run the country and make it secure both at home and abroad. Instead, these were local party hacks whose major concern was securing patronage from the federal government. They saw the outcome of the Presidential election mainly in terms of what it did to their own power bases. Mayor Daley cared less about whether the Democratic Presidential candidate knew where Afghanistan was than whether he could carry Illinois. Doing so would increase the number of politically controlled jobs available to the Chicago Democratic machine.

Where are the party leaders who do care about governing and want to secure nominees who know about the issues? They are in Washington, where they have always been. Now, perhaps more than ever before, they are the leaders of the parties' national committees. But is it realistic to expect them to guide the parties toward "better" nominees? It hardly seems likely. Party leaders now are expected to be neutral in the nominating game, lest their actions tear the parties apart. National committees do raise money, but such funds do not go to candidates in primaries and no one seems to be suggesting that the party organizations fund only favored candidates. The only other thing that national committees do of any great importance is run the party conventions. Now such conventions are little more than ratifying bodies for the decisions made in primaries and caucuses. The pre-reform days of the 1950s and 1960s were hardly eras of national parties that secured the nominations for preferred candidates. The leading study of the national committees during that period had the paradoxical title: *Politics Without Power*.[7]

## WHAT IS TO BE DONE?

Making the primary season shorter will not resolve any fundamental issues. The problem is with the nominating system itself. There is no indication that the pre-reform system was any better than what we have now.[8] In any event, the strong political machines that used to dominate our politics have since passed. Even such machine strongholds as Chicago and Baltimore are now governed by shifting coalitions of old and new style politicians. Some thoughtful observers, going back to the years before there were so many primaries and caucuses, wish for more deliberative party conventions. Such meetings would not be tied to voters' whims. Gerald Pomper has suggested that primaries should not take place until *after* party leaders selected appropriate candidates to compete for the public's affection at conventions.[9] Lloyd N. Cutler, a former advisor to President Carter, has argued for a "two-house" nominating system. One house would be a group of delegates selected in primaries and caucuses. The other house would consist of party leaders. Candidates would have to secure the support of both houses to be nominated.[10]

These proposals, like the regional primaries espoused by Taylor, would accomplish little. What group of party leaders would reject candidates with broad popular appeal, as expressed in primaries and caucuses? Which of them would deny the basic right to run in primaries to virtually any candidate, save extremists such as Lyndon LaRouche? The Democrats already give key party leaders (645 of them) "superdelegate" status. These officials do not have to compete for anyone's votes. Yet, as Jesse Jackson argued, such leaders could not in good conscience deny the nomination to a candidate who led in elected delegates at the convention. Regional primaries would do nothing to change this.

Consider a much more radical alternative: Do away with primaries and caucuses altogether. *Give the power of nominations to the parties' members of the House of Representatives and the Senate*. These men and women are, after all, the people with whom the new President will have to work and bargain. Such legislators would not necessarily choose one of their own. In 1932, for example, almost *any* conceivable Democratic nominating body would have selected New York Governor Franklin D. Roosevelt. Even if there were some predisposition to choosing members of Congress, this would hardly be a cause for concern. The well-qualified candidates—typically passed over in the President-by-primary process—largely come from the Congress. At a minimum, the members of Congress would have a very large stake in rejecting "outsiders" who not only lack experience in Washington but persist in running against it and find themselves unable to master the system once they are in power. Nominations made by members of Congress have another advantage. The current convention system is dominated by delegates who meet for a week and then disband. Few serve at more than one convention. Members of Congress, on the other hand, are more accountable since they face the electorate every two years.

Some might argue that this proposal is little more than a reversion to the bad old days of the 1820s when such a system was used to select Presidents and ultimately found wanting. And yet four of the ten Presidents who served two full and consecutive four-year terms in American history were nominated by this system in the first thirty-five years of the new nation (Washington, Jefferson, Madison, and Monroe). Moreover, in rankings of Presidents by historians, all four finished in the top half, with two achieving the rating of "Great."[11] Today the need for executive leadership is more critical than ever before. In the founding years national politics was little more than patronage. Indeed, not until the late nineteenth century did the federal government play much of a role in the lives of its citizens.[12] In contrast, by 1988 the United States government had a budget of over $1 trillion.

Some might object that such a system would discriminate against states that have one-party representation in the Congress. But this is hardly a major problem. There are, as of 1988, only four states where the Congressional delegation is one-party.[13] Most of these states are safe for that party in the Presidential race anyway. A more serious objection is that such a system might promote better coordination between the President and Congress, but at the cost of short-circuiting democratic procedures. Would not such a system be antidemocratic? Would it not ignore the "will of the people"?

It most certainly would. But we must realize that there is more than one conception of democracy. Political parties in the United States are perhaps unique among democratic nations in that they permit anyone who says that he or she identifies with them to participate in the nominating process. In some states with open primaries, Republicans and Independents can vote in Democratic primaries. No wonder American parties are in such dire straits. They cannot control their own nominating procedures. An equally "democratic" perspective argues that what democracy is all about is choosing among competing parties that offer real alternatives to the voters. Such parties *retain control* over their nominees. Voters are more than spectators, but are not full-fledged participants. They do not, in current terminology, "micro-manage" all party decisions. The most important thing that a party can do is to select candidates who can govern the country. This is, after all, what politics is all about.[14] We have come to believe that the election is all that matters. We have forgotten that we elect people to run the country. The tensions between the legislative and executive branches over domestic and foreign policy in recent years can in part be traced to the way we select our Presidents. If we have a penchant for selecting outsiders, we are doomed to get Presidents who have trouble working with the insiders. We do not take our politics seriously enough. If the stakes were only those of the NCAA Final Four, we could perhaps shrug off our mistakes and wait until the next round (election). But we all know how much more is at issue. So asking for some assistance from people (i.e., members of Congress) who must take governing seriously hardly seems like such a wild idea.

# NOTES

1  Broder, "Why Can't the Campaign Be Like the NCAA?" *Washington Post* (March 23, 1988), p. A27.
2  Greenfield, "The Cult of the Amateur," *Washington Post* (June 11, 1980), p. A19.
3  Theodore Lowi, *The Personal President* (Ithaca, NY: Cornell University Press, 1985).

4 R. W. Apple, Jr., "Blue-Collar Contrast," *New York Times* (April 2, 1988), p. 9.

5 Woodrow Wilson, *Congressional Government* (Cleveland: Meridian Books, 1967), p. 171. Originally published in 1885.

6 James Bryce, *The American Commonwealth,* vol. 1, revised ed. (New York: Macmillan, 1915), p. 77.

7 Cornelius P. Cotter and Bernard C. Hennessy, *Politics Without Power* (New York: Atherton, 1964).

8 In 1964, Alabama Governor George Wallace challenged President Lyndon B. Johnson for the Democratic nomination. This is just one of the many pieces of evidence that the nominating system had gone awry before the reforms of 1972. For a more detailed discussion of this general thesis, see Howard L. Reiter, *Selecting the President* (Philadelphia: University of Pennsylvania Press, 1985).

9 Pomper, "Primaries *After* Conventions," *New York Times* (January 2, 1988), p. 23.

10 Cutler, "To Form a Government," *Foreign Affairs* (Fall 1980), pp. 126–143.

11 See Robert DiClerico and Eric Uslaner, *Few Are Chosen: Problems in Presidential Selection* (New York: McGraw-Hill, 1984), pp. 187, 188.

12 See Stephen Skowronek, *Building a New American State* (New York: Cambridge University Press, 1982), esp. ch. 1.

13 They are: Alaska (Republican), North Dakota (Democratic), West Virginia (Democratic), and Wyoming (Republican).

14 See E. E. Schattschneider, *Party Government* (New York: Holt, Rinehart and Winston, 1942), ch. 3.

# Elections

*At least once every four years, as the nation approaches the election of the president, political commentators raise the issue of the electoral college mechanism for electing the president, claiming that something ought to be done to correct it. One such critic, political scientist Lawrence Longley, in the first of the two selections in this section, argues that the electoral college is both undemocratic and politically dangerous: undemocratic because voters and votes are treated unequally; dangerous because there exists the possibility that it could lead to a major disruption of the normal electoral process.*

*In the second selection, however, Robert Weissberg takes the view that we should retain the electoral college. While acknowledging that the present arrangement is not perfect, he maintains that the defects of the electoral college are not as serious as critics would have us believe. Moreover, he argues that several positive features associated with the electoral college more than compensate for its shortcomings, not the least of which is that it works!*

# The Case against the Electoral College

## Lawrence D. Longley

The contemporary electoral college is a curious political institution.[1] Obscure and even unknown to the average citizen,[2] it serves as a crucial mechanism for transforming popular votes cast for President into electoral votes which actually elect the President. If the electoral college were only a neutral and sure means for counting and aggregating votes, it would likely be the subject of little controversy. The electoral college does not, however, just tabulate popular votes in the form of electoral votes. Instead, it is an institution that operates with noteworthy inequality—it favors some interests and hurts others. In addition, its operations are by no means certain or smooth. The electoral college can—and has—deadlocked, forcing a resort to extraordinarily awkward contingency procedures. Other flaws and difficulties with the system can also develop under various electoral situations. In short, the electoral college system has important political consequences, multiple flaws, possible grave consequences, and inherent gross inequalities. Yet, it continues to exist as a central part of our Presidential electoral machinery. . . .

## THE FAITHLESS ELECTOR

The first characteristic arises out of the fact that the electoral college today is not the assembly of wise and learned elders as assumed by its creators, but is rather a state by state assembly of political hacks and fat cats.[3] Neither in the quality of the electors nor in law is there any assurance that the electors will vote as expected. Pledges, apparently unenforceable by law,[4] and party and personal loyalty seem to be the only guarantee of electoral voting consistent with the will of a state's electorate.

The problem of the "faithless elector" is neither theoretical nor unimportant. Republican elector Doctor Lloyd W. Bailey of North Carolina, who decided to vote for Wallace after the 1968 election rather than for his pledged candidate Nixon, and Republican elector Roger MacBride of Virginia who likewise deserted Nixon in 1972 to vote for Libertarian Party candidate John Hospers, are two examples of "faithless electors." In the . . . 1976 election, we once again had a faithless elector—and curiously enough once again a deviant Republican elector. Washington Republican Mike Padden decided, six weeks after the November election, that he preferred not to support Re-

Lawrence D. Longley is professor of political science at Lawrence University, Appleton, Wisconsin. From Lawrence D. Longley, "The Case against the Electoral College," paper delivered at the annual meeting of the American Political Science Association, Washington, D.C., 1977. Used with permission.

publican nominee Ford, and cast his electoral vote for Ronald Reagan. Similar defections from the voter expectations also occurred in 1948, 1956, . . . 1960 [and 1988]. . . . Even more important is that the likelihood of this occurring on a multiple basis would be greatly heightened in the case of an electoral vote majority resting on one or two votes—a very real possibility in 1976 as in other recent elections.

In fact, when one looks at the election returns for the . . . 1976 election, one can observe that if about 5,560 votes had switched from Carter to Ford in Ohio, Carter would have lost that state and had only 272 electoral votes, two more than the absolute minimum needed of 270. In that case, two or three individual electors seeking personal recognition or attention to a pet cause could withhold their electoral votes, and thus make the election outcome very uncertain.

A startling reminder of the possibilities inherent in such a close electoral vote election as 1976 was provided . . . by Republican Vice President nominee Robert Dole. Testifying before the Senate Judiciary Committee on January 27, 1977, in *favor* of abolishing the electoral college, Senator Dole remarked that during the election count:

> We were looking around on the theory that maybe Ohio might turn around because they had an automatic recount.
>
> We were shopping—not shopping, excuse me. Looking around for electors. Some took a look at Missouri, some were looking at Louisiana, some in Mississippi, because their laws are a little bit different. And we might have picked up one or two in Louisiana. There were allegations of fraud maybe in Mississippi, and something else in Missouri.
>
> We need to pick up three or four after Ohio. So that may happen in any event.
>
> But it just seems to me that the temptation is there for that elector in a very tight race to really negotiate quite a bunch.[5]

## THE WINNER-TAKE-ALL SYSTEM

The second problem of the contemporary electoral college system lies in the almost universal custom of granting all of a state's electoral votes to the winner of a state's popular vote plurality—not even a majority. This can lead to interesting results, such as in Arkansas in 1968 where Humphrey and Nixon together split slightly over 61 percent of the popular vote, while Wallace, with 38 percent, received 100 percent of the state's electoral votes. Even more significant, however, is the fact that the unit voting of state electors tends to magnify tremendously the relative voting power of residents of the larger states, since each of their voters may, by his vote, decide not just one vote, but how 41 or 45 electoral votes are cast—if electors are faithful.

As a result, the electoral college has a major impact on candidate strategy—as shown by the obsession of Carter and Ford strategists, in the closing weeks of the 1976 campaign, with the nine big electoral vote states with 245 of the 270 electoral votes necessary to win. Seven of these nine states were, in fact, to be exceedingly close, with both candidates receiving at least 48 percent of the state vote.

The electoral college does not treat voters alike—a thousand voters in Scranton, Pennsylvania, are far more strategically important than a similar number of voters in Wilmington, Delaware. This also places a premium on the support of key political leaders in large electoral vote states. This could be observed in the 1976 election in the desperate wooing of Mayors Rizzo of Philadelphia and Daley of Chicago by Carter because of the major roles these political leaders might have in determining the outcome in Pennsylvania and Illinois. The electoral college treats political leaders as well as voters unequally—those in large marginal states are vigorously courted.

The electoral college also encourages fraud—or at least fear and rumor of fraud. New York, with more than enough electoral votes to elect Ford, went to Carter by 290,000 popular votes. Claims of voting irregularities and calls for a recount were made on election night, but later withdrawn because of Carter's clear national popular vote win. *If* fraud was present in New York, only 290,000 votes determined the election; under direct election, at least 1,700,000 votes would have to have been irregular to determine the outcome.

The electoral college also provides opportunity for third-party candidates to exercise magnified political influence in the election of the President when they can gather votes in large, closely balanced states. In 1976, third-party candidate Eugene McCarthy, with less than 1 percent of the popular vote, came close to tilting the election through his strength in close pivotal states. In four states (Iowa, Maine, Oklahoma, and Oregon) totaling 26 electoral votes, McCarthy's vote exceeded the margin by which Ford defeated Carter. In those states, McCarthy's candidacy *may* have swung those states to Ford.[6] Even more significantly, had McCarthy been on the New York ballot, it is likely Ford would have carried that state with its 41 electoral votes, and with it the election—despite Carter's national vote majority.

## THE CONSTANT TWO ELECTORAL VOTES

A third feature of the electoral college system lies in the apportionment of electoral votes among the states. The consitutional formula is simple: one vote per state per senator and representative. A significant distortion from equality appears here because of "the constant two" electoral votes, regardless of population, which correspond to the senators. Because of this, inhabitants of the very small states are advantaged to the extent that they "control" three electoral votes (one for each senator and one for the representative), while their population might otherwise entitle them to but one or two votes. This is weighting by states, not by population—however, the importance of this feature, as shown below, is greatly outweighed by the previously mentioned winner-take-all system.

## THE CONTINGENCY ELECTION PROCEDURE

The fourth feature of the contemporary electoral college system is probably the most complex—and probably also the most dangerous in terms of the stability of the political system. This is the requirement that if no candidate receives an absolute majority of the electoral vote—in recent years, 270—the election is thrown into the House of Representatives for voting among the top three candidates. Two questions need to be asked: Is such an electoral college deadlock likely to occur in terms of contemporary politics? and, Would the consequences likely be disastrous? A simple answer to both questions is yes.

Taking some recent examples, it has been shown that, in 1960, a switch of less than 9,000 popular votes from Kennedy to Nixon in Illinois and Missouri would have prevented either man from receiving an electoral college majority.[7] Similarly, in 1968, a 53,000 vote shift in New Jersey, Missouri, and New Hampshire would have resulted in an electoral college deadlock, with Nixon receiving 269 votes—one short of a majority. Finally, in the . . . 1976 election, if slightly less than 11,950 popular votes in Delaware and Ohio had shifted from Carter to Ford, Ford would have carried these two states. The result of the 1976 election would then have been an exact tie in electoral votes—269–269. The presidency would have been decided *not* on election night, but through deals or switches at the electoral college meetings on December 13, or the later uncertainties of the House of Representatives.

What specifically might happen in the case of an apparent electoral college nonmajority or deadlock? A first possibility, of course, is that a faithless elector or two, pledged to one candidate or another, might switch at the time of the actual meetings of the electoral college so as to create a majority for one of the candidates. This might resolve the crisis, although it is sad to think of the presidency as being mandated on such a thin reed of legitimacy.

If, however, no deals or actions at the time of the December 13 meetings of the electoral college were successful in forming a majority, then the action would shift to the House of Representatives, meeting at noon on January 6, 1977, only 14 days before the constitutionally scheduled Inauguration Day for the new President.

The House of Representatives contingency procedure which would now be followed is an unfortunate relic of the compromises of the writing of the Constitution. . . . Serious problems of equity exist, certainly, in following the constitutionally prescribed one-vote-per-state procedure. Beyond this problem of voter fairness lurks an even more serious problem—what if the House itself should deadlock and be unable to agree on a President?

In a two-candidate race, this is unlikely to be a real problem; however, in a three-candidate contest, such as 1968, there might well be enormous difficulties in getting a majority of states behind one candidate, as House members agonized over choosing between partisan labels and support for the candidate (especially Wallace) who carried their district. The result, in 1968, might well have been no immediate majority forthcoming of 26 states and political uncertainty and chaos as the nation approached Inauguration Day.

## THE UNCERTAINTY OF THE WINNER WINNING

Besides the four aspects of the electoral college system so far discussed, "the faithless elector," "the winner-take-all system," "the constant two votes per state," and "the contingency election procedure," one last aspect should be described. This is that, under the present system, there is no assurance that the winner of the popular vote will win the election. This problem is a fundamental one—can an American President operate effectively in our democracy if he has received *less* votes than the loser? I suggest that the effect upon the legitimacy of a contemporary presidency would be disastrous if a president were elected by the electoral college after losing in the popular vote—yet this *can* and *has* happened two or three times, the most recent undisputable case being the election of 1888, when the 100,000 popular vote plurality of Grover Cleveland was turned into a losing 42 percent of the electoral vote.

Was there a real possibility of such a divided verdict in 1976? An analysis of the election shows that if 9,245 votes had shifted to Ford in Ohio and Hawaii, Ford would have become President with 270 electoral votes, the absolute minimum,[8] despite Carter's 51 percent of the popular vote and margin of 1.7 million votes.

One hesitates to contemplate the consequences of a nonelected President being inaugurated for four more years despite having been rejected by a majority of the American voters in his only presidential election. . . .

## NOTES

1 Some of the material contained in this paper was originally prepared and presented as "Statement of Lawrence D. Longley Before the Committee on the Judiciary, United States Senate," *Hearings on the Electoral College and Direct Election,* 95th Cong., 1st sess., February 1, 1977, pp. 88–105. Earlier research drawn upon for this paper include: Lawrence D. Longley and Alan G. Braun, *The Politics of Electoral College Reform* (New Haven: Yale University Press, 1972, 2nd ed., 1975); Lawrence D. Longley, "The Electoral College," *Current History,* vol. 67 (August 1974), pp. 64–69 ff; and John H. Yunker and Lawrence D. Longley, *The Electoral College: Its Biases Newly Measured for the 1960s and 1970s* (Beverly Hills, Calif.: Sage Professional Papers in American Politics, 1976).

2 In another publication, the following "man-on-the-street" interviews are cited: "Every boy and girl should go to college, if they can't afford Yale or Harvard, why,

Electoral is just as good, if you work''; ''The group at the bar poor-mouth Electoral somethin' awful. Wasn't they mixed up in a basketball scandal or something?'' quoted in Longley and Braun, *The Politics of Electoral College Reform,* p. 1.

3  See Lawrence C. Longley, ''Why the Electoral College Should Be Abolished,'' speech to the 1976 Electoral College, Madison, Wis., December 3, 1976. Despite being referred to as ''political hacks and fat cats,'' the Wisconsin electors there assembled proceeded to go on record supporting the abolishment of their office.

4  Only sixteen states have laws requiring electors to vote according to their pledge, and these laws themselves are of doubtful constitutionality. See James C. Kirby, Jr., ''Limitations on the Power of State Legislatures over Presidential Elections,'' *Law and Contemporary Problems,* vol. 27 (Spring 1962), pp. 495–509.

5  ''Testimony of Honorable Robert Dole, U.S. Senator from the State of Kansas,'' *Hearings on Electoral College and Direct Election,* 95th Cong., 1st sess., January 27, 1977, pp. 36–37.

6  Testimony of Neal Peirce, *National Journal,* Author, February 1977 Senate Hearings, p. 248.

7  Neal R. Peirce, *The People's President: The Electoral College in American History* and *The Direct-Vote Alternative* (New York: Simon & Schuster, 1968), pp. 317–21. The concept of hairbreadth elections is also discussed in Longley and Braun, *The Politics of Electoral College Reform,* pp. 37–41.

8  This analysis assumes, of course, the nondefection of Republican elector Mike Padden of Washington. If he had nevertheless declined to vote for Ford, then the election would have been inconclusive and would have gone to the House in January 1977.

# In Defense of the Electoral College

**Robert Weissberg**

Defending the electoral college is like defending sin. Almost every responsible person is against it; defenders are rare, yet it somehow survives. However, while sin may be beyond eradication, the electoral college is not deeply rooted in human nature. The electoral college can be abolished just as we abolished other archaic portions of the Constitution. Clearly, then, a defense of this system of selecting our President must be defended on grounds other than its inevitability. Our defense will be divided into two parts. We shall first show that its alleged defects are not as serious as some critics would have us believe. Second, we shall argue that there are in fact several virtues of this electoral arrangement, which the American Bar Association has characterized as "archaic, undemocratic, complex, ambiguous, and dangerous"!

## CRITICISMS OF THE ELECTORAL COLLEGE

Criticisms of the electoral college basically fall into two groups. The first emphasize the unpredictable and unintended outcomes that are conceivable under the present system. In a nutshell, from the perspective of these critics, here is what *could* have happened [for example] in the 1980 presidential election: Ronald Reagan overwhelmingly wins the popular vote, but by barely winning several populous states, Jimmy Carter wins the electoral college vote and appears to have been reelected. However, several electors pledged to Carter refuse to honor this pledge, thereby depriving him of a majority in the electoral college. The contest is thus thrown into the House, and after months of deals and bitter debate, John Anderson is elected president.

The second basic criticism accuses the electoral college of overvaluing some votes at the expense of other votes. Some disagreement occurs over just who benefits from these distortions, but most experts claim that voters in populous states, especially members of certain urban ethnic and racial groups, are overrepresented. Would-be presidents pay more attention to some New York and California voters at the expense of votes in places like North Dakota.

## THE NIGHTMARE OF UNINTENDED CONSEQUENCES

These are serious charges. Let us first consider what may be called the nightmare of unintended political outcomes. Two points may be made concerning this criticism. First, the odds of any one of these events occurring is remote.

Robert Weissberg is professor of political science at the University of Illinois at Urbana-Champaign. This article was written especially for *Points of View* in 1983.

Only once in U.S. history—in 1888—has the undisputed winner of the popular vote lost the electoral college vote. Electors have voted contrary to their popular instructions, but this has been extremely rare, and most important, such "unfaithful electors" have never affected who won and have almost never tried to influence the election's outcome (their actions were largely symbolic in a clearly decided contest). Nor has the last 150 years seen a presidential election decided by the House, despite some efforts by minor-party candidates to bring this about. All in all, the odds of any one event happening are low, and the odds of several such events occurring and making a difference in the same election are remote.

A second rejoinder to this nightmare of unintended, undesirable consequences is that hypothetical catastrophes are possible under *any* electoral system. Take, for example, a direct popular election with the provision for a runoff in the event no candidate receives a majority. It is conceivable that the initial election brings forth a wide range of candidates. A large number of moderate candidates each gets 5 or 7 percent from the middle of the political spectrum, and for the runoff, the public faces a contest between two unpopular extremists who together received 25 percent of the vote in the first election. *All* electoral mechanisms contain so-called time bombs waiting to go off.

## MISREPRESENTATION CAUSED BY THE ELECTORAL COLLEGE

This alleged defect of misrepresentation derives from both the electoral college as stated in the Constitution plus individual requirements that all of a state's electoral votes go to the candidate receiving the largest number of votes (though Maine since 1969 does allow a division of its electoral vote). The effect of this unit voting is that to win the presidency a candidate must win in several populous states. New York, California, Texas, Illinois, and a few other big states are the valuable prizes in the election and thus a few thousand New Yorkers have more electoral clout than a few thousand voters in South Dakota. It supposedly follows, then, that the desires of these strategically placed voters are given greater attention by those seeking the presidency.

Four points can be made in response to this inequality-of-voters argument. First, it is far from self-evident just who those overadvantaged voters are and whether these big groups can be the cornerstone of electoral victory. It has been said, for example, that since there are many blacks in New York, the black vote can determine who carries New York. However, New York, like all populous states, has a varied population, so in principle the same argument can be applied to farmers, young people, white Protestants, middle-class suburbanites—any group comprising at least 10 percent of the electorate. This "key-voting-bloc-in-a-key-state" argument is largely the creation of statistical manipulation. Of course, it makes considerable sense for a group to *claim* that its vote, given its strategic position, put a candidate in the White House.

Second, it is a great exaggeration to assert that these strategically placed, "overrepresented" voters can exert control or significantly influence the election. Let's suppose that a candidate said that to win the presidency one must win the big states; to win the big states one must do very well among blacks, Jews, and union workers because these groups are overrepresented in these big states. Not only might it be difficult to appeal to all groups simultaneously (promising jobs to blacks may anger union workers), but also, even if one's appeals are successful, these "key" votes alone are not enough. The idea of certain well-situated minorities running the electoral show via the electoral college ignores the problems of creating large, diverse voting coalitions and the relatively small size of these "key" groups. At best, the electoral college may provide a disproportionate influence to voters—not a specific group—in large states in close elections (and since World War II national elections have been close only about half the time).

Third, the relationship between overrepresentation caused by the electoral college and disproportionate government benefits has never been demonstrated. The relationship has appeared so reasonable and been mentioned so often that it is now reiterated as if it were a truism. Actual evidence, however, has never been marshaled. Obviously, presidents have endorsed some policies favorable to supposed key groups in large states, but presidents have also opposed policies favorable to these same groups. It may be true that presidents have occasionally taken the operation of the electoral college into account in their policy calculations, but such action has not been sufficiently blatant to draw widespread attention.

Finally, the electoral system embodied in the electoral college may be biased in favor of some voters, but bias is part of *every* system of election. To reject a system because it is somehow "unfair" makes sense only if some perfectly fair system did exist. In fact, no such system does exist. As we did before, let us take as an example the simple majority rule plus a runoff system commonly advocated by opponents of the electoral college. This seemingly "pure" system is "unfair" for several reasons. Unlike the systems of proportional representation used by many European democracies, it provides no representation to citizens whose candidate received less than a majority—49.9 percent of all voters may get nothing. Moreover, it can be easily demonstrated that by allowing each citizen only one yes or no vote, the system does not allow citizens to rank candidates so that the candidate most acceptable to the most people is selected. In other words, a candidate who is not the first choice of a majority, but is still highly acceptable to almost everyone, is shut out under a simple majority system. In short, the issue is not one of "fair" versus "unfair," but what type of unfairness will be present.

## DEFENDING THE ELECTORAL COLLEGE

Thus far we have argued that the major criticisms against the electoral college either rest on exaggerations and misunderstandings or are simply unproven. Is there, however, anything positive to be said for the frequently maligned system? At least four virtues of the electoral college seem reasonably clear and are probably advantageous to most people: (1) it is a proven, workable system; (2) it makes campaigns more manageable; (3) it discourages election fraud; and (4) it preserves a moderate two-party system.

The first virtue—*it is a proven, workable system*—is basically a conservative argument. Conservatives believe that when something works, though somewhat imperfectly, it should not be easily abandoned for the promise of perfection. That is, on paper almost every alternative to the electoral college is without defect. However, as anyone familiar with the success rates of proposed reforms knows well, political changes do not always work as intended. The nightmare and inequalities of the status quo are hypothetical and alleged; a change might bring real and consequential problems despite promises of perfection. Constitutional changes should be made only if the *real* costs of the electoral college are heavy.

The second virtue—*it makes campaigns more manageable*—derives from two facts. First, in terms of time, money, and energy, the present electoral system is already very demanding on candidates. Running for president is so exhausting physically that some have said, half jokingly, that only the mentally unbalanced are attracted to this activity. Second, the electoral college, plus the "winner-take-all" role in forty-nine of the fifty states, means that some votes are not as important as others. Swaying a few thousand uncommitted voters in a closely divided populous state is much more important than an appeal to the same number of voters in a small, one-party-dominated state. Obviously, then, without some division of voters into important and unimportant voters, campaigning for president would become even more hectic and overwhelming than ever. A rational candidate might even lock himself in a television studio rather than attempt the impossible task of trying to wage an effective nationwide personal campaign.

The third virtue—*it discourages election fraud*—also derives from the present system's divisions of votes into important and less important. In a state with a relatively small number of electoral votes, where the outcome is not in much doubt, little incentive exists for widespread election fraud. Such manipulation is only worthwhile in big states like New York or Illinois where presidential elections tend to be close and a large bloc of electoral votes may hinge on a few thousand votes. Under a direct popular election system, however, all votes are equally valuable and thus equally worth manipulating. Practices such as multiple voting, voting the dead, and intimidating the opposition, which were once limited to a few localities, might very well become national in scope.

The fourth and final virtue—*it preserves a moderate two-party system*—is perhaps the most important. Under the existing system, winning the presidency means winning numerous electoral votes. Since to win electoral votes you must win pluralities in many states, it takes a formidable political organization to win these big prizes. A group that won, say, 5 or 10 percent of the vote in a few states would be doomed. Even an organization that wins a few million votes usually comes up with very little where the prizes are big blocs of electoral votes. In contemporary politics, the only organizations capable of such a massive electoral undertaking are large, diverse, compromise-oriented political parties such as the Democratic and Republican parties.

To appreciate this contribution of the existing electoral college system, imagine presidential campaigns *without* the two major parties. Instead of two major candidates and a dozen or two inconsequential candidates, there would be numerous hopefuls with some reasonable chance of success. These candidates would likely draw most of their support from relatively small segments of the population. There might be an anti-abortion candidate, a strong civil rights candidate, an anti-school-busing candidate, and a few others closely associated with one or two specific issues. The incentive to create broad-based coalitions to capture a majority in twenty or thirty states would be considerably reduced and thus the two major parties would virtually disappear.

This type of campaign politics would suffer from several problems. The narrow basis of candidate appeal would likely generate much sharper conflict and deepen group antagonism (for example, blacks might see for the first time in modern times an explicitly anti-civil rights candidate who could win). Perhaps most important, postelection governance would become difficult. Not only would a president have a much smaller base of popular support, but he or she would likely have to deal with a Congress composed of people with no party attachment whose primary purpose was to advance a particular group or regional interest. Of course, the present system of Democratic and Republican party politics does not eliminate the advancement of narrow interests and interbranch conflict. However, the situation would probably be even worse if numerous single-issue groups replaced the present two major political parties. In short, the electoral college, plus the winner-take-all-system, encourages the current two-party system, and this system moderates conflict and promotes effective postelection governance.

We began by noting that defending the electoral college is like defending sin. We have argued that, as some have said of sin, it is not nearly as bad as is claimed, and it may even be beneficial. We have not argued that the present system is beyond reproach. The system has been modified numerous times since its inception, and future changes are certainly possible. It is a serious mistake, however, to believe that abolishing the electoral college will be as beneficial as finally ridding ourselves of sin.

# 8

# Political Parties

*Political analysts have for years sought to make sense out of national presidential and congressional elections by classifying them on the basis of two major considerations: First, as a result of the election, is the party in power returned to office? Second, during the course of one or several elections, do the people retain or change their party identification? Thus, depending on the outcome of the election, an election is called "maintaining" if the party is continued in power and the people do not change their basic loyalties; it is called "deviating" if the party in power loses the election but there continues to be no basic change in party identification; and it is called "realigning" if the party in power is defeated and, concurrently, a majority of the electorate "switch" allegiance permanently to the other party.*

*With the election of President Ronald Reagan in 1980, his landslide reelection victory in 1984, the subsequent election of Republican George Bush in 1988, and the weakening of party loyalties, political analysts have speculated that a new realignment has occurred or is occurring—that is, the old Democratic dominance is passing and a majority of the people are shifting loyalties (and votes) to the Republican Party.*

*The following two articles address the question of whether or not a realignment has occurred. In the first article, political scientist Everett Carll Ladd argues that, at least at the presidential level, realignment is well underway. Ladd sees in the current "realignment drama" a shift in party identification, new patterns of group voting, and a distinct "generational conversion" to the Republican Party—all of which has resulted in the Republicans winning five out of the last six presidential elections. The final unfolding of the realignment drama, according to Ladd, will depend on how well the American people view the performance of the Republican Party these past several years.*

*Subsequent to Ladd's analysis, the 1986 congressional elections were held. In these elections, the Democrats regained control of the Senate and increased their strength in the House of Representatives by five seats. And, of course, the Democrats continued their dominance of Congress in the 1988 elections. The result of these elections, together with other evidence showing continuing support for the Democratic Party, leads our second author, political scientist Larry Sabato, to conclude that at least from the perspective of the Democrats, the argument could be made that realignment has not occurred and will not occur. Sabato presents several reasons for his conclusions. First, he argues that the Republicans have been unable to make enduring electoral gains in races below the presidential level. Second, while acknowledging that Republicans have eroded the Democratic majority, they have nonetheless not been able to erase the loyalties of Democratic voters and the popularity of issues for which the Democratic Party stands. Third, the Democrats have in recent times moved to change themselves organizationally and philosophically to meet the challenge of the Republicans. Finally, Sabato stresses the fact that in the future, the Republicans themselves are likely to undergo strain as a result of tensions among competing factions within the party, hastening the day when the Democrats, with the proper candidate, will once again win the presidency.*

# As the Realignment Turns:
## A Drama in Many Acts
### Everett Carll Ladd

## REALIGNMENT AND DEALIGNMENT

For two decades now, political scientists and other commentators have stumbled and sloshed around the conceptual swamp we have created for ourselves called *realignment*. The main reason we have had such difficulty dealing with contemporary partisan realignment is that we have expected it to be like the one acted out in the 1930s—the Great New Deal realignment, presided over by Franklin D. Roosevelt—that brought the Democrats to power as the new majority party. The New Deal realignment came like a flash of lightning. While the Republicans' majority status had been eroded by earlier developments, such as the changing ethnic makeup of the United States following the big immigration of 1900–1924, the GOP was still clearly ascendant when the Depression began. By 1936, however, the GOP had been humbled and tossed aside, a thoroughly beaten and confused minority. The New Deal realignment was as complete and decisive as it was rapid. By 1936 the Democrats were unquestionably the majority party at all levels: They were the presidential majority, they dominated Congress, they held sway in the state houses, and they had a substantial lead over the Republicans in party identification. The New Deal realignment was accompanied by an unambiguous strengthening of Democratic party loyalties across the electorate.

Clearly, nothing like the above has occurred in American electoral politics since the 1930s. If a set of changes in the partisan balance must closely resemble those of the New Deal, we have not had a realignment in recent years. There has been no galvanizing event comparable to the Depression. The Republicans have been dominating presidential elections, but the Democrats have maintained ample majorities in the U.S. House of Representatives, governorships, and state legislatures. Growing numbers of Americans vote independently—splitting their tickets and deciding their votes on the basis of the candidates and issues in individual elections, rather than going down the line for "my party."

There seems no good reason, however, why "realignment" must be reserved for partisan developments like those of the 1930s. Something substantial has happened, and realignment is a good word for it. First, major shifts in

Everett Carll Ladd is professor of political science and director of the Roper Center for Public Opinion Research, University of Connecticut. This article is from Everett Carll Ladd, "As the Realignment Turns: A Drama in Many Acts," *Public Opinion,* December–January 1985, pp. 4–7. Reprinted with permission of American Enterprise Institute for Public Policy Research.

voter alignments have been evident in recent years. Second, there is a new majority party in presidential voting, the Republicans. Third, the mix of issues differs greatly from that of the New Deal period. Fourth, dealignment, the weakening of voters' ties to the parties, seems better understood as a distinguishing feature of the present realignment than as an alternative to realignment. The proper question seems not whether a realignment has occurred, but rather where it is being pushed by the experiences of the Reagan era.

## NEW PATTERNS IN GROUP VOTING

If one wants to locate the time and place of the curtain raiser in our modern realignment drama, it would almost certainly have to be the year 1948 in the American South. White southerners had been the strongest link in the New Deal coalition, and indeed were the most loyal supporters of the Democratic party since the Civil War. In 1948, however, they began their long march away from the Democrats. The States' Rights party, led by Strom Thurmond of South Carolina, seized on white racial protest against Truman policies, split off from the national Democratic party, and carried four southern states. Democrat Harry Truman won the support of just 53 percent of white southerners. In subsequent elections over the 1950s and 1960s, regional opposition to the national Democrats' civil rights policies combined with the increasing attraction that a rapidly industrializing and newly prosperous South felt for the Republicans to produce a massive presidential swing to the GOP. Jimmy Carter, the first true southerner to be nominated for president by a major party since the Civil War, and clearly the beneficiary of substantial regional loyalties, was nonetheless unable in 1976 to win a majority of the vote among southern whites, and in 1980 he got only about one-third of this vote. Whereas 85 percent of white southerners voted for FDR in 1936, just over a quarter of them backed Walter Mondale in 1984. . . .[1]

Over the last three decades a number of other groups that had been mainstays of the New Deal coalition have swung gradually to the Republicans. Labor leaders went all out for Mondale, but the blue-collar vote went for Reagan and the union vote (that is, voters from households where at least one adult was a union member) gave Mondale only a modest margin. Catholics have swung from their historic attachment to the Democratic party, and a majority of them voted for Reagan this year. These and other important shifts were influenced by Ronald Reagan's personal popularity, but they antedated the Reagan presidency by many years and reflected deep-rooted social changes.

The group alignments evident in the 1984 presidential voting represent an extraordinary shift from those of the New Deal era. Even in cases where a group comes down on the same partisan side now that it did then, its position in the larger electoral scheme is often different. Black Americans, for example, gave a majority of their votes to the Democrats during the New Deal, and they do so now, but the Democratic share has grown much bigger since 1964, and blacks are now a much larger component of the Democrats' electorate than ever before.

## A REPUBLICAN PRESIDENTIAL MAJORITY

Another element we have in mind when we speak of partisan realignment is the displacement of the previous majority party and the emergence of a new majority. At the presidential level such a shift has occurred. The GOP has been victorious in four of the last five presidential elections, winning 55 percent of the total two-party vote over this span. Three of the Republican victories have been landslides—in 1972, 1980, and 1984. The one election the Democrats won, in 1976, is in a sense the most graphic confirmation of the GOP's ascendancy: Jimmy Carter and the Democrats managed the narrowest win in 1976, even though the Republican party had been decimated by the Watergate scandals.

Americans don't elect their presidents by national popular vote majorities, of course, but by electoral votes, all of which go to the popular vote victor in each state. In 1984, Reagan showed the extraordinary breadth of his support by winning 49 of the 50 states. Moreover, for the last five contests the electoral vote maps have looked even more decisively Republican than the popular vote distributions. There are 23 "N$^2$FR$^2$" states: carried by Nixon in 1968 and 1972, Ford in 1976, and Reagan in 1980 and 1984. These states have 202 electoral votes, about three-fourths of the 270 electoral votes needed for a presidential victory. By contrast, there are no "HMC$^2$M" states; only the District of Columbia has given its support to all of the recent Democratic nominees—Humphrey in 1968, McGovern in 1972, Carter in 1976 and 1980, and Mondale in 1984.

### Shifts in Party Identification

Throughout the 1984 campaign, politicians and pollsters perused survey data for indications of whether party identification was beginning to shift toward the Republicans, reflecting the GOP's persisting margin in presidential balloting. Party loyalties usually change only after actual voting behavior shifts; at any point they reflect yesterday's, not today's, political agenda. In view of this lag, there is special interest in the partisan attachments of young voters. The young are not wholly cut loose from yesterday, because family socialization continues to shape them; but their partisan ties reflect more of today's commitments than do those of older voters.

### Generational Conversion?

Does the current political generation differ from its predecessors? Perhaps. In the late 1970s, polls for the first time began showing the Republicans doing their best at the extremes of the age continuum, among those 18–24 and among the

**TABLE 1  Most and Least Democratic Age Groups**

|  | Democrat | Republican | Independent | % Democratic minus % Republican |
|---|---|---|---|---|
| All ages | 39% | 25% | 36% | +14 |
| Ages 62–65 | 48 | 22 | 30 | +26 |
| Ages 30–33 | 43 | 18 | 39 | +25 |
| Ages 22–25 | 31 | 27 | 42 | + 4 |
| Age 78 and older | 31 | 43 | 26 | −12 |

Source: General Social Surveys, National Opinion Research Center; composite of surveys conducted in 1983 and 1984.

very oldest voters, who came of age before the Great Depression. This pattern has become firmer. The National Opinion Research Center (NORC) surveys taken in 1983 and 1984 suggest, for example, that current generational experience is more supportive of the GOP than any other reaching back to the 1930s (Table 1). The Democrats do best among the generations that reached maturity in the height of the Roosevelt years, and in the late 1960s and early 1970s. The Republicans' best groups are those that came of age politically in the Roaring Twenties and since 1975. The contrast shown by the NORC data between representatives of the Sixties generation and those of the late Seventies is especially striking. The Democrats' edge over the Republicans is 25 points among those 30–33 years of age, compared to just 4 points among those in their early to mid-twenties.

Some surveys taken around the time of the 1984 presidential elections indicate that, for the first time since the Depression, the Republicans may have even more support than the Democrats among the young. For example, a poll taken by CBS News and the *New York Times* between September 30 and October 4, 1984, found 53 percent of persons 18–29 years of age either clearly identifying with the GOP or leaning to it, compared to just 37 percent for the Democrats. Similarly, the *Times*/CBS News poll of November 8–14, 1984, showed the GOP with its biggest advantage in the 18–29-year cohort, where it led the Democrats 50 percent to 42 percent when "leaners" were included.

## A Stronger Republican Showing

Looking at all age groups in the population and the findings of a number of different surveys, one sees clear Republican gains. The results of a number of questions on party identification, using various wordings and different samples are shown on page 156. Clearly, the Republicans got a lift out of the decision made by voters to cast their ballots for the incumbent Republican president. How lasting these GOP gains in party identification prove to be will depend on future performance. What we can conclude is that the Republicans have now closed the gap on the Democrats more than at any time in the last five decades. Four Gallup polls taken in September and October, 1984, showed the Republican percentage in party identification only four points below the Democratic percentage—the smallest gap shown by a sustained series of Gallup polls since 1940.

## The Political Transformation of the White South

The shift in party preference of certain groups is especially striking. Long after they began voting Republican presidentially, southern whites still gave the Democrats a large margin over the Republicans in party identification. But according to the exit poll taken by the *Los Angeles Times* on election day 1984, 37 percent of the southern white electorate described themselves as Republicans, compared to just 23 percent Democrats. This is a historic first. Never before the 1984 campaign had a plurality of white southerners identified with the party that had once sent the Grand Army of the Republic marching through Georgia. Perhaps more striking is [pollster] Peter Hart's finding. . . . In Alabama, Hart found a net swing of 41 percentage points in party identification from December 1983 to November 1984, to the Republicans' favor.

These extraordinary shifts in professed partisan ties obviously point to a big change in party fortunes. But what do they say about the present-day meaning of party identification? We have long assumed that party identification reflected deep loyalties—not easily changed. A group might vote for another party in a given presidential election, even in a number of elections, and still not abandon its ancestral party ties. White southerners managed to keep their Democratic identities in 1948, 1968, 1972, and 1980—when political currents were pushing them away from the Democrats and toward the Republicans at the presidential level. Why did they swing so massively to the GOP in professed party ties in 1984? Was there a straw that broke the proverbial camel's vertebrae? The shift was especially striking in the white South, but all across the electorate there was unprecedented movement in partisan identification during Campaign '84. Is party identification ceasing—in this age of dealignment—to suggest any psychological imperative? Is it becoming something more casual than it has ever before been—little more than a reflection of current political preferences?

## DEALIGNMENT

The present realignment is accompanied, indeed distinguished, by the continued weakening of voter loyalties to political parties in general. I erred four years ago when I argued that the question was whether a realignment *or* a dealignment was occurring. The larger change in voter alignments we are experiencing includes a greater reluctance on the part of many voters to express any underlying party preference, and an increased willingness to leave the candidate of their professed party with little hesitancy. In general party identification is a more casual matter than it ever before has been. Whatever their future assessment of Reagan administration and Republican performance, or of the Democrats, voters are not going to re-create the extent and degree of stability in party ties that they displayed in the New Deal era. It takes less to move this electorate from one party to the other, from one election to the next.

One manifestation of the diminished strength of party ties is a high frequency of split-ticket voting. In this regard, 1984 fitted neatly into the experience of modern U.S. elections. Gallup regularly asks: "For the various political offices, did you vote for all the candidates of one party, that is, a straight ticket, or did you vote for the candidates of different parties?" For the last five presidential elections the proportions saying they voted a *straight ticket* have been a fairly *consistent minority:* 37 percent in 1968, 44 percent in

# OPINION ROUNDUP

# PARTY IDENTIFICATION

QUESTION: Generally speaking, do you usually consider yourself a Republican, a Democrat, an Independent, or what? (CBS News/*New York Times*) Do you usually think of yourself as a Republican, Democrat, or Independent? (CBS News/*New York Times* 1980) Do you usually think of yourself as a Democrat, Independent, or Republican? (CBS News/*New York Times* 1984) Regardless of how you may have voted in the past, what do you usually consider yourself—a Democrat, a Republican, some other party, or what? (Roper) In politics, as of today, do you consider yourself a Republican, Democrat, or Independent? (Gallup) Regardless of how you may vote what do you usually consider yourself—a Republican, a Democrat, an Independent or what? (ABC News/Harris and Harris) Regardless of how you voted, in politics today do you consider yourself a Democrat, Republican, Independent, or something else? (ABC News 1980 Exit poll) Generally speaking, do you think of yourself as a Republican, Democrat, or Independent? (ABC News/*Washington Post*) Do you consider yourself a very strong Democrat, a fairly strong Democrat, an Independent, a fairly strong Republican, a very strong Republican, or something else? (*Los Angeles Times* 1984 Exit poll)

| | | 1980 | | | | 1984 | | |
|---|---|---|---|---|---|---|---|---|
| | | Dem. | Rep. | Ind. | | Dem. | Rep. | Ind. |
| CBS News/*New York Times* | 9/10–14 | 46% | 23% | 31% | 10/14–17 | 41% | 26% | 33% |
| | 11/7–12 | 46 | 24 | 30 | 11/8–14 | 32 | 32 | 36 |
| CBS News/*New York Times* Exit poll | 11/4 | 45 | 30 | 26 | 11/6 | 38 | 35 | 26 |
| Roper | 9/27–10/4 | 48 | 25 | 26 | 9/15–22 | 44 | 31 | 25 |
| Gallup | 10/10–13 | 45 | 26 | 29 | 10/26–29 | 39 | 35 | 26 |
| | 11/7–10 | 42 | 26 | 32 | 11/30–12/3 | 40 | 31 | 29 |
| ABC News/Harris | 8/14–18 | 46 | 29 | 25 | 10/26–11/5 | 44 | 34 | 21 |
| ABC News Exit poll | 11/4 | 42 | 29 | 29 | 11/6 | 39 | 33 | 29 |
| ABC News/*Washington Post* | | | | | 9/7–11 | 39 | 26 | 34 |
| *Los Angeles Times* Exit poll | | | | | 11/6 | 34 | 30 | 36 |

Table from "Opinion Roundup," *Public Opinion*, December/January, 1985, p. 39. Reprinted with permission of American Enterprise Institute for Public Policy Research.

1972, 41 percent in 1976, 37 percent in 1980, and 43 percent in 1984. The specific consequences of this proclivity for ticket-splitting can be quite dramatic—as in Nebraska where Democratic Senator J. J. Exon edged out Republican challenger Nancy Hoch, even though Reagan overwhelmed Mondale 71 percent to 29 percent in that state's presidential balloting.

## THE TWO-TIER ELECTORAL SYSTEM

The present realignment also manifests a kind of split personality: As we have noted, the presidency has been dominated by the Republicans in recent elections, but Congress, state legislatures, and other offices have hardly become GOP bastions.

Some observers explain the two-tier electoral system as Americans' liking for separation of powers and checks and balances. If the direction the Republicans propose for national policy is to be encouraged by the election of Republican presidents, isn't some check on it useful in Congress and the state houses? Besides, a great many people are highly ambivalent about the role of government and other central policy issues. What better way to express their mixed feelings than by ordaining divided party control?

Other observers stress the importance of structural factors that influence voting at the various levels. For example, members of Congress now have large staffs and other resources of incumbency that are useful in advancing their reelection. Gaining high levels of name recognition and emphasizing their nonpartisan service to constituents, they can often divorce their own electoral fortunes from those of their parties' presidential nominees. In addition, incumbents frequently outspend their challengers by substantial margins. . . .

The Democrats entered the modern period with a big edge in congressional seats, and the advantages of incumbency have been theirs more than the Republicans'.

Both of these explanations of the two-tier voting system seem to have some validity. A great many people are ambivalent on many big policy issues and express that ambivalence by dividing governmental control—easily done given the American separation of powers. And the resources of incumbency are such that many candidates can insulate themselves from broader swings in public preferences. The precise mix of these two sets of factors isn't known.

We do know that the present realignment with a split personality is proving to be remarkably enduring and strong. Some of the most dramatic testimony to that strength comes from a comparison of congressional voting in 1982 and 1984. In 1982, of course, the country was in a deep recession—a big negative for the Republicans. In 1984, in contrast, the economy was doing very well and a popular incumbent was running for reelection. Nineteen eighty-four was as good a year to be a Republican as 1982 was a bad year. This makes all the more striking the fact that in the 340 House races where Republican and Democratic candidates confronted each other in both elections, the average net swing toward the GOP, from 1982 to 1984, was just 3.7 percentage points. Presidential and congressional voting are two distinct systems.

We encounter little disagreement in general on the changes that have occurred, on the shape of partisan competition in the contemporary electoral era. But what will the next act be like? It was hard in 1980 to envision the context for the 1984 election, and it is no easier now looking to 1988. Since the Republicans control the White House, the greatest likelihood of some significant change in the story line of our long-playing realignment drama is likely to be found in the public's perceptions of GOP performance in serving the country's social and economic well-being. Will the approach of the Reagan administration ultimately be seen as *successful,* not merely *promising?* Or will it crash against deepening economic problems and social conflict? In the last analysis American voters are performance oriented, as they have always been. If there is to be a deeper, broader Republican majority, it will result from the public's finding the GOP a successful governing party.

## NOTES

1 For further discussion of the long-term shift in group voting, see Everett Ladd (with Charles Hadley), *Transformations of the American Party System* (New York: Norton; 2nd revised edition, 1978).

# A Republican Realignment?
## The Democrats' Rejoinder

**Larry Sabato**

By now the reader may be convinced that not only has a major realignment transpired but that the Democratic party's electoral position is resting somewhere between hopeless and terminal. Nothing could be further from the truth, as a glance at congressional election results during the Reagan era would suggest. Even though historically, realignment usually has been accompanied by large House gains for the ascendant party, the Republicans control only eighteen more House seats in the twilight of Reagan's presidential tenure than they did before his initial election. And despite a sustained effort the GOP has not succeeded in building a broad grassroots party at the local level in many areas, and this has enabled the Democrats to maintain control of a large majority of state legislatures and local offices.[1] The ongoing revitalization of Democratic fundraising and organizational capacity will probably help to reduce somewhat the GOP's technological advantage and aid Democrats in holding their own in congressional, state, and local contests in the post-Reagan era.

The electoral auguries for that era are not as forbidding for the Democrats as many analysts have claimed. First of all, in an age of loosened party ties and candidate-centered campaigns, much depends on the identities of the presidential nominees in 1988 and beyond. Not only does a president have the opportunity to reshape his or her party's image but victory alone frequently boosts the public's evaluation of and identification with the presidential party.[2] Obviously Democrats will have to win the presidency to reap these rewards, but their chances of doing that are not at all bad. Even before the Iran-contra scandal, only 30 percent of the electorate agreed with the statement, "Given President Reagan's success in governing the country, we should stick with a Republican as our next president.[3] After the scandal broke Democrats quickly gained a substantial advantage as the party people preferred to win the White House in 1988,[4] and other important perceptions were also reversed. In September 1986, for example, the GOP was chosen as the party better equipped to cope with the main problems facing the country by a 47 percent to 36 percent margin, but by January the Democrats held the advantage by a nearly identical plurality of 46 percent to 38 percent.[5] Whether the Democrats prevail in 1988 or not, these figures suggest how rapidly political events can reverse field. They also cast doubt on the belief that any lasting realignment has taken place, since

Larry Sabato is professor of political science at the University of Virginia. From Larry Sabato, *The Party's Just Begun: Political Parties for America's Future,* pp. 164–170. Copyright © 1988 by Larry J. Sabato. Reprinted by permission of HarperCollins Publishers.

one would expect deeply held partisan loyalties to weather storms of the Iran-contra variety better than early indications suggest they have. Absent a major realignment and given the natural cycle of American politics, it is almost inevitable that the Democrats will capture the presidency again in the next several elections, and with a new leader will come a fresh start and partial absolution for the party's past sins (in anticipation, perhaps, of new transgressions).

Moreover, as Table 1 shows, there has been no massive shift in party identification during Reagan's presidency. Until the Iran-contra scandal Republicans had gained marginally and Democrats had drifted downward slightly, but the overall Democratic advantage, while reduced, was never really eliminated. And . . . few radical alterations have occurred in the coalition of population groups that comprise each party's base.[6] The New Deal coalition has eroded but is still clearly visible, and while it may well be fading, it has staged one of the longest goodbyes in American history.[7] Obviously, the arrival of a new electoral majority does not require the complete destruction of its predecessor,[8] and the ascending coalition may be simply a relatively minor rearrangement of the old one. Still, one is struck by the enduring quality and stability of the political alliance that continues to fuel most Democratic victories in subpresidential contests.

The Democratic party's coalition has proven lasting partially because of the popular staying power of many of the party's issues and ideas.[9] Public support for trimming government expenditure does not imply backing for a dismantling of the welfare state. On the contrary, Democratic innovations such as Social Security, Medicare, and even basic support programs for the poor are considered politically sacrosanct—untouchable by the Republicans when they hold office. Protection of the environment, equal rights for women and minorities, opposition to policies unfairly benefiting big business and the wealthy— all positions clearly associated in the public mind with the Democrats—are also as popular or more popular today than in the pre-Reagan period. So long as issues and principles this fundamental to American politics are strongly identi-

**TABLE 1 Party Identification During the Reagan Presidency[a]**

| | Date of Survey | | | | | |
| Partisan Affiliation | Nov. 1981 | Nov. 1982 | Nov. 1984 | June 1986 | Nov. 1986 | July 1987 |
|---|---|---|---|---|---|---|
| Democrat | 51% | 46% | 46% | 45% | 45% | 47% |
| Republican | 35 | 34 | 41 | 40 | 36 | 38 |
| Independent[b] | 13 | 16 | 11 | 13 | 17 | 14 |
| Net Democratic advantage | +16 | +12 | +5 | +5 | +9 | +9 |

[a] Column percentages do not add up to 100% because "don't know," "refuse to answer," and "other party" answers are not included. All surveys were random-sample telephone polls taken by William R. Hamilton and Staff. Sample sizes were as follows: Nov. 1981 (N = 1261), Nov. 1982 (N = 1401), Nov. 1984 (N = 1351), June 1986 (N = 1400), Nov. 1986 (N = 1399), July 1987 (N = 1200).

[b] Pure Independents only. Party leaners are included in Democrat and Republican totals.

fied with the Democratic party, it is difficult to believe the party would be forced into a permanently secondary electoral role. Reagan's broad personal appeal often has obscured the fact that a large portion of his supporters are not in sympathy with many of his policies. Fully 41 percent of those who gave Reagan a favorable personal popularity rating in one of our polls admitted that they like only "about half" to "almost none" of the Reagan administration's policies.[10] Clearly, many of these individuals may prove susceptible to the charms of a *likeable* Democratic candidate with whom they *do* agree.

The Democratic party has not been condemned to the past, then, because voters consider many of its main concerns to be central to contemporary life. As Table 2 shows, voters during the Reagan presidency have consistently disagreed, usually by 2 to 1, with the statement, "The Democratic party is the party of the past—holding onto tired, outdated ideals that no longer work." Furthermore, by 1986, 34 percent strongly disagreed with that proposition and only 9 percent strongly agreed. And while Americans in the heyday of Reagan's Republican renaissance were closely divided about whether or not "the Republican party is the party of the future [with] the fresh ideas to deal with America's problems," support for that belief has dropped to near the pre-1982 level. Once again, by 1986, those who strongly disagreed outnumbered those who strongly agree (by 21 percent to 12 percent). Incidentally, Reagan's own successes may be at least as responsible as his most prominent failure (the Iran-contra fiasco) for the resurgence in Democratic fortunes. By his second term, the most antigovernment president since Calvin Coolidge had restored the public's faith in the federal government by reducing some of its perceived excesses; he had bolstered support for domestic spending programs by allegedly cutting the waste out of them; and he had built up the nation's defenses

**TABLE 2 Party Perceptions in the Reagan Years in Percentages**

| | Date of Survey[a] | | | | |
| --- | --- | --- | --- | --- | --- |
| | Nov. 1981 | Nov. 1982 | Nov. 1984 | Nov. 1986 | July 1987 |
| *Statement:* "The Democratic party is the party of the past—holding onto tired, outdated ideas that no longer work." | | | | | |
| Agree | 30 | 33 | 46 | 30 | 34 |
| Disagree | 60 | 60 | 49 | 68 | 62 |
| Don't know | 10 | 7 | 5 | 4 | 4 |
| *Statement:* "The Republican party is the party of the future—it has the fresh ideas to deal with America's problems." | | | | | |
| Agree | 39 | 46 | 48 | 44 | 40 |
| Disagree | 49 | 46 | 47 | 50 | 56 |
| Don't know | 12 | 8 | 5 | 6 | 4 |

[a] All surveys were random-sample telephone polls taken by William R. Hamilton and Staff. Sample sizes were as follows: November 1981 (N = 1261), Nov. 1982 (N = 1401), Nov. 1984 (N = 1351), Nov. 1986 (N = 1399), July 1987 (N = 1200).

so fully that backing for further defense spending had plummeted.[11] In dissipating anger directed at Washington and scaling back government about as far as most people wanted to go, Reagan also calmed the passions of those who blamed the Democratic party for the problems, and indirectly and unintentionally prepared the way for the Democrats' eventual comeback.

It is also inevitable that the Democrats will sooner or later draw considerable strength from the inherent tensions and contradictions in the current GOP coalition. The flammable mix of the predominantly blue-collar, socially traditionalist fundamentalist Christians, the libertarian young (especially affluent yuppies), and the Main Street business establishment cannot forever coexist without political combustion. Recent economic and foreign policy issues as well as Reagan's personal appeal have united these disparate groups. But as cultural issues (lifestyle choice, creationism, etc.) become more prominent and as the fundamentalists become more insistent that "their issues" be moved to the top of the agenda, the GOP could easily be torn by dissension and deserted by a significant share of its base.[12] A possible harbinger of future elections is apparent in a survey conducted for this study. Voters under the age of 35 believed that "we need to adapt our thinking to the modern changes that are occurring" rather than "America needs more conservative, traditional values of earlier days" by the decisive margin of 52 percent to 34 percent. The "born-again" population was the mirror image, choosing tradition over change by 52 percent to 35 percent. (Other predominantly Republican groups were closely split on the question.[13]) It is certainly true that for many decades the Democrats held together groups at least as diverse as the modern GOP's, but conditions were quite different. Broad-based education, instant mass communications, the growth of issue-oriented politics, and the weakening of party identification all make it much more difficult to submerge disputes and paper over disagreements. Put another way, the costs today of changing parties and the stimulus necessary to do so probably both are reduced compared to the New Deal's period of dominance. This may be especially true for the volatile young, whose partisan identities are not firmly set and who can sometimes swing dramatically in their voting choices from election to election.[14]

Finally, the Democrats themselves deserve some credit for staving off what might have turned into a realignment of sorts had they proved oblivious to their own faults and to the lessons of recent party defeats. In essence, the Democrats changed organizationally and adapted philosophically to survive. They are rapidly and with a measure of success becoming technologically and financially modernized, enabling them to compete on more equal terms. Additionally, the Democrats undeniably have moderated in tone and substance. . . . [T]he "special-interest" caucuses (representing various minority groups) no longer have official recognition in party councils. And just as major parties incorporate the popular planks of third party platforms, so too does each major party absorb most of the ideas made broadly acceptable by the other major party. The Republicans might never have won the presidency again if they had not made their peace (however uneasy) with the New Deal, and pledged preservation of the major social welfare gains achieved in that era. Similarly, the Democrats have come to understand that the presidency may continue to elude their grasp without the party's acquiescence to the public's desire for lower taxes and less government "giveaway" waste. After the Democrats recaptured the Senate in 1986, the proposals made by new committee chairs were remarkably cautious and frugal compared to those of their previous tenure.[15] Instead of comprehensive national health insurance, a system of private insurance with fairly minimal governmental requirements was suggested. Instead of a flood of new educational aid, a mere trickle to targeted needy districts was slated for action. Instead of massive government "makework" jobs programs, states might be rewarded with some additional federal aid for getting citizens off the welfare rolls and into productive employment. The crown prince of American liberalism, Senator Edward Kennedy (D-Massachusetts), gave the party's shift to the right an unmistakable imprimatur when he declared, "America does not have to spend more to do more."[16] The Democrats' programmatic sights have been lowered, but their party's chances for victory have been raised as a consequence.

## NOTES

1 Between 1978 and 1986, for instance, the Democrats controlled between 63 and 71 of the 99 legislative chambers (counting each House and Senate separately). Republicans were in charge of only 26 to 35 chambers. (In each year a few chambers were tied or—for Nebraska's unicameral legislature alone—nonpartisan.)

2 The same phenomenon is often observed on the state level. For instance, after Virginia's Democrats swept all statewide posts in November 1985, Democratic party identification increased by six percentage points, and GOP identification fell by five compared to the preelection period. The surveys were taken by Mason-Dixon Opinion Research and reported in Kent Jenkins, "Poll Shows Shift to Democratic Party in Virginia," *Virginian-Pilot*, December 6, 1985, A1, A3.

3 Fifty-two percent disagreed, and 18 percent said "not sure," in a Yankelovich Clancy Shulman random-sample telephone survey for *Time* magazine, September 8–10, 1986. N = 1,014 adults.

4 In a random-sample telephone survey of 781 registered voters conducted December 7–8, 1986 by the *New York Times* and CBS News, 39 percent said they "will probably vote" for the Democratic presidential candidate in 1988, 27 percent for the Republican, and 34 percent were unsure. In October 1986 the parties had been essentially tied on this question, with 32 percent preferring the Democrat and 33 percent the Republican.

5 Both random-sample telephone polls were conducted by the *Washington Post* and ABC News. See the *Washington Post*, January 27, 1987, A4.

6 See Figure 4.2 in Chapter Four [in original text—eds.].

7 See Harold Stanley, William Bianco, and Richard Niemi, "Partisanship and Group Support Over Time: A Multivariate Analysis," *American Political Science Review* 80 (September 1986): 970–976; and Seymour Martin Lipset, "Beyond 1984: The Anomalies of American Politics," *PS* 19 (Spring 1986): 222–236.

8 See James L. Sundquist, "Whither the American Party System?—Revisited," *Political Science Quarterly* 99 (Winter 1983–1984): 573–593.

9 See Lipset, "Beyond 1984"; Thomas Ferguson and Joel Rogers, *Right Turn: The Decline of the Democrats and the Future of American Politics* (New York: Hill and Wang, 1986); and William Schneider, "Win Now, Pay Later," *The New Republic* 192 (August 21, 1986): 19–20.

10 Poll I (see Appendix) [in original text—eds.]. Of the 72 percent who said they had a "very favorable" or "somewhat favorable" opinion of Reagan, 7 percent liked "all the policies of his administration," 51 percent supported "most" of them, 36 percent liked "about half," and 5 percent supported "almost none" (1 percent said "not sure").

11 Note the surveys cited in *National Journal* 18 (August 2, 1986): 1891.

12 This clash has already occurred in some state, local, and congressional contests. See, for example, *Congressional Quarterly Weekly* 44 (April 12, 1986): 802–803.

13 Poll I (see Appendix) [in original text—eds.].

14 See the surveys cited in the *Washington Post,* September 14, 1986, D1, and November 5, 1986, A36.

15 See Helen DeWar, "Reagan's Themes, Deficits Alter Course of Democratic Mainstream," *Washington Post,* March 9, 1987, A3.

16 As quoted ibid.

# 9

# Interest Groups

*One of the most significant political developments in recent times has been the emergence and spectacular growth of political action committees, or PACs. PACs are specially organized political campaign finance groups, functioning outside of the traditional political parties, whose primary purpose is to raise and spend money on behalf of candidates running for office. Modern PACs, with members numbering in the thousands, represent all sorts of special interests, from organized labor, to professional and business organizations, to liberal and conservative ideological groups.*

*Although PACs clearly have every right to exist in a democratic political system and contribute significantly to our free system of elections, there are those who allege that PACs have come to exercise too much political and governmental power—that they affect electoral and legislative outcomes far more than they should, often to the detriment of the public interest.*

*Among the critics is David Corn, Washington, D.C., editor of* The Nation *magazine and frequent critic of the national political scene. Corn's view of the matter is suggested by the title of his article—"Shilling in the Senate," which refers to the process whereby senators serve as "pitchmen" for special interests. With a fascinating inside look at some rather obscure dealings in the Senate, Corn gives us in several case studies a not too favorable view of how senators look out after special interests—the interests that all too frequently have been major contributors to their campaigns.*

*The selection offered in rebuttal to Corn is written by political scientist Larry Sabato, considered one of the nation's leading authorities on PACs. While admitting some faults with PACs, Professor Sabato strongly defends the existence of these new political organizations and the contributions they make to our system of democracy. In Sabato's view, PACs have been the victim of a bum rap, neither causing the current excesses in campaign finance nor unduly influencing individual legislators or the Congress as a whole.*

# Interest Groups on Capitol Hill:
## Shilling in the Senate

**David Corn**

The amendment concerned the testing of prospective pesticides, and the language seemed altogether innocuous. "Whenever tests . . . are required by more than one state or federal agency, such tests . . . shall be coordinated and synchronized among the agencies so as to avoid unnecessary repetition and redundancy." Who could be in favor of unnecessary redundancy?

But Senator Rudy Boschwitz, who was pushing the amendment to the Federal Insecticide, Fungicide and Rodenticide Act at a session of the Senate Agriculture Committee last year, was not acting solely in the name of efficiency. Boschwitz was shilling for a very special interest: small manufacturers of pesticides. And he was doing so in the fashion that occurs in Congress daily: maneuvering at a "mark-up," the underreported committee meetings where legislation gets modified.

North Carolina's Jesse Helms and tobacco, Connecticut's Christopher Dodd and insurance, West Virginia's Robert Byrd and coal—these are well-known partnerships. But many less visible joint enterprises exist in both houses of Congress, engaged in by both liberals and conservatives. I have selected Boschwitz and three of his colleagues—Bennett Johnston, Orrin Hatch and Alan Cranston—as four not-too-extraordinary examples of how the system operates. They may not necessarily be the worst offenders; such an honor is difficult to award, given the number of contenders. These are just tales of business as usual, which is what makes them alarming.

Boschwitz claimed his pesticide amendment would help small firms develop new products and save consumers from bearing the "inordinate costs," via higher prices, of too much product testing. But to those familiar with pesticide law the amendment had another intent: to subvert the efforts of individual states that write pesticide regulations stiffer than the Federal requirements. Most of the committee saw through Boschwitz. His fellow Republican Pete Wilson put it bluntly: "I think [the amendment] is frankly an effort to achieve a uniformity [of pesticide testing] for the convenience of manufacturers." In fact, prior to the session, the amendment had been widely referred to as the "C.S.M.A. amendment," after the Chemical Specialties Manufacturers Assocation, a trade group representing firms that manufacture home-use pesticides.

Some C.S.M.A. members are based in Minnesota, the state Boschwitz represents. Would that justify supporting a bill that could weaken pesticide

David Corn is a Washington bureau editor for *The Nation* magazine. From David Corn, "The Art of Capitol Hill: Shilling in the Senate," *The Nation*, July 17, 1989, pp. 84–87. *The Nation* magazine/ The Nation Co., Inc. © 1989.

regulation nationwide? The *Minneapolis Star Tribune* didn't see a home-state interest and chastised Boschwitz for pushing the amendment. But there was another local connection. A key lobbyist for the provision was Jon Grunseth, vice president of the Minneapolis-based Economics Laboratory, which owns ChemLawn and is part of C.S.M.A. Grunseth, whose wife is a major Republican fund-raiser in Minnesota, is himself a player in Republican politics and is considering running for governor. Moreover, the political action committees of C.S.M.A. members gave Boschwitz at least $30,000 when he ran for re-election in 1984.

At the end of the debate on the amendment, when it became clear that Boschwitz could not persuade a majority of the committee, C.S.M.A. representatives were willing to throw in the towel, according to Janet Hathaway, an attorney for the Natural Resouces Defense Council, who was at the session. But Boschwitz, to the surprise of some present, pressed for a vote. "C.S.M.A. didn't communicate [its willingness to surrender] to Boschwitz," Hathaway recalls. "It's a little embarrassing to pass a note to the Senator saying, 'C.S.M.A. says to give up.'" The committee rejected his amendment, 14 to 4.

On March 24, Bennett Johnston, the powerful chair of the Senate Energy and Natural Resources Committee, must have realized that a pet project of his was sunk. That was the day that the *Exxon Valdez* struck a reef and dumped 10 million gallons of crude oil into Prince William Sound. Only nine days earlier, Johnston, a Louisiana Democrat, had carefully navigated through his committee a bill to open the coastal plain of the Arctic National Wildlife Refuge in Alaska to oil and gas drilling.

For the past two years, Johnston has tried to deliver a piece of the wildlife refuge, the nation's sole unspoiled Arctic ecosystem, to the oil industry. But Johnston could not sell the measure to his fellow Democrats. When the committee voted on his bill in February 1988, eight of the ten Democrats refused to support the chair. The bill, however, squeaked out of committee on an 11-to-8 vote; but it didn't move on the Senate floor. This year it was a top priority of Johnston, until the oil spill. He then deep-sixed the measure, explaining it would be "politically foolish" to push it.

Johnston's affection for big energy goes well beyond oil. In 1986 he successfully pushed a bill that favored privately owned utilities over public utilities in Federal licensing involving hydroelectric power. Last year he fought back proposed legislation that would make contractors at Department of Energy–owned nuclear facilities—including General Electric, Rockwell and Westinghouse—liable for accidents caused by their own gross negligence. Johnston has now revived a bill that would save the nuclear industry billions of dollars.

In 1969 the government began enriching uranium for the burgeoning commercial nuclear power industry. The 1954 Atomic Energy Act requires the Department of Energy to price its enrichment services so that it recovers the program's cost. But the General Accounting Office reported in 1987 that the D.O.E., as of 1986, had not recovered $8.8 billion; that sum may now have risen to more than $10 billion. The utilities claim this debt is solely the result of accounting trickery. Last year, Johnston was one of the proponents of a measure that would restructure the uranium industry and set the amount of unrecovered costs at about $364 million, a figure acceptable to the utilities. In 1988 he succeeded in ushering the bill through the Senate but it died in the House.

On a complex issue such as this, there may be room for honest disagreement; but the room would have to be quite large to accommodate the range between $364 million and $10 billion. Johnston argues that maintaining a healthy nuclear industry is in the national interest. It certainly is in his interest. His finance reports overflow with money from a host of energy concerns. When he was running for re-election in 1983 and 1984, he received more than $121,000 from energy PACs and at least $84,000 from individuals who work in the business. Last year, he earned $8,000 in honorariums from G.E., Chevron and electric utilities.

Johnston has taken special-interest campaign financing to creative heights via his own Pelican PAC, established in 1987 and named after the Louisiana state bird. As detailed by *Congressional Quarterly*, this PAC has been managed by a small group of former Johnston aides who now lobby for big energy interests. Many of its funds came from individuals who work for energy companies, according to Federal Election Commission records. Two of the prime movers behind Pelican, both former Johnston aides, are Robert Szabo, who has lobbied for electric utilities, the Uranium Producers of America and the corporation that owns the drilling rights in the Arctic refuge; and Charles McBride, who has lobbied for the American Nuclear Energy Council and nuclear utilities. Pelican's mission was to raise money that Johnston, then contending for the majority leader's job in the Senate, could funnel to the senatorial campaigns of other Democrats. Johnston doled out over $200,000 in 1987 and 1988, but his largesse failed to win him the votes he needed from his colleagues.

Asked about the propriety of his Pelican scheme, Johnston said, "I'm very much playing by the rules." He's right. By Washington rules, there is nothing wrong when a senator recruits aides turned lobbyists to hit up special interests—whose profits the senator can greatly affect—to finance an effort to obtain the top Senate leadership post.

Orrin Hatch is the ranking Republican on the Senate Labor and Human Resource Committee, which oversees health legislation. He is also the beneficiary of great wads of cash from health-related industry, whose interests frequently come before his committee. For example, in the years before Hatch's 1988 re-election he took in more than $30,000 from company officials and PACs of Eli Lilly, Bristol-Myers and Pfizer.

Last year the House passed the Medical Device Improvements Act, which was intended to better regulate such items as pacemakers, incubators and X-ray machines. The bill was the product of extensive negotiations between Congressional staff and the Health Industry Manufacturers Association, according to Congressional sources and Jerry Connor, a former lobbyist for H.I.M.A. Consumer advocates felt that the bill did not go far enough, but it did tighten a loophole that had allowed medical device manufacturers to escape Federal review of many new products.

Three medical device companies and H.I.M.A. members—Pfizer, Bristol-Myers and Eli Lilly—bolted and vowed to sink the bill in the Senate. They found an ally in Hatch. He and Representative John Dingell, chair of the House Energy and Commerce Committee, which had responsibility for the medical device bill, began negotiating. Hatch provided Dingell with a list of several proposed changes in the legislation, most of which appeared reasonable to the House side and did not seem, at first blush, to be linked to Pfizer, which had taken the lead in opposing the bill.

But Hatch's list included a measure that previously had been introduced on its own as a bill by Senator Howell Heflin and Representative Dan Glickman. This proposal would prevent foreign citizens from using U.S. courts to sue American manufacturers of defective products. Pfizer had a well-publicized and pressing interest in the measure due to trouble it had with its Bjork-Shiley heart valve. Between 1979 and 1986, 85,000 valves had been implanted in patients, about half of whom were foreigners; as of June 1988 the valve had been linked to 123 deaths. At that time at least forty foreign citizens were suing Pfizer in California.

The Pfizer bailout provision Hatch proposed adding to the medical device bill fell outside the scope of Dingell's committee, so that Dingell could not have attached it to the medical device bill whether he wanted to or not. Though Hatch failed to deliver this favor to Pfizer, he did succeed in blocking the medical device bill in the Senate, where it expired when Congress adjourned last year. A Hatch spokesperson maintains that the Senator was not acting at the behest of Pfizer but on behalf of a number of senators who had various objections to the House bill. But, according to a Congressional aide, Pfizer was boasting that Hatch had killed the bill for the company. . . .

On March 27, 1987, Senator Pete Domenici, a Republican from New Mexico, took to the Senate floor to offer Amendment 59 to the Competitive Equality Banking Act, a major piece of financial legislation. Domenici's measure was quite simple. It would limit the amount of junk bonds a state-chartered and federally insured savings and loan institution could hold in its portfolio. Domenici noted that limits already applied to federally chartered S&Ls and that it seemed unreasonable to allow state-chartered thrifts to engage in high-risk investment yet receive the same insurance. The amendment did not please junk-bond peddlers like Drexel Burnham, Lambert or the state-regulated S&Ls in California that hold a lot of these bonds; both forces lobbied against the provision.

Several senators spoke out against Domenici's amendment, among them Alan Cranston, the Democratic liberal from California. For Cranston, the majority whip and a member of the Banking Committee, this must have been a special moment. He was helping two of his good friends—the S&L industry and Drexel—at the same time. To Cranston's re-election campaign of 1986, Drexel executives and the firm's PAC contributed at least $42,800, and thrift industry PACs, $47,000. With Cranston and others in opposition, Domenici's endeavor failed.

If you're looking for senators who front for industry, one Federal Elections Commission official says, check out the Banking Committee. This is where the titanic forces of the U.S. economy do battle. Insurance interests oppose banks eager to get into the insurance field. The securities industry tries to keep banks from underwriting securities. Major financial firms seek to get a piece of banking. Thrifts vie for less regulation and greater powers. Each bloc has its champions. Cranston, according to former committee aides, usually does double time, helping both S&Ls and the financial services industry. Once, says a committee source, a Cranston aide submitted amendments to a banking bill without the Senator's having read them. They were put in at the request of a trade association of financial services firms.

Cranston consistently has fought efforts to strengthen the capital-reserve standards for S&Ls and pressed measures that would allow them to be more freewheeling. In 1987, in committee caucuses, he urged a lower recapitalization of the Federal Savings and Loan Insurance Corporation. This is what Speaker Jim Wright pushed in the House. Thrifts were not eager to see a large refinancing of the F.S.L.I.C. for several reasons: They would have to pay the tab; the money would be used to close down ailing S&Ls, an admission that the S&L industry faced a severe problem; and they realized that if only a small recapitalization at that stage was set up, it could lead to a taxpayer bailout down the road. Which it did.

"Alan Cranston is not playing a large role in the public interest on that committee," says Peggy Miller, a banking lobbyist for the Consumers Federation of America. As an example, she points to community reinvestment legislation, which she maintains should interest a liberal well known for his advocacy of housing programs. Miller complains that groups backing community reinvestment legislation, which would require banks to take into account local needs when they review their lending patterns, cannot get help from Cranston: "With the exception of housing, whenever we try to have an impact on the financial community we don't bother with him."

One of Cranston's more notorious actions occurred in April 1987. As reported in the *National Thrift News,* Cranston and four other Senators— Dennis DeConcini, John McCain, John Glenn and Donald Riegle, Jr.—held a meeting with four representatives of the San Francisco Federal Home Loan Bank and urged the regulators to reappraise the real estate investments of a California-based thrift, Lincoln Savings and Loan. This was "an unprecedented display of Senatorial effort on behalf of a thrift," the publication observed. Last year, *The Detroit News* noted that Cranston had received $41,900 in campaign contributions from executives connected to the American Continental Corporation, the owner of Lincoln Savings. . . .

Recently, Cranston was given the chance to relive his 1987 small victory on the issue of junk bonds and thrifts. In April, when the Senate passed the S&L bailout, the bill emerged with a provision that allows S&Ls to count as capital their investment in subsidiaries that hold junk bonds. Because the Banking Committee prepared much of the bill in secret, the author of this provision was never publicly identified. But Congressional sources told *The Washington Post* that Cranston was the culprit and that the bill's main beneficiary was a Beverly Hills S&L.

As long as members of Congress need to turn to well-heeled individuals, corporations, trade associations, labor unions and other special interests to finance their runs for office, the favors will fly and the taxpayer will pick up the tab. As long as they accept from the same gang honorariums (which are direct personal income) and free travel, motives will always be questioned. And as long as key legislative work goes on in secrecy, suspicion will be well justified. Take the case of Cranston's opposition to Domenici's Amendment 59. Senator William Proxmire, then chair of the Banking, Housing, and Urban Affairs Committee, also opposed the measure. But Proxmire, who retired last year, did not accept PAC money and declined honorariums from any group with an interest in Banking Committee legislation. In fact, he spent only $145.10 in his last re-election bid.

The big lie on Capitol Hill is that the flow of money doesn't pervert the legislative process. The system has become so poisoned (and the public and news media so cynical) that most episodes of special-interest legislating no longer outrage anyone. In a year marked by scandal and greed on Capitol Hill, the need for reform is obvious. The time is long past to close off the financial tap and open the committee room doors. If there is no noticeable change in the way Congress does business, then we can return to the old ways. The money will always be there.

# The Misplaced Obsession with PACs

**Larry Sabato**

The disturbing statistics and the horror stories about political action committees seem to flow like a swollen river, week after week, year in and year out.
Outrage extends across the ideological spectrum: the liberal interest group
Common Cause has called the system "scandalous," while conservative former senator Barry Goldwater (R-Ariz.) has bluntly declared, "PAC money is
destroying the election process. . . ."[1]

\* \* \*

PAC-bashing is undeniably a popular campaign sport,[2] but the "big PAC
attack" is an opiate that obscures the more vital concerns and problems in
campaign finance. PAC excesses are merely a symptom of other serious mal-
adies in the area of political money, but the near-obsessive focus by public
interest groups and the news media on the PAC evils has diverted attention
from more fundamental matters. The PAC controversy, including the charges
most frequently made against them, can help explain why PACs are best
described as agents of pseudo corruption.[3]

## THE PAC ERA

While a good number of PACs of all political persuasions existed prior to the
1970s, it was during that decade of campaign reform that the modern PAC era
began. Spawned by the Watergate-inspired revisions of the campaign finance
laws, PACs grew in number from 113 in 1972 to 4,196 by 1988, and their
contributions to congressional candidates multiplied more than fifteenfold,
from $8.5 million in 1971–72 to $130.3 million in 1985–86.

The rapid rise of PACs has engendered much criticism, yet many of the
charges made against political action committees are exaggerated and dubious.
While the widespread use of the PAC structure is new, special interest money
of all types has always found its way into politics. Before the 1970s it simply did
so in less traceable and far more disturbing and unsavory ways. And while, in
absolute terms, PACs contribute a massive sum to candidates, it is not clear
that there is proportionately more interest-group money in the system than
before. As political scientist Michael Malbin has argued, we will never know
the truth because the earlier record is so incomplete.[4]

The proportion of House and Senate campaign funds provided by PACs
has certainly increased since the early 1970s, but individuals, most of whom are

Larry Sabato is professor of political science at the University of Virginia. From Chapter 1 of Larry
Sabato, *Paying for Elections: The Campaign Finance Thicket,* A Twentieth Century Fund Paper,
© 1989 by the Twentieth Century Fund, New York.

unaffiliated with PACs, together with the political parties, still supply about three-fifths of all the money spent by or on behalf of House candidates and three-quarters of the campaign expenditures for Senate contenders. So while the importance of PAC spending has grown, PACs clearly remain secondary as a source of election funding. PACs, then, seem rather less awesome when considered within the entire spectrum of campaign finance.

Apart from the argument over the relative weight of PAC funds, PAC critics claim that political action committees are making it more expensive to run for office. There is some validity to this assertion. Money provided to one candidate funds the purchase of campaign tools that the other candidate must match in order to stay competitive.

In the aggregate, American campaign expenditures seem huge. In 1988, the total amount spent by all U.S. House of Representatives candidates taken together was about $256 million, and the campaign cost of the winning House nominee averaged over $392,000. Will Rogers's 1931 remark has never been more true: "Politics has got so expensive that it takes lots of money to even get beat with."

Yet $256 million is far less than the annual advertising budgets of many individual commercial enterprises. These days it is expensive to communicate, whether the message is political or commercial. Television time, polling costs, consultants' fees, direct-mail investment, and other standard campaign expenditures have been soaring in price, over and above inflation.[5] PACs have been fueling the use of new campaign techniques, but a reasonable case can be made that such expenses are necessary, and that more and better communication is required between candidates and an electorate that often appears woefully uninformed about politics. PACs therefore may be making a positive contribution by providing the means to increase the flow of information during elections.

PACs are also accused of being biased toward the incumbent, and except for the ideological committees, they do display a clear and overwhelming preference for those already in office. But the same bias is apparent in contributions from individuals, who ask the same reasonable, perhaps decisive, economic question: Why waste money on contenders if incumbents almost always win? On the other hand, the best challengers—those perceived as having fair-to-good chances to win—are usually generously funded by PACs. Well-targeted PAC challenger money clearly helped the GOP win a majority in the U.S. Senate in 1980, for instance, and in turn aided the Democrats in their 1986 Senate takeover.

The charge that PACs limit the number of strong challengers is true, because by giving so much money so early in the race to incumbents, they deter potential opponents from declaring their candidacies. On the other hand, the money that PACs channel to competitive challengers late in the election season may actually help increase the turnover of officeholders on election day. PAC money also tends to invigorate competitiveness in open-seat congressional races where there is no incumbent. . . .

# PAC MONEY AND CONGRESSIONAL "CORRUPTION"

The most serious charge leveled at PACs is that they succeed in buying the votes of legislators on issues important to their individual constituencies. It seems hardly worth arguing that many PACs are shopping for congressional votes and that PAC money buys access, or opens doors, to congressmen. But the "vote-buying" allegation is generally not supported by a careful examination of the facts.[6] PAC contributions do make a difference, at least on some occasions, in securing access and influencing the course of events, but those occasions are not nearly as frequent as anti-PAC spokesmen, even congressmen themselves, often suggest.

PACs affect legislative proceedings to a decisive degree only when certain conditions prevail. First, the less visible the issue, the more likely that PAC funds can change or influence congressional votes. A corollary is that PAC money has more effect in the early stages of the legislative process, such as agenda setting and votes in subcommittee meetings, than in later and more public floor deliberations. Press, public, and even "watchdog" groups are not nearly as attentive to initial legislative proceedings.

PAC contributions are also more likely to influence the legislature when the issue is specialized and narrow, or unopposed by other organized interests. PAC gifts are less likely to be decisive on broad national issues such as American policy in Nicaragua or the adoption of a Star Wars missile defense system. But the more technical measures seem tailor-made for the special interests. Additionally, PAC influence in Congress is greater when large PACs or groups of PACs (such as business and labor PACs) are allied. In recent years, despite their natural enmity, business and labor have lobbied together on a number of issues, including defense spending, trade policy, environmental regulation, maritime legislation, trucking legislation, and nuclear power.[7] The combination is a weighty one, checked in many instances only by a tendency for business and labor in one industry (say, the railroads) to combine and oppose their cooperating counterparts in another industry (perhaps the truckers and teamsters).

It is worth stressing, however, that most congressmen are *not* unduly influenced by PAC money on most votes. The special conditions simply do not apply to most legislative issues, and the overriding factors in determining a legislator's votes include party affiliation, ideology, and constituents' needs and desires. Much has been made of the passage of large tax cuts for oil and business interests in the 1981 omnibus tax package. The journalist Elizabeth Drew said there was a "bidding war" to trade campaign contributions for tax breaks benefiting independent oil producers.[8] Ralph Nader's Public Citizen group charged that the $280,000 in corporate PAC money accepted by members of the House Ways and Means Committee helped to produce a bill that "contained everything business ever dared to ask for, and more."[9] Yet as Robert Samuelson has convincingly argued, the "bidding war" between Democrats and Republicans was waged not for PAC money but for control of a House of Representatives sharply divided between Reaganite Republicans and liberal Democrats, with conservative "boll weevil" Democrats from the southern oil states as the crucial swing votes.[10] The Ways and Means Committee actions cited by Nader were also more correctly explained in partisan terms. After all, if these special interests were so influential in writing the 1981 omnibus tax package, how could they fail so completely to derail the much more important (and, for them, threatening) tax reform legislation of 1986?

If party loyalty can have a stronger pull than PAC contributions, then surely the views of a congressman's constituents can also take precedence over those of political action committees. If an incumbent is faced with choice of either voting for a PAC-backed bill that is very unpopular in his district or forgoing the PAC's money, the odds are that any politician who depends on a majority of votes to remain in office is going to side with his constituency and vote against the PAC's interest. PAC gifts are merely a means to an end: re-election. If accepting money will cause a candidate embarrassment, then even a maximum donation will likely be rejected. The flip side of this proposition makes sense as well: if a PAC's parent organization has many members or a major financial stake in the congressman's home district, he is much more likely to vote the PAC's way—not so much because he receives PAC money but because the group accounts for an important part of his electorate. Does a U.S. senator from a dairy state vote for dairy price supports because he received a significant percentage of his PAC contributions from agriculture, or because the farm population of his state is relatively large and politically active? When congressmen vote the National Rifle Association's preferences is it because of the money the NRA's PAC distributes, or because the NRA, unlike gun-control advocates, has repeatedly demonstrated the ability to produce a sizable number of votes in many legislative districts?

If PACs have appeared more influential than they actually are, it is partly because many people believe legislators are looking for opportunities to exclaim (as one did during the Abscam scandal) "I've got larceny in my blood!" It is certainly disturbing that the National Republican Congressional Committee believed it necessary to warn its PAC-soliciting candidates: "Don't *ever* suggest to the PAC that it is 'buying' your vote, should you get elected.[11] Yet knowledgeable Capitol Hill observers agree that there are few truly corrupt congressmen. Simple correlations notwithstanding, when most legislators vote for a PAC-supported bill, it is because of the *merits* of the case, or the entreaties of their party leaders, peers, or constituents, and not because of PAC money.

When the PAC phenomenon is viewed in the broad perspective of issues, party allegiance, and constituent interests, it is clear that *merit* matters most in the votes most congressmen cast. It is naive to contend that PAC money never influences decisions, but it is unjustifiably cynical to believe that PACs always, or even usually, push the voting buttons in Congress.

## PACs IN PERSPECTIVE

As the largely unsubstantiated "vote-buying" controversy suggests, PACs are often misrepresented and unfairly maligned as the embodiment of corrupt special interests. Political action committees are a contemporary manifestation of what James Madison called "factions." In his *Federalist, No. 10,* Madison wrote that through the flourishing of these competing interest groups, or factions, liberty would be preserved.[12]

In any democracy, and particularly in one as pluralistic as the United States, it is essential that groups be relatively unrestricted in advocating their interests and positions. Not only is that the mark of a free society, it also provides a safety valve for the competitive pressures that build on all fronts in a capitalistic democracy. And it provides another means to keep representatives responsive to legitimate needs.

This is not to say that all groups pursue legitimate interests, or that vigorously competing interests ensure that the public good prevails. The press, the public, and valuable watchdog groups such as Common Cause must always be alert to instances in which narrow private interests prevail over the commonweal—occurrences that generally happen when no one is looking.

Besides the press and various public interest organizations, there are two major institutional checks on the potential abuses wrought by factions, associations, and now PACs. The most fundamental of these is regular free elections with general suffrage. As Tocqueville commented:

> Perhaps the most powerful of the causes which tend to mitigate the excesses of political association in the United States is Universal Suffrage. In countries in which universal suffrage exists, the majority is never doubtful, because neither party can pretend to represent that portion of the community which has not voted.
>
> The associations which are formed are aware, as well as the nation at large, that they do not represent the majority: this is, indeed, a condition inseparable from their existence; for if they did represent the prepondering power, they would change the law instead of soliciting its reform.[13]

Senator Robert Dole (R-Kan.) has said, "There aren't any Poor PACs or Food Stamp PACs or Nutrition PACs or Medicare PACs,"[14] and PAC critics frequently make the point that certain segments of the electorate are underrepresented in the PAC community. Yet without much support from PACs, there are food stamps, poverty and nutrition programs, and Medicare. Why? Because the recipients of governmental assistance constitute a hefty slice of the electorate, and *votes matter more than dollars to politicians.* Furthermore, many citizens *outside* the affected groups have also made known their support of aid to the poor and elderly—making yet a stronger electoral case for these PAC-less programs.

The other major institution that checks PAC influence is the two-party system. While PACs represent particular interests, the political parties build coalitions of groups and attempt to represent a national interest. They arbitrate among competing claims, and they seek to reach a consensus on matters of overriding importance to the nation. The parties are one of the few unifying forces in an exceptionally diverse country. . . .

However limited and checkmated by political realities PACs may be, they are still regarded by a skeptical public as thoroughly unsavory. PACs have become the embodiment of greedy special interest politics, rising campaign costs, and corruption. It does not seem to matter that most experts in the field of campaign finance take considerable exception to the prevailing characterization of political action committees. PACs have become, in the public's mind, a powerful symbol of much that is wrong with America's campaign process, and candidates for public office naturally manipulate this symbol as well as others for their own ends. It is a circumstance as old as the Republic.

PACs, however, have done little to change their image for the better. Other than the business-oriented Public Affairs Council, few groups or committees have moved to correct one-sided press coverage or educate the public on campaign financing's fundamentals. In fact, many PACs fuel the fires of discontent by refusing to defend themselves while not seeming to care about appearances. Giving to both candidates in the same race, for example—an all-too-common practice—may be justifiable in theory, but it strikes most people as unprincipled, rank influence purchasing. Even worse, perhaps, are PACs that "correct their mistakes" soon after an election by sending a donation to the winning, but not originally PAC-supported, candidate. In the seven 1986 U.S. Senate races where a Democratic challenger defeated a Republican incumbent, there were 150 instances in which a PAC gave to the GOP candidate *before* the election and to the victorious Democrat once the votes were counted.[15] These practices PACs themselves should stop. Every PAC should internally ban double giving, and there should be a moratorium on gifts to previously opposed candidates until at least the halfway point of the officeholder's term.

Whether PACs undertake some necessary rehabilitative steps or not, any fair appraisal of their role in American elections must be balanced. PACs are neither political innocents nor selfless civic boosters. But, neither are they cesspools of corruption and greed, nor modern-day versions of Tammany Hall.

PACs will never be popular with idealistic reformers because they represent the rough, cutting edge of a democracy teeming with different peoples and conflicting interests. Indeed, PACs may never be hailed even by natural allies; it was the business-oriented *Wall Street Journal,* after all, that editorially referred to Washington, D.C., as "a place where politicians, PACs, lawyers, and lobbyists for unions, business or you-name-it shake each other down full time for political money and political support."[16]

Viewed in perspective, the root of the problem in campaign finance is not PACs; it is money. Americans have an enduring mistrust of the mix of money (particularly business money) and politics, as Finley Peter Dunne's Mr. Dooley revealed:

I niver knew a pollytician to go wrong ontil he'd been contaminated be contact with a business man. . . . It seems to me that th' only thing to do is to keep pollyticians an' business men apart. They seem to have a bad infloonce on each other. Whiniver I see an alderman an' a banker walkin' down th' street together I know th' Recordin' Angel will have to ordher another bottle iv ink.[17]

As a result of the new campaign finance rules of the 1970s, political action committees superseded the "fat cats" of old as the public focus and symbol of the role of money in politics, and PACs inherited the suspicions that go with the territory. Those suspicions are valuable because they keep the spotlight on PACs and guard against undue influence. It may be regrettable that such supervision is required, but human nature—not PACs—demands it.

# NOTES

1 Quotations from Common Cause direct-mail package to members, January 1987.
2 *The New Republic,* May 28, 1984, p. 9.
3 For a much more extended discussion of these subjects, see Larry Sabato, *PAC POWER: Inside the World of Political Action Committees,* rev. ed. (New York: Report of the Twentieth Century Fund Task Force on Political Action Committees, 1984).
4 Michael J. Malbin, "The Problem of PAC-Journalism," *Public Opinion,* December/January 1983, pp. 15–16, 59.
5 See Larry Sabato, *The Rise of Political Consultants* (New York: Basic Books, 1981); see also *National Journal,* April 16, 1983, pp. 780–81.
6 See Sabato, *PAC POWER,* pp. 122–59, 222–28.
7 See, for example, Edwin M. Epstein, "An Irony of Electoral Reform," *Regulation,* May/June 1979, pp. 35–44; and Christopher Madison, "Federal Subsidy Programs under Attack by Unlikely Marriage of Labor and Right," *National Journal,* December 31, 1983, pp. 2682–84.
8 Elizabeth Drew, "Politics and Money, Part I" *The New Yorker,* December 6, 1982, pp. 38–45.
9 Herbert E. Alexander, *Financing the 1980 Election* (Lexington, Mass.: D.C. Heath, 1983), p. 379.
10 Robert J. Samuelson, "The Campaign Reform Failure," *The New Republic,* September 5, 1983, pp. 32–33.
11 From the NRCC publication "Working with PACs" (1982).
12 See *The Federalist, No. 10,* for a much fuller discussion of the role of factions in a democratic society.
13 Alexis de Tocqueville, *Democracy in America,* vol. 1 (New York: Vintage Books, 1954), p. 224.
14 As quoted in Drew, "Politics and Money," p. 147.
15 Common Cause "If At First You Don't Succeed, Give, Give Again" (Press release, Washington, D.C., March 20, 1987).
16 "Cleaning Up Reform," *Wall Street Journal,* November 10, 1983, p. 26.
17 Finley Peter Dunne, *The World of Mr. Dooley,* edited with an introduction by Louis Filler (New York: Collier Books, 1962), pp. 155–56.

# 10

# Congress
## Representation

*The three selections in this section are illustrative of a long-standing debate among political theorists and elected officials alike—namely, whose views should prevail on a given issue, the constituents' or the representatives'. In the first selection, taken from an early debate in the General Assembly of the State of Virginia, the argument is made that legislators are obliged to act as instructed* delegates—*that is, that they must vote in accordance with the will of their constituents. In the second selection, former Massachusetts Senator and President, John F. Kennedy, writing in 1956, argued that legislators should act as* trustees, *voting according to their own conscience, regardless of whether their choices reflect the sentiments of their constituents. Finally, George Galloway, a former staff assistant in Congress, contends that on some occasions legislators must follow public opinion, while on others they are obliged to vote according to their own conscience. This view, which combines both the delegate and the trustee approach, is characterized as the* politico *role.*

# The Legislator as Delegate

## General Assembly of Virginia

There can be no doubt that the scheme of a representative republic was derived to our forefathers from the constitution of the English House of Commons; and that that branch of the English government . . . was in its origin, and in theory always has been, purely republican. It is certain, too, that the statesmen of America, in assuming that as the model of our own institutions, designed to adopt it here in its purest form, and with its strictest republican tenets and principles. It becomes, therefore, an inquiry of yet greater utility than curiosity, to ascertain the sound doctrines of the constitution of the English House of Commons in regard to this right of the constituent to instruct the representative. For the position may safely be assumed that the wise and virtuous men who framed our constitutions designed, that, in the United States, the constituent should have at least as much, if not a great deal more, influence over the representative than was known to have existed from time immemorial in England. Let us then interrogate the history of the British nation; let us consult the opinions of their wise men.

Instances abound in parliamentary history of formal instructions from the constituent to the representative, of which . . . the following may suffice: In 1640, the knights of the shire for Dorset and Kent informed the commons *that they had in charge from their constituents* seven articles of grievances, which they accordingly laid before the House, where they were received and acted on. In the 33rd year of Charles II, the citizens of London instructed their members to insist on the bill for excluding the Duke of York (afterward King James II) from the succession to the throne; and their representative said "that his *duty* to his electors *obliged* him to vote the bill." At a subsequent election, in 1681, in many places, formal instructions were given to the members returned, to insist on the same exclusion bill; we know, from history, how uniformly and faithfully those instructions were obeyed. . . . In 1741, the citizens of London instructed their members to vote against standing armies, excise laws, the septennial bill, and a long train of evil measures, already felt, or anticipated; and expressly affirm their right of instruction—"We think it" (say they) "our *duty,* as it is *our undoubted right,* to acquaint you, with *what we desire and expect from you, in discharge of the great trust we repose in you,* and what we take to be *your duty as our representative,* etc." In the same year,

From Commonwealth of Virginia, General Assembly, *Journal of the Senate,* 1812, pp. 82–89. In some instances, spelling and punctuation have been altered from the original in order to achieve greater clarity—*Editors.*

instructions of a similar character were sent from all parts of England. In 1742, the cities of London, Bristol, Edinburgh, York, and many others, instructed their members in parliament to seek redress against certain individuals suspected to have betrayed and deserted the cause of the people. . . .

Instances also are on record of the deliberate formal knowledgement of the right of instruction by the House of Commons itself, especially in old times. Thus the commons hesitated to grant supplies to King Edward III *till they had the consent of their constituents,* and desired that a new parliament might be summoned, which might be *prepared with authority from their constituents.* . . .

"Instructions" (says a member of the House of Commons) "ought to be *followed implicitly,"* after the member has *respectfully* given his constituents *his opinion* of them: *"Far be it from me to oppose my judgment to that of 6000 of my fellow citizens."* "The practice" (says another) "of consulting our constituents was good. I wish it was continued. *We can discharge our duty no better, than in the direction of those who sent us hither. What the people choose is right, because they choose it."* . . .

Without referring to the minor political authors . . . who have maintained these positions (quoted from one of them)—"that the people have a right to instruct their representatives; that no man ought to be chosen that will not receive instructions; that the people understand enough of the interests of the country to give general instructions; that it was the custom formerly to instruct all the members; and the nature of deputation shows that the custom was well grounded"—it is proper to mention that the great constitutional lawyer Coke . . . says, "It is the *custom of parliament,* when any new device is moved for on the king's behalf, for his aid and the like, that the commons may answer, *they dare not agree to it without conference with their counties."* And Sydney . . . maintains "that members derive their power from those that choose them; that those who give power do not give an unreserved power; that many members, in all ages, and sometimes the whole body of the commons have refused to vote until they consulted with those who sent them; that the houses have often adjourned to give them time to do so and if this were done more frequently, or if cities, towns and counties had on some occasions given instructions to their deputies, matters would probably have gone better in parliament than they have done.". . . The celebrated Edmund Burke, a man, it must be admitted, of profound knowledge, deep foresight, and transcendent abilities, disobeyed the instructions of his constituents; yet, by placing his excuse on the ground that the instructions were but the clamour of the day, he seems to admit the authority of instructions soberly and deliberately given; for he agrees, "he ought to look to their opinions" (which he explains to mean their permanent settled opinions) "but not the flash of the day"; and he says elsewhere, that he could not bear to show himself "a representative, whose face did not reflect the face of his constituents—a face that did not joy in their joys and sorrow in their sorrows." It is remarkable that, notwithstanding a most splendid display of warm and touching eloquence, the people of Bristol would not reelect Mr. Burke, for this very offense of disobeying instructions. . . .

It appears, therefore, that the right of the constituent to instruct the representative, is firmly established in England, on the broad basis of the nature of representation. The existence of that right, there, has been demonstrated by the only practicable evidence, by which the principles of an unwritten constitution can be ascertained—history and precedent.

To view the subject upon principle, the right of the constituent to instruct the representative, seems to result, clearly and conclusively, from the very nature of the representative system. Through means of that noble institution, the largest nation may, almost as conveniently as the smallest, enjoy all the advantages of a government by the people, without any of the evils of democracy—precipitation, confusion, turbulence, distraction from the ordinary and useful pursuits of industry. And it is only to avoid those and the like mischiefs, that representation is substituted for the direct suffrage of the people in the office of legislation. The representative, therefore, must in the nature of things, represent his own particular constituents only. He must, indeed, look to the general good of the nation, but he must look also, and especially to the interests of his particular constituents as concerned in the commonweal; because the general good is but the aggregate of individual happiness. He must legislate for the whole nation; but laws are expressions of the general will; and the general will is only the result of individual wills fairly collected and compared. In order . . . to express the general will . . . it is plain that the representative must express the will and speak the opinions of the constituents that depute him.

It cannot be pretended that a representative is to be the organ of his own will alone; for then, he would be so far despotic. *He must be the organ of others*—of whom? Not of the nation, for the nation deputes him not; but of his constituents, who alone know, alone have trusted, and can alone displace him. And if it be his province and his duty, in general, to express the will of his constituents, to the best of his knowledge, without being particularly informed thereof, it seems impossible to contend that he is not bound to do so when he is so especially informed and instructed.

The right of the constituent to instruct the representative, therefore, is an essential principle of the representative system. It may be remarked that wherever representation has been introduced, however unfavorable the circumstances under which it existed, however short its duration, however unimportant its functions, however dimly understood, the right of instruction has always been regarded as inseparably incidental to it. . . .

A representative has indeed a wide field of discretion left to him; and great is the confidence reposed in his integrity, fidelity, wisdom, zeal; but neither is the field of discretion boundless, nor the extent of confidence infinite; and the very discretion allowed him, and the very confidence he enjoys, is grounded on the supposition that he is charged with the will, acquainted with the opinions, and devoted to the interests of his constituents. . . .

Various objections have been urged to this claim of the constituent, of a right to instruct the representative, on which it may be proper to bestow some attention.

The first objection that comes to be considered . . . is grounded on the supposed impossibility of fairly ascertaining the sense of the constituent body. The *impossibility* is denied. It may often be a matter of great *difficulty;* but then the duty of obedience resolves itself into a question, not of principle, but of fact: whether the right of instruction has been exercised or not. The representative cannot be bound by an instruction that is not given; but that is no objection to the obligation of an instruction *actually given.* . . .

It has been urged that the representatives are not bound to obey the instructions of their constituents because the constituents do not hear the debates, and therefore, cannot be supposed judges of the matter to be voted. If this objection has force enough to defeat the right of instruction, it ought to take away, also, the right of rejecting the representative at the subsequent election. For it might be equally urged on that occasion, as against the right of instruction, that the people heard not the debate that enlightened the representative's mind—the reasons that convinced his judgment and governed his conduct. . . . In other words, the principle that mankind is competent to self-government should be renounced. The truth is, that our institutions suppose that although the representative ought to be, and generally will be, selected for superior virtue and intelligence, yet a greater mass of wisdom and virtue still reside in the constituent body than the utmost portion allotted to any individual. . . .

Finally, it has been objected, that the instructions of the constituent are not obligatory on the representative because the obligation insisted on is fortified with no sanction—the representative cannot be punished for his disobedience, and his vote is valid notwithstanding his disobedience. It is true that there is no mode of legal punishment provided for this . . . default of duty and that the act of disobedience will not invalidate the vote. It is true, too, that a representative may perversely advocate a measure which he knows to be ruinous to his country; and that neither his vote will be invalidated by his depravity, nor can he be punished by law for his crime, heinous as it surely is. But it does not follow that the one representative is *not bound to obey the instructions* of his constituents any more than that the other is not bound to obey the dictates of his conscience. Both duties stand upon the same foundation, with almost all the great political and moral obligations. The noblest duties of man are without any legal sanction: the great mass of social duties . . . , our duties to our parents, to our children, to our wives, to our families, to our neighbor, to our country, our duties to God, are, for the most part, without legal sanction, yet surely not without the strongest obligation. The duty of the *representative* to obey the instructions of the *constituent* body cannot be placed on higher ground.

Such are the opinions of the General Assembly of Virginia, on the subject of this great right of instruction, and such the general reasons on which those opinions are founded. . . .

# The Legislator as Trustee

**John F. Kennedy**

The primary responsibility of a senator, most people assume, is to represent the views of his state. Ours is a federal system—a union of relatively sovereign states whose needs differ greatly—and my constitutional obligations as senator would thus appear to require me to represent the interests of my state. Who will speak for Massachusetts if her own senators do not? Her rights and even her identity become submerged. Her equal representation in Congress is lost. Her aspirations, however much they may from time to time be in the minority, are denied that equal opportunity to be heard to which all minority views are entitled.

Any senator need not look very long to realize that his colleagues are representing *their* local interests. And if such interests are ever to be abandoned in favor of the national good, let the constituents—not the senator—decide when and to what extent. For he is their agent in Washington, the protector of their rights, recognized by the vice president in the Senate Chamber as "the senator from Massachusetts" or "the senator from Texas."

But when all of this is said and admitted, we have not yet told the full story. For in Washington we are "United States senators" and members of the Senate of the United States as well as senators from Massachusetts and Texas. Our oath of office is administered by the vice president, not by the governors of our respective states; and we come to Washington, to paraphrase Edmund Burke, not as hostile ambassadors or special pleaders for our state or section, in opposition to advocates and agents of other areas, but as members of the deliberative assembly of one nation with one interest. Of course, we should not ignore the needs of our area—nor could we easily as products of that area—but none could be found to look out for the national interest if local interests wholly dominated the role of each of us.

There are other obligations in addition to those of state and region—the obligations of the party. . . . Even if I can disregard those pressures, do I not have an obligation to go along with the party that placed me in office? We believe in this country in the principle of party responsibility, and we recognize the necessity of adhering to party platforms—if the party label is to mean anything to the voters. Only in this way can our basically two-party nation avoid the pitfalls of multiple splinter parties, whose purity and rigidity of principle, I might add—if I may suggest a sort of Gresham's Law of politics—increase inversely with the size of their membership.

John F. Kennedy, thirty-fifth president of the United States, was a Democratic member of the U.S. Senate from the State of Massachusetts from 1952 to 1960 and a member of the U.S. House of Representatives from 1947 to 1952. This selection is from pp. 33–39 in *Profiles in Courage* by John F. Kennedy. Copyright © 1955, 1956 by John F. Kennedy. Reprinted by permission of HarperCollins Publishers.

And yet we cannot permit the pressures of party responsibility to submerge on every issue the call of personal responsibility. For the party which, in its drive for unity, discipline and success, ever decides to exclude new ideas, independent conduct or insurgent members, is in danger. . . .

Of course, both major parties today seek to serve the national interest. They would do so in order to obtain the broadest base of support, if for no nobler reason. But when party and officeholder differ as to how the national interest is to be served, we must place first the responsibility we owe not to our party or even to our constituents but to our individual consciences.

But it is a little easier to dismiss one's obligations to local interests and party ties to face squarely the problem of one's responsibility to the will of his constituents. A senator who avoids this responsibility would appear to be accountable to no one, and the basic safeguards of our democratic system would thus have vanished. He is no longer representative in the true sense, he has violated his public trust, he has betrayed the confidence demonstrated by those who voted for him to carry out their views. "Is the creature," as John Tyler asked the House of Representatives in his maiden speech, "to set himself in opposition to his Creator? Is the servant to disobey the wishes of his master?"

> How can he be regarded as representing the people when he speaks, not their language, but his own? He ceases to be their representative when he does so, and represents himself alone.

In short, according to this school of thought, if I am to be properly responsive to the will of my constituents, it is my duty to place their principles, not mine, above all else. This may not always be easy, but it nevertheless is the essence of democracy, faith in the wisdom of the people and their views. To be sure, the people will make mistakes—they will get no better government than they deserve—but that is far better than the representative of the people arrogating for himself the right to say he knows better than they what is good for them. Is he not chosen, the argument closes, to vote as they would vote were they in his place?

It is difficult to accept such a narrow view of the role of United States senator—a view that assumes the people of Massachusetts sent me to Washington to serve merely as a seismograph to record shifts in popular opinion. I reject this view not because I lack faith in the "wisdom of the people," but because this concept of democracy actually puts too little faith in the people. Those who would deny the obligation of the representative to be bound by every impulse of the electorate—regardless of the conclusions his own deliberations direct—do trust in the wisdom of the people. They have faith in their ultimate sense of justice, faith in their ability to honor courage and respect judgment, and faith that in the long run they will act unselfishly for the good of the nation. It is that kind of faith on which democracy is based, not simply the often frustrated hope that public opinion will at all times under all circumstances promptly identify itself with the public interest.

The voters selected us, in short, because they had confidence in our judgment and our ability to exercise that judgment from a position where we could determine what were their own best interests, as a part of the nation's interests. This may mean that we must on occasion lead, inform, correct and sometimes even ignore constituent opinion, if we are to exercise fully that judgment for which we were elected. But acting without selfish motive or private bias, those who follow the dictates of an intelligent conscience are not aristocrats, demagogues, eccentrics, or callous politicians insensitive to the feelings of the public. They expect—and not without considerable trepidation—their constituents to be the final judges of the wisdom of their course; but they have faith that those constituents—today, tomorrow, or even in another generation—will at least respect the principles that motivated their independent stand.

If their careers are temporarily or even permanently buried under an avalanche of abusive editorials, poison-pen letters, and opposition votes at the polls—as they sometimes are, for that is the risk they take—they await the future with hope and confidence, aware of the fact that the voting public frequently suffers from what ex-Congressman T. V. Smith called the lag "between our way of thought and our way of life." . . .

Moreover, I question whether any senator, before we vote on a measure, can state with certainty exactly how the majority of his constituents feel on the issue as it is presented to the Senate. All of us in the Senate live in an iron lung—the iron lung of politics, and it is no easy task to emerge from that rarefied atmosphere in order to breathe the same fresh air our constituents breathe. It is difficult, too, to see in person an appreciable number of voters besides those professional hangers-on and vocal elements who gather about the politician on a trip home. In Washington I frequently find myself believing that forty or fifty letters, six visits from professional politicians and lobbyists, and three editorials in Massachusetts newspapers constitute public opinion on a given issue. Yet in truth I rarely know how the great majority of the voters feel, or even how much they know of the issues that seem so burning in Washington.

Today the challenge of political courage looms larger than ever before. For our everyday life is becoming so saturated with the tremendous power of mass communications that any unpopular or unorthodox course arouses a storm of protests. . . . Our political life is becoming so expensive, so mechanized, and so dominated by professional politicians and public relations men that the idealist who dreams of independent statesmanship is rudely awakened by the necessities of election and accomplishment. . . .

And thus, in the days ahead, only the very courageous will be able to take the hard and unpopular decisions necessary for our survival. . . .

# The Legislator as Politico

**George B. Galloway**

One question which the conscientious congressman must often ask himself, especially when conflicts arise between local or regional attitudes and interests and the national welfare, is this: "As a member of Congress, am I merely a delegate from my district or state, restricted to act and vote as the majority which elected me desire, bound by the instructions of my constituents and subservient to their will? Or am I, once elected, a representative of the people of the United States, free to act as I think best for the country generally?

In a country as large as the United States, with such diverse interests and such a heterogeneous population, the economic interests and social prejudices of particular states and regions often clash with those of other sections and with conceptions of the general interest of the whole nation. The perennial demand of the silver-mining and wool interests in certain western states for purchase and protection, the struggle over slavery, and the recent filibuster of southern senators against the attempt to outlaw racial discrimination in employment are familiar examples of recurring conflicts between local interests and prejudices and the common welfare. These political quarrels are rooted in the varying stages of cultural development attained by the different parts of the country. It is the peculiar task of the politician to compose these differences, to reconcile conflicting national and local attitudes, and to determine when public opinion is ripe for legislative action. Some conflicts will yield in time to political adjustment; others must wait for their legal sanction upon the gradual evolution of the conscience of society. No act of Congress can abolish unemployment or barking dogs or racial prejudices. . . .

## TYPES OF PRESSURES ON CONGRESS

One can sympathize with the plight of the conscientious congressman who is the focal point of all these competing pressures. The district or state he represents may need and want certain roads, post offices, courthouses, or schools. Irrigation dams or projects may be needed for the development of the area's resources. If the representative is to prove himself successful in the eyes of the people back home, he must be able to show, at least occasionally, some visible and concrete results of his congressional activity. Or else he must be able to give good reasons why he has not been able to carry out his pledges.

George B. Galloway (1898–1967) was senior specialist in American Government with the Legislative Reference Service of the Library of Congress. This article is abridged from pp. 284–85, 301, 319–22, in *Congress at the Crossroads* by George B. Galloway (Thomas Y. Crowell). Copyright 1946 by George B. Galloway. Reprinted by permission of HarperCollins Publishers.

The local residence rule for congressmen multiplies the pressures that impinge upon him. Faithful party workers who have helped elect him will expect the congressman to pay his political debts by getting them jobs in the federal service. Constituents affected by proposed legislation may send him an avalanche of letters, telegrams, and petitions which must be acknowledged and followed up. The region from which he comes will expect him to protect and advance its interests in Washington. All the various organized groups will press their claims upon him and threaten him if he does not jump when they crack the whip. Party leaders may urge a congressman to support or oppose the administration program or to "trade" votes for the sake of party harmony or various sectional interests. He is also under pressure from his own conscience as to what he should do both to help the people who have elected him and to advance the best interests of the nation. Besieged by all these competing pressures, a congressman is often faced with the choice of compromising between various pressures, of trading votes, of resisting special interests of one sort or another, of staying off the floor when a vote is taken on some measure he prefers not to take a stand on, of getting support here and at the same time running the risk of losing support there. Dealing with pressure blocs is a problem in political psychology which involves a careful calculation of the power of the blocs, the reaction of the voters on election day, and the long-haul interests of the district, state, and nation. . . .

## SHOULD CONGRESS LEAD
## OR FOLLOW PUBLIC OPINION?

It is axiomatic to say that in a democracy public opinion is the source of law. Unless legislation is sanctioned by the sense of right of the people, it becomes a dead letter on the statute books, like Prohibition and the Hatch Act. But public opinion is a mercurial force; now quiescent, now vociferous, it has various moods and qualities. It reacts to events and is often vague and hard to weigh.

Nor is public opinion infallible. Most people are naturally preoccupied with their personal problems and daily affairs; national problems and legislative decisions seem complex and remote to them, despite press and radio and occasional Capitol tours. Comparatively few adults understand the technicalities of foreign loans or reciprocal trade treaties, although congressional action on these aspects of our foreign economic policy may have far-reaching effects upon our standard of living. . . .

In practice, a congressman both leads and follows public opinion. The desires of his constituents, of his party, and of this or that pressure group all enter into his decisions on matters of major importance. The influence of these factors varies from member to member and measure to measure. Some congressmen consider it their duty to follow closely what they think is the majority opinion of their constituents, especially just before an election. Others feel that they should make their decisions without regard to their constituents' wishes in the first place, and then try to educate and convert them afterward. Some members are strong party men and follow more or less blindly the program of the party leaders. Except when they are very powerful in the home district, the pressure groups are more of a nuisance than a deciding influence on the average member. When a legislator is caught between the conflicting pressures of his constituents and his colleagues, he perforce compromises between them and follows his own judgment.

The average legislator discovers early in his career that certain interests or prejudices of his constituents are dangerous to trifle with. Some of these prejudices may not be of fundamental importance to the welfare of the nation, in which case he is justified in humoring them, even though he may disapprove. The difficult case occurs where the prejudice concerns some fundamental policy affecting the national welfare. A sound sense of values, the ability to discriminate between that which is of fundamental importance and that which is only superficial, is an indispensable qualification of a good legislator.

Senator Fulbright* gives an interesting example of this distinction in his stand on the poll-tax issue and isolationism. "Regardless of how persuasive my colleagues or the national press may be about the evils of the poll tax, I do not see its fundamental importance, and I shall follow the views of the people of my state. Although it may be symbolic of conditions which many deplore, it is exceedingly doubtful that its abolition will cure any of our major problems. On the other hand, regardless of how strongly opposed my constituents may prove to be to the creation of, and participation in, an ever stronger United Nations Organization, I could not follow such a policy in that field unless it becomes clearly hopeless."[1]

## A TWO-WAY JOB

As believers in democracy, probably most Americans would agree that it is the duty of congressmen to follow public opinion insofar as it expresses the desires, wants, needs, aspirations, and ideals of the people. Most Americans probably would also consider it essential for their representatives to make as careful an appraisal of these needs and desires as they can, and to consider, in connection with such an appraisal, the ways and means of accomplishing them. Legislators have at hand more information about legal structures, economic problems, productive capacities, manpower possibilities, and the like, than the average citizen they represent. They can draw upon that information to inform and lead the people—by showing the extent to which their desires can be realized.

In other words, a true representative of the people would follow the people's desires and at the same time lead the people in formulating ways of

*At the time this article was written, J. William Fulbright was a U.S. senator from the state of Arkansas—*Editors.*

accomplishing those desires. He would lead the people in the sense of calling to their attention the difficulties of achieving those aims and the ways to overcome the difficulties. This means also that, where necessary, he would show special interest groups or even majorities how, according to his own interpretation and his own conscience, their desires need to be tempered in the common interest or for the future good of the nation.

Thus the job of a congressman is a two-way one. He represents his local area and interests in the national capital, and he also informs the people back home of the problems arising at the seat of government and how these problems affect them. It is in the nature of the congressman's job that he should determine, as far as he can, public opinion in his own constituency and in the whole nation, analyze it, measure it in terms of the practicability of turning it into public policy, and consider it in the light of his own knowledge, conscience, and convictions. Occasionally he may be obliged to go against public opinion, with the consequent task of educating or reeducating the people along lines that seem to him more sound. And finally, since he is a human being eager to succeed at his important job of statesmanship and politics, he is realistic enough to keep his eyes on the voters in terms of the next election. But he understands that a mere weather-vane following of majority public opinion is not always the path to reelection. . . .

## NOTES

1 In an address on "The Legislator" delivered at the University of Chicago on February 19, 1946. *Vital Speeches,* May 15, 1946, pp. 468–72.

# Congressional Reform: Term Limitation

Take a poll—any poll—and ask people what they think of Congress, and the response is likely to be, "Throw the bums out!" Indeed, in any popularity contest between the three branches of government—Congress, the Presidency, and the Supreme Court—the Congress will almost always end up a poor third.

What are the voters so angry about? The easy answer is—almost everything: the budget, pay raises for representatives, abuses of the franking privilege, undue influences by pressure groups, legislative ethics, the seemingly endless gridlocks in government—a veritable litany of complaints.

Given the high level of public criticism and disgust, what might be done to improve the situation? The two articles in this section address what has become a favorite reform proposal of late—limiting the term of representatives to twelve years.

The first of these articles, written by Hendrik Hertzberg, advances the basic argument of those who would limit congressional terms: term limitation would encourage real political competition, severely limit the influence of seniority, produce energetic legislators, invigorate the two-party system, and open up public office to the average person. Indeed, Hertzberg argues that the mere "threat" of limiting incumbents would have such salutary effects.

Taking issue with these arguments is law professor Peter Kahn, who, in rebuttal, rejects the "simple answer" of the anti-incumbent reformers. According to Kahn, if the American people think Congress is in chaos now, they might want to think what it would be like with term limitations—a very weak body lacking in experience and encouraging shortsightedness and personal corruption.

# A Simple Cure for Chronic Incumbency: Twelve Is Enough

## Hendrik Hertzberg

Before you automatically reject the proposal now making the rounds for a twelve-year limit for members of Congress as a dreadful idea—an anti-democratic, anti-political, mechanistic "reform" that like so many other "reforms" would most likely end up making things worse, a bit of mischievous tinkering with the precious Constitution that has served us so well for 200 years, a misguided gimmick that ignores the *real* problem (PACs, polls, gerrymandering, special interests, negative ads, cowardly politicians, ignorant citizens, whatever) and is probably nothing but a Republican plot anyway—before you agree with all these dismissals and turn your attention to more pressing matters, consider three numbers.

Number number one: 37.1. Yes, it's a voter turnout figure, the op-ed writer's best friend. This particular figure represents the percentage of American over-eighteens who bestirred themselves to go to the polls in 1986, the last time the citizenry was invited to vote for members of Congress without the added glitz of a presidential contest. Compared with the turnout in any other arguably democratic country—France, Nicaragua, Norway, Hungary, El Salvador, Israel, Turkey, Italy, Lithuania, you name it—this is pathetic. It was the lowest since 1926, not counting 1944, when World War II made voting inconvenient for large numbers of people. And the public's true interest in House elections is even lower. According to *Congressional Quarterly*'s Rhodes Cook, if you factor out districts where there was a contest for governor or U.S. senator to lure people out, the turnout was a scandalous 27.6 percent. Only the most perverse elitists argue that this state of affairs is anything but a symptom of extreme political ill health.

Number number two: 98.3. This is the percentage of incumbent members of the House of Representatives who won their "races" for re-election in 1988, up from 98 percent flat in 1966. According to a recent study by David C. Huckabee of the Congressional Research Service of the Library of Congress, this number has remained in the 90s ever since 1974, and it is currently the highest it has ever been since the middle of President Washington's first term. And because more incumbents now choose to run than ever before, the re-election rate for the House as a whole is now in the 90s, too—92.4 percent last time out, to be exact. In the 19th century this figure tended to hover somewhere between 40 percent and 70 percent, once dropping to as low as 24 percent (in 1842); it hit the 70s after World War I and has been climbing more or less steadily ever since.

Hendrik Hertzberg is editor of *The New Republic* magazine. This article is from "Twelve Is Enough," by Hendrik Hertzberg, *The New Republic*, May 14, 1990, pp. 22–26.

**192**

The 98.3 figure actually understates the political stasis of the House. Of the 409 incumbents who ran for re-election, six were defeated in November. But five of these had been tainted by one sort of scandal or another. So the grand total of representatives who lost their seats as a consequence of what we normally think of as politics—that is, a process in which the electorate chooses between competing sets of programs and policies—was exactly one.

Number number three: 36. This is how many years a single party, the Democrats, has controlled the lower house of the national legislature of the United States. By contrast, the British House of Commons has changed hands four times since 1954, the French Chamber of Deputies three times, the West German Bundestag five times, the Canadian House of Commons five times, and the Indian Lok Sabha three times. When it comes to one-party legislative dominance in serious countries, only Japan, Mexico, South Africa, and the Soviet Union are even in our league. And in the last two, unlike in the United States, the ruling party is a pretty good bet to lose the next election. No moral equivalence intended, of course. Or deserved.

In the light of numbers number two and three, the wonder is that number number one is so high. In the overwhelming majority of congressional districts, voting is increasingly an irrational act. Why bother, when 85 percent of the incumbents are getting more than 60 percent of the vote in their districts, when the *average* incumbent is getting 73.5 percent, when sixty-three members are returned with Brezhnevian majorities exceeding 94 percent? Except in the handful of districts where there are open seats or close races, voting may still make sense as a civic sacrament—as a way of refreshing one's soul with a sense of belonging to a democratic community—but it makes no sense as a form of political action. Better to spend the hour or so it takes to vote writing checks and sending them off to candidates in contested districts.

Against this background, the idea of a twelve-year limit begins to acquire a certain logic. Such proposals are neither new nor flakily marginal. A limit on congressional service was considered at the founding constitutional convention (which laid it aside as "entering too much into detail"), and the idea has won the support, over the decades, of a bipartisan list of luminaries including Abraham Lincoln, Harry Truman, Dwight D. Eisenhower, and John F. Kennedy. The current campaign for a constitutional amendment that would limit service to six two-year terms for House members and two six-year terms for senators (with an exemption for the present crew of incumbents, of course) is led by Senators Gordon Humphrey, Republican of New Hampshire, and Dennis DeConcini, Democrat of Arizona. Their ten co-sponsors span the Senate's ideological spectrum, from Jake Garn on the right to Nancy Kassebaum in the center to Tom Daschle on the left. . . .

The arguments for the term limit are surprisingly persuasive, especially where the House is concerned. Almost all of them are variations on a single theme: breaking the Gordian knot of entrenched incumbency, which distorts our democracy from the polling place clear up to the Senate and (especially) House chambers. Out in that fabled land beyond the Beltway, the term limit would mean that at least once every twelve years (and probably more frequently), every citizen would get a fighting chance to vote in a genuinely *political* congressional election, which is to say one that would turn not on the goodies that good old Congressman Thing has procured for the district or the Social Security checks he has expedited or the campaign funds he has raised or the newsletters he has franked, but rather on the competing political visions and programs of parties and candidates. But the most interesting, and salutary, effects of the limit would be the ways in which it would change the political ecology of Congress itself.

A twelve-year limit would necessarily bring an end to the much-reformed but still pervasive and undemocratic rule of seniority. The House Speaker, the chairmen of important committees, and the other potentates of Congress have long been elevated by a decades-long, quasi-feudal process of favor-trading, personal alliance-building, ladder-climbing, and "getting along by going along." The term limit would leave Congress little choice but to elect its chiefs democratically, on the basis of the policies and the leadership qualities of the candidates. Like the Speakers of many of our state legislatures, these leaders would tend to be vigorous men and women in their forties and fifties—people in the mold of Bill Gray, Stephen Solarz, and Henry Hyde. The Dingells and Rostenkowskis would remain where they belong, on the back benches or in private life. This would be an important gain. And the frequent turnover of leaders—one who served more than six years would be a rarity—would be a spur both to brisk accomplishment and to attentiveness to the concerns and needs of the country.

The seniority system occasionally produces good leaders as well as bad ones, but there is no denying that it is grossly biased in favor of the most politically sluggish and unchanging parts of the nation. A swing district—one marked by close elections, and the robust debate and clamorous participation that close elections bring—has a hard time keeping somebody in office long enough to survive the glacial process by which congressional power is accumulated. It is precisely such districts that are most likely to elect representatives alive to the cutting-edge problems that most urgently require action. Systematically disempowering these districts and the people representing them, as the current arrangement so efficiently does, is insane.

A Congress invigorated by frequent infusions of new blood would be a more responsive, more democratic, more varied place. So would a Congress whose majority regularly changed from one party to the other, which a term limit would unquestionably promote. However bad this might be for the short-term partisan interests of Democrats like me, it would be good for the long-term interests of the country—and the party, too. Critics of the term limit idea argue that it would "weaken" Congress; and so it would, but in ways that would strengthen both its most useful functions and democratic governance in general. The one-party Congress has become a world unto itself, and the long period of Republican control of the presidency and Democratic control of Congress has produced an insidious mentality on Capitol Hill. The leaders of the Democratic congressional majority, veterans of decades of supremacy in their own little universe, no longer constitute an opposition. They conceive of themselves as ins, not outs—as leaders of one-half of a permanent coalition government. They may imagine that their own fiefdoms are secure, but their party is reaping almost all of the penalties of incumbency and almost none of the benefits. The foundations of Democratic congressional dominance are being relentlessly undermined, and once the structure topples, as eventually it must, rebuilding it will seem as hopeless a task as destroying it does now. A Congress shaped by a term limit would have a different and healthier mentality. During periods when it was controlled by the party that also controls the White House, it would be energetic in pursuit of that party's program; when in opposition, it would—for a change, and just as energetically—oppose.

The many Americans who deplore the decline of political parties in this country ought especially to welcome the term limit idea. By routinely undermining the totally independent, totally personal power bases that long-serving senators and representatives are able to build and maintain under the current system, and by dramatically increasing the number of elections fought on the basis of national issues, the term limit would enhance the strength and coherence of both national parties.

The term limit would mean that at any given moment something like sixty or seventy representatives, and perhaps half that number of senators, would be ineligible to run again. To critics of the proposal, this is one of its worst features. The lame ducks, say the critics, would be "unaccountable" and unresponsive to their constituents' wishes. But Congress's problem is hardly that its members are insufficiently obsessed with re-election, insufficiently attentive to polling data, and insufficiently ardent in pursuit of district pork barrel. The broader public good could only benefit from having a cohort of comparatively disinterested legislators, relieved from re-election pressures and free to consult their consciences as well as their pollsters and contributors. The critics add that the lame ducks might fall prey to corruption, legal or illegal. This phenomenon is not exactly unknown under present arrangements. But it would not be more likely to happen if most of the departing members are still relatively young and still ambitious. Why should they feather their nests at the cost of their reputations?

It's true, as the critics also say, that the term limit would deprive Congress of the services of legislators whom experience has made wise. This would be a real cost. But it would be a cost worth paying to be rid of the much larger number of timeservers who have learned nothing from longevity in office except cynicism, complacency, and a sense of diminished possibility. And it's not as if the job of being a congressman is so difficult that it takes decades to master. It's easier than being a first-rate schoolteacher, for example, and no harder than such jobs as president, governor, or mayor—all of which are regularly performed very well indeed by people who have had no on-the-job experience at all.

In any case, the senators and representatives obliged to seek other employment after twelve years will not vanish from the face of the earth. They will be available for service in the executive branch, in industry, in advocacy groups, and in the academy. Few will become lobbyists, because the turnover on the Hill will quickly make their contacts obsolete and their influence unpeddlable. Many will run for other public offices. Representatives will run for senator, senators will run for representative, and both will run for president, governor, mayor, and state legislator. The result will be more and better competition for these jobs, too. This would not be such a bad thing. Membership in Congress would no longer be a life calling or a lifetime sinecure, but this would not be such a bad thing either. A shot at Congress would be an attractive option for the young and ambitious, for the old but still energetic, and for men and women in midlife who want something more meaningful than whatever success they have earned elsewhere. There would be no shortage of candidates. Though harder to keep, the job would be easier to get.

A Gallup Poll taken in December found that 70 percent of the American public favors the idea of a term limit. This is uncannily close to the percentages of the public that (*a*) think Congress is doing a lousy job and (*b*) keep on voting to re-elect the same old incumbents. Opponents of the term limit say that if voters are so fed up with Congress, there is a simple way for them to do something about it without tinkering with the Constitution: "Throw the rascals out," as *The Chicago Tribune* suggests. So why don't they? "The explanation," writes my friend Michael Kinsley ("Voters in Chains," TNR, April 2), "is that the voters are lazy hypocrites." Maybe they are, but that's not the explanation. A given voter can vote to throw out a maximum of one rascal—three if you count senators. The problem is not individual incumbents; it's chronic incumbency, and trying to solve it by removing one's own incumbent is like treating tuberculosis with a cough drop. To tell a voter he can solve the problem of chronic incumbency by voting against his own representative is to recommend a particularly fruitless form of single-issue politics. The public's disgust is with Congress as an institution, and defeating one member out of 535 won't revamp Congress any more than firing the Deputy Assistant to the President for Scheduling would revamp the White House.

Thanks to seniority, voting to remove a long-serving congressman necessarily means voting to replace him with someone who will have less power. It therefore means voting to deprive one's district (and oneself) of clout. That's fine if you truly think your representative is a rascal. But what if you simply think he's a mediocrity?

There has to be a better way, and the twelve-year limit just might be it. The movement for it deserves the support of all who think Congress is broke and needs fixing—even those who, unlike me, don't think the limit itself is a particularly good idea. Let's be realistic: the chances a term limit amendment will actually get enacted are pretty remote. Congress, for obvious reasons, is not likely to pass it, and the other route—a constitutional convention called by two-thirds of the state legislatures—has never been successfully traveled. But the movement to impose a limit, if it catches fire, could throw enough of a scare into the Congress we've got to induce it to make changes—in campaign financing, PAC spending, access to television, mandatory campaign debates, and so on—that would accomplish most if not all of the same salutary results. The term limit movement is potentially like the nuclear freeze movement of the early 1980s. As a policy blueprint the freeze proposal left a lot to be desired. But the movement did a world of good by forcing the Reagan administration to offer serious arms control proposals of its own, most of which the Russians eventually accepted. The freeze movement was a cri de coeur. So is the term limit movement. Listen, Congress.

# A Word in Defense of Incumbents

## Peter L. Kahn

The next earthquake in California will probably be a political one. Proposals to limit the time politicians hold office are on the November ballot, and likely to pass. A measure to throw the rascals out just passed in Oklahoma, and others are under consideration in Colorado, Missouri and elsewhere. There is even talk of a constitutional amendment that would, in the name of good government, sweep from office the likes of Sam Nunn, Bill Bradley and Pete Domenici.

Thanks, but I'd rather keep those rascals in. Few proposals seem less likely to produce good government.

Limiting tenure limits the expertise and experience of those facing the complex and subtle problems of government. This is not just because less time passes while a politician holds office. Because his time is limited, he has less reason to spend time understanding policy issues. Though it may seem those clowns don't have expertise anyway, think what the military might look like without a Sam Nunn or Barry Goldwater to keep tabs on it. Power inevitably will be transferred to bureaucrats and lobbyists around long before and long after the brief life span of the legislator.

Officeholders can spend time saved not thinking about their present job by thinking about the next. They'd only be sensible to consider the opportunities they'll have when their short time in government is over. While some might trust to the fates, others will take more direct action to ensure their futures. Incumbents will not only be less able; they'll be more corrupt.

Weak incumbents invite weak challengers. It takes less to beat them. Possible candidates with attractive private careers are less likely to disrupt those careers to participate briefly in government. The field will offer unusual opportunities to the undesirable. Fringe candidates like David Duke might well be attracted to such opportunities.

Imagine, then, a contest between two poor candidates, each with a weak grasp of issues and little record. The result seems sure to be ever more vicious and irrelevant campaigns and a premium on image and innuendo, cheapening an already degraded electoral process.

And once these brave new legislators get into office, they'll have just a few short years to make their mark. Better get busy. No climbing the ladder of leadership for them: pull out all the stops to get your program, or just to get attention. If they're all short-timers, there will be no leaders to corral the

Peter L. Kahn is a professor of law at the Catholic University of America, Washington, D.C. From Peter L. Kahn, "A Word in Defense of Incumbents," *The Washington Post*, October 23, 1990, A-21. © *The Washington Post*.

disruptive, teach the unwashed, or frame balanced policies. If you think Congress is chaotic now, just wait.

It's hard to see why we'd want these measures. The idea seems to be that term limits will make politicians more responsive to the voters. But a lame-duck incumbent, without hope of re-election and immune to the voters' wrath, can pursue his own agenda. The term-limited legislature will contain a large number of members in their last terms contemplating retirement. That government would be less—not more—responsive.

Incumbents do win with almost disgusting regularity. That's not completely strange: people win the first time because they have some appeal for the voters, a characteristic not all challengers share. But they also have some powerful advantages, due largely to the bizarre system of campaign finance created after the Watergate scandal. That's a system ripe for reform.

But the dramatic unintended results of the Watergate reforms tell us it's not easy to improve the electoral process. Term limits have a lot in common with Mr. Bush's "read my lips" tax pledge: lots of quick fix and sex appeal, not much attention to unpleasant details. Simple answers aren't always so simple.

The citizen-legislator has almost a mythic appeal as a Mr. Smith who'd go to Washington and give voice to the plain common sense of the people. Mr. Smith, of course, was a Hollywood creation, designed to appeal to our vanity. It's comfortable to think we'd have good government if only those politicians would listen to us. But the budget mess arose because they were already trying too hard to give us what we wanted. We have met the enemy and, as usual, it is us.

What term limitation advocates have in common is the belief that Congress fouled things up. They want to stick it to politicians who didn't do what they should have. But what should the politicians do? Agreement on that little issue will be no greater after term limitation than before.

To quote Jack Gargan, a leader of the term limitation movement, "we can't do any worse" than the current incumbents. Oh, yes we can. Just wait and see.

# 11

# Presidential Power

In the first selection, George McGovern, a former U.S. senator and one-time Democratic presidential nominee (1972), reflects upon the state of the presidency and finds reason to be concerned—a concern, incidentally, he insists would be shared by the Founding Fathers were they alive today. Nearly all our post–World War II presidents, he charges, have at one time or another embarked upon foreign policy ventures that were in clear violation of the Constitution and the laws. Not only were these initiatives illegal, but many were misguided as well, damaging our reputation abroad and/or the credibility of the presidency at home. As he sees it, there is only one sure antidote to this disturbing pattern of presidential behavior, and that is electing a president committed to the constitutional principles set forth by the framers.

R. Gordon Hoxie, who currently serves as president of the Center for the Study of the Presidency, is unpersuaded by McGovern's analysis. He contends that the former senator misunderstands how the framers and other early statesmen conceived of the president's foreign policy role. Nor does he agree that the foreign policy initiatives cited by McGovern were necessarily illegal, unwise, or undertaken only by our more recent presidents. Finally, in contrast to McGovern, Hoxie concludes that whatever misfirings have occurred in American foreign policy since World War II, they are attributable more to a meddling Congress than to an unrestrained president.

# We Need a Constitutional Presidency

**George McGovern**

. . . My modest and practical hope is that the President elected in 1988 will pursue his policies, however different from mine, within the framework of the Constitution. America does not need another imperial Presidency; we urgently need a *constitutional Presidency*.

When a new President takes office, he raises his right hand, places his left hand on the bible, looks the Chief Justice of the Supreme Court in the eye and then swears to "preserve, protect and defend the Constitution of the United States." Included in Article II of the Constitution under the President's responsibilities are these words: "he shall take Care that the Laws be faithfully executed."

This is the only pledge a President is legally bound to execute. No one really expects (or wants, in all probability) a new President to execute every plank in his campaign platform. But we do have a right to expect a President to honor his constitutional oath and to execute the laws of the land—even those laws he may not personally like.

Unfortunately, many of our Presidents since the end of World War II have violated the law and the Constitution. From Korea, the Bay of Pigs and Vietnam to Watergate, Iran and the covert war in Nicaragua, Presidents have weakened the nation and their own credibility by dishonoring the Constitution.

Most of these violations have been made in the name of national security; most were schemes hatched in secret by a handful of people around the President; most were not only illegal, but also poorly conceived ideas that embarrassed the nation. These constitutional crises know no party preference; they have afflicted Democratic and Republican administrations alike.

In 1947, with the cold war gathering momentum, President Harry Truman created the Central Intelligence Agency to strengthen and coordinate the gathering of foreign intelligence. Almost from the beginning, the CIA engaged not only in the collection of intelligence information, but also in covert operations which involved rigging elections and manipulating labor unions abroad, carrying on paramilitary operations, overturning governments, assassinating foreign officials, protecting former Nazis and lying to Congress.

In later years, Truman expressed deep regret over these operations. But the practices have continued, and, what is more significant, they seem to have infected the behavior of our national-security officials from the President on down the line. If it is acceptable for the CIA to break the law in the name of

George McGovern is a former member of the U.S. Senate from the state of South Dakota (1962–1980) and Democratic candidate for President in 1972. From George McGovern, "We Need a *Constitutional* Presidency," *Parade Magazine,* August 9, 1987, pp. 12–14.

national security, why shouldn't others place national security above and beyond the reach of the Constitution?

President Truman's quick decision in 1950 to enter the Korean war without waiting for a Congressional debate and declaration of war is generally hailed as an example of courageous and decisive leadership. But it was an unconstitutional act that quickly turned sour with the American public and Congress.

In 1954, during the Eisenhower Administration, the CIA under Allen Dulles successfully plotted a covert military coup that overthrew the newly elected Guatemalan leader, President Jacobo Arbenz, a socialist. This action, of which Dulles boasted publicly, was not only a violation of American and international law; it was also a repudiation of America's traditional commitment to self-determination of people.

This kind of crass interference in Central America—both covert and overt—has cost the U.S. dearly, weakening our standing in the eyes of Latin Americans. Such cynical, illegal tactics may serve the short-term interests of a few corporations doing business in Central America; they do not serve the interests of peace and justice or the long-term interests of the American people.

The Bay of Pigs debacle early in the administration of John F. Kennedy was another classic example of a secretive, illegal and badly conceived plan that not only violated the constitutional system of checks and balances but also damaged the international position of the U.S. It also was one of several factors that caused President Kennedy to deepen U.S. military involvement in Vietnam.

President Lyndon Johnson expanded that involvement into a major war. President Richard Nixon continued the war for four more years, including a secret 14-month bombing campaign against Cambodia in 1969–1970. He and his associates consistently denied that they were bombing neutral Cambodia while ordering the Air Force to fake the records and continue bombing. The whole disastrous intervention finally collapsed in defeat with the fall of Saigon and the ignominious airlift of the American Ambassador from the roof of our embassy in 1975.

This calamitous, enormously costly American military venture was for the most part an Executive Branch war. There was never a Congressional declaration of war, nor was one ever requested.

And it was the Nixon Administration's effort to plug the leaks to the press on the illegal bombing of Cambodia that led to the creation of the "plumbers" at the White House with their illegal taps on the phones of key White House aides and members of the press. A strong case can be made that the conspiratorial atmosphere that led to the Watergate scandals and the destruction of the Nixon Administration had its origin in the Indochina war. An unconstitutional and ill-conceived policy abroad came home to poison the wells of our domestic politics.

One of the plusses of the Watergate affair was that it was supposed to have been such a painful lesson that the nation could reasonably hope that no subsequent President would repeat it for a long time to come. But in the fall of 1986—only 14 years after Watergate—it was revealed that the [Reagan] Administration was secretly selling arms to the worst terrorist government in the world and illegally diverting the proceeds to the Contra forces seeking to sabotage the Nicaraguan government.

Both ends of this bizarre operation appeared to be in violation of the law. The much-debated Boland Amendment prohibited the government from supplying military aid to the Contras. Federal law—in addition to the Administration's announced foreign policy—prohibits the sale of arms to terrorist states. The law does give the President authority to set this barrier aside if he finds such arms sales in the national interest, but only if he so informs the Congress. No such finding was provided, and, in fact, the Administration made a conscious decision to withhold knowledge of the sales from the Congress and key members of the Administration. Clearly, it seems to me, a number of federal statutes appear to have been violated. And for what end?

When Franklin D. Roosevelt made 50 overage destroyers available to the British at the time when the U.S. was still officially a neutral nation, he broke the law—but he did so to advance the security interest of this country. In the Iran-Contra scam, it would appear that the law was set aside for an operation that ran counter to both the national interest and the stated foreign policy of our government. These factors have led many of our friends abroad to the conclusion that the current violations are more serious than the Watergate affair.

Iran represents the kind of extreme and dangerous fanaticism that threatens to end hope for peace and stability in the Middle East. Yet, the anti-aircraft and anti-tank weapons that the [Reagan] Administration provided were precisely the weapons Iran needed to overcome the advantage Iraq had in planes and tanks to offset the greater Iranian manpower.

The earlier support of the invasion of Grenada in 1983 and the bombing of Libya in 1986—both in violation of international and American law—doubtless contributed to the feeling inside the White House that illegal, high-handed tactics were acceptable for a popular President.

Perhaps if Congress, the media and the public had insisted all along on constitutional behavior, the Administration might have been less inclined to ignore the laws relating to Iran and Nicaragua.

The greatest irony in virtually all the cases of illegal, covert actions that have come to light is that they have not only weakened our constitutional democracy, but also have been foreign-policy mistakes. Some have seriously weakened our credibility in the world. All have been counterproductive in their aftereffects.

There may have been illegal covert activities that were successful in advancing American interests which I do not know about. But, as a long-time Senator and member of the Foreign Relations Committee vitally interested in foreign relations, I am convinced that the net result of all these operations, including undeclared wars, has been to weaken the nation.

The constitutional framers foresaw the dangers of unchecked executive power. They constructed a system of checks and balances, which placed the war-declaring power in the Congress and the execution of war in the President's hands. They would have been appalled by the secretive, unchecked unilateral operations that have been carried out by Presidents and their staffs in recent decades. They would not have been surprised by the dangerous and self-defeating results of this imperial behavior.

. . . [In 1987, we observed] the Bicentennial of the Constitution, marking the 200th anniversary of that historic convention in Philadelphia when 55 statesmen struggled throughout the summer to lay the foundations of the world's greatest and oldest constitutional democracy. Some historians believe that Madison, Hamilton, Franklin, Washington and their fellow delegates comprised the ablest group of political leaders assembled in American history. They, of course, reflected some of the prejudices of their age in omitting political rights for women and tolerating the evil of slavery. But it is easy to accept Franklin's assessment that the new Constitution provided the horizon for "a rising sun" in the young nation.

Recognizing that changing needs and perspectives would result in amendments of the founding document, Washington—who had presided over the constitutional deliberations and was to become the first President to serve under the newly drafted charter—wrote to his nephew Bushrod on November 10, 1987: "I do not think we are more inspired, have more wisdom, or possess more virtue, than those who will come after us."

The most important contribution we can make in this Bicentennial period to redeem Washington's faith is to elect a President who, in keeping with his oath, will truly honor the Constitution.

# We Have a Constitutional Presidency: What We Need Is a Constitutional Congress

## R. Gordon Hoxie

In a recent essay, looking toward the 1988 Presidential election, former United States Senator George McGovern asserts, "America does not need another imperial Presidency; we urgently need a *constitutional Presidency.*"[1] My position is diametrically different from that of Senator McGovern, albeit I respect him for his illustrious careers as a teacher, senator, and now senior statesman. Far from our having an "imperial presidency," we have had, at least since 1973, an *imperiled* presidency, imperiled by a Congress seeking to go outside its own constitutional parameters. Hence, I conclude we need a *constitutional Congress.*

First, I shall examine the historical examples Senator McGovern uses to illustrate his charges of unconstitutional presidential actions in foreign policy. His selective recall is limited to the so-called modern presidency, from Franklin Roosevelt to the present. However, it is my contention that the precedents for many of the presidential actions McGovern criticizes were established as early as the first Washington administration by those who had been Framers of the Constitution, notably Alexander Hamilton and George Washington himself. Further, I shall contend that the Framers desired an energetic presidency with primacy vis-à-vis Congress in the conduct of foreign affairs; that the Supreme Court has affirmed that primacy; and that Congress has unwisely attempted to preempt the president's role in foreign affairs.

## THE MCGOVERN CHARGES

With the curious exception of President Carter, Senator McGovern charges every president from Franklin Roosevelt to the present with unconstitutional actions in the conduct of American foreign policy. He lets Roosevelt off easiest with his transfer of "50 overage destroyers" to Great Britain in the early part of World War II "when the U.S. was still officially a neutral nation," since he says this was designed "to advance the security interest of this country." The same could be said for the motivation of the other presidents he criticizes, beginning with Truman. He terms Truman's commitment of U.S. armed forces in the Korean War "without waiting for a Congressional debate and declaration of war" as being "an unconstitutional act." But the simple fact is that had Truman awaited such congressional action, North Korea's conquest of South

R. Gordon Hoxie is president of the Center for the Study of the Presidency, Washington, D.C. This essay was written especially for *Points of View* in 1988.

Korea would have been completed. Moreover, Truman did cite the United Nations Charter and the resolution of the U.N. Security Council as justification for his action. With the lightning speed of military operations in modern warfare, it is doubtful whether it will ever again be possible to await a declaration of war before commencing decisive military action. McGovern condemns Eisenhower's covert intervention in Guatemala, in which the United States helped to overthrow a regime hostile to the United States, as "a repudiation of America's traditional commitment to self-determination of people." However, earlier presidents, notably Theodore Roosevelt in the Panamanian revolt against Colombia, also intervened on behalf of certain Colombian factions sympathetic to the security interests (in that instance, the Panama Canal) of the United States.

But it was the U.S. participation in the Vietnam war which, in retrospect, was particularly upsetting to McGovern, who calls that effort "an Executive Branch War." He ignores the Gulf of Tonkin Resolution whereby Congress registered its support for preventing further aggression by North Vietnam. He further ignores the fact that if the Congress had been as uninvolved or opposed to the war as he implies, it would not have appropriated the funds for the war's support. He condemns President Nixon's "bombing neutral Cambodia," but there was nothing "neutral" about the Communist forces there. On March 27, 1973, President Nixon announced that the bombing of Communist troops in Cambodia would continue until the Communists agreed to a cease-fire. It was Congress on August 15, 1973, that passed legislation ending all military action in Southeast Asia. Two years later, of course, both South Vietnam and Cambodia came under the control of Communist North Vietnam. McGovern refers to "the ignominious airlift of the American Ambassador from the roof of our embassy in 1975." It was Congress, not the president, that had terminated support and caused this debacle. Whether the United States should have been involved in Vietnam is questionable, although we and seven other nations had been signators to the 1954 Southeast Asia Collective Defense Treaty pledging joint action to protect South Vietnam and other nations in the area. But having participated in the involvement, Congress should have supported the effort to take such diplomatic, economic, and military measures as would have precluded the Communist victory, the fall of the South Vietnamese and Cambodian governments, and the tragedy that has subsequently befallen millions of people in these two countries.

Perhaps most far-fetched is McGovern's allegation "that the conspiratorial atmosphere that led to the Watergate scandals . . . had its origins in the Indochina war." The war had nothing to do with the Watergate break-in or President Nixon's effort to protect his staff, the so-called cover-up which, under congressional pressure, led to Nixon's resignation.

McGovern finds "the invasion of Grenada in 1983 and the bombing of Libya in 1986 both a violation of international and American law." The American students rescued have a different view of the Grenada effort and so doubtless would such a concerned constitutionalist as Thomas Jefferson of the

Libyan bombing. Without consulting the Congress, in 1802 Jefferson sent the United States Navy to do its own bombing on the North African coast. Historians of an earlier era had no constitutional qualms in writing of such events. Professor Andrew C. McLaughlin, a distinguised constitutional scholar, wrote in 1900: "The American navy won the honor of teaching these robber nations that they must behave themselves and that blackmailing must cease." As much could be said of the U.S. Air Force bombing of Libya under the direction of the Commander-in-Chief in 1986.

Finally, McGovern voices his indignation over the Iran-Contra affair and his approval of "the much debated Boland Amendment" which cut off aid to the Contras seeking to overthrow the Soviet-supported Sandinista regime in Nicaragua. Actually, from 1982 to 1985 there were five Boland Amendments, which vacillated between granting aid and cutting it off. It was the uncertainty created by this on-again, off-again approach that led to the desperate attempt to find other sources of aid, including the "Iran-Contra Caper" which, according to McGovern, was seeking "to sabotage the Nicaraguan government." And why not "sabotage" Daniel Ortega's efforts to build a military dictatorship in Nicaragua hostile to its neighbors, especially El Salvador, which was seeking to establish a democratic government? The president of the United States was endeavoring to prevent the spread of communism from Nicaragua to El Salvador, Honduras, Guatemala, and even to Mexico. The congressional prohibitions were largely inspired by public relations polls indicating that the majority of those polled believed the United States had no vital concern in that area and a Vietnam-type war might result.

The Boland Amendments were as ill-conceived as the 1976 congressional legislation cutting off aid to the anti-Communist forces in Angola. As a result of congressional ineptitude in 1976, abetted by substantial Soviet and Cuban support for the Marxists in Angola, that strategically important land with major oil resources became a Communist state. After the Communist governments became entrenched in Angola and Nicaragua, Congress in both instances repealed its prohibition of aid to the anti-Communist guerrillas. In June 1986, Congress voted $100 million in aid for the Contras. In February 1988, however, by a narrow margin the House again cut off aid to the Contras, although both the Senate and the President would have continued the assistance.

Both the Angolan and the Nicaraguan experiences exemplify the fact that Congress cannot effectively direct foreign policy operations. The Angolan Communist regime is propped up by 30,000 Cuban troops battling the anti-Communist guerrillas and American oil companies which generate the funds to keep the Communist government intact, even though the United States does not officially recognize that government. In the case of Nicaragua, President Ortega* alternates between visiting the Soviet Union and seven other Communist governments to get funds and meeting with members of the U.S. Congress

---

*Daniel Ortega was defeated in a bid to become the popularly elected president of Nicaragua in 1990—*Editors.*

to get them to stop aid to the Contras. Assuredly, the constitutional Framers would never have countenanced such confusion in foreign policy.

## THE VIEWS OF THE CONSTITUTIONAL FRAMERS

Senator McGovern's reading of post–World War II history is even more distracting in a bicentennial period by his endeavoring to relate his views to those of the Framers in 1787. McGovern asserts, "Madison, Hamilton, Franklin, Washington, and their fellow delegates," would have been shocked by the "imperial behavior" of the modern presidency. He concludes: "The most important contribution we can make in this Bicentennial period to redeem Washington's faith is to elect a president, who in keeping with his oath, will truly honor the Constitution."

What were the *real* views of the Framers, especially of Washington and those who worked with him in launching the government under the Constitution? Early in his essay, Senator McGovern cites from Article II of the Constitution, as regards the President: "he shall take Care that the Laws be faithfully executed." He contends, "This is the only pledge a President is legally bound to execute." Thus, McGovern would appear to conceive of the president as a caretaker, not as the initiator and interpreter of the Constitution. McGovern portrays Congress, the media, and the public (not the Courts) as telling the president what is "constitutional behavior." Yet the Framers who created the presidency, notably James Wilson, Gouverneur Morris, Washington, and Hamilton, had a different view. They envisioned an energetic executive.

The presidency clearly established its dominant position in the foreign policy sphere during the first Washington administration (1789–1793). As early as 1790, the first Secretary of State, Thomas Jefferson, asserted: "The transaction of business with foreign nations is *Executive altogether . . . Exceptions are to be construed strictly"* [emphasis added]. Likewise, Hamilton contended that the Constitution granted the president full authority in foreign relations except when it provided otherwise for Congress by specifically enumerated powers. (These included declarations of war and appropriation of funds and, for the Senate, its advice and consent functions on appointments and treaties). Writing in 1793, Hamilton asserted: "The President is the Constitutional EXECUTOR of the laws. . . . He who is to execute the laws," Hamilton concluded, "must first judge for himself of their meaning." These observations were precipitated by an incident between Washington and Hamilton on the one hand and Secretary of State Jefferson (who for political reasons had broken with Hamilton and taken Congressman Madison with him) and Congress on the other as to who or what body was the interpreter of the meaning of the 1778 treaty of alliance with France. By his Neutrality Proclamation in the war between France and Great Britain, Washington in effect annulled Article XI of the treaty. Congress, egged on by Jefferson and Madison, was annoyed by this action but nonetheless accepted Washington's position. Contrast this with the present Congress. As of this writing, Senator majority leader Robert C. Byrd and Senator Sam Nunn, chairman of the Armed Services Committee, are threatening to hold up approval of the new Soviet-American treaty banning ground-launched medium- and shorter-range missiles (INF) unless the Reagan administration accepts their interpretation of the 1972 Antiballistic Missile Treaty. Further, though the administration protests such actions as unconstitutional, the Senate majority is proposing a binding attachment to the INF Treaty that the president must have Senate approval on future interpretations of the treaty. This is completely counter to the 1793 Washington view that since the initiation of treaties resided with the president, the president alone should determine whether treaties should be, as Hamilton expressed it, "continued or suspended."

Further jockeying between Congress and president occurred in both the first and second Washington administrations with respect to establishing the principle of executive privilege (denying to the Congress correspondence within the executive branch). In the first instance in 1793, when a House committee was investigating the defeat of General Arthur St. Clair by the Indians, Washington told his Cabinet: "There might be papers of so select a nature, as they might not be given up." Having established the principle, with Hamilton's assurance that "there was not a paper which might not be properly produced," the papers were produced. In a second instance in 1794, a communication from Gouverneur Morris, then representing the United States in Paris, was withheld from the Senate. Finally, in 1796 a defiant House of Representatives, before approving an appropriation bill related to the Jay Treaty with Great Britain, demanded correspondence between Jay and the administration. Reasserting the executive privilege principle, however, President Washington still withheld certain papers. Ultimately, the House approved appropriating funds to put the treaty in force, but only by a margin of one vote.

Clearly Senator McGovern views all covert actions by the government with derision, finding them "counterproductive" and "illegal." But what was the opinion of the Framers and members of the first Washington administration? They believed the early establishment of an intelligence community was an urgent need for the nation. In arguing for the adoption of the Constitution, John Jay, who had managed foreign affairs under the old Articles of Confederation, wrote in *The Federalist* that by the authority of the new Constitution, the president "will be able to manage the business of intelligence in such manner as prudence may suggest." Subsequently, Hamilton recognized that there should be a congressional oversight role in intelligence operations, but proposed that it be limited to three members of the House and three members of the Senate. To include more, he believed, would create security problems. Yet today both Senate and House have large intelligence committees. Of course, covert operations should be appropriately reviewed. The recent Tower Commission, which investigated President Reagan's handling of the Iran-Contra affair, recommended that ". . . each administration formulate precise procedures for restricted consideration of covert action and, once formulated, those procedures be strictly adhered to.'' Still, the number of people involved in the review process should not be so great as to compromise the necessary secrecy that must be maintained in a covert operation.

Clearly the views of the Framers, underscored by the record of the first administration, established the principle of presidential primacy in foreign policy, including the interpretation of treaties, executive privilege, and the conduct of covert operations.

## THE CONTINUING STRUGGLE, 1800–1945

Despite congressional misgivings, the principles of presidential primacy in foreign policy, conceived by the Framers and established in the Washington administration, were continued in subsequent administrations. The requirements Hamilton had enunciated for the successful conduct of foreign policy— "decision, activity, secrecy, and dispatch"—could not characterize a body as large and unwieldy as Congress. Washington's successors—John Adams, Jefferson, Madison, Monroe, John Quincy Adams, and Jackson—all broadly interpreted their executive authority. Jefferson, for example, seized upon the opportunity to increase the national domain by the Louisiana Purchase, even though he could find no authority for it in the Constitution. He assuaged his conscience by suggesting a constitutional amendment for future similar actions, something which was not acted upon. Ironically, where both he and Madison had sought to stir up congressional opposition to the Washington-Hamilton foreign policy initiatives, they in turn were bitterly attacked by Congress for their own policies. In the case of Jefferson, the opposition to his embargo cutting off trade with both Britain and France as a neutral measure in the Napoleonic Wars literally forced him to retreat to Monticello in the last months of the presidency. Congress would also turn on President James Madison in the War of 1812 with Britain. They called it "Mr. Madison's War," and New England threatened secession.

During all these early presidencies, the national authority in foreign affairs was strengthened by the nation's greatest Chief Justice, John Marshall, who had long recognized presidential primacy in foreign policy. While serving in the House of Representatives (1799–1800), Marshall declared: "The President is the sole organ of the nation in its external relations and its sole representative with foreign nations. He possesses the whole Executive power. He holds and directs the force of the Nation." President Adams rewarded Marshall for his support by making him secretary of state in 1800 and, just before leaving the presidency in 1801, appointed him as Chief Justice.

It was the nation's greatest president, Abraham Lincoln, who most fully and effectively found authority in the constitutional mandate to "take care that the laws be faithfully executed" to assert a strong leadership role in foreign and military affairs. Through this and his interpretation of "executive power" and his role as commander-in-chief, he took such steps as he deemed necessary to preserve the Union: raising an army, blockading the southern ports, and even suspending the writ of habeas corpus, thereby throwing conspirators into jail without due process. Only after these extraordinary actions did he ask for and secure congressional approval. Only after the South was defeated and Lincoln was assassinated did the Supreme Court criticize his action. Still, a much later Chief Justice, William Howard Taft, contended: "Lincoln always pointed out the sources of authority which in his opinion justified his acts, and there was always a strong ground for maintaining the view which he held."

Theodore Roosevelt (1901–1909) too epitomized the energetic presidency. As a demonstration of American military strength, Roosevelt determined to send the Great White Fleet around the world. Despite the fact that Congress refused to fund this venture, Roosevelt as commander-in-chief directed the fleet to set sail anyway. Once it was halfway round the world, Congress capitulated and appropriated the money. President Wilson was also a strong foreign policy leader, dominating policymaking during World War I. But in the fight over America becoming a member of the League of Nations, which had been Wilson's creation, he was defeated. The Senate thereafter seized control of foreign policy, and did not relinquish it until the beginning of World War II, during the presidency of Franklin Roosevelt.

Meanwhile, in 1936, the Supreme Court reiterated the assertion earlier made by Hamilton, Jefferson, and Madison. More specifically, in the Curtis-Wright case, the Court stated: "In this vast external realm [i.e., foreign affairs] . . . the President alone has the power to speak or listen as a representative of the nation."

## THE POST–WORLD WAR II ERA

From 1946 to 1949 the relationship between the presidency and Congress in foreign affairs was a model of cooperation. Such harmony was due in no small part to the leadership of Republican Senator Arthur Vandenberg, whose bipartisan approach was instrumental in helping a Democratic president realize such landmark foreign policy initiatives as the Marshall Plan and the creation of NATO. Unfortunately, this relationship was shattered by Vandenberg's death in 1950 and by the lack of effective consultation between the presidency and Congress in the Korean War. Indeed, during this war, both Congress and Court rebuffed the President, the latter particularly in the Youngstown Sheet and Tube case (1952) where it overturned Truman's seizure of the steel mills which, during a labor dispute, he had ordered on grounds of national security.

Congress was also uneasy about the executive agreements Roosevelt and then Truman had concluded with the Soviet Union at Yalta and at Potsdam. When Eisenhower became President in 1953, he was immediately confronted with the proposed Bricker Amendment to the Constitution, which would have prevented presidents from entering into such executive agreements without congressional consent. After rereading the views of constitutional Framers

Hamilton and Madison, and also the views of John Jay in *The Federalist*, Eisenhower concluded such an amendment would have been a major step to "put us back" to the kind of government existing under the Articles of Confederation. Still, Congress came close to sending such an amendment to the states for ratification, defeating it by only a narrow margin.

Actually Eisenhower was the last president to enjoy relatively cordial relations with Congress. He was masterful in seeking out congressional advice. They protested it was unnecessary, but were obviously pleased that he did so. Indeed, following the end of the Eisenhower presidency, Senator J. William Fulbright, chairman of the Senate Foreign Relations Committee, wrote in 1961: ". . . for the existing requirements of American foreign policy we have hobbled the President by too niggardly a grant of power." A decade later Fulbright and other critics were singing another tune. As tensions mounted, Congress enacted a series of restrictive measures related to arms sales, foreign aid, human rights, intelligence, and trade. By the mid-1970s, Congress had again wrested from the presidency control of national security and foreign policy. *The New York Times* editorially observed that the congressional investigations of the intelligence community in this period were characterized by "a counterproductive rash of leaked reports and premature disclosures." Indeed, in the judgment of many, its restrictions on covert intelligence operations significantly diminished the nation's intelligence capabilities and lowered morale in the intelligence community. In addition, as noted earlier, it was at this time that Congress cut off aid to the democratic forces in Angola, thereby insuring Communist domination. Nor was this all. Inspired by pro-Greek lobbyists, Congress terminated aid to a strategically vital NATO ally, Turkey.

Perhaps the most confusing congressional measure to check the presidency during the 1970s was the 1973 War Powers Resolution, which barely passed over President Nixon's veto during the Watergate controversy. Each president has since called it unconstitutional and unsound. It defies the principle set forth by Hamilton in *Federalist* No. 74: "Of all the cares or concerns of government, the direction of war most peculiarly demands those qualities which distinguish the exercise of power by a single hand." By the War Powers Resolution, Congress contravenes the president's responsibilities as commander-in-chief. Most repugnant, the act allows Congress, by taking no action at all, to force the withdrawal of troops at the end of 90 days. In protest, President Ford put it this way in his final State of the Union Address on January 12, 1977: "There can be only one Commander-in-Chief." Indeed, Ford, Carter, and Reagan have all condemned having 535 commanders-in-chief and 535 chief diplomats in Congress.

By 1979 both Democratic and Republican leaders of the Senate had begun to reflect on these ill-advised efforts to control foreign policy operations. That year former Senator Fulbright wrote: "I confess to increasingly serious misgivings about the ability of the Congress to play a constructive role in our foreign relations." In 1981 the ranking Republican member of the Senate Armed Services Committee, John Tower, concluded: "Congress has inhibited the President's freedom of action and denied him the tools necessary for the formulation and implementation of American foreign policy." By 1984 William Bundy, long-time editor of *Foreign Affairs,* had reached a similar conclusion: "I cannot believe that the Founding Fathers, if they were brought back today, would have wished their (and our) treasured principle of checks and balances to be carried to the extent visible in far too many examples today. . . ." Moreover, this concern has been echoed on both sides of the aisle by such leading congressmen as Richard Cheney (R.–Wyo.) and Lee Hamilton (D.–Ind.). In a similar vein, Caspar Weinberger warned in his farewell address as Secretary of Defense, in November 1987: "Very few members of Congress see any danger in seizing control of the smallest and largest details of our nation's foreign and defense policies."

The congressional-executive balance in formulating and executing foreign policy should be restored. In the modern presidency, this balance was best epitomized in the Eisenhower years, which were characterized by effective consultation and disciplined leadership. The Eisenhower presidency was well staffed and well structured. It included the creation of an eight-member legislative liaison office with Congress. National security policy issues and programs were thoroughly studied through the National Security Council. Regrettably, in several subsequent administrations they have *not* been. The Special Assistant for National Security Affairs, a position created by Eisenhower, was low-keyed. Unfortunately, in several subsequent administrations they have not been. In the Eisenhower administration the secretary of state was clearly the principal foreign policy advisor to the president. Eisenhower, a Republican, sought out and worked effectively with the Democratic leadership of both houses of Congress. On the congressional side, there was far more disciplined leadership in the 1950s than exists today and far fewer congressional committees and subcommittees. Today there are 85 congressional subcommittees related to foreign policy. Congressional staffing has swollen enormously. Interest groups and political action committees have multiplied. The conduct of foreign policy has become much more difficult, and the national interest has become blurred.

As we embark on the third century of government under the Constitution, it is to be hoped that the delicate balance between president and Congress can and will be restored. Congress and the presidency should return to being partners in foreign policy, not adversaries. As [former] Secretary of State Schultz expressed it: "Trust is the coin of the realm." But that trust cannot be achieved by Congress seeking to straitjacket the presidency and micromanage foreign policy.

## NOTES

1 George McGovern, "We Need a Constitutional Presidency," in *Parade Magazine,* August 9, 1987, pp. 12–14.

# 12

# President and Congress

*While political observers are constantly taking the pulse of the American po-*
*litical system, the bicentennial of our Constitution understandably*
*occasioned more than the usual amount of introspection and self-examina-*
*tion. Certainly one of the most ambitious efforts in this regard was that of*
*the Committee on the Constitutional System (CCS). Composed of more than*
*fifty scholars and current or former public officials, its report on the state of*
*the American political system serves as the first selection in this chapter.*

*The CCS believes that our political system is in some trouble and*
*traces its source to legislative-executive branch conflict generated by the*
*separation of powers. The Founding Fathers, of course, fully expected that*
*the division of power in our national government would create tensions be-*
*tween the executive and legislative branches. Indeed, they believed that*
*interbranch rivalry would help prevent government from becoming too*
*powerful. For much of our history, however, political parties served to mute*
*such conflict by establishing a bond between the president and his respec-*
*tive party members in Congress. But political parties have grown*
*considerably weaker in recent decades, and the relationship between presi-*
*dent and Congress has become decidedly more confrontational. The result,*
*according to the CCS, is a stalemated government that for some time now*
*has been incapable of addressing the critical domestic and foreign policy is-*
*sues facing the nation. This unfortunate state of affairs, the CCS believes,*
*can be overcome only by making constitutional changes designed to foster*
*greater collaboration between president and Congress. While these changes*
*do not go so far as to institute a parliamentary form of government in which*
*executive and legislative power are fused, they certainly take us in that di-*
*rection.*

*In the second article, James Q. Wilson makes clear that he is unsym-*
*pathetic to the arguments and recommendations made in the CCS report*
*and to those set forth by some of its members (Lloyd Cutler and Douglas*

*Dillon) in other writings. Not only does Wilson contend that the separation of powers principle has served us well, but he challenges the characterization of "stalemated" government and argues that the constitutional changes contemplated by the CCS would not in any event resolve the deficiencies it alleges to exist.*

# Rethinking the Separation of Powers:
## Less Separation and More Power
### Committee on the Constitutional System

## SIGNS OF STRAIN

. . . The signs of strain in our governing processes are unmistakable.

Perhaps the most alarming evidence is the mounting national debt, fueled anew each year by outsized and unsustainable deficits that defy the good intentions of legislators and Presidents.

Consistency in our foreign and national security policies is also frustrated by an institutional contest of wills between Presidents and shifting, cross-party coalitions within the Congress. Over forty treaties submitted to the Senate for ratification since World War II have either been rejected or have never come to a vote. Among those that have never come to a vote are SALT II, the 1974 and 1976 treaties with Mexico and Canada, several UN and OAS human rights conventions, and a wide variety of bilateral trade, tax and environmental treaties. Meanwhile presidential concern over "leaks" and frustration with congressionally imposed restrictions have led Presidents and their staffs to launch important diplomatic, military and covert activities in secret and without consulting Congress . . .

## CAUSES

Sensing the failures and weaknesses in governmental performance, people tend to blame particular politicians or the complexity of the modern world. But our public officials are no less competent, either individually or as a group, than they used to be. Nor do our problems, as complex as they are, defy rational solutions consistent with our basic constitutional liberties. The difficulty lies mainly in the diffuse structure of the executive-legislative process and in the decline of party loyalty and cohesion at all levels of the political system.

The separation of powers, as a principle of constitutional structure, has served us well in preventing tyranny and the abuse of high office, but it has

The Committee on the Constitutional System was established to study and analyze the American constitutional system on the occasion of the two hundredth anniversary of the Constitution. The Committee was co-chaired by U.S. Senator Nancy Landon Kassebaum (Rep.–Kansas), C. Douglas Dillon, former Secretary of the Treasury, and Lloyd N. Cutler, former Counsel to the President. This selection is excerpted from a *Bicentennial Analysis of the American Political Structure*. Report and Recommendations of the Committee on the Constitutional System (Washington, D.C.: Committee on the Constitutional System, January 1987), pp. 3–8, 10–12, 14–16, 20.

done so by encouraging confrontation, indecision and deadlock, and by diffusing accountability for the results.

Ideally our two-party system should counteract the centrifugal tendencies of the separation of powers, with each party's politicians committed to a common philosophy of government and to specific program goals for which they stand accountable at the next election. In fact, throughout most of the nineteenth century and until after the end of World War II, the loyalty of most politicians to their party was deeply felt. They ran for office on a ticket selected by the party's leaders. Once in office, they recognized a common stake in the success of their party's governance and their joint accountability as candidates of the party at the next election.

In recent decades, however, political reforms and technological changes have worked together to weaken the parties and undermine their ability to draw the separated parts of the government into coherent action. Beginning in the late nineteenth century, Congress enacted a series of measures that redistributed functions previously performed by the parties. Civil service systems stripped the parties of much of their patronage.

The rise of the welfare state took away many opportunities for service by which the parties had won and held the loyalty of their followers. The secret ballot replaced the "tickets" which had previously been prepared by the parties and handed to the voters to cast into the ballot box. The 17th Amendment (ratified in 1913), which required the direct election of Senators, dealt another blow to party cohesiveness. So did the direct primary, which came to dominate the nomination of presidential candidates, particularly after 1968.

Modern technology has enabled candidates to appeal to voters directly, through television, computer-assisted mailings and telephone campaigns, and by quick visits in jet airplaines, all of which have lessened their dependence on party organizations and leaders. The key to these technologies is money, but candidates found they could raise it directly for themselves better than through the party organization. At the same time, interest groups found they could exercise more power over legislative votes by contributing directly to selected candidates rather than to a party.

The habits of voters also changed in this new environment. Party loyalty had been the rule for most of the nineteenth century, but by the last quarter of the twentieth century, one-third of all voters were registered as independents, and even among voters registering with parties, ticket-splitting became the norm.

Many of these changes resulted from laudable reforms and were, in any case, inevitable. No one wants to roll the clock back to the time when party bosses and local "machines" dominated the political process.

Nevertheless, we need to recognize that the weakening of parties in the electoral arena has contributed to the disintegration of party cohesion among the officials we elect to public office. Members of Congress who owe their election less to their party than to their own endeavors and their own sources of funds have little incentive to cooperate with party leaders in the Congress, much less their party's incumbent in the White House. And the proliferation of congressional committees and subcommittees has increased the disarray. There are now so many that almost every member is the chairman or ranking minority member of at least one committee or subcommittee, with all the political influence, proliferating staffs, publicity and fund-raising potential needed to remain in office.

## EFFECTS

Because the separation of powers encourages conflict between the branches and because the parties are weak, the capacity of the federal government to fashion, enact and administer coherent public policy has diminished and the ability of elected officials to avoid accountability for governmental failures has grown. More specifically, the problems include:

### Brief Honeymoons

Only the first few months of each four-year presidential term provide an opportunity for decisive action on domestic problems. By the second year, congressional incumbents are engrossed in the mid-term election and defer difficult decisions that will offend any important interest group.

The mid-term election usually results in a setback for the President's party that weakens his leadership and increases the stalemate and deadlock in the Congress. After the mid-term election, the government comes close to immobility as the President and Congress focus their energies on the imminent presidential election.

### Divided Government

We have had divided government (one party winning the White House and the other a majority in one or both houses of Congress) 60 percent of the time since 1956 and 80 percent of the time since 1968, compared to less than 25 percent of the time from the adoption of the Constitution until World War II.

This has led to inconsistency, incoherence and even stagnation in national policy. Affirmative policy decisions, as well as the nondecisions resulting from frequent deadlocks that block any action at all, are reached by shifting majorities built out of cross-party coalitions that change from one issue to the next.

Divided government in turn reflects the decline in party loyalty and the growing practice of ticket-splitting among the electorate. In 1900 only four percent of all congressional districts were carried by one party's presidential candidate and the other party's candidate for Member of the House. By 1984, because of the growth of ticket-splitting, this happened in 44 percent of all congressional districts.

One of Woodrow Wilson's themes during the campaign of 1912—a time of divided government—was that only party government (with one party success-fully bridging the separated powers by winning control of the Presidency and both houses of Congress) could carry a coherent program into effect. The voters in 1912 responded by choosing party government, and Wilson's New Freedom program was successfully legislated.

## Lack of Party Cohesion in Congress

Even in times of united government, disunity persists between the branches—and between and within the two houses of Congress—because many members of both the President's party and the opposition party reject the positions taken by their leaders. Legislators today have less reason to stick with their party's position and more reason to follow the urgings of non-party political action committees, which provide more of their campaign funds than the party does. The summary rejection of President Reagan's budget in 1986, even by members of his own party in the Republican-controlled Senate, dramatically illustrates the lack of party cohesion in the current political environment. This lack of cohesion induces Presidents and their staffs, as noted above, to conceal impor-tant foreign policy initiatives even from the leaders of their own party in Congress.

## Loss of Accountability

Divided government and party disunity also lead to diffused accountability. No elected official defends the sum of all the inconsistent policy decisions made by so many shifting cross-party coalitions, and each successfully shifts the blame to others. Polls show the public is dissatisfied with the governmental institu-tions—especially Congress and the bureaucracy—that legislate and administer this hodge-podge of policies. But the public seldom holds a party accountable for these failures, and it hardly ever holds individual legislators responsible.

Since World War II, 90 percent of each party's incumbent legislators who sought another term have been reelected, even in years when their party lost the White House. In 1986 the figure was 97 percent. Benjamin Franklin's famous maxim, "We must all hang together, or assuredly we shall all hang separately," no longer applies to the Members of Congress of either party.

## Lack of a Mechanism for Replacing Failed or Deadlocked Government

Presently there is no way between our fixed election dates to resolve basic disagreements between the President and Congress by referring them to the electorate. The only way to remove a failed President is by a House impeach-ment and Senate trial for "treason, bribery, or other high crimes and misde-meanors." And between the fixed election dates there is no way to reorient a Congress in which one or both houses obstruct an important and popular presidential program.

# REMEDIES

In seeking to adjust the constitutional system to modern conditions, we must be careful to preserve its enduring virtues. We must continue to respect the Bill of Rights, protected by an independent judiciary, and we must continue to insist that elected officials be able to monitor one another's performance and call another to account.

Consistent with these principles, it should be possible to design improvements that would encourage party cohesion and lessen the deadlock between the executive and legislative branches without sacrificing essential checks and balances. The Committee on the Constitutional System offers the following proposals as sufficiently meritorious to warrant national consideration and debate. Some of these proposals call only for adopting new party rules or statutes, while others would require amendments to the Constitution. . . .

## Improving Collaboration Between the Executive and Legislative Branches

**1.** *Four-Year Terms for House Members and Eight-Year Terms for Senators, with Federal Elections Every Fourth Year.* The present system of staggered elections has the effect of pulling the branches apart. Members of the House, who run every two years, feel a political need to demonstrate their independence from the White House, particularly in off-year elections. So do the one-third of the Senators who face an election within two years. Every other time an incumbent in either house runs for reelection, there is no presidential campaign.

The effect is to encourage legislators to distance themselves from the President and from presidential programs that may involve a difficult, short-term adjustment on the way to a worthwhile, longer-term result.

The Constitution could be amended so that the President and Members of the House would serve concurrent, four-year terms, and one Senator from each state would be elected for an eight-year term at each presidential election. This would eliminate the present House and Senate elections in the middle of the presidential term. It would lengthen and coordinate the political horizons of all incumbents. Presidents and legislators could join to enact necessary measures with the promise of longer-run benefits, without having to worry about an imminent election before the benefits were realized.

With fewer elections, the aggregate cost of campaign financing should go down, and legislators would be less frequently or immediately in thrall to the interest groups on whom they depend for funds. The honeymoon for enacting a President's program would be longer. With a four-year life for each Congress, the legislative process for the budget and other measures could be made more orderly and deliberate.

**Alternatives:** If the eight-year term for Senators were deemed too long, the Senate term could be shortened to four years, concurrent with the terms of the President and the House, which would also eliminate the mid-term election. Or, if the Senate would not accept a shortened term, we could keep the present six-year term. This would retain a limited mid-term election (for one-third of the Senate), permitting a partial referendum on government policy, at the cost of shortening the political horizon of one-third of the Senate.

**2.** *Permitting Members of Congress to Serve in the Cabinet.* The Constitution now bars members of Congress from serving as heads of administrative departments or agencies or holding any other executive-branch position. This provision was intended to prevent the President from dominating Congress by offering executive positions to key legislators. But its principal effect has been to deprive the nation of administrators who would have the confidence of both the executive and legislative branches.

If the barrier were removed from the Constitution, Presidents would have the option of appointing leading legislators to cabinet positions, and legislators would have the option of accepting such offers, without being required to give up their seats in Congress. Such ties between the branches might encourage closer collaboration and help to prevent stalemates. They would broaden both the range of talent available to a President informing his administration and the base of political leadership in the executive branch.

Under such an amendment, of course, a President would not be obliged to appoint any members of Congress to his cabinet, nor would they be obliged to accept.

Woodrow Wilson strongly favored this amendment, as a means to encourage closer collaboration between the branches. While modern legislators may have less time and incentive to join the cabinet than earlier generations, there is no longer any reason for a constitutional barrier to an experiment that has considerable promise and little risk.

**3.** *Relaxing the Requirements for Treaty Ratification.* The ability to enter into formal agreements with other nations is vital to effective national government in an increasingly interdependent world. The present constitutional requirement that treaties require the approval of two-thirds of the Senate has been a major barrier to the use of treaties and has led to evasion of the treaty process by way of executive agreements.

To restore an appropriate congressional role in the making of agreements with foreign powers, this provision should be amended to require that treaties can take effect with the approving vote of a constitutional majority of both houses. If the Senate does not join in proposing such an amendment, it should at least approve an amendment reducing the present requirement of approval by two-thirds of the Senate to 60 percent. . . .

The changes recommended in the previous section command majority support among members of the Committee on the Constitutional System. A number of other ideas have found less than majority support to date, but some members believe they are important enough to deserve further discussion. They fall into four categories.

## Strengthening Party Cohesion and Party Accountability

**1.** *Encouraging Presidential Appearances Before Congress.* Congress and the President should work out mutually agreeable voluntary arrangements for periodic presidential appearances before major congressional committees. These appearances would be used to present presidential positions and to answer congressional questions about presidential actions and proposals. Such arrangements would be consistent with the provision in Article II that the President "shall from time to time give to the Congress information on the State of the Union." They would also encourage greater cohesion between the President and the members of his party in Congress.

**2.** *Creating a Shadow Cabinet for the Legislative Opposition.* Legislators of the party losing the presidential election should organize a "shadow cabinet." The party's leaders in each house might alternate annually as leader and spokesman of the shadow cabinet, and the party's chairman or ranking member of the major committees in each house might alternate annually as shadow spokesmen in their particular fields, with their counterparts in the other house serving as deputy spokesmen. The shadow cabinet could coordinate party positions on legislative issues and act as party spokesmen before the public.

## Reducing the Likelihood of Divided Government

For 20 of the last 32 years—and for 14 out of the last 18—the White House and at least one house of Congress have been controlled by opposing parties. Some of the measures suggested above should reduce the likelihood of divided government, but they may be insufficient to eliminate it. If divided government is recognized as the preeminent cause of interbranch conflict and policy stalemate and deadlock, two stronger approaches are worth considering.

**1.** *Mandatory Straight Tickets.* The first approach is to make straight-ticket voting not merely easier, as suggested above, but compulsory. By constitutional amendment, each party's nominees for President, Vice President, Senate and House could be placed on the ballot as a single slate, with the voter required to cast his or her vote for one of the party slates in its entirety.

The drawback to this idea is that Americans are strongly committed to voting for the person rather than the party. They would not be easily convinced to sacrifice this freedom in the interest of party loyalty and cohesion.

**2.** *Sequential Elections.* The second approach is for Congress to enact a statute providing for sequential elections in presidential years, with the voting for President and Vice President to be conducted two to four weeks before the voting for members of Congress. Under such a proposal voters would already know, at the time they balloted for members of Congress, which party they have entrusted with the presidency. This would give the newly elected President an opportunity to persuade voters to elect a majority of the same party to Congress and thus give the party a better opportunity to carry out its program.

The drawbacks here are that in the congressional election Americans might still vote for the person rather than the party. Also, there would probably be a considerable fall-off in the number of voters in the congressional election.

## Calling New Elections in the Event of Deadlock or Governmental Failure

If it were possible for a President to call new elections, or for Congress to do so, we would have a mechanism for resolving deadlocks over fundamental policy issues. Indeed, the very existence of such a mechanism would be an inducement to avoid a deadlock that could trigger new elections. It would also make it possible to reconstitute a government that had palpably failed for any other reason.

There are formidable obstacles to incorporating such a device in our present system. Should the President alone, or Congress alone, or both the President and Congress be empowered to call for new elections? How soon should they follow after the passage of the resolution calling for them? Are we prepared to vote in a month other than November? Should there be full new terms for the winners (perhaps adjusted to the regular January expiration dates), or should they fill just the unexpired terms?

These questions can probably be answered. The real questions are whether we need such a strong device for breaking deadlocks or for removing Presidents who have failed for reasons other than impeachable conduct, and whether it is likely that in a special election the electorate would break the deadlock or would simply reelect all the incumbents.

Most constitutional democracies employ such a device, and it deserves serious consideration. It is not inconsistent with separated powers, and it might well operate to encourage cooperation between the branches in order to fore-stall the ordeal of special elections.

## CONCLUSION

In presenting this analysis and list of proposals, the Committee wishes to stress its central conviction. The best way to honor the framers of the Constitution during the bicentennial era is to follow their example.

When the parlous state of affairs under the Continental Congress raised doubts about the fitness of the new nation's frame of government, George Washington and his associates took steps to meet the challenge. They adopted the changes necessary (in the words of the resolution that called the Convention of 1787 into being) to "render the federal constitution adequate to the exigencies of government and the preservation of the union."

Two hundred years later, we stand in awe of their achievement. We disserve their memory, however, if we ignore signs that our political system today faces challenges that it is not equipped to meet.

We need to face up to these shortcomings in the capacity of our two-hundred-year-old political structure to cope with a global economy and prevent a nuclear war. We may ultimately conclude that these shortcomings can be remedied without major structural changes, or that any major changes needed to correct them would create even greater problems. But we cannot be confident of having reached the right conclusions until we confront the problems, trace them to their roots and examine the alternatives.

It is in this spirit that we offer these proposals.

# Leave the Separation of Powers Alone

## James Q. Wilson

. . . If one is asked what is wrong with American government, the odds are great—maybe not eight in ten, but better than one in two—that the reply will refer to some aspect of our politics that can be explained by the separation of powers: "The president cannot negotiate for the United States on delicate foreign policy matters." "Congress meddles in the work of bureaucratic agencies." "There are too many government leaks to the press." "The Pentagon is not under strong, unified management." "There are too many patronage (i.e., political) appointees in government agencies." "There are too few policy-oriented (i.e., political) appointees in government agencies."

If one makes a list of the most frequently proposed alterations in our constitutional arrangements, the odds are high that these proposals will call for a reduction in the separation of powers: "Let the president put some members of Congress in his cabinet." "Have the president and members of Congress who are from the president's party run as a team." "Allow the president to dissolve Congress." "Allow Congress to call for a special presidential election." "Curb the power of judicial review."

If one listens to the reflections of presidents and their aides, no matter whether they are liberals or conservatives, the most common complaint is that the president does not have enough power. Roosevelt, Truman, Eisenhower, Kennedy, Nixon, Carter, Reagan: All have remarked on how little the president can do compared to what the public expects him to do. Roosevelt, Truman, and Nixon appointed commissions (the President's Commission on Administrative Management [PCAM], the Hoover Commission, and the Ash Commission) to advise them on how best to extend their control over the bureaucracy; Nixon (like many presidents before him) tried to impound funds that Congress had ordered him to spend; Carter made a largely futile effort to weaken congressional control over the bureaucracy; Ford and Reagan have argued that the War Powers Act, which requires congressional participation in presidential decisions to commit armed forces, is unconstitutional. And on and on. . . .

## THE CASE AGAINST THE SEPARATION OF POWERS

There have always been two distinct though often intertwined strands in the case against the separation of powers. One is the *liberal* case: *The federal government should play a large and active role in human affairs by supplying*

James Q. Wilson is Collins Professor of Management at the University of California–Los Angeles. From James Q. Wilson, "Does the Separation of Powers Still Work?" *The Public Interest*, No. 86 (Winter 1987), pp. 36–37, 39–52.

*services, reducing economic inequality, and catering to the demands of those who find themselves at a disadvantage in the marketplace* [italics added]. During most of this century, presidents have been more sensitive to the urban and industrial constituencies who make these demands than has Congress. Therefore, the powers of the president should be enlarged and those of Congress (or those parts of Congress that are "obstructionist") should be reduced. From this perspective, it made sense to weaken the authority of congressional committees, or at least the committees headed by powerful conservatives (such as the House Rules Committee under the leadership of the legendary Judge Howard Smith of Virginia). It also made sense to call, as did James MacGregor Burns and E. E. Schattschneider, for strong political parties headed by the president, or presidential candidates, that would be able to command the loyalty of party members in Congress to the president's program and supplant the loyalty those members gave to committee chairmen. When Burns wrote of the "deadlock of democracy," he was writing of the political barriers to the enactment of a liberal agenda.

The other case is the *rationalist* one. *Whether policies are liberal or conservative, they should be made decisively, efficiently, and on the basis of comprehensive principles* [italics added]. The public interest was not well served by simply adding up individual preferences into a "patchwork" or "crazy quilt" of inconsistent programs administered in "wasteful" ways by "duplicative" agencies. The public interest was better served by having a unitary view of what was good for the nation "as a whole." Only a single official could design and propose an internally consistent set of policies based on some overriding principle. In our system that person is the president. Therefore, the president should have more power. In this view, it made sense to give the president firmer control over the bureaucracy, equip him with sufficient staff to develop programs and oversee their administration, empower him to recognize government agencies, and strengthen his hand in dealing with Congress. In theory, a rationalized national government could serve either liberal ends (by enacting broad welfare and regulatory programs) or conservative ones (by cutting waste, reducing spending, and simplifying or minimizing regulation). The rationalist view especially emphasized the foreign policy role of the president. With Tocqueville, it noted that diplomacy is especially difficult in a democracy owing to the need for secrecy, speed, and unity of action, all hampered by the fact that the president must share power with Congress. . . .

Liberals achieved the enactment of a large part of their agenda as a consequence of two windows of opportunity that opened thirty years apart. The Great Depression enabled an overwhelming Democratic majority in Congress, aided (after 1935) by a slim but solid majority on the Supreme Court, to lay the foundations for the modern welfare state. In 1965, a landslide electoral victory by Lyndon Johnson and the arrival of a liberal majority in both houses of Congress set the stage for a vast expansion of the welfare state and the enactment of dozens of consumer- and environmental-protection laws.

Rationalists made some gains in wartime, when the president gained enhanced authority over the government and the economy, but most of these gains faded with the return to peace. Otherwise, rationalists have had to plug away at small, painfully won changes—the passage of the Budget and Accounting Act in 1921 (that created the Bureau of the Budget and the General Accounting Office), the acquisition by the president in 1935 of the power to reorganize by executive order (subject to a legislative veto), the expansion of the White House office pursuant to the recommendations of the PCAM, the passage of the Legislative Reorganization Act of 1946 that reduced the number of standing committees of Congress and laid the groundwork for the growth in congressional staff, and the creation in 1978 of the Senior Executive Service (SES) to permit more flexible use of high-level bureaucrats. Some of these changes, especially the creation of the Bureau of the Budget and the attendant growth of presidential control over the budget and the legislative agenda, were of great moment, but many proved to be short-lived or chimerical gains. The power to reorganize expired, and now that the legislative veto has been deemed unconstitutional, it probably cannot be revived. The White House staff has grown so much that it has become a bureaucratic problem in its own right. The reduction in the number of congressional committees was quickly followed by the growth in the number of subcommittees, leaving authority in Congress at least as decentralized as it had once been. The Senior Executive Service has been a disappointment: Not many top-level bureaucrats moved from one agency to another, rarely was a SES member fired, and the availability of cash bonuses did not seem to enhance performance.

Moreover, the very success of the liberals in supplying the agenda for and expanding the role of the federal government was achieved at the cost of major setbacks for the rationalist cause. The government became big before the president became institutionally (as opposed to personally) powerful. What Roosevelt and Johnson created, their successors could not easily manage. Moreover, the liberal gains in the late 1960s and early 1970s were accompanied by a radical decentralization of Congress. Liberal majorities in the House and Senate confronted the conservatives holding power as chairmen of certain key committees, such as the House Rules Committee and the House Ways and Means Committee. To move their agenda onto the floor where its passage was assured, liberals had to unseat committee chairmen they regarded as obstructionist, enhance the power of individual members at the expense of committee chairmen, modify the rules to make it harder to bottle up legislation in committee, and (in the Senate) alter, slightly, the cloture rule to reduce the threat of a filibuster. The effect of these changes, chiefly wrought by the House Democratic caucus, was to increase the power of individual congressmen and reduce the power of congressional leaders.

Politically, if not constitutionally, powers became more rather than less separated. The president now was held responsible for every imaginable domestic and foreign problem, but his capacity to make a systematic response to these problems was reduced by two changes: The growth in the size of the government had contributed to the growth in the number and variety of interest groups that sought to block presidential initiatives, and the decentralization of Congress reduced the president's ability to negotiate with a handful of congressional leaders who could help build legislative majorities.

Critics of the separation of powers could have made one of two responses to this state of affairs. The rationalist might have argued for a reduction in the size and scope of the federal government on the grounds that our policy commitments now exceeded our capacity to manage them. Or the rationalist could have reaffirmed his alliance with the liberals by arguing for more profound and sweeping changes—necessarily involving constitutional revision—in order to reduce the separation of powers sufficiently to permit the president to direct affairs in the new order. By and large, rationalists have chosen the second course, and so we have such groups as the Committee on the Constitutional System (CCS), led by Lloyd Cutler, C. Douglas Dillon, and Senator Nancy Landon Kassebaum. . . .

To the CCS and its supporters, the need for fundamental change is almost self-evident. Perhaps that is why so little of their writing is devoted to making the case for change. The most important essay, Lloyd Cutler's "To Form a Government,"[1] is almost the only systematic effort to explain why we need to modify the separation of powers. Given their premises, of course, the need for change is virtually self-evident. To them, the public interest is a discoverable set of principles and goals from which right actions can be inferred. The means to achieve these ends must be comprehensively and efficiently related to those ends. This is more easily done by one mind than by 535, by an official responsible to a national electorate than by one beholden to many small electorates, and by a person able to carry out his policies subject to the check of electoral defeat than by one who cannot carry out any policies at all without first overcoming countless checks by subcommittees, committees, interest groups, and houses of Congress. The rationalist position, like rationality itself, seems to require little defense.

## THE INTENT OF THE FRAMERS

But of course the Framers of the Constitution were not trying to create a government that would discern national goals and serve them efficiently and with dispatch; they were trying to create a limited government that would serve only those goals that could survive a process of consultation and bargaining designed to prevent the mischief of factions and the tyranny of passionate majorities or ambitious politicians. The CCS and its allies understand this but argue that conditions have changed since 1787: Public affairs today are more complex, interdependent, and fraught with peril than they were in the nineteenth century, and so we must modify our governing arrangements in order to meet these new challenges.

It is not difficult, of course, to produce a litany of difficulties facing the nation: a large budget and trade deficit, the threat of nuclear war, a complex array of international competition, the cancer of crime and drug abuse, and so on. But it is not clear that these "new realities" are fundamentally different from the kinds of problems faced by Washington's first administration and it is certainly far from clear that they constitute a case for constitutional change.

The first administrations had to salvage a disrupted economy, pay off or otherwise settle a crushing war debt funded by worthless paper, worry about the presence of hostile British forces in Canada and a British navy at sea, cope with French control of the Mississippi River valley and Spanish control of Florida, put down a rebellion of Pennsylvania farmers protesting the tax on whiskey, reconcile the deep ideological divisions stirred up by the French Revolution, make legitimate the government in the eyes of skeptical Anti-Federalists and Jeffersonian Democrats, do battle with Indians waging war on the periphery of the new republic, and settle the hotly contested Jefferson-Adams presidential race by going to thirty-six ballots in the House of Representatives. Hardly simple times; hardly an easy test for the new constitutional order. It survived.

Today, the case for constitutional change is being made to a nation prosperous and at peace whose political institutions enjoy unquestioned legitimacy. Decision making is as contentious and protracted now as it was two hundred years ago, but under circumstances that are far more conducive to success and popular support than once was the case. In 1986, one can only be amused to reread the 1974 essay by Charles Hardin on why our government was then in crisis and why only major "constitutional surgery" could correct it. Watergate, the supposedly "imperial presidency," and popular distrust of government were the crisis; the cure required these changes: electing the president and Congress for coterminous four-year terms, abolishing the office of vice president, allowing Congress to remove a president by a vote of no confidence, giving the president an automatic majority in the House of Representatives, and so on. Of course, the "crisis" ended without any of these "cures." Watergate was handled by the normal constitutional procedures—congressional investigations, criminal trials, and the prospect of impeachment—and the presidency and the president are once again in high repute.

## REAL AND IMAGINED PROBLEMS

But generalities cannot settle the matter. Let us look at the specific ways in which the constitutional system is allegedly defective: the deficit, economic policy, and foreign affairs.

### 1. The Deficit

C. Douglas Dillon has argued for a parliamentary democracy because, unlike our system, it would more effectively address the problem of the deficit. There are two things wrong with this argument. The first is that there is no evidence at all that the deficit is a consequence of the separation of powers. At the President's [Reagan] request, taxes were cut. At the President's request, defense spending was increased. At the President's request, the Social Security system was preserved intact, with minor adjustments in tax and benefit levels. At the President's request, budgets were submitted that were not in balance. There are important differences between what the President has requested and Congress has approved with respect to many spending bills, but all of these differences, if resolved in the president's favor, would not produce a balanced budget. The deficit would be somewhat less, but not substantially so, if all presidential requests were automatically enacted by a subservient Congress. If Mr. Dillon is worried about the deficit, he need not vote for constitutional reform; he need only have voted against Mr. Reagan.

The second difficulty with the Dillon argument is immediately apparent when we examine the budgets of parliamentary democracies. There are important conceptual problems in comparing deficits across nations—consider, for example, the problem of comparing governments that do and do not own major industries, or that of comparing deficits between high- and low-inflation countries. Taking into account all these problems, Vito Tanzi of the International Monetary Fund, using data from the Organization for Economic Cooperation and Development (OECD), produces estimates for the 1984 deficit, measured in percentage of gross national product, that are arranged from high to low in Table 1.

Every nation on this list with a fiscal deficit except ours has a parliamentary democracy: that is to say, it is not governed in accordance with the separation of powers. Japan, Germany, and Norway have deficits smaller than ours; Italy, Ireland, Belgium, Greece, Denmark, the Netherlands, Spain, and

**TABLE 1 Deficit Comparison Across Nations for 1984**

| Country | Percentage of GNP |
| --- | --- |
| Italy | 12.4 |
| Ireland | 12.3 |
| Belgium | 10.3 |
| Greece | 9.8 |
| Denmark | 6.0 |
| Netherlands | 5.9 |
| Spain | 5.7 |
| Canada | 5.3 |
| Sweden | 3.5 |
| UNITED STATES | 3.1 |
| United Kingdom | 2.8 |
| Japan | 2.3 |
| Germany | 1.4 |
| Norway | −2.4 |

Source: Vito Tanzi, "The Deficit Experience in Industrial Countries," in Philip Cagan, ed., *The Economy in Deficit* (Washington, D.C.: American Enterprise Institute, 1955), pp. 94–95.

Canada have much larger ones; France, Sweden, and the United Kingdom are
about on a par with us. The safest conclusion that can be drawn from this list is
that form of government has no effect on the size of the deficit. . . .

## 2. Economic Policy

We are constantly reminded that we live in an interdependent world undergoing
rapid technological and economic change. Those who remind us of this situation claim that the United States does not respond to that change very well. We
save and invest too little. We import too much. We allow jobs to be destroyed
by Asian competitors. We fail to rebuild our smokestack industries. We regulate in cumbersome ways. We have too many small farmers. Our legal system
imposes costly delays.

The implication of these criticisms is that there is a correct economic
policy that a bold president would implement. (Among my students at UCLA,
there is a widespread belief that a sufficiently bold president would turn out to
be either Lee Iaccoca or Peter Ueberroth.) If the right president can be found,
then he should be given the freedom to design and carry out his economic
policy. If he fails, the voters will punish him at the next election; if he succeeds,
the voters will reward him (unless, of course, constitutional reformers have
succeeded in limiting him to a single six-year term).

In support of the virtues of greater decisiveness and comprehensiveness
in economic policymaking, one can point to the fact that many other industrial
nations have been more successful than the United States in taxing consump-
tion (for example, the value added tax) and rewarding investment (for example,
by not taxing capital gains). There is also evidence from several studies of other
countries that their system of environmental regulation is less adversarial and
less legalistic but just as effective as that in the United States.[2]

These are weighty arguments, but it is not clear they weigh in favor of
movement toward a parliamentary regime. First, it is not obvious what economic policy is correct. Of course, advocates of a rationalist governing system
will respond that, though no one knows for certain what policies will work, at
least a strong, executive-centered system will permit us to try a given policy.
Their view is that a yes-or-no referendum by the public is a better check on
economic policymaking than a detailed scrutiny and amendment by Congress. I
am not convinced. We may make new economic policy in half-hearted steps or
tolerate inconsistent economic programs, but we thereby hedge our bets and
avoid the extreme swings in policy that are characteristic of some other regimes. Britain nationalized, denationalized, renationalized, and then denationalized again several of its basic industries. France appears on the verge of
doing the same.

Second, it is increasingly implausible to use "deadlock" as a word to
describe economic policymaking in America. After many decades of increased
regulation of prices and conditions of entry in such industries as domestic
banking, aviation, securities trading, and telecommunications, a more or less

measured and careful process of deregulation began that, though far from constituting a revolution, has revealed this nation's capacity for learning and self-correction. After decades during which Democrats demanded steeply progressive tax rates and Republicans went along in return for extensive deductions, the president and Congress renegotiated the terms of that old compact in favor of a system with less steep rates and fewer loopholes.

Third, the adversarial and legalistic nature of economic regulation here, while indisputable, reflects many factors in addition to the separation of powers. No doubt the separation of powers intensifies the adversarial nature of our regulatory system by empowering congressional critics of current regulatory law and enabling the courts to play a large role in reviewing and reversing regulatory decisions. But we live in an adversarial culture, the product of centuries devoted to defining politics as a struggle over rights. We are deeply imbued with a populist suspicion of the sort of behind-the-scenes negotiations that characterize regulatory policymaking in England and Sweden. The centralized nature of political and economic life abroad facilitates the settlement of issues by negotiations among peak associations, whereas here the decentralized political order and the more competitive economic one make it impossible to commit either the government or economic actors to the syndicalist pattern of decision making so often seen in Europe.

## 3. Foreign Policy

Lloyd Cutler makes much of President Carter's inability to get the Senate to ratify the SALT II treaty in 1979. A president able to "form a government" would have been able to commit this country to such a treaty. Cutler points out that no prime minister is faced with the need to obtain senatorial ratification of treaties.

True enough. But one moment: The Senate rarely fails to ratify a treaty. It has approved something approaching a thousand treaties and turned down about twenty and just five in this century, of which only the Treaty of Versailles, establishing the League of Nations, was an important defeat. Of course, it can talk a treaty to death, as it almost did with SALT II (the *coup de grace* was not Senate but Soviet behavior—the USSR invaded Afghanistan before the treaty could come to a vote). But in general the Senate tends to go along.

The crucial question should not be whether the president should have more power over the Senate but whether the treaties that failed ratification were in the public interest. Just before describing Carter's problems with SALT II, Cutler speaks of the need for "making those decisions we all know must be made." Was SALT II such a decision? If so, Cutler leaves the argument unstated. Strong arguments can be and were made against it. Many thoughtful people believed that it was a bad treaty. The notion that ratification should be made easier so that the real check on the success of the president's policy is public reaction at the next election is chimerical: People rarely, if ever, vote for or against presidents because of the treaties they have signed, for the obvious reason that, barring some dramatic incident, the people have no way of knowing whether the treaty was a good or bad idea.

Foreign policy is more than treaties, of course. It is not hard to think of circumstances in which one would want the president to have a freer hand. It is not hard to think of ways of giving him a freer hand. If constitutional reformers are so keen on supplying a freer hand, it is curious that they spend so much time discussing quasi-parliamentary procedures and so little time discussing the virtues of repealing the War Powers Act, modifying congressional supervision of the Central Intelligence Agency, and eliminating the legislative veto over arms sales, none of which requires a constitutional amendment. One wonders whether the rationalists are really rationalists and not actually liberals in rationalist clothing, eager to have a president powerful enough to sign arms-control and nuclear-test-ban agreements but not strong enough to commit troops to Grenada or Lebanon or provide aid to anti-Marxist rebels in Central America or Angola.

Still, a strong case can be made that in negotiating with foreign powers, the president of the United States is in an awkward position, not simply or even mainly because he must get the Senate to ratify his treaties, but because he must publicly negotiate simultaneously with both Congress (and congressionally amplified domestic pressures) and the foreign power. When President Nixon was negotiating with the North Vietnamese to end the war in Southeast Asia, he had to make concessions to both Congress and the enemy, reducing any incentive the enemy had to make concessions in return. As President Reagan negotiates with the Soviet Union over arms control [as at the time of this writing—Editors], it would be difficult for him to make credible and useful offers to constrain deployment of antisatellite weapons or the "Star Wars" defense system if Congress, in advance of the negotiations, places, on its own initiative, constraints on these weapons. It is hard to play poker if someone on your side frequently proclaims that you will give away certain chips regardless of what your opponent may do.

But it is unlikely that any of the most frequently discussed constitutional changes would materially improve the president's bargaining position. Putting members of Congress in the cabinet, letting the president serve a six-year term, or having the president and House members run as a team would leave the president and Congress in essentially the same relationship they are now: rivals for control over the direction of foreign policy.

## THE UNWRITTEN CONSTITUTION

There are two fundamental arguments for a constitutional system of separate institutions sharing powers: It helps preserve liberty and it slows the pace of political change. Those arguments are as valid today as they were in 1787. Individual liberties are more secure when the actions of one part of the national government can be checked by, or appealed to, another. Political change is slower, and so the growth of new programs and public spending is slower, when any new proposal must survive the political obstacle course of bureaus, subcommittees, committees, and houses of Congress. . . .

Defending the principle of separation of powers, [however], is not the same as defending the practices that have developed around these constitutional principles. Don K. Price, like me, argues against constitutional change but argues in favor of changes in the "unwritten constitution," those customs and arrangements that allow a government of separate institutions to work at all.[3]

The most important provision of the unwritten constitution is the internal organization and procedures of Congress. The Constitution requires that the House and the Senate as a whole enact legislation, but it is silent on how many additional "enactments" must occur within the House and the Senate. At one time, there were virtually no congressional committees and no chairmen, at another time there were many powerful chairmen; at one time members of the House had great autonomy, at another time they yielded immense authority to the Speaker; at one time the House Rules Committee dominated the legislative process, at another time it played a smaller role; at one time seniority alone determined who should be chairman, at another time the party caucus influenced the choice of chairmen.

\* \* \*

The Congress of the United States . . . is extremely decentralized and individualized. Speaker Sam Rayburn during the 1950s was not nearly as powerful as Speaker Thomas Reed in the 1890s, but he was far more powerful than Speaker Tip O'Neill in the 1980s. Congress, especially the House, has chosen to have weak leadership; in principle it could choose to have strong leadership. The methods are neither obscure nor unconstitutional: vest in the speaker or the majority leader the power to select and remove committee chairmen; change campaign finance laws so that the House and Senate campaign committees could raise and spend large sums of money on behalf of individual candidates and place control of these entities firmly in the hands of the speaker or majority leader; reduce the ability of individual members to create their own political action committees or to receive funds directly from the political action committees of others; and strengthen the power of the speaker or the majority leader to choose which committees shall consider bills and which bills will come to the floor for a vote. All of these things are done in state governments operating under essentially the same separation of powers principles as shape the national government. . . .

I am not optimistic that Congress will restore strong leadership. As I have written elsewhere,[4] there are very few examples in American history of people who possess certain powers voting to give them up or of people deciding they favored less democracy rather than more. And even if congressional leadership is strengthened, the president will certainly not be able to dominate the leaders who emerge. But it is in this area of the unwritten constitution that remedies for the defeats of the separation of powers must be found. There are no constitutional remedies short of the abolition of the principle itself, and that is a price that two hundred years of successful constitutional government should have taught us is too high to pay.

## NOTES

1 Lloyd N. Cutler, "To Form a Government," *Foreign Affairs,* Fall 1980, pp. 126–143.
2 David Vogel, *National Styles of Regulation* (Ithaca, N.Y.: Cornell University Press, 1986); Steven J. Kelman, *Regulating America, Regulating Sweden* (Cambridge, Mass.: MIT Press, 1981).
3 Don K. Price, *America's Unwritten Constitution* (Baton Rouge, La.: Louisiana State University Press, 1983).
4 James Q. Wilson, "Political Parties and the Separation of Powers," in Robert A. Goldwin and Art Kaufman, eds., *Separation of Powers—Does It Still Work?* (Washington, D.C.: American Enterprise Institute, 1986), pp. 18–37.

# 13

# Bureaucracy

*It has become commonplace among business leaders, politicians, and the public alike to criticize government for waste and inefficiency. Former U.S. Senator William Proxmire (D.–Wis.), for example, used to present the Golden Fleece award to bureaucrats or government agencies that wasted the taxpayers' money. And former President Ronald Reagan made one of his administration's major themes the elimination of government waste. So it was not surprising that, shortly after taking office, Reagan took the lead in establishing a commission charged with finding ways to reduce government spending and eliminate bureaucratic waste and mismanangement. Known as the Grace Commission (for its chairman, Peter Grace, one of America's top corporate executives), it issued a thick report outlining ways to make the government more efficient.*

*In the first of the articles in this chapter, Edward Meadows reviews the work of the Grace Commission and agrees with its conclusion that "the government is the worst-run enterprise in America." Citing examples from the report, Meadows paints a dismal picture of bureaucratic waste, including a government that overly indulges its workers, tolerates the spending of the taxpayers' money to an excessively high degree, and is blind to the need to get government out of doing what the free market itself should be doing.*

*In the second selection, Steven Kelman offers a rebuttal to the Grace Commission findings. In a point-by-point refutation of ten of the commission's examples of bureaucratic waste, Kelman concludes that popular conceptions of waste in the federal government, fueled by the commission and others, are at best, "gross exaggerations." According to Kelman, the government is simply not as poorly run as everyone supposes. The reader is left to judge, of course, which is the more accurate view, based on the evidence.*

# The Government Is the Worst-Run Enterprise in America

**Edward Meadows**

. . . When President Reagan named Peter Grace chairman of his new budget-study commission, back on February 18, 1982, the President bade him and his men go forth like tireless bloodhounds. The President asked Mr. Grace to command troops of corporate volunteers—accountants, staff officers, management experts—who would stalk the government's red-tape jungle, sniffing out inefficiency. In order not to add to the problem it was investigating, the commission would be funded privately, the President decreed, by corporate donations of time and money. Such a scheme had worked in California under his governorship, and it would work again in Washington. . . .

Bloodcurdling pig screams echoed down the Washington Mall as the Grace Commission began to release its findings in 1983. One task force proposed, for instance, that military commissaries be shut down. The military press ranted, and Defense Secretary Weinberger agreed that the matter needed "more study." This was typical and predictable.

A listing of the commission's executive committee reads like an honor roll of blue-chip corporate America, names like Frank Cary, chairman of IBM; William Agee, chairman of Bendix; John W. Hanley, chairman of Monsanto; and 157 other top-ranking executives. They remanded some two thousand of their employees to root in government files for evidence of mismanagement. The volunteer inspectors ended up writing 47 hefty blue-bound reports, many of them two inches thick, all chock-full of fascinating detail. They wrote 23,000 pages in all, suggesting budget cuts ranging from half a million dollars to $59 billion. All the work was done at a cost of $75 million in donated manpower, equipment, and materials, plus $3.3 million in cash contributions. Corporations footed the entire bill. Not a cent of the money came from the federal government. . . .

. . . The government is the worst-run enterprise in America. Thus it is the thesis of the Grace Commission that the country can save that $454 billion simply by curbing outright, blatant, casebook mismanagement, without ripping the social safety net, or even cutting some government services that many people, libertarians especially, would deem unwarranted on principle.

To begin, here is a random sampler of this mismangement. Read and be outraged:

• The Health and Human Services Department has been paying Medicare benefits to 8,500 dead people.

Edward Meadows is a professional journalist and writer who frequently comments on economic issues. From Edward Meadows, "Peter Grace Knows 2,478 Ways to Cut the Deficit," *National Review*, March 9, 1984, pp. 26–36. Copyright © 1984 by National Review, Inc., 150 East 35th Street, New York, N.Y. 10016. Reprinted by permission.

- A Mississippi supplier bought a gravity timer from the sole manufacturer for $11 and sold it to the Navy for $256—a 2,227 percent markup.
- The Minority Business Development Agency didn't notice when a management consulting firm used part of its $4 million MBDA grant to rent a townhouse and two cars for its executives, buy unauthorized gifts for its employees, and promote "questionable activities." The firm also neglected to pay some $315,000 in federal and state taxes, consulting fees, and salaries.
- It costs the Veterans Administration from $100 to $140 just to process a single medical claim, while the average for private insurance companies is $3 to $6 per claim.
- But the VA is a paragon of efficiency in letter-writing. It requires only twenty days to finish a letter. Compare with Health and Human Services, where a single piece of correspondence needing the signature of the Secretary takes 47 days to get done and involves about sixty people.
- The Army spends $4.20 to issue each payroll check, compared to the private-sector cost of $1. This wastes $40 million a year.
- Some unsuspecting citizens open their mailboxes to find 29 or more copies of pamphlets with titles like *How to Serve Nuts,* because the Government Printing Office uses out-of-date, duplicate, and incorrect mailing lists to post its myriad free publications. The lack of centralized correct mailing lists costs an estimated $96 million a year.

Say, is this Ubanga or the Central Banana Republic we're talking about? No, it's glittering Washington, and you're paying the tab. How does one get a firm hold on such maddeningly diverse ways of wasting taxpayers' money? The Grace Commission has broken down the inefficiencies by government agency and by function. For simplicity's sake, here are some specific categories of inefficiency, and what the Grace Commission thinks ought to be done to get things in shape.

## INFORMATION PROCESSING

The federal government uses 17,000 computers, operated by 250,000 employees. But they are mostly obsolete—on average, they are twice as old as computers in private business. Half of them are so old they can no longer be supported by the manufacturer. And these ancient computers can't tie in with each other. Beyond that, government decision-makers mostly don't know what information they need, where to get it, or how to analyze it. Witness the results:

- The Social Security Administration's computers stay four to six weeks behind in issuing new Social Security cards, and the agency has a three-year backlog in posting retirement contributions. It is unable to process the 7.5 million new claims each year on time or correctly.
- Some 20 percent of all tax returns for 1978, that's right, 1978—have yet to be

entered into the IRS computer system, a twenty-year-old dinosaur that pre-dates most modern computer technology. Delinquent accounts are therefore at $23.2 billion and growing.

- Though the Urban Mass Transportation Administration spent $10 million to buy new computers to keep track of the $25 billion in grants it hands out, the agency has been unable to close its accounting books since 1979. No account reconciliations have been possible since 1977. The UMTA has no central ledger showing who owes what to whom. Despite the computers, the agency must do its financial data by hand.
- The cost of the Army's business computer systems can only be estimated (at $1.5 billion), because the Army simply doesn't know how much it has spent on these computers, what kinds of computers it has, where they are, how many there are, or whether they should be replaced.

The Grace Commission argues that, for starters, some $20 billion can be saved over a three-year period by straightening out the computer mess. The commission recommends naming a manager to oversee computer operations throughout the government; hiring competent professionals; upgrading the obsolete systems; and using common payroll, personnel, property-management, and other such systems throughout the government. And if the government went even further in closing its information gap, by such means as figuring out what information it needs and then setting up mechanisms to get it, some $78 billion could be saved.

## ASSET MANAGEMENT

Any businessman worth his P&L statement knows how to manage financial assets, mainly by putting idle money in interest-bearing accounts, and timing his own payments to avoid costing himself interest. Another way is to cut down the "float" that offers free credit as a payment takes its time getting to its destination. The federal government, however, is ignorant of these common techniques. Because of this, it loses millions of your dollars a year. Consider the evidence:

- In 1982 the Justice Department seized $317 million in the form of cash and of property, such as dope-smuggling planes. But the captured cash, $79 million of the total, wasn't put into interest-bearing bank accounts. Instead, the Justice Department just let it sit. Noncash assets are allowed to depreciate to as little as 65 percent of their value before they are sold off.
- At the Transportation Department, some $473 million in recent grants was paid to contractors an average of 13 days sooner than necessary, costing the government $13 million in interest payments. If payments were made only when due, and bills collected promptly, the department could save $144 million per year.

- The State Department squandered some $17 million over a three-year period by failing to acquire foreign currency before it was actually needed. (And when the dollar weakens, State should delay buying foreign currency.)
- Some $635 million could be saved over three years if the government used direct deposit for the 48 million payments it makes each month. This would allow the money to remain on deposit longer.
- The Education Department could generate some $4.68 billion in cash-flow improvements and $1 billion in interest savings over three years merely by making loans to students in increments rather than in lump sums. Consolidating the student-loan programs could return at least $290 million per year to the Treasury.

In spite of a daily cash flow of $6.8 billion, the federal government obviously hasn't got a handle on the management of its financial assets. The Grace Commission says the government could save up to $79 billion if it ran its asset management as business does.

## PERSONNEL

The federal government employs nearly three times the number of high-grade white-collar workers found in the private sector. They tend to be overpaid and underworked, given to absenteeism and job-hopping. They get 35 percent more vacation time than private-industry workers and health benefits that cost $134 a month per family, versus the private-sector average of $93. They like to file such things as on-the-job injury claims (6.3 percent of federal employees filed in 1980, versus 1.7 percent of private-industry employees).

- In 1981, a typical year, Postal Service workers took an average of nearly nine sick days each, versus the 5.3-day average in private enterprise. This lost 21.734 workweeks, at a cost to the taxpayers of $652 million.
- The Department of Energy has one supervisor for every three employees, twice the number of supervisors in the rest of the federal government, not to mention the private sector. Just bringing the Energy Department into line with the rest of the government would save a tidy $19 million over three years.
- The Education Department overpays nearly 30 percent of its workers, since that many are "overclassified" and there hasn't been a classification audit since the department was formed in 1980. Education Department employees don't mind. Nor do they complain about cost-of-living raises. The average increase was 17.3 percent in 1980 and 27.3 percent in 1981.
- Government pensions are twice as generous as private ones, and military pensions are 600 percent higher than those in the private sector. These pensions are sweetened by lavish cost-of-living increases, such that between 1977 and 1981, civil-service pension pay rose by 50 percent. Between 1973

and 1982, the government handed out more than $200 billion in pension checks to civil-service and military retirees. These costs will more than double over the next decade, rising to $500 billion, not including an unfunded pension liability of a trillion dollars over that period. (For example, there are a million retired railroad workers and only 450,000 active workers in the Railroad Retirement System—that is, 2.2 retirees per worker. The system already has an unfunded liability of $30 billion and will run out of funds sometime before next year.)

- To decide how much to pay its workers, the government surveys salaries in the private sector. But this "comparability survey" covers only a quarter of federal jobs and excludes 95 percent of companies in major industries. Thus the survey is biased toward high salaries. The average blue-collar salary is 8 percent higher in government enterprises than in private industry. In any case, about half of all federal job-classification standards are more than ten years out of date, with excessively detailed requirements and time-consuming procedures.
- One government study determined that word-processing operators weren't as skilled as regular secretaries, so it cut word-processing pay by $3,000 a year. The predictable result was that word-processing operators disappeared from federal word-processing pools, only to turn up as secretaries. Some word-processing centers went idle for lack of operators. Productivity fell.
- The VA has a hospital construction staff of eight hundred, while the Hospital Corporation of America does the same work with a staff of fifty. As a result of overstaffing, it takes the VA seven years to finish a project, versus two years at the HCA. Administrative costs are 8 percent, versus 2 percent in the private sector.

The Grace Commission says the government could save a neat $58 billion over three years by such things as raising the retirement age to 62 (it now can be as low as 55 for civil service and 40 for the military), imposing early-retirement penalties, offering more reasonable cost-of-living adjustments, and redesigning the job-comparability surveys and the job-classification system. More savings would come just from bringing government pay and work customs into line with those in private business.

## PROCUREMENT

One-fifth of the federal budget goes for buying equipment and supplies. In fiscal 1982, for instance, procurement totaled nearly $160 billion, with more than three-fourths of that sum going for Defense Department purchases. Add to the total some $88 billion in inventories that government agencies hold stored all over the country in hundreds of locations.

To do all the federal shopping, some 130,000 federal procurement officers take part in about 18 million "procurement actions" per year. They do all this while entangled in more than eighty thousand pages of regulations, plus twenty thousand new pages of revisions each year.

Here are some examples of what federal procurement has wrought:

- The Navy's Training Equipment Center in Orlando paid $511 for bulbs that cost 60 cents in the grocery store.
- The Navy paid $100 last year for aircraft simulator parts that cost a nickel at the hardware store.
- Costs for 25 major weapons systems that were started between 1971 and 1978 have risen an average of 323 percent. One reason is that defense contractors typically underbid on contracts—sometimes as much as 80 percent below true costs—to get government work. Then, as they proceed, they double and even triple the cost estimates. But by then it is too late to do anything about it.
- The government compounds the cost-overrun problem by allowing a defense contractor that underbids to become the government's monopoly supplier of a system or product for up to twenty years. During that time, the contractor has a free hand to raise and re-raise the price as much as he pleases. Costs are typically doubled and tripled again by these monopoly contractors.
- When the Agency for International Development bought 399 cars and trucks for projects in the Middle East, an audit found that five were missing, 93 had been diverted to personal or nonproject use; 84 had been sitting idle in parking lots, some for two years; and many of the remaining vehicles had been commandeered by host-country government officials for their private use.
- The U.S. Coast Guard pays $100 per week for the use of an office trailer, while the Environmental Protection Agency pays $100 per day to the same supplier for the identical trailer. The EPA's unwitting generosity is blamed on the way the agency deals with its suppliers, and on the fact that the contractor forgot to mention that the $100 was a weekly rate, not a daily one.

More than $28 billion could be saved in procurement over a three-year span, says the Grace Commission, if the government would tighten up its procedures. It could cure cost overruns by using two competing contractors for production of things like weapons systems; by spreading procurement funding over several years to allow better monitoring; and by purchasing spare parts from a source other than the manufacturer (who tends to mark up spare parts outrageously). Federal agencies should also hold smaller inventories, in line with the practice in private business, and they should consider past perform-ance when deciding on a bid award, and ride herd on bidders' cost estimates.

## PRIVATIZATION

The federal government is the world's largest (and worst-run) conglomerate. It is at once the nation's largest insurer, lender, borrower, hospital-system operator, power producer, landowner, tenant, holder of grazing land and timberland, grain owner, warehouse operator, ship owner, and truck-fleet operator.

This unnatural situation evolved from the assumption that only government can provide some services. That might have been true years ago when the feds got into most of the businesses they run today. But now it is often nonsensical:

- In the 1860s the government decided to provide cheap food for soldiers in isolated frontier outposts by setting up government grocery stores, the military commissaries. Nowadays, a wild frontier town like Washington, D.C., has six commissaries; San Francisco and San Antonio have five each; there are four each in San Diego and in Norfolk. The government has 358 commissary stores, 238 of them in the continental United States, duplicating private supermarkets, but without the profit motive. The result is an uncompetitive and inefficient government grocery chain with annual sales of $4.2 billion, at an annual cost to taxpayers of $597 million.
- Europe and Japan are beginning to cut into the U.S. monopoly on outer space, because semiprivate companies like Arianespace can undercut NASA. If the United States is to compete in this growing high-tech business, it should let private companies in on space launches, especially since, by the government's own estimates, it won't be able to meet the commercial demand for space launches in this decade.
- The Department of Energy operates 123 hydroelectric dams and 622 substations, supplying 45 percent of the nation's hydroelectric power. But revenues aren't enough to cover the federal investment, the pricing doesn't make sense, and the account books are a mess.
- Federal agencies try to do everything in-house. The Defense Department has 11,700 employees doing such things as providing food service, maintenance, laundry service, firefighting, etc. Contracting out this kind of work would save $70 million a year at the Department of Defense.

The Grace Commission has found $28.4 billion of potential savings over three years through privatization. Of these savings, $20 billion would come from selling off the government's hydroelectric dams and substations, some $2.5 billion would come from selling off military commissaries, and the rest would come from contracting out services like VA hospital management and turning over redundant operations to the private sector.

## SUBSIDIES

The federal government handed out nearly $500 billion in 1983 to individuals, businesses, and other government agencies. The Department of Health and Human Services alone gives away two out of every five tax dollars—$269 billion last year. Not counting such earned entitlements as Social Security and VA benefits, the federal government offers 64 different welfare programs, costing close to $100 billion a year. In 1983, there were an estimated 22 million Medicaid recipients, 19 million food-stamp recipients, 4.1 million Supplemental Security Income recipients, and 11 million recipients of Aid to Families with Dependent Children. Aside from welfare, there are billions more in subsidies paid to industry and even foreign governments. Without debating the basic validity of some of those programs, here are a few of the obvious abuses:

- Food-stamp cheating amounted to $1 billion in 1981, 10 percent of the whole program. It happens largely because recipients lie about their income and the government never checks.
- An estimated 206,100 aliens living abroad collect U.S. Social Security benefits. The average alien family gets $24 in benefits for every dollar paid in FICA taxes.
- Most of the subsidized mortgage loans made by the government in 1982 went to folks who could have bought homes without help. The typical mortgage revenue bond buyer had an income between $20,000 and $40,000. Some 53 percent were among the more affluent families in their states, with several making over $50,000 a year.
- An audit revealed nearly $1 billion in rail-modernization money lying idle at the Urban Mass Transportation Administration because the agency has no system for awarding urban discretionary grants.

Some $59 billion could be saved over three years, according to the Grace Commission, by better management of subsidy programs. One recommendation is to tax subsidy payments above a certain income level or corporate tax bracket. Benefit programs ought to be consolidated, and agency accounting systems need to be improved to provide accurate, up-to-date information. The commission says poverty statistics should be redefined to include in-kind transfer payments such as food stamps and Medicaid.

These broad management categories account for some $330 billion in savings over three years, 78 percent of the total. The rest comes from applying the principles of good business management in diverse cases; for example, the Agriculture Department could save an extra $7 billion over three years by cutting out the overlap and duplication in its services; by shifting the FHA's activities from direct loans to loan guarantees and transferring its housing functions to HUD; by charging for such things as maps, soil survey reports, and firewood, all of which are now given away free; and by increasing user fees for grazing, recreation, and the like.

The Grace Commission calls for an Office of Federal Management to be set up in the executive office of the President. Such an office would guide and coordinate management of the government's $800 billion conglomerate. It would institute the kind of budgeting and strategic planning that large corporations practice, and develop common government-wide software for standardized receivables, payroll, pension-plan, and fixed-asset accounting.

After Peter Grace presented the final report to the President in a White House ceremony on January 16 [1984,] the networks dutifully ran stories on the evening news, usually ending with the remark that here is another commission report to be filed away. Who, in an election year, was going to propose serious budgetary pigsticking? The *New York Times* wanly editorialized that the Grace Commission was "wishful, but worthwhile, on waste." Some of the Grace Commission's recommendations are already being carried out, but three-quarters of them need congressional approval. Hence, the question lingers: Can it really be done? And we are led to the crux of the issue: psychology.

News that the government pays $30 million in Medicare checks to the deceased, and loses track of $10 billion in block-grant money, seems almost beyond reality, somewhere in the realm of the absurd. It makes neat newspaper filler material, American black humor, good for a chuckle over coffee. It's another little confirmation of what most Americans have suspected of the government since the time of Thomas Jefferson.

Upon reflection, the unreality of the abuses becomes as overwhelming and unimaginable as the sheer size of the expenditures. More discouraging still is the realization that this sort of thing has obviously been going on for ages. So one shakes one's head and flips the page. What's to be done. *Nada, niente, rien du tout.*

The irony is that something can indeed be done, if enough citizens believe it can be, and make their wish known in Washington. Only by the force of widespread dissatisfaction can Congress find the courage to stick some pigs. In this sense, Peter Grace's work has only begun.

# How Much Waste in Government?
## An Alternate View

**Steven Kelman**

There are few beliefs more deeply embedded in the popular consciousness than that government wastes a lot of money. Seymour Martin Lipset and William Schneider, in their book *The Confidence Gap,* report that in surveys asking people how much of each tax dollar they think the federal government wastes, the median response is 48¢. Lipset and Schneider argue that the paradox of simultaneous public support for tax cuts, and for maintaining or increasing spending in all major categories of government programs, is explained by the perception that waste in government is so rampant that there can be big spending reductions without service rollbacks.

Last January the President's Private Sector Survey on Cost Control (generally known as the "Grace Commission" after its head, J. Peter Grace, Chief Executive Officer of W.R. Grace & Co.) delivered its final reports. The Grace Commission recruited over 2,000 corporate executives to scrutinize the government. Announcing the report, Peter Grace told the press that President Reagan had asked him to look at government agencies as if considering a merger or takeover. "The President's private sector survey would not acquire the government" was the conclusion, he stated. No wonder. He found that, over a three-year period, a total of $424 *billion* in savings could be obtained from controlling waste, "without weakening America's needed defense build-up and without in any way harming necessary social welfare programs." These were stupendous numbers, almost enough to eliminate federal deficits.

But they were not uncontroversial. With the perspective of someone interested in how government can be managed better, I spent time examining some specific allegations of waste the Grace Commission made in areas where, first, there is general agreement—public and governmental—that the activity being undertaken is worthwhile, and second, there are examples of the private sector producing the same output, so that the relative costs to government and to the private sector can be compared. The Grace Commission issued 48 reports and made a now-notorious 2,478 recommendations, so it was obviously impossible to examine any significant percentage. But in the press packet accompanying the Grace Commission report, there was a chart entitled "Ten Random Examples of Bureaucratic Absurdity" (which was picked up in the *New York Times* story on the Commission), and I examined those ten.[1] Also, I

Steven Kelman is a professor of public policy at the Kennedy School of Government at Harvard University. From "The Grace Commission: How Much Waste in Government?" by Steven Kelman. Reprinted with permission of the author from *The Public Interest,* No. 78 (Winter 1985), pp. 62–74, 77–78 © 1985 by National Affairs, Inc.

examined recommendations the Commission made involving the General Services Administration (GSA) and the Veterans Administration (VA), because
the responsibilities of both agencies include tasks very similar to ones private
firms undertake.

## THE CASE OF THE $91 SCREW

(1) *"The Pentagon has been buying screws, available in any hardware store for
3 cents, for $91 each."*

There have been many widely publicized examples of the apparently
outrageous prices paid for spare parts for weapons—$110 for a 4¢ diode, $9,609
for a 12¢ Allen wrench, and $1,118 for a plastic cap for a navigator's seat.

One has reason to doubt these stories, even before further investigation,
on strictly logical grounds. To suggest that defense contractors could routinely
charge the government $110 for something they got for a few pennies is to
suggest that the defense contracting business is the easiest avenue to unearned
fortune since the invention of plunder. In fact, it turns out that the Defense
Department has not negligently allowed itself to be hoodwinked. Most of these
cases have a common explanation, which involves an accounting quirk in
pricing material purchased from contractors.

Any time anybody buys something, the price includes not only the direct
cost of the materials, machines, and labor to produce it, but also a share of the
company's overhead expenses—ranging from running the legal department to
renting corporate headquarters. Defense Department acquisition rules prescribe that a defense contractor's overhead expenses be allocated to each
shipment at some fixed proportion of the value of the procurement. Thus, if the
direct cost of a weapon is $5 million, a company might be authorized to tack on,
illustratively, 20 percent or $1 million, for overhead expenses. The same
percentage may also be added to the direct costs of other items procured, such
as spare parts. Thus $1 million would be added to a spare parts order for $5
million, just as it would be to a fighter plane order.

The Pentagon orders many different spare parts at one time. Often in the
past, contractors have, simply as a matter of accounting convenience, allocated
the overhead to the individual parts on an "item" basis rather than a "value"
basis. Say that the $20 million order is for 10,000 parts, some of which have a
direct cost of $25,000 each and others of 4¢ each. Instead of apportioning the $1
million total overhead such that the $25,000 part gets a lot and the 4¢ part a
little, the computer printout will allocate $100 to each part. This produces a
charge to the government of $25,100 for the expensive part and $100.04 for the
cheap one.

Although this produces horror stories, nothing horrible has occurred. The
total overhead represents real resources legitimately charged to the government. If the $100 doesn't get allocated to the 4¢ diode, the diode no longer

appears to be so outrageously expensive. But the $100 doesn't disappear, nor should it. The overhead is just allocated elsewhere.

There is one mildly distressing aspect of this practice. The spreading of overhead costs over a contractor's entire production appears to reduce the up-front costs of new weapons systems, since research and development for the weapon is charged to spare parts as well. This, in turn, makes new weapons systems appear less expensive than they really are, and distorts political discussions of a system's costs and benefits. But that has nothing to do with "not minding the store."

Other horror stories have a different explanation. Many parts the Defense Department procures are "common use items," the same as commercially produced parts that might be used in a car as well as a tank. Other items need to be custom designed, which often produces an extremely high price per unit, because, unlike Chevrolets, much military equipment is produced in very small quantities and thus requires only a few of the same spare parts. The initial cost to design the part, and make the machine die or molding to produce it, must then be spread out over only a few units. (If it costs $3,000 to design and tool up a plastic cap, that will add only 1¢ to the cost of the cap if 300,000 are produced, but $1,000 if three are produced.)

The economics of tooling-up do suggest that common-use parts be used when possible, and the Defense Department does make efforts to get common-use items. Spare parts are frequently procured on a sole-source basis from the contractors for the original weapon. When the contractor submits designs for spare parts, he must designate those which are common-use. This list is reviewed by a Defense Department contracting officer, who makes suggestions for expanding common-use procurement when appropriate. After the contractor proposes prices, the contracting officer requests an independent evaluation of the offer by Defense Department value engineers, who may question whether a newly designated part is sufficiently different from common-use items to justify special tooling-up. But special design *is* sometimes necessary.

Contractors have something of an incentive to propose custom-designed parts, since a contractor is allowed to take a standard percentage profit, which in dollar terms is of course far greater for a $1,000 item than a $1 item. Cheating is presumably discouraged by the negative impact repeated discovery would have on the contractor's relations with the Defense Department. But the Department has an enormous review task—there are about 300,000 parts in an airplane—and sometimes an item that should have been classified as common-use ends up getting designed to order. This is what happened in the case of the $1,118 plastic cap. In the widely publicized case of the $9,609 Allen wrench, however, the system did work. General Dynamics proposed a custom-designed wrench, but the Pentagon's value review engineer found that the function could be performed equally well by an ordinary wrench. The Defense Department never ordered the custom-designed version, and is now increasing its scrutiny for common-use items. The additional scrutiny may cost more than it saves, but the issue to the Defense Department at this point is the credibility of the defense buildup.

## THE OUTRAGEOUS CASE OF BUILDING MANAGEMENT

(2) *"In comparison to a private sector company, managing comparable building space, the General Services Administration employs 17 times as many people and spends almost 14 times as much on total management costs."*

This contention is so wildly inaccurate that it is hard to know where to begin. The best place to start is with two whopping errors in the numbers the Grace Commission provided on the private sector firm being compared with GSA. The chart the Commission provided stated that the property management division of a large life insurance firm was managing 10,000 buildings, "comparable building space" to GSA. In fact, no insurance company has a portfolio anywhere near that large. The correct number for the insurance company is not 10,000 buildings, but *1,000*, which is not comparable to GSA at all. Furthermore, the Grace Commission states that the insurance company employs a total of 300 professionals, 100 in central administration, and 200 under contract. It turns out, however, that the company in question does not employ 200 *individuals* under contract, but rather hires 200 property management *firms* actually to manage its buildings. Each of these firms in turn has many professionals working for it.

The figure the Commission chart provided for GSA professionals— 5,000—is also exaggerated. About one-third of these are clerical and often non-professional employees (the Grace Commission simply looked at total white-collar employment at the Public Buildings Service). And about 800 of this number manage GSA design and construction, overseeing the contract process for construction of new buildings as well as repairs and alterations of existing buildings; the people who do this for the insurance company work in a different division, and thus aren't included in the employment figures the Grace Commission provided. So the number of professionals working on building management at GSA is really around 2,700, rather than 5,000.

Although all this indicates that the Grace Commission is monumentally mistaken, a precise comparison is difficult to make. One would need to know how many professionals the building management contractors employ, and the insurance company itself doesn't know that. Beyond that, the nature of the GSA portfolio and the insurance company's portfolio is different. Over two-thirds of the GSA buildings are leased space rather than owned space; this requires people to work on initial lease bids and on lease renewals (neither of which applies to the insurance company), but does not require government-provided building management services. Over 1,000 of the GSA buildings are (owned or leased) local social security offices, which are considerably smaller than the properties an insurance company owns. GSA officials would themselves concede that they probably have a larger staff for comparable functions than a private sector counterpart, because GSA requires more levels of review on contracting and leasing decisions to assure due process and to minimize corruption. But the difference is nothing like 17 to 1.

## THE $61,250 NURSING HOME BED

(3) *"The VA spends $61,250 per bed to construct nursing homes—almost four times the $16,000 per bed cost of a major private sector nursing home operator."*

The Grace Commission averaged the cost of six VA nursing homes, and the average was raised dramatically by the reported $113,500 per-bed cost of construction of a home in Martinsburg, West Virginia. This nursing home was being built simultaneously with a VA hospital adjacent to it, and the cost the Grace Commission reported included construction costs for a domiciliary that was part of the whole medical center, as well as site preparation and utilities for the entire complex. The actual cost for the nursing home at that site was $29,000 per bed, bringing the average cost per bed for the six facilities down from $61,000 to $47,000. Furthermore, the cost of three of the VA homes was significantly higher than usual because of unfavorable site conditions (such as confined space for construction, thus requiring off-site warehousing of building materials). Site conditions were unfavorable because the nursing homes were being built next to already-existing VA hospitals, pursuant to VA policy. The average cost of the remaining three homes, built under normal site conditions, was $39,000 a bed. So while the Commission exaggerates, there remains a substantial difference compared with the private sector, even if one considers only the homes constructed on normal site conditions.

Why these differences? Whatever the answer, one can be relatively confident that it is not the result of lazy government construction workers or bloated construction material prices paid by government. In fact, the VA does not construct nursing homes itself. It takes its nursing home specifications and puts them out to bid by building contractors. The low bid wins.

The truth is that what the VA calls a nursing home is in many ways of much higher quality than what private-sector chains produce. These quality differences increase the cost of a VA nursing home relative to a private one.

The most obvious differences involve the physical designs. VA facilities have been top-of-the-line. Homes have routinely included balconies in each room, occupational therapy areas, quiet rooms, extensive recreation space, and on-premises artwork. The VA policy of building homes contiguous to VA hospitals rather than freestanding, as the private company Beverly does, is also quality-driven; it provides nursing home residents quick access to hospital services and allows more rapid treatment of medical emergencies. That policy drives up costs in a number of ways, however. The VA got into the nursing home business relatively recently, and most homes are built on existing hospital sites. Often, however, these sites are too small to be ideal for new construction. That can raise costs by requiring construction in cramped or otherwise difficult situations. And frequently there is not enough land to build single-story homes, which are marginally cheaper to construct than the two-story homes the VA often must build. Is it worthwhile to produce this level of quality? That is a matter of debate. But it is not an issue of "waste," as the term is typically used.

The cost of constructing VA nursing homes *can* be reduced by decreasing quality. In 1981 the VA established a task force on nursing home construction cost reduction, after private nursing home chains had called cost differences to the attention of congressional oversight committees. The task force proposed a number of design changes that will reduce the cost of new VA nursing homes by about $12,000 per bed. They include eliminating balconies, making ceilings eight rather than nine feet high, reducing recreation room and dining room space by 35 percent, and reducing landscaping by half.

Another part of higher VA construction costs stems from the special requirements of government procurement. The most obvious are ones such as Davis-Bacon, and the preference given to American-made products and to minority and small-business enterprises. When the government builds a nursing home, it has decided not just to build a home but also to aid small business and American-made products. Again, this is not "waste," but rather government policy.

The entire mode of procurement in government is a less obvious, but very important, source of additional costs. Private sector nursing home chains generally establish ongoing relationships with construction firms in an area (often two firms, each to serve as a competitive check on the other), to whom they turn again and again. This allows them to avoid the costs of gearing up for new bidding procedures for each job. By contracting for several jobs at the same time, it allows the general contractor to obtain lower prices from subcontractors and suppliers, who give quantity discounts for the larger volume of work. It allows the contractors to become familiar with the details of how the firm wants the home built and to look for ways to build more economically, since investments in such efforts can be capitalized over a number of projects. The VA, by contrast, must gear up for a *de novo* bidding procedure, open to all, for each construction contract, with detailed functional specifications (rather than brand-specific ones) so that nobody is excluded from bidding. There are many layers of review within the VA to ensure that specifications inhibit no one, and to clear any deviations by the procurement or project staff from the rule that the lowest bid must be accepted. These procurement methods entail extensive additional costs, both because any individual act of procurement is more complicated (developing functional specifications, layers of review) and personnel-intensive, and because there are far more separate procurement decisions to be made (the *de novo* bidding process). Although the monetary costs of these procedures outweigh their monetary benefits (or else private firms would follow similar procedures) none of them, again, constitutes a clear example of waste. At worst, they reflect mistaken policies. They produce outputs with "quality" features not found in private home construction such as equal opportunity for all businesses to compete and a minimization of kickbacks.

Where does all this leave the VA/private sector comparison? I start with a $39,000 per bed average figure for the nursing homes built on normal site conditions, and I subtract $6,000 per bed in savings from the cost-control task force.[2] This brings the VA cost down to $33,000 a bed, compared with $16,000 in the private sector: about twice as much, rather than four times as much. The costs of Davis-Bacon and various statutory procurement preferences, of complex procurement procedures that must be repeated each time a home is built, of any remaining quality difference compared with private sector homes, and of any extra costs from two-story construction, reduce the differences further. Since no study exists of the accumulated effect of those factors, it is impossible to say how much of the VA/private sector difference that does remain is simple waste. My suspicion is that something does remain, but that the differences are not dramatic.

## THE FREIGHT-CHARGES BOONDOGGLE

(4) *"The government spends almost $5 billion annually on freight charges but doesn't bother to negotiate volume discounts with suppliers."*

The Grace Commission's own backup material regarding this claim turns out not even to make the contention that the government "doesn't bother to negotiate volume discounts." In fact, it turns out that virtually all government freight is moved at rates discounted for volume.

The problem is a more subtle one. Before trucking deregulation, freight tariffs were fixed. Deregulation in 1980 produced an avalanche of different rates (similar to the situation for airline travelers). Suddenly, there were differences in fares charged for a given route and many lower tariffs for full-load shipments.

Deregulation opened up opportunities for savings on freight expenses, but the proliferation of rates increased the information-processing requirements for taking advantage of those possibilities. Very quickly, computer software companies began offering packages that allow a shipper to determine the cheapest available rate, and also to determine what shipments from several sources within the organization might be going to the same place at the same time, so that full-load discounts can be obtained. These systems have spread quickly in the private sector since 1980.

In 1981 the General Services Administration, which administers shipping for most of the government, began to look at these new computer systems, but decided they were still too new to try. In the summer of 1983 they decided to procure one, and the system they selected went on-line in March 1984.

## THE MAILING LIST FIASCO

(5) *"Government mailing lists erroneously repeat the same addresses as many as 29 times."*

This statement, though ambiguous, seems to suggest that somewhere there is a government mailing list that has the same address on it 29 times, causing 29 copies of the same publication to be sent to one location. The implication is that government officials simply never bothered to check the list for such wasteful duplication.

This example of 29 repetitions comes from a 1980 effort by the Office of Human Development Services in HHS to improve its management of mailing lists. The Office was formed in the mid-1970s as an umbrella organization for a large number of already existing agencies, such as the Administration on Aging and the Administration for Children, Youth and Families. Each of these separate organizations, quite naturally, maintained its own mailing lists—usually, in fact, a number of different mailing lists, such as lists of subscribers to an agency magazine, media contacts, libraries, or recipients of grant award information. There were about 300 different mailing lists in all.

In 1979, a newly appointed manager of the Office of Public Affairs at Human Development Services persuaded his boss to authorize a project to centralize and modernize the organization's mailing lists. The 300 lists were combined into one master list. A "positive purge" was conducted, whereby every person on any of the lists had to return a card in order to stay on. The Public Affairs Office also began to rent commercially available lists—of libraries, professors of social work, etc.—as an alternative to maintaining and updating its own lists.

In the course of this project, it was discovered that one address (a social service agency) appeared 29 times. But this was 29 times on 300 different lists, and these 300 lists generally received different publications. In other words, the addressee might have been on one list to receive the *Mental Disability Law Reporter,* on another for press releases from the Administration on Aging, and on a third for information about grant availability from the Office of Handicapped Individuals. The addressee wasn't receiving 29 copies of any one publication. At worst, as the person in charge of the reform effort told me, an addressee appearing 29 times might receive five copies of a single publication—but only in the rare cases when a mailing went to several of the agency's *different* lists. There were certainly some examples of duplications on the same list: Although federal law requires annual canvassing of individual agency lists for duplication, compliance is mixed.

Although the quality of mailing list management within the government varies, there is no doubt that significant improvements could be made. There have been major changes in the mailing list business during the last decade, with the increased use of computers for list generation and management. Simple software now exists to purge lists of duplication, and with the growth of list brokers there is no longer any need for an organization to attempt to maintain its own lists of nursing home administrators, libraries, or public health professors. The government is now beginning to adapt to these changes.

## THE SCANDAL OF SEIZED ASSETS

(6)*"The Justice Department just sits on the cash seized from criminals, not bothering to deposit the money in interest bearing accounts while cases are being adjudicated."*

Traditionally, cash seized from criminals was indeed not deposited in interest-bearing accounts. "Not bothering," however, was not the reason. Prosecuting attorneys wanted the actual bills in hand, to impress juries with wads of ill-gotten lucre. Depositing the money would have meant losing the ability to show it to juries: The only thing available would have been a statement in a government bank account! Furthermore, some jurisdictions require that actual bills be submitted as evidence.

Until quite recently, very little cash was seized from criminal suspects. In the late 1970s, however, the Justice Department began actively to seize cash and physical assets (such as cars and boats)—and to seek their forfeiture—as a tactic against organized crime.

Soon thereafter, the Department realized that this vast quantity of physical assets had created a management problem. The Justice Department's policy was not to question legitimate third-party liens on seized assets, so that if there was $110,000 loan outstanding on a $150,000 boat, the government would not contest the bank's right to collect $110,000 from the sale of the boat. The frequent problem is that the hypothetical boat might deteriorate badly while in the government's possession. When sold after being forfeited, less than $110,000 might be realized; the government would have to make up the difference. The local U.S. Attorney offices had no capability to manage seized assets while they awaited disposition (lawyers are experts at trying cases, not managing property), and no centralized management system had ever been developed because there were so few seized assets.

In 1981, the Justice Department appointed a task force to examine the management of seized assets. It issued a report in 1982, recommending that the Department establish a central organizational capability, through the U.S. Marshal Service, to manage seized assets for local U.S. Attorney offices. Agreement having been obtained within the Department (including from the U.S. Attorney offices), this new capability is now being established.

## THE SHOCKING SLOTH OF LOAN COLLECTORS

(7) *"HUD makes only 3 attempts to collect loans versus 24 to 36 tries in the private sector."*

This refers to loan collection procedures for two programs—a Housing and Urban Development credit insurance program for regular property improvement loans (Title I), and HUD's direct, subsidized loan program for property-improvement loans in disadvantaged areas (Section 312). Title I is an old program (enacted in 1934) that does not have income restrictions; Section 312 is a War on Poverty-era program that is targeted to poorer neighborhoods.

Again, the comparison the Grace Commission presents is exaggerated. First, the Grace Commission's own backup material refers to two or three loan collection tries per month in the private sector (compared to a total of three in HUD), but collection activity, in both the private sector and HUD, proceeds for only four months before legal action is commenced or the loan abandoned. The press packet figure of "24 to 36 tries in the private sector" comes from incorrectly assuming that collection activity at private banks goes on for an entire year. Even accepting the Grace Commission comparison at face value, the proper number is thus eight to 12 tries in the private sector, not 24 to 36. Second, HUD loan collection officers generally do not make a written record of telephone calls they make to delinquents, so Grace Commission investigators looking only at the written record underestimated the number of collection tries HUD made. Finally, and crucially, there has been collection activity on these loans *before* they are sent to HUD. Title I loans are made by regular banks, and Title I regulations mandate that the banks pursue their own normal debt-collection efforts before passing the loans on to HUD; for the Section 312 loans that HUD makes directly, Fannie Mae (the Federal National Mortgage Association), which services the loans, engages in some mild collection activity (dunning letters but no phone calls or contacts with an employer) before passing the loans on. HUD isn't starting from scratch on collections, as the Grace Commission's comparison suggests.

None of this is to suggest that there have been no problems with debt-collection at HUD. Although the regulations call for banks to pursue normal debt-collection efforts first, HUD officials concede that compliance is mixed. Also, when their own collection efforts fail, private banks give potentially collectible loans to private-collection agencies, and HUD gives them to the Department of Justice for prosecution. Attorneys there have regarded these as low-priority cases and have not prosecuted them in a timely way—something that debt-collection experts regard as crucial to any chance of recovery. Finally, at least for Section 312 loans, management at HUD has probably always regarded these loans as a sort of disguised social assistance program, and has seen the idea of banging on the doors of poor people to get them to pay as distasteful. Loan collection efforts for the 312 program traditionally received little attention from top management. (The Title I program, by contrast, turns a profit for the government.)

The organization of debt collection at HUD has also failed to reflect changes in private debt collection practices. HUD standard operating procedures continued to call for personal dunning visits to delinquents, although banks had concluded over a decade ago that such efforts (earlier traditional in the industry) were generally not cost-effective. And HUD was very slow to computerize debt information, which resulted both in a great deal of clerical work for loan collectors (reducing the time available for collection activities) and in poor control over the status of files. The Section 312 program began to move toward computerization (and now to contracting out its debt collection to a private firm) after a critical report by the General Accounting Office in 1979; Title I has only recently computerized its collection activities, after a decision to do so was made by the assistant secretary appointed by President Reagan.

\* \* \*

## WASTE IN GOVERNMENT?

There are a number of conclusions one can draw from all of this. First, the horror stories one hears are almost always gross exaggerations. What we have seen suggests that those responsible for the activities in question generally pay attention to costs, and have a fairly good sense of ways to keep them down. People are too quick to conclude that programs are wasteful when they think the programs are not worthwhile. But if the government efficiently delivers a worthless product, the criticism should be directed at the decision to deliver the product, not vented in charges of incompetence and venality against those making the deliveries.

Second, some differences between relative costs to government and to the private sector occur because the government, superficial similarities notwithstanding, is in fact producing something very different. This is most obviously the case when, for instance, the VA puts balconies outside its nursing home rooms. But it is also the case when agencies follow cumbersome procurement procedures designed not solely to procure certain goods, but also to ensure due process for vendors and special aid for disadvantaged businesses. There may indeed be incentives in some government programs, such as those administered by the VA, to overproduce quality. And it may be that we are spending too much for due process. But the extra money entailed has not simply disappeared down a black hole.

Third, even after taking account of quality differences, it is probably true that government generally produces a given output less efficiently than the private sector. If I had to hazard a guess, I would say that the government might typically use, not 4 times or 17 times as many resources as the private sector to produce a given output, but perhaps 1.2 times. That is less dramatic, but it does add up. Even if it adds up only to several billion dollars, rather than to the Grace Commission's fantasy figures, such a sum is negligible only to those who, to paraphrase [former U.S. Senator] Everett Dirksen, have gotten so used to spending a billion here and a billion there that they forget it eventually adds up to real money.

Fourth, government is not very good at turning on a dime. As we have seen, there are many situations in which the environment changed—computer programs becoming available, for example—and it took more time for government to adapt than for the private sector. But, as we have also seen, the government does in fact adapt. . . .

## NOTES

1 Of these, four proved not to be "bureaucratic absurdity" after all, but rather policies enacted by Congress. So only six cases were investigated. In addition, I examined the issue of Defense Department spare parts prices (which appeared in the press packet under another listing) because the issue had received so much media attention and because it had the horror-story sound of the other examples of "bureaucratic absurdity."

2 I subtract $6,000 rather than the estimated $12,000 in savings because some of the changes the VA is making bring VA nursing homes below Beverly's standards—for example, the ceilings in VA homes will now be lower than those in Beverly homes. Lacking time, or expertise in architecture, to allow an exact estimate of the cost-reduction steps that bring the VA homes to the *same* level as Beverly's, I have taken a figure of one-half, the arbitrary nature of which the reader should be aware of.

# 14

## The Supreme Court

*While few would question the Supreme Court's authority to interpret the Constitution, there has long been disagreement over how the nine justices should approach this awesome responsibility. This debate grew in intensity during the Reagan era as the president and his attorney general inveighed against the Supreme Court, charging that justices had all too often substituted their own values and principles for those contained in the Constitution.*

*In the selection which immediately follows, Edwin Meese, U.S. Attorney General during part of the Reagan administration, calls upon judges to interpret the Constitution in accordance with the intent of those who wrote and ratified it. Insisting that the Founding Fathers expected as much from the members of the Supreme Court, Meese goes on to suggest how the justices should approach this task. He remains convinced that the application of original intent—undistorted by the personal values of well-meaning judges—will best preserve the principles of democratic government.*

*The second selection offers a markedly different perspective from someone who has had the responsibility of interpreting our Constitution. Irving Kaufman, Chief Judge of the United States Court of Appeals for the Second Circuit, maintains that ascertaining the original intent of the Founding Fathers is decidedly more difficult than Edwin Meese would lead us to believe. Nor, for that matter, is the strict application of original intent necessarily desirable in every instance. This is not to say that judges are at liberty to read whatever they choose into the wording of our Constitution. On the contrary, Kaufman points to several factors which serve to restrain judges from doing so.*

# A Jurisprudence of Original Intention

## Edwin Meese III

. . . Today I would like to discuss further the meaning of constitutional fidelity. In particular, I would like to describe in more detail this administration's approach.

Before doing so, I would like to make a few commonplace observations about the original document itself. . . .

The period surrounding the creation of the Constitution is not a dark and mythical realm. The young America of the 1780s and '90s was a vibrant place, alive with pamphlets, newspapers and books chronicling and commenting upon the great issues of the day. We know how the Founding Fathers lived, and much of what they read, thought, and believed. The disputes and compromises of the Constitutional Convention were carefully recorded. The minutes of the convention are a matter of public record. Several of the most important participants—including James Madison, the "father" of the Constitution—wrote comprehensive accounts of the convention. Others, Federalists and Anti-Federalists alike, committed their arguments for and against ratification, as well as their understandings of the Constitution, to paper, so that their ideas and conclusions could be widely circulated, read, and understood.

In short, the Constitution is not buried in the mists of time. We know a tremendous amount of the history of its genesis. . . .

With these thoughts in mind, I would like to discuss the administration's approach to constitutional interpretation. . . .

Our approach . . . begins with the document itself. The plain fact is, it exists. It is something that has been written down. Walter Berns of the American Enterprise Institute has noted that the central object of American constitutionalism was "the effort" of the Founders "to express fundamental governmental arrangements in a legal document—to 'get it in writing.'"

Indeed, judicial review has been grounded in the fact that the Constitution is a written, as opposed to an unwritten, document. In *Marbury v. Madison* John Marshall rested his rationale for judicial review on the fact that we have a written constitution with meaning that is binding upon judges. "[I]t is apparent," he wrote, "that the framers of the Constitution contemplated that instrument as a rule for the government of *courts,* as well as of the legislature. Why otherwise does it direct the judges to take an oath to support it?"

The presumption of a written document is that it conveys meaning. As Thomas Grey of the Stanford Law School has said, it makes "relatively definite and explicit what otherwise would be relatively indefinite and tacit."

Edwin Meese III served as U.S. Attorney General under President Ronald Reagan. Excerpted from a speech by Attorney General Meese before the Washington, D.C., Chapter of the Federalist Society, Lawyers Division, November 15, 1985, pp. 2–14.

We know that those who framed the Constitution chose their words carefully. They debated at great length the most minute points. The language they chose meant something. They proposed, they substituted, they edited, and they carefully revised. Their words were studied with equal care by state ratifying conventions.

This is not to suggest that there was unanimity among the framers and ratifiers on all points. The Constitution and the Bill of Rights, and some of the subsequent amendments, emerged after protracted debate. Nobody got everything they wanted. What's more, the framers were not clairvoyants—they could not foresee every issue that would be submitted for judicial review. Nor could they predict how all foreseeable disputes would be resolved under the Constitution. But the point is, the meaning of the Constitution can be known.

What does this written Constitution mean? In places it is exactingly specific. Where it says that Presidents of the United States must be at least 35 years of age it means exactly that. (I have not heard of any claim that 35 means 30 or 25 or 20.) Where it specifies how the House and Senate are to be organized, it means what it says.

The Constitution also expresses particular principles. One is the right to be free of an unreasonable search or seizure. Another concerns religious liberty. Another is the right to equal protection of the laws.

Those who framed these principles meant something by them. And the meanings can be found. The Constitution itself is also an expression of certain general principles. These principles reflect the deepest purpose of the Constitution—that of establishing a political system through which Americans can best govern themselves consistent with the goal of securing liberty.

The text and structure of the Constitution is instructive. It contains very little in the way of specific political solutions. It speaks volumes on how problems should be approached, and by *whom*. For example, the first three articles set out clearly the scope and limits of three distinct branches of national government. The powers of each being carefully and specifically enumerated. In this scheme it is no accident to find the legislative branch described first, as the framers had fought and sacrificed to secure the right of democratic self-governance. Naturally, this faith in republicanism was not unbounded, as the next two articles make clear.

Yet the Constitution remains a document of powers and principles. And its undergirding premise remains that democratic self government is subject only to the limits of certain constitutional principles. This respect for the political process was made explicit early on. When John Marshall upheld the act of Congress chartering a national bank in *McCulloch v. Maryland* he wrote: "The Constitution [was] intended to endure for ages to come, and, consequently, to be adapted to the various crises of human affairs." But to use *McCulloch*, as some have tried, as support for the idea that the Constitution is a protean, changeable thing is to stand history on its head. Marshall was keeping faith with the original intention that Congress be free to elaborate and apply constitutional powers and principles. He was not saying that the Court must invent some new constitutional value in order to keep pace with the times. In Walter Berns's words: "Marshall's meaning is not that the Constitution may be adapted to the 'various crises of human affairs,' but that the legislative powers granted by the Constitution are adaptable to meet these crises."

The approach this administration advocates is rooted in the text of the Constitution as illuminated by those who drafted, proposed, and ratified it. In his famous Commentary on the Constitution of the United States Justice Joseph Story explained that:

> The first and fundamental rule in the interpretation of all instruments is, to construe them according to the sense of the terms, and the intention of the parties.

Our approach understands the significance of a written document and seeks to discern the particular and general principles it expresses. It recognizes that there may be debate at times over the application of these principles. But it does not mean these principles cannot be identified.

Constitutional adjudication is obviously not a mechanical process. It requires an appeal to reason and discretion. The text and intention of the Constitution must be understood to constitute the banks within which constitutional interpretation must flow. As James Madison said, if "the sense in which the Constitution was accepted and ratified by the nation . . . be not the guide in expounding it, there can be no security for a consistent and stable, more than for a faithful exercise of its powers."

Thomas Jefferson, so often cited incorrectly as a framer of the Constitution, in fact shared Madison's view: "Our peculiar security is in the possession of a written Constitution. Let us not make it a blank paper by construction."

Jefferson was even more explicit in his personal correspondence:

> On every question of construction [we should] carry ourselves back to the time, when the constitution was adopted; recollect the spirit manifested in the debates; and instead of trying [to find], what meaning may be squeezed out of the text, or invented against it, conform to the probable one, in which it was passed.

In the main a jurisprudence that seeks to be faithful to our Constitution— a jurisprudence of original intention, as I have called it—is not difficult to describe. Where the language of the Constitution is specific, it must be obeyed. Where there is a demonstrable consensus among the framers and ratifiers as to a principle stated or implied by the Constitution, it should be followed. Where there is ambiguity as to the precise meaning or reach of a constitutional provision, it should be interpreted and applied in a manner so as to at least not contradict the text of the Constitution itself.

Sadly, while almost everyone participating in the current constitutional debate would give assent to these propositions, the techniques and conclusions of some of the debaters do violence to them. What is the source of this violence? In large part I believe that it is the misuse of history stemming from the neglect of the idea of a written constitution.

There is a frank proclamation by some judges and commentators that what matters most about the Constitution is not its words but its so-called "spirit." These individuals focus less on the language of specific provisions than on what they describe as the "vision" or "concepts of human dignity" they find embodied in the Constitution. This approach to jurisprudence has led to some remarkable and tragic conclusions.

In the 1850s, the Supreme Court under Chief Justice Roger B. Taney read blacks out of the Constitution in order to invalidate Congress's attempt to limit the spread of slavery. The *Dred Scott* decision, famously described as a judicial "self-inflicted wound," helped bring on civil war.

There is a lesson in this history. There is danger in seeing the Constitution as an empty vessel into which each generation may pour its passion and prejudice.

Our own time has its own fashions and passions. In recent decades many have come to view the Constitution—more accurately, part of the Constitution, provisions of the Bill of Rights and the Fourteenth Amendment—as a charter for judicial activism on behalf of various constituencies. Those who hold this view often have lacked demonstrable textual or historical support for their conclusions. Instead they have "grounded" their rulings in appeals to social theories, to moral philosophies or personal notions of human dignity, or to "penumbras," somehow emanating ghostlike from various provisions— identified and not identified—in the Bill of Rights. The problem with this approach, as John Hart Ely, Dean of the Stanford Law School, has observed with respect to one such decision, is not that it is bad constitutional law, but that it is not constitutional law in any meaningful sense, at all.

Despite this fact, the perceived popularity of some results in particular cases has encouraged some observers to believe that any critique of the methodology of those decisions is an attack on the results. This perception is sufficiently widespread that it deserves an answer. My answer is to look at history.

When the Supreme Court, in *Brown v. Board of Education,* sounded the death knell for official segregation in the country, it earned all the plaudits it received. But the Supreme Court in that case was not giving new life to old words, or adapting a "living," "flexible" Constitution to new reality. It was restoring the original principle of the Constitution to constitutional law. The *Brown* Court was correcting the damage done 50 years earlier, when in *Plessy v. Ferguson* an earlier Supreme Court had disregarded the clear intent of the framers of the Civil War amendments to eliminate the legal degradation of blacks, and had contrived a theory of the Constitution to support the charade of "separate but equal" discrimination.

Similarly, the decisions of the New Deal and beyond that freed Congress to regulate commerce and enact a plethora of social legislation were not judicial adaptations of the Constitution to new realities. They were in fact removals of encrustations of earlier courts that had strayed from the original intent of the framers regarding the power of the legislature to make policy.

It is amazing how so much of what passes for social and political progress is really the undoing of old judicial mistakes.

Mistakes occur when the principles of specific constitutional provisions—such as those contained in the Bill of Rights—are taken by some as invitations to read into the Constitution values that contradict the clear language of other provisions.

Acceptances to this illusory invitation have proliferated in recent decades. One Supreme Court justice identified the proper judicial standard as asking "what's best for this country." Another said it is important to "keep the Court out in front" of the general society. Various academic commentators have poured rhetorical grease on this judicial fire, suggesting that constitutional interpretation appropriately be guided by such standards as whether a public policy "personifies justice" or "comports with the notion of moral evolution" or confers "an identity" upon our society or was consistent with "natural ethical law" or was consistent with some "right of equal citizenship."

Unfortunately, as I've noted, navigation by such lodestars has in the past given us questionable economics, governmental disorder, and racism—all in the guise of constitutional law. Recently one of the distinguished judges of one of our federal appeals courts got it about right when he wrote: "The truth is that the judge who looks outside the Constitution always looks inside himself and nowhere else." Or, as we recently put it before the Supreme Court in an important brief: "The further afield interpretation travels from its point of departure in the text, the greater the danger that constitutional adjudication will be like a picnic to which the framers bring the words and the judges the meaning."

In the *Osborne v. Bank of United States* decision 21 years after *Marbury,* Chief Justice Marshall further elaborated his view of the relationship between the judge and the law, be it statutory or constitutional:

> Judicial power, as contradistinguished from the power of the laws, has no existence. Courts are the mere instruments of the law, and can will nothing. When they are said to exercise a discretion, it is a mere legal discretion, a discretion to be exercised in discerning the course prescribed by law; and, when that is discerned, it is the duty of the Court to follow it.

Any true approach to constitutional interpretation must respect the document in all its parts and be faithful to the Constitution in its entirety.

What must be remembered in the current debate is that interpretation does not imply results. The framers were not trying to anticipate every answer. They were trying to create a tripartite national government, within a federal system, that would have the flexibility to adapt to face new exigencies—as it did, for example, in chartering a national bank. Their great interest was in the distribution of power and responsibility in order to secure the great goal of liberty for all.

A jurisprudence that seeks fidelity to the Constitution—a jurisprudence of original intention—is not a jurisprudence of political results. It is very much concerned with process, and it is a jurisprudence that in our day seeks to de-politicize the law. The great genius of the constitutional blueprint is found in its creation and respect for spheres of authority and the limits it places on govern-mental power. In this scheme the framers did not see the courts as the ex-clusive custodians of the Constitution. Indeed, because the document posits so few conclusions it leaves to the more political branches the matter of adapting and vivifying its principles in each generation. It also leaves to the people of the states, in the Tenth Amendment, those responsibilities and rights not commit-ted to federal care. The power to declare acts of Congress and laws of the states null and void is truly awesome. This power must be used when the Constitution clearly speaks. It should not be used when the Constitution does not.

In *Marbury v. Madison,* at the same time he vindicated the concept of judicial review, Marshall wrote that the "principles" of the Constitution "are deemed fundamental and permanent," and except for formal amendment, "unchangeable." If we want a change in our Constitution or in our laws we must seek it through the formal mechanisms presented in that organizing document of our government.

In summary, I would emphasize that what is at issue here is not an agenda of issues or a menu of results. At issue is a way of government. A jurisprudence based on first principles is neither conservative nor liberal, neither right nor left. It is a jurisprudence that cares about committing and limiting to each organ of government the proper ambit of its responsibilities. It is a jurisprudence faithful to our Constitution.

By the same token, an activist jurisprudence, one which anchors the Constitution only in the consciences of jurists, is a chameleon jurisprudence, changing color and form in each era. The same activism hailed today may threaten the capacity for decision through democratic consensus tomorrow, as it has in many yesterdays. Ultimately, as the early democrats wrote into the Massachusetts state constitution, the best defense of our liberties is a govern-ment of laws and not men.

On this point it is helpful to recall the words of the late Justice Frank-furter. As he wrote:

> [T]here is not under our Constitution a judicial remedy for every political mis-chief, for every undesirable exercise of legislative power. The framers carefully and with deliberate forethought refused so to enthrone the judiciary. In this sit-uation, as in others of like nature, appeal for relief does not belong here. Appeal must be to an informed, civically militant electorate. . . .

# What Did the Founding Fathers Intend?

## Irving R. Kaufman

. . . In the ongoing debate over original intent, almost all Federal judges hold to
the notion that judicial decisions should be based on the text of the Constitution
or the structure it creates. Yet, in requiring judges to be guided solely by the
expressed views of the framers, current advocates of original intent seem to
call for a narrower concept. Jurists who disregard this interpretation, the
argument runs, act lawlessly because they are imposing their own moral standards and political preferences on the community.

As a Federal judge, I have found it often difficult to ascertain the "intent
of the framers," and even more problematic to try to dispose of a constitutional
question by giving great weight to the intent argument. Indeed, even if it were
possible to decide hard cases on the basis of a strict interpretation of original
intent, or originalism, that methodology would conflict with a judge's duty to
apply the Constitution's underlying principles to changing circumstances. Furthermore, by attempting to erode the base for judicial affirmation of the freedoms guaranteed by the Bill of Rights and the 14th Amendment (no state shall
"deprive any person of life, liberty, or property without due process of law; nor
deny to any person . . . the equal protection of the laws"), the intent theory
threatens some of the greatest achievements of the Federal judiciary.

Ultimately, the debate centers on the nature of judicial review, or the
power of courts to act as the ultimate arbiters of constitutional meaning. This
responsibility has been acknowledged ever since the celebrated 1803 case of
*Marbury v. Madison,* in which Chief Justice John Marshall struck down a
congressional grant of jurisdiction to the Supreme Court not authorized by
Article III of the Constitution. But here again, originalists would accept judicial
review only if it adhered to the allegedly neutral principles embalmed in
historical intent.

In the course of 36 years on the Federal bench, I have had to make many
difficult constitutional interpretations. I have had to determine whether a
teacher could wear a black armband as a protest against the Vietnam War;
whether newspapers have a nonactionable right to report accusatory statements; and whether a school system might be guilty of de facto segregation.
Unfortunately, the framers' intentions are not made sufficiently clear to provide easy answers. A judge must first determine what the intent was (or would
have been)—a notoriously formidable task.

An initial problem is the paucity of materials. Both the official minutes of
the Philadelphia Convention of 1787 and James Madison's famous notes of the

Irving R. Kaufman is a judge of the Second U.S. Circuit Court of Appeals. From "What Did the
Founding Fathers Intend?" by Irving R. Kaufman, *New York Times Magazine,* February 23, 1986,
pp. 59–69. Copyright © 1986 by the New York Times Company. Reprinted by permission.

266

proceedings, published in 1840, tend toward the terse and cursory, especially in relation to the judiciary. The congressional debates over the proposed Bill of Rights, which became effective in 1791, are scarcely better. Even Justice William Rehnquist, one of the most articulate spokesmen for original intent, admitted in a recent dissent in a case concerning school prayer that the legislative history behind the provision against the establishment of an official religion "does not seem particularly illuminating."

One source deserves special mention. *The Federalist Papers*—the series of essays written by Alexander Hamilton, James Madison and John Jay in 1787 and 1788—have long been esteemed as the earliest constitutional commentary. In 1825, for example, Thomas Jefferson noted that *The Federalist* was regularly appealed to "as evidence of the general opinion of those who framed and of those who accepted the Constitution of the United States."

*The Federalist,* however, did not discuss the Bill of Rights or the Civil War amendments, which were yet to be written. Moreover, the essays were part of a political campaign—the authors wrote them in support of New York's ratification of the Constitution. The essays, therefore, tended to enunciate general democratic theory or rebut anti-Federalist arguments, neither of which offers much help to modern jurists. (In light of the following passage from *The Federalist,* No. 14, I believe Madison would be surprised to find his words of 200 years ago deciding today's cases: "Is it not the glory of the people of America that . . . they have not suffered a blind veneration for antiquity . . . to overrule the suggestions of their own good sense . . .?")

Another problem with original intent is this: Who were the framers? Generally, they are taken to be the delegates to the Philadelphia Convention and the congressional sponsors of subsequent amendments. All constitutional provisions, however, have been ratified by state conventions or legislatures on behalf of the people they represented. Is the relevant intention, then, that of the drafters, the ratifiers or the general populace?

The elusiveness of the framers' intent leads to another, more telling problem. Originalist doctrine presumes that intent can be discovered by historical sleuthing or psychological rumination. In fact, this is not possible. Judges are constantly required to resolve questions that 18th-century statesmen, no matter how prescient, simply could not or did not foresee and resolve. On most issues, to look for a collective intention held by either drafters or ratifiers is to hunt for a chimera.

A reading of the Constitution highlights this problem. The principles of our great charter are cast in grand, yet cryptic, phrases. Accordingly, judges usually confront what Justice Robert Jackson in the 1940s termed the "majestic generalities" of the Bill of Rights, or the terse commands of "due process of law," or "equal protection" contained in the 14th Amendment. The use of such open-ended provisions would indicate that the framers did not want the Constitution to become a straitjacket on all events for all times. In contrast, when the framers held a clear intention, they did not mince words. Article II, for example, specifies a minimum Presidential age of 35 years instead of merely requiring "maturity" or "adequate age."

The First Amendment is a good example of a vaguer provision. In guaranteeing freedom of the press, some of our forefathers perhaps had specific thoughts on what publications fell within its purview. Some historians believe, in light of Colonial debates, that the main concern of the framers was to prevent governmental licensing of newspapers. If that were all the First Amendment meant today, then many important decisions protecting the press would have to be overruled. One of them would be the landmark *New York Times v. Sullivan* ruling of 1964, giving the press added protection in libel cases brought by public figures. Another would be *Near v. Minnesota,* a case involving Jay Near, a newspaper publisher who had run afoul of a Minnesota statute outlawing "malicious, scandalous and defamatory" publications. The Supreme Court struck down the statute in 1931, forbidding governmental prior restraints on publication; this ruling was the precursor of the 1971 Pentagon Papers decision.

The Founding Fathers focused not on particularities but on principles, such as the need in a democracy for people to engage in free and robust discourse. James Madison considered a popular government without popular information a "Prologue to a Farce or a Tragedy." Judges, then, must focus on underlying principles when going about their delicate duty of applying the First Amendment's precepts to today's world.

In fact, our nation's first debate over constitutional interpretation centered on grand principles. Angered at John Adams's Federalist Administration, advocates of states' rights in the late 18th century argued that original intent meant that the Constitution, like the Articles of Confederation, should be construed narrowly—as a compact among separate sovereigns. The 1798 Virginia and Kentucky Resolutions, which sought to reserve to the states the power of ultimate constitutional interpretation, were the most extreme expressions of this view. In rejecting this outlook, a nationalistic Supreme Court construed the Constitution more broadly.

The important point here is that neither side of this debate looked to the stated views of the framers to resolve the issue. Because of his leading role at the Philadelphia Convention, Madison's position is especially illuminating. "Whatever veneration might be entertained for the body of men who formed our Constitution," he declaimed on the floor of Congress in 1796, "the sense of that body could never be regarded as the oracular guide in expounding the Constitution."

Yet, I doubt if strict proponents of original intent will be deterred by such considerations. Their goal is not to venerate dead framers but to restrain living judges from imposing their own values. This restraint is most troublesome when it threatens the protection of individual rights against governmental encroachment.

According to current constitutional doctrine, the due process clause of the 14th Amendment incorporates key provisions of the Bill of Rights, which keeps in check only the Federal Government. Unless the due process clause is construed to include the most important parts of the first eight amendments in the Bill of Rights, then the states would be free, in theory, to establish an official church or inflict cruel and unusual punishments. This doctrine is called incorporation.

Aside from the late Justice Hugo Black, few have believed that history alone is a sufficient basis for applying the Bill of Rights to the states. In his Georgetown University address, Justice Brennan noted that the crucial liberties embodied in the Bill of Rights are so central to our national identity that we cannot imagine any definition of "liberty" without them.

In fact, a cramped reading of the Bill of Rights jeopardizes what I regard as the true original intent—the rationale for having a written Constitution at all. The principal reason for a charter was to restrain government. In 1787, the idea of a fundamental law set down in black and white was revolutionary. Hanoverian England in the 18th century did not have a fully written, unified constitution, having long believed in a partially written one, based on ancient custom and grants from the Crown like the Magna Carta. To this day, the British have kept their democracy alive without one. In theory, the "King-in-Parliament" was and is unlimited in sovereign might, and leading political theorists, such as Thomas Hobbes and John Locke, agreed that governments, once established by a social contract, could not then be fettered.

Although not a Bill of Rights, the Magna Carta—King John's concessions to his barons in 1215—was symbolic of the notion that even the Crown was not all-powerful. Moreover, certain judges believed that Parliament, like the king, had to respect the traditions of the common law. This staunch belief in perpetual rights, in turn, was an important spark for the Revolutionary conflagration of 1776.

In gaining independence, Americans formed the bold concept that sovereignty continually resided with the people, who cede power to governments only to achieve certain specific ends. This view dominated the Philadelphia Convention. Instead of merely improving on the Articles of Confederation, as they had been directed to do, the framers devised a government where certain powers—defined and thereby limited—flowed from the people to the Congress, the President and the Federal judiciary.

Alexander Hamilton recognized that the basic tenets of this scheme mandated judicial review. Individual rights, he observed in *The Federalist*, No. 78, "can be preserved in practice no other way than through the medium of courts of justice, whose duty it must be to declare all acts contrary to the manifest tenor of the Constitution void." Through a written constitution and judicial enforcement, the framers intended to preserve the inchoate rights they had lost as Englishmen.

The narrow interpretation of original intent is especially unfortunate because I doubt that many of its proponents are in favor of freeing the states from the constraints of the Bill of Rights. In fact, I believe the concern of many modern "intentionalists" is quite specific: outrage over the right-of-privacy cases, especially *Roe v. Wade,* the 1973 Supreme Court decision recognizing a woman's right to an abortion. (The right of privacy, of course, is not mention-ed in the Constitution.) Whether one agrees with this controversial decision or not, I would submit that concern over the outcome of one difficult case is not sufficient cause to embrace a theory that calls for so many changes in existing law.

* * *

. . . [I]f original intent is an uncertain guide, does some other, more functional approach to interpreting the Constitution exist?

One suggestion is to emphasize the importance of democratic "process." As John Hart Ely, dean of the Stanford Law School forcefully advocates, this approach would direct the courts to make a distinction between "process" (the rules of the game, so to speak) and "substance" (the results of the game). Laws dealing with process include those affecting voting rights or participation in society; the Supreme Court correctly prohibited segregation, for example, because it imposed on blacks the continuing stigma of slavery. Judges, how-ever, would not have the power to review the substantive decisions of elected officials, such as the distribution of welfare benefits.

Basically, such an approach makes courts the guardians of democracy, but a focus on process affords little help when judges decide between difficult and competing values. Judicial formulation of a democratic vision, for exam-ple, requires substantive decision-making. The dignities of human liberty en-shrined in the Bill of Rights are not merely a means to an end, even so noble an end as democratic governance. For example, we cherish freedom of speech not only because it is necessary for meaningful elections, but also for its own sake.

The truth is that no litmus test exists by which judges can confidently and consistently measure the constitutionality of their decisions. Notwithstanding the clear need for judicial restraint, judges do not constitute what Prof. Raoul Berger, a retired Harvard Law School fellow, has termed an "imperial judici-ary." I would argue that the judicial process itself limits the reach of a jurist's arm.

First, judges do not and cannot deliberately contravene specific constitu-tional rules or clear indications of original intent. No one would seriously argue or expect, for instance, that the Supreme Court could or would twist the Presidential minimum-age provision into a call for "sufficient maturity," so as to forbid the seating of a 36-year-old.

I doubt, in any event, that Federal judges would ever hear such a ques-tion. The Constitution limits our power to traditional "cases" and "controver-sies" capable of judicial resolution. In cases like the hypothetical one regarding the Presidential age, the High Court employs doctrines of standing (proving injury) and "political question" to keep citizens from suing merely out of a desire to have the government run a certain way.

Moreover, the issues properly before a judge are not presented on a tabula rasa. Even the vaguest constitutional provisions have received the judicial gloss of prior decisions. Precedent alone, of course, should not preserve clearly erroneous decisions; the abhorrent "separate but equal" doctrine survived for more than 50 years before the Warren Court struck it down in 1954.

The conventions of our judicial system also limit a jurist's ability to impose his or her own will. One important restraint, often overlooked, is the tradition that appellate judges issue written opinions. That is, we must support our decisions with reasons instead of whims and indicate how our constitutional rulings relate to the document. A written statement is open to the dissent of colleagues, possible review by a higher court and the judgment, sometimes scathing, of legal scholars.

In addition, the facts of a given case play a pivotal role. Facts delineate the reach of a legal decision and remind us of the "cases and controversies" requirement. Our respect for such ground rules reassures the public that, even in the most controversial case, the outcome is not just a political ruling.

Judges are also mindful that the ultimate justification for their power is public acceptance—acceptance not of every decision, but of the role they play. Without popular support, the power of judicial review would have been eviscerated by political forces long ago.

Lacking the power of the purse or the sword, the courts must rely on the elected branches to enforce their decisions. The school desegregation cases would have been a dead letter unless President Eisenhower had been willing to order out the National Guard—in support of a decision authored by a Chief Justice, Earl Warren, whose appointment the President had called "the biggest damned-fool mistake I ever made."

Instead of achieving the purple of philosopher-kings, an unprincipled judiciary would risk becoming modern King Canutes, with the cold tide of political reality and popular opprobrium lapping at their robes.

My revered predecessor on the Court of Appeals, Judge Learned Hand, remarked in a lecture at Harvard in the late 1950s that he would not want to be ruled by "a bevy of Platonic Guardians." The Constitution balances the danger of judicial abuse against the threat of a temporary majority trampling individual rights. The current debate is a continuation of an age-old, and perhaps endless, struggle to reach a balance between our commitments to democracy and to the rule of law. . . .

# 15

# Civil Liberties
## Free Speech

*Intolerance of one kind or another, long a feature of American society, has nevertheless been more in evidence during some periods of our history than others. Events of the last several years suggest that we have once again entered a cycle in which bigotry is being expressed more publicly. Regrettably, this phenomenon has also manifested itself on our campuses, where university property has been defiled by racial epithets and black students have been subject to verbal and physical abuse. Alarmed by the growing number of such incidents, several universities have instituted regulations prohibiting discriminatory behavior, with violators thereof subject to disciplinary action.*

*Some observers, however, believe that these regulations are just as distasteful as the behavior they are designed to discourage. Thus, in the first essay which follows, Professor Chester Finn contends that a university—of all places—should be characterized by unfettered freedom of expression. In his judgment, there were disturbing signs that "unpopular" views were being stifled on many campuses even before these regulations were adopted. The presence of such regulations—often vaguely worded—can only have the effect of further dampening the robust expression of opinions and ideas in and outside the classroom.*

*Charles Lawrence, in the second essay, readily admits that under some circumstances even the most offensive speech must be tolerated on campus and believes that university regulations should be carefully crafted to allow for it. At the same time, however, he also insists that neither the First Amendment nor Supreme Court rulings require a university to tolerate racist expression within its walls under any and all circumstances.*

# The Campus:
## "An Island of Repression in a Sea of Freedom"
**Chester E. Finn, Jr.**

Two weeks before the Supreme Court held that the First Amendment protects one's right to burn the flag, the regents of the University of Wisconsin decreed that students on their twelve campuses no longer possess the right to say anything ugly to or about one another. Though depicted as an anti-discrimination measure, this revision of the student-conduct code declares that "certain types of expressive behavior directed at individuals and intended to demean and to create a hostile environment for education or other university-authorized activities would be prohibited and made subject to disciplinary sanctions." Penalties range from written warnings to expulsion.

Several months earlier, the University of Michigan adopted a six-page "anti-bias code" that provides for punishment of students who engage in conduct that "stigmatizes or victimizes an individual on the basis of race, ethnicity, religion, sex, sexual orientation, creed, national origin, ancestry, age, marital status, handicap, or Vietnam-era veteran status." (Presumably this last bizarre provision applies whether the "victim" is labeled a war hero or a draft dodger.)

Nor are Wisconsin and Michigan the only state universities to have gone this route. In June, the higher-education regents of Massachusetts prohibited "racism, anti-Semitism, ethnic, cultural, and religious intolerance" on their 27 campuses. A kindred regulation took effect on July 1 at the Chapel Hill campus of the University of North Carolina. And in place for some time at the law school of the State University of New York at Buffalo has been the practice of noting a student's use of racist language on his academic record and alerting prospective employers and the bar association.

Not to be outdone by the huge state schools, a number of private universities, like Emory in Atlanta and Stanford in California, have also made efforts to regulate unpleasant discourse and what the National Education Association terms "ethnoviolence," a comprehensive neologism that includes "acts of insensitivity."

Proponents of such measures are straightforward about their intentions. Says University of Wisconsin President Kenneth Shaw of the new rule: "It can particularly send a message to minority students that the board and its administration do care." Comments Emory's director of equal opportunity: "We just wanted to ensure that at a time when other universities were having problems that we made it clear that we wouldn't tolerate graffiti on walls or comments in

Chester E. Finn, Jr. is professor of education and public policy at Vanderbilt University and former assistant secretary, U.S. Department of Education (1985–1988). Reprinted from *Commentary*, September 1989, by permission; all rights reserved.

**274**

classes.'' And in Massachusettes, the regents concluded that ''There must be a unity and cohesion in the diversity which we seek to achieve, thereby creating an atmosphere of pluralism.''

This ''pluralism'' is not to be confused with the version endorsed by the First Amendment. Elsewhere we are expected, like it or not, to attend to what Justice Brennan calls the ''bedrock principles . . . that the government may not prohibit the expression of an idea simply because society finds the idea itself offensive or disagreeable.'' Not so for those running universities. ''What we are proposing is not completely in line with the First Amendment,'' a leader of Stanford's student government has acknowledged to a reporter, but ''I'm not sure it should be. We . . . are trying to set a standard different from what society at large is trying to accomplish.'' Explains the Emory official: ''I don't believe freedom of speech on campus was designed to allow people to demean others on campus.'' And a Stanford law professor contends that ''racial epithets and sexually haranguing speech silences rather than furthers discussion.''

Disregard the hubris and the sanctimony. Academics and their youthful apprentices have long viewed their own institutions and causes as nobler than the workaday world and humdrum pursuits of ordinary mortals. Forget, too, the manifest evidence of what some of the nation's most esteemed universities are teaching their students about basic civics. Consider only the two large issues that these developments pose, each freighted with a hefty burden of irony.

The first can still evoke a wry smile. We are, after all, seeing students pleading for controls to be imposed on campus behavior in the name of decency and morality. Yet these same students would be outraged if their colleges and universities were once again to function *in loco parentis* by constraining personal liberty in any other way. What is more, faculties, administrators, and trustees are complying with the student demands; they are adopting and—one must assume—enforcing these behavior codes. By and large, these are the same campuses that have long since shrugged off any serious responsibility for student conduct with respect to alcohol, drugs, and promiscuity (indeed, have cheerily collaborated in making the last of these behaviors more heedless by installing condom dispensers in the dorms). These are colleges that do not oblige anyone to attend class regularly, to exercise in the gym, to drive safely, or to eat a balanced diet. A student may do anything he likes with or to his fellow students, it appears, including things that are indisputably illegal, unhealthy, and dangerous for everyone concerned, and the university turns a blind eye. But a student may not, under any circumstances, speak ill of another student's origins, inclinations, or appearance.

The larger—and not the least bit amusing—issue is, of course, the matter of freedom of expression and efforts to limit it. That the emotionally charged flag-burning decision emerged from the Supreme Court the same month as authorities in China shot hundreds of students (and others) demonstrating for democracy in the streets of Beijing is as stark an illustration as one will ever see of the gravity and passion embedded in every aspect of this question.

In the Western world, the university has historically been the locus of the freest expression to be found anywhere. One might say that the precepts embodied in the First Amendment have applied there with exceptional clarity, and long before they were vouchsafed in other areas of society. For while private colleges are not formally bound by the Bill of Rights, they, like their public-sector counterparts, are heirs to an even older tradition. The campus was a sanctuary in which knowledge and truth might be pursued—and imparted—with impunity, no matter how unpopular, distasteful, or politically heterodox the process might sometimes be. That is the essence of academic freedom and it is the only truly significant distinction between the universities of the democracies and those operating under totalitarian regimes. Wretched though the food and lodging are for students on Chinese campuses, these were not the provocations that made martyrs in Tiananmen Square. It was the idea of freedom that stirred China's students and professors (and millions of others, as well). And it was the fear of allowing such ideas to take root that prompted the government's brutal response.

Having enjoyed almost untrammeled freedom of thought and expression for three and a half centuries, and having vigorously and, for the most part, successfully fended off efforts by outsiders (state legislators and congressional subcommittees, big donors, influential alumni, etc.) to constrain that freedom, American colleges and universities are now muzzling themselves. The anti-discrimination and anti-harassment rules being adopted will delimit what can be said and done on campus. Inevitably, this must govern what can be taught and written in lab, library, and lecture hall, as well as the sordid antics of fraternity houses and the crude nastiness of inebriated teenagers. ("The calls for a ban on 'harassment by vilification' reached a peak last fall" at Stanford, explained the New York *Times,* "after two drunken freshmen turned a symphony recruiting poster into a black-face caricature of Beethoven and posted it near a black student's room.")

Constraints on free expression and open inquiry do not, of course, depend on the adoption of a formal code of conduct. Guest speakers with controversial views have for some years now risked being harassed, heckled, even shouted down by hostile campus audiences, just as scholars engaging in certain forms of research, treading into sensitive topics, or reaching unwelcome conclusions have risked calumny from academic "colleagues." More recently, students have begun to monitor their professors and to take action if what is said in class irks or offends them.

Thus, at Harvard Law School this past spring, Bonnie Savage, the aptly-named leader of the Harvard Women's Law Association (HWLA), sent professor Ian Macneil a multicount allegation of sexism in his course on contracts. The first offense cited was Macneil's quoting (on page 963 of his textbook) Byron's well-known line, "And whispering, 'I will ne'er consent,'—consented." This, and much else that he had said and written, the HWLA found objectionable. "A professor in any position at any school," Savage pronounced, "has no right or privilege to use the classroom in such a way as to offend, at the very least, 40 percent of the students. . . ."

This was no private communication. Savage dispatched copies to sundry deans and the chairman of the faculty-appointments committee because, she later explained, "We thought he might be considered for tenure." The whole affair, Macneil responded in the *Harvard Law Record,* was "shoddy, un-lawyerlike, reminiscent of Senator McCarthy, and entirely consistent with HWLA's prior conduct." As for the Byron passage, it "is in fact a perfect summary of what happens in the Battle of Forms" (a part of the contract-making process).

Macneil is not the only Harvard professor to have been given a hard time in recent years for writing or uttering words that upset students, however well-suited they might be to the lesson at hand. Not long ago, the historian Stephan Thernstrom was accused by a student vigilante of such classroom errors as "read[ing] aloud from white plantation owners' journals 'without also giving the slaves' point of view.'" Episodes of this kind, says Thernstrom, serve to discourage him and other scholars from even teaching courses on topics that bear on race and ethnicity.*

Nor is Harvard the only major university where student allegations, unremonstrated by the administration, have produced such a result. At Michigan last fall, the distinguished demographer, Reynolds Farley, was teaching an undergraduate course in "race and cultural contact," as he had done for the previous ten years, when a column appeared in the Michigan *Daily* alleging racial insensitivity on his part, citing—wholly out of context, of course—half a dozen so-called examples, and demanding that the sociology department make amends. Farley was not amused and, rather than invite more unjust attacks, is discontinuing the course. Consequently 50 to 125 Michigan students a year will be deprived of the opportunity to examine issues of ethnicity and the history of race relations in America under the tutelage of this world-class scholar. And to make matters even worse, Farley notes that several faculty colleagues have mentioned that they are dropping any discussion of various important race-related issues from their courses, lest similar treatment befall them.

This might seem perverse, not least from the standpoint of "aggrieved" students and their faculty mentors, because another of their major goals is to oblige everyone to take more courses on precisely these topics. "I would like to see colleges engage all incoming students in mandatory racial-education programs," writes William Damon, professor of psychology and chairman of the education department at Clark University, in the *Chronicle of Higher Education.* And his call is being answered on a growing number of campuses, including the state colleges of Massachusetts, the University of Wisconsin, and the University of California at Berkeley.

Ironies abound here, too, since the faculties and governing boards adopting these course requirements are generally the very bodies that resist any suggestion of a "core curriculum" or tight "distribution requirements" on the ground that diverse student preferences should be accommodated and that, in any case, there are no disciplines, writings, or ideas of such general importance

*See "A New Racism on Campus?" by Thomas Short, *Commentary,* August 1988.

that everyone should be obliged to study them. Curricular relativism can be suspended, though, when "pluralism" is itself the subject to be studied." "It is important to make such programs mandatory," Professor Damon explains, "so that they can reach students who otherwise might not be inclined to participate."

* * *

Diversity and tolerance, evenhandedly applied, are estimable precepts. But that is not how they are construed in the academy today. Nor do the narrowing limits on free expression lead only to penalties for individuals who engage in "biased" talk or "hostile" behavior. They also leave little room for opinion that deviates from campus political norms or for grievances from unexpected directions. During Harvard's race-awareness week last spring, when a white student dared to complain that she had experienced "minority ethnocentrism" on campus—black and Hispanic students, it seems, often ignored her—she was given short shrift and no sympathy by the speaker (who had already suggested that Harvard and Dartmouth were "genocidal" institutions).

More commonly, however, it is rambunctious student newspapers and magazines that get into trouble with academic authorities for printing something that contravenes the conventional wisdom. Given the predominant campus climate, it is not surprising that these are often publications with a moderate or Right-of-Center orientation. Sometimes, clearly, they do mischievous, stupid, and offensive things, but for such things the degree of toleration in higher education seems to vary with the ideology of the perpetrator. (Acts of discrimination and oppression based on political views, it should be observed, are *not* among the categories proscribed in the new codes of behavior.) In addition to a much-reported sequence of events at Dartmouth, there have been recent efforts to censor or suppress student publications, and sometimes to discipline their staff members, at Brown, Berkeley, UCLA, Vassar, and California State University at Northridge.

The last of these prompted one of the most extraordinary media events of 1989, a joint press conference on May 16 featuring—no one could have made this up—former Attorney General Edwin Meese III and the director of the Washington office of the American Civil Liberties Union (ACLU), Morton Halperin. What brought them together was shared outrage over what Halperin termed the "double standard" on campus. "Our position," he reminded the attending journalists, "is that there is an absolute right to express views even if others find those views repugnant." He could cite numerous instances, he said, where campus authorities were making life difficult for outspoken conservative students, yet could find "no cases where universities discipline students for views or opinions on the Left, or for racist comments against non-minorities."

Meese, not surprisingly, concurred, as did James Taranto, the former Northridge student journalist whose lawsuit settlement afforded the specific occasion for the press conference. In 1987, Taranto, then news editor of his campus paper, had written a column faulting UCLA officials for suspending a student editor who had published a cartoon mocking affirmative action. Taranto reproduced the offending cartoon in the Northridge paper, whereupon its faculty adviser suspended *him* from his position for two weeks because he had printed "controversial" material without her permission. The ACLU agreed to represent him in a First Amendment suit—"We were as outraged as he was by the attempt to censor the press," Halperin recalled—and two years later a settlement was reached.

While we are accumulating ironies, let it be noted that the ACLU, the selfsame organization in which Michael Dukakis's "card-carrying membership" yielded George Bush considerable mileage in the 1988 election campaign, has been conspicuously more vigilant and outspoken about campus assaults on free expression in 1989 than has the Bush administration. The Secretary of Education, Lauro Cavazos (himself a former university president), has been silent. The White House has been mute. During an incident at Brown in May, when an art professor canceled a long-planned screening of the classic film, *Birth of a Nation,* because the Providence branch of the NAACP had denounced it, the local ACLU affiliate was the only voice raised in dismay. "University officials," declared its executive director, "have now opened the door to numerous pressure groups who may wish to ban from the campus other films that they too deem 'offensive.'" Indeed. A colleague of mine recently revived a long-lapsed membership in the ACLU on the straightforward ground that no other national entity is resisting the spread of attitude-adjustment, censorship, and behavior codes in higher education.

* * *

. . . Meanwhile, in the realms of intellectual inquiry and expression, [colleges] permit ever less diversity, turning the campus (in the memorable phrase of civil-rights scholar Abigail Thernstrom) into "an island of repression in a sea of freedom."

# The Justification for Curbing Racist Speech on Campus

## Charles R. Lawrence III

I have spent the better part of my life as a dissenter. As a high-school student, I was threatened with suspension for my refusal to participate in a civil-defense drill, and I have been a conspicuous consumer of my First Amendment liberties ever since. There are very strong reasons for protecting even racist speech. Perhaps the most important of these is that such protection reinforces our society's commitment to tolerance as a value, and that by protecting bad speech from government regulation, we will be forced to combat it as a community.

But I also have a deeply felt apprehension about the resurgence of racial violence and the corresponding rise in the incidence of verbal and symbolic assault and harassment to which blacks and other traditionally subjugated and excluded groups are subjected. I am troubled by the way the debate has been framed in response to the recent surge of racist incidents on college and university campuses and in response to some universities' attempts to regulate harassing speech. The problem has been framed as one in which the liberty of free speech is in conflict with the elimination of racism. I believe this has placed the bigot on the moral high ground and fanned the rising flames of racism.

Above all, I am troubled that we have not listened to the real victims, that we have shown so little understanding of their injury, and that we have abandoned those whose race, gender, or sexual preference continues to make them second-class citizens. It seems to me a very sad irony that the first instinct of civil libertarians has been to challenge even the smallest, most narrowly framed efforts by universities to provide black and other minority students with the protection the Constitution guarantees them.

The landmark case of *Brown v. Board of Education* is not a case that we normally think of as a case about speech. But *Brown* can be broadly read as articulating the principle of equal citizenship. *Brown* held that segregated schools were inherently unequal because of the *message* that segregation conveyed—that black children were an untouchable caste, unfit to go to school with white children. If we understand the necessity of eliminating the system of signs and symbols that signal the inferiority of blacks, then we should hesitate before proclaiming that all racist speech that stops short of physical violence must be defended.

University officials who have formulated policies to respond to incidents of racial harassment have been characterized in the press as "thought police,"

Charles R. Lawrence III is visiting professor of law at the University of Southern California Law Center. Reprinted with permission of the author from *The Chronicle of Higher Education* Oct. 25, 1989 B1–B3. This article is adapted from a longer article: "If He Hollers Let Him Go: Regulating Racist Speech on Campus," by Charles R. Lawrence III, vol. 1990 (no. 3) *Duke Law Journal* 431–483 (1990).

but such policies generally do nothing more than impose sanctions against intentional face-to-face insults. When racist speech takes the form of face-to-face insults, catcalls, or other assaultive speech aimed at an individual or small group of persons, it falls directly within the "fighting words" exception to First Amendment protection. The Supreme Court has held that words which "by their very utterance inflict injury or tend to incite an immediate breach of the peace" are not protected by the First Amendment.

If the purpose of the First Amendment is to foster the greatest amount of speech, racial insults disserve that purpose. Assaultive racist speech functions as a preemptive strike. The invective is experienced as a blow, not as a proffered idea, and once the blow is struck, it is unlikely that a dialogue will follow. Racial insults are particularly undeserving of First Amendment protection because the perpetrator's intention is not to discover truth or initiate dialogue but to injure the victim. In most situations, members of minority groups realize that they are likely to lose if they respond to epithets by fighting and are forced to remain silent and submissive.

Courts have held that offensive speech may not be regulated in public forums such as streets where the listener may avoid the speech by moving on, but the regulation of otherwise protected speech has been permitted when the speech invades the privacy of the unwilling listener's home or when the unwilling listener cannot avoid the speech. Racist posters, fliers, and graffiti in dormitories, bathrooms, and other common living spaces would seem to clearly fall within the reasoning of these cases. Minority students should not be required to remain in their rooms in order to avoid racial assault. Minimally, they should find a safe haven in their dorms and in all other common rooms that are a part of their daily routine.

I would also argue that the university's responsibility for insuring that these students receive an equal educational opportunity provides a compelling justification for regulations that insure them safe passage in all common areas. A minority student should not have to risk becoming the target of racially assaulting speech every time he or she chooses to walk across campus. Regulating vilifying speech that cannot be anticipated or avoided would not preclude announced speeches and rallies—situations that would give minority-group members and their allies the chance to organize counter-demonstrations or avoid the speech altogether.

The most commonly advanced argument against the regulation of racist speech proceeds something like this: We recognize that minority groups suffer pain and injury as the result of racist speech, but we must allow this hate mongering for the benefit of society as a whole. Freedom of speech is the lifeblood of our democratic system. It is especially important for minorities because often it is their only vehicle for rallying support for the redress of their grievances. It will be impossible to formulate a prohibition so precise that it will present the racist speech you want to suppress without catching in the same net all kinds of speech that it would be unconscionable for a democratic society to suppress.

Whenever we make such arguments, we are striking a balance on the one hand between our concern for the continued free flow of ideas and the democratic process dependent on that flow, and, on the other, our desire to further the cause of equality. There can be no meaningful discussion of how we should reconcile our commitment to equality and our commitment to free speech until it is acknowledged that there is real harm inflicted by racist speech and that this harm is far from trivial.

To engage in a debate about the First Amendment and racist speech without a full understanding of the nature and extent of that harm is to risk making the First Amendment an instrument of domination rather than a vehicle of liberation. We have not all known the experience of victimization by racist, misogynist, and homophobic speech, nor do we equally share the burden of the societal harm it inflicts. We are often quick to say that we have heard the cry of the victims when we have not.

The *Brown* case is again instructive because it speaks directly to the psychic injury inflicted by racist speech by noting that the symbolic message of segregation affected "the hearts and minds" of Negro children "in a way unlikely ever to be undone." Racial epithets and harassment often cause deep emotional scarring and feelings of anxiety and fear that pervade every aspect of a victim's life.

*Brown* also recognized that black children did not have an equal opportunity to learn and participate in the school community if they bore the additional burden of being subjected to the humiliation and psychic assault contained in the message of segregation. University students bear an analogous burden when they are forced to live and work in an environment where at any moment they may be subjected to denigrating verbal harassment and assault. The same injury was addressed by the Supreme Court when it held that sexual harassment that creates a hostile or abusive work environment violates the ban on sex discrimination in employment of Title VII of the Civil Rights Act of 1964.

Carefully drafted university regulations would bar the use of words as assault weapons and leave unregulated even the most heinous of ideas when those ideas are presented at times and places and in manners that provide an opportunity for reasoned rebuttal or escape from immediate injury. The history of the development of the right to free speech has been one of carefully evaluating the importance of free expression and its effects on other important societal interests. We have drawn the line between protected and unprotected speech before without dire results. (Courts have, for example, exempted from the protection of the First Amendment obscene speech and speech that disseminates official secrets, that defames or libels another person, or that is used to form a conspiracy or monopoly.)

Blacks and other people of color are skeptical about the argument that even the most injurious speech must remain unregulated because, in an unregulated marketplace of ideas, the best ones will rise to the top and gain acceptance. Our experience tells us quite the opposite. We have seen too many demagogues elected by appealing to America's racism. We have seen too many good liberal politicians shy away from the issues that might brand them as being too closely allied with us.

Whenever we decide that racist speech must be tolerated because of the importance of maintaining societal tolerance for all unpopular speech, we are asking blacks and other subordinated groups to bear the burden for the good of all. We must be careful that the ease with which we strike the balance against the regulation of racist speech is in no way influenced by the fact that the cost will be borne by others. We must be certain that those who will pay that price are fairly represented in our deliberations and that they are heard.

At the core of the argument that we should resist all government regulation of speech is the ideal that the best cure for bad speech is good, that ideas that affirm equality and the worth of all individuals will ultimately prevail. This is an empty ideal unless those of us who would fight racism are vigilant and unequivocal in that fight. We must look for ways to offer assistance and support to students whose speech and political participation are chilled in a climate of racial harassment.

Civil-rights lawyers might consider suing on behalf of blacks whose right to an equal education is denied by a university's failure to insure a non-discriminatory educational climate or conditions of employment. We must embark upon the development of a First Amendment jurisprudence grounded in the reality of our history and our contemporary experience. We must think hard about how best to launch legal attacks against the most indefensible forms of hate speech. Good lawyers can create exceptions and narrow interpretations that limit the harm of hate speech without opening the floodgates of censorship.

Everyone concerned with these issues must find ways to engage actively in actions that resist and counter the racist ideas that we would have the First Amendment protect. If we fail in this, the victims of hate speech must rightly assume that we are on the oppressors' side.

# Pornography

*The two previous selections highlighted the difference of opinion over what we should be free to say. Similar disagreement exists over what we should be free to see, read and hear, when the subject matter in question is "obscene" or "pornographic" in character.*

*In the first of the following essays, Ernest van den Haag is concerned with two basic questions. First, is pornographic material clearly definable so that it may be distinguished from other kinds of expression we would not want to suppress? Second, even if we can define it, is there any public interest to be served by prohibiting our citizens from having access to it? Van den Haag answers both questions in the affirmative.*

*Geoffrey Stone does not object to laws against child pornography nor to age and zoning restrictions limiting access to pornography in general. In contrast to van den Haag, however, he wholly opposes any attempt to limit the distribution of obscene material to consenting adults. In his judgment, a careful weighing of the costs and benefits associated with censorship clearly reveals that the individual incurs very great costs, while the society derives very little benefit.*

# Pornography and Censorship

## Ernest van den Haag

Ultramoralists want to prohibit any display of nudity while ultralibertarians feel that even the most scabrously prurient display must be tolerated. However, most people are not that extreme. They are uneasy about obscene incitements to lechery; but uncertain about what to do about them. They wonder whether distaste, even when shared by a majority, is reason enough to prohibit what a minority evidently wants. Beyond distaste, is there enough actual harm in pornography? Where will suppression end? and how harmful might it be? Can we legally distinguish the valuable from the pornographic, the erotic from the obscene? Would courts have to act as art critics? Not least, we wonder about our own disapproval of obscenity. We are aware, however dimly, of some part of us which is attracted to it. We disapprove of our own attraction—but also worry whether we may be afraid or hypocritical when we suppress what attracts us as well as many others.

Still, most people want something done about pornography. As so often in our public life, we turn to the Constitution for a rule. "Congress" it tells us "shall make no law . . . abridging the freedom of speech or of the press." Although addressed to the federal government only, the First Amendment has been echoed in many state constitutions and applied to all states by the courts. Further, its scope has been broadened, perhaps unduly so, by court decisions which hold that all expressions rather than just words are protected by the First Amendment. Yet speech—words, spoken, or printed, or otherwise re-produced—is a narrow subclass of expression and the only one protected by the First Amendment. Music, painting, dance, uniforms, or flags—expressions but not words—are not.[1] The framers wanted to protect political and intellec-tual discourse—they thought free verbal interchange of ideas indispensable to consensual government. But obscenity hardly qualifies as an interchange of ideas, and is no more protected than music is. Whatever their merits, neither addresses the intellect, nor is indispensable to free government. For that matter words without cognitive content, words not used as vehicles for ideas—e.g., "dirty words" or expletives—may not be constitutionally protected. And even the constitutional right to unfettered verbal communication of ideas is limited by other rights and by the rights of others. Else there could be no libel or copyright laws and no restrictions on incitements to illicit or harmful action.

The Constitution, then, gives us the right to outlaw pornography. Should we exercise it? Is there a sufficient social interest in suppression? And how can

Ernest van den Haag was John M. Olin Professor of Jurisprudence and Public Policy at Fordham University before joining the Heritage Foundation as Distinguished Scholar in 1981. From Ernest van den Haag, "Pornography and Censorship," *Policy Review*, 13 (Summer 1980), pp. 73–81.

we separate pornography from things we constitutionally cannot or do not want to suppress?

Some people feel that there can be no objective standard of obscenity: "Beauty is in the eye of the beholder—and so is obscenity," they argue. This notion is popular among pseudo-sophisticates; but it seems wildly exaggerated. Is the difference between your mother-in-law and the current Miss America merely in the eye of the beholder (yours)? How come everyone sees the difference you see? Is the distinction between pictures which focus on exposed human genitals or on sexual intercourse, and other pictures only in the eye of the beholder? To be sure, judgments of beauty, or of obscenity, do have subjective components—as most judgments do. But they are not altogether subjective. Why else do even my best friends not rate me a competitor to Apollo? For that matter judgments of art are not altogether subjective either. Museums persistently prefer Rembrandt's paintings to mine. Do they all have a subjective bias against me?

Pornography seems a reasonably objective matter which can be separated from other things. Laws, if drawn sensibly, might effectively prohibit its display or sale. An in-between zone between the obscene and the nonobscene may well remain, just as there is such a twilight zone between brightly lit and dark areas. But we still can tell which is which; and where necessary we can draw an arbitrary, but consistent (i.e., non-capricious), line. The law often draws such a line: to enable the courts to deal with them the law treats as discontinuous things that in nature may be continuous. The law quite often leaves things to the judgment of the courts: just how much spanking is cruelty to children? Just when does behavior become reckless?—courts always have to decide cases near the dividing line. But courts would have to decide only the few cases near the line which divides obscene from nonobscene matters. Most of the obscene stuff now displayed is not even near that line. With sensible laws it will no longer be displayed or offered for sale. The doubtful cases will be decided by juries applying prevailing standards. Such standards vary greatly over time and space, but at any given time, in any place, they are fairly definite and knowable. Lawyers who argue otherwise never appear in court, or for that matter in public places, without pants (or skirts, as the case may be). They seem to know what is contrary to the standards prevailing in the community in which they practice—however much they pretend otherwise.

A word on the current legal situation may not be amiss. The courts have not covered themselves with glory in clarifying the notion of obscenity. At present they regard the portrayal of sex acts, or of genitalia, or of excretion, as obscene if (a) patently offensive by contemporary community standards and if (b) taken as a whole[2] it appeals dominantly to a prurient (morbid or shameful) interest in sex and if (c) it lacks serious scientific, literary or artistic merit. The courts imply that not all appeals to sexual interest are wrong—only prurient ones are. They have not said directly which appeals are prurient. The courts might have been more explicit but they are not unintelligible.

An appeal to sexual interest need not be obscene per se; only attempts to arouse sexual interest by patently offensive, morbid, shameful means are. By contemporary standards a nude is not obscene. But an appeal to sexual interest is, when carried out by focusing on exposed genitalia, or on the explicit, detailed portrayal of sex acts. Detailed portrayals of excretion may be patently offensive too, but since they scarcely appeal to the sexual interest of most people they may pass under present law unless specifically listed as unlawful; so may portrayals of sexual relations with animals for the same reason—if the jury is as confused as the law is. The courts never quite made up their minds on the relative weight to be given to "offensive," to "prurient" and to "sexual." Thus intercourse with animals may be offensive to most people and prurient, i.e., morbid and shameful, but not necessarily sexual in its appeal to the average person. Therefore some exhibitors of such spectacles have been let off. But should the fact that some sexual acts are so disgusting to the majority as to extinguish any sexual appeal they might otherwise have legitimize these acts? Offensiveness, since in effect it is also a criterion for the prurience of a sexual appeal, is a decisive element of obscenity; yet the other two elements must be present.

If more clearly drawn laws would leave few doubtful cases for juries to decide, why do many literary, sociological, or psychological experts find it so hard to determine what is obscene? Why do they deny that such laws can be fashioned? Most people who protest that they cannot draw the line dividing the pornographic from the non-pornographic are deliberately unhelpful. "None so blind as they that won't see." They don't want to see because they oppose any pornography laws. They certainly have a right to oppose them. But this right does not entitle anyone to pretend that he cannot see what he does see. Critics who testify in court that they cannot distinguish pornography from literature, or that merely pornographic stuff has great literary or educational merit, usually know better. If they didn't they would have no business being critics or experts. To oppose pornography laws is one thing. It is quite another thing to attempt to sabotage them by testifying that hardcore stuff cannot be separated from literature or art, pornographic from aesthetic experience. Such testimony is either muddleheaded beyond belief or dishonest.

Once we have decided that the obscene is not inseparable from the nonobscene, we can address the real issue: are there compelling grounds for legally restraining public obscenity?

Some argue that pornography has no actual influence. This seems unpersuasive. Even before print had been invented Francesca blamed a book for her sin: "Galeotto fu il libro" (the book was the panderer) she told Dante in the *Divine Comedy*. Did she imagine the book's influence? Literature—from the Bible to Karl Marx or to Hitler's *Mein Kampf*—does influence people's attitudes and actions, as do all communications, words or pictures. That is why people write, or, for that matter, advertise. The influence of communications varies, depending on their own character, the character of the person exposed to them, and on many other circumstances. Some persons are much influenced by the Bible—or by pornography—others not. Nor is the direction of the influence, and the action to which it may lead altogether predictable in each case. But there is little doubt that for the average person the Bible fosters a religious disposition in some degree and pornography a lecherous one.

Granted that it has some influence, does pornography harm non-consenting persons? Does it lead to crime? Almost anything—beer, books, poverty, wealth, or existentialism—can "lead" to crime in some cases. So can pornography. We cannot remove all possible causes of crime—even though we might remove those that can be removed without much difficulty or loss. But crime scarcely seems the major issue. We legally prohibit many things that do not lead to crime, such as polygamy, cocaine, or dueling. Many of these things can easily be avoided by those who do not wish to participate; others cannot be shown to be actually harmful to anyone. We prohibit whatever is *perceived* as socially harmful, even if merely contrary to our customs, as polygamy is.

When we prohibit cartels, or the sale of marijuana, when we impose specific taxes, or prohibit unlicensed taxis from taking fares, we believe our laws to be useful, or to prevent harm. That belief may be wrong. Perhaps the tax is actually harmful or unjust, perhaps we would all be better off without licensing any taxis, perhaps cartels are economically useful, perhaps marijuana smoking is harmless or beneficial. All that is needed to justify legislation is a rational social interest in accomplishing the goals of the legislation. Thus, an activity (such as marijuana smoking) can be prohibited because it is *perceived* to be socially harmful, or even merely distasteful. Pornography is. The harm it actually may do cannot be shown the way a man can be shown to be guilty of a crime. But such a demonstration of harm or guilt is not required for making laws—it is required only if someone is to be convicted of breaking them.

Still, unless we are convinced that pornography is harmful the whole exercise makes little sense. Wherein then is pornography harmful? The basic aim of pornographic communication is to arouse impersonal lust, by, in the words of Susan Sontag (incidentally a defender of pornography), driving "a wedge between one's existence as a full human being and one's sexual being . . . a healthy person prevents such a gap from opening up. . . ." A healthy society too must help "prevent such gaps from opening up," for, to be healthy, a society needs "full human beings," "healthy persons" who integrate their libidinal impulses with the rest of their personality, with love and with personal relationships.

We all have had pre-adolescent fantasies which ignore the burdens of reality, of commitment, concern, conflict, thought, consideration and love as they become heavier. In these fantasies others are mere objects, puppets for our pleasure, means to our gratification, not ends in themselves. The Marquis de Sade explored such fantasies most radically; but all pornographers cater to them: they invite us to treat others merely as means to our gratification. Sometimes they suggest that these others enjoy being so treated; sometimes they suggest, as the Marquis de Sade did, that pleasure lies in compelling unwilling others to suffer. Either way pornography invites us to reduce fellow humans to mere means. The cravings pornography appeals to—the craving for contextless, impersonal, anonymous, totally deindividualized, as it were abstract, sex—are not easy to control and are, therefore, felt as threats by many persons, threats to their own impulse-control and integration. The fear is real and enough sex crimes certainly occur . . . to give plausibility to it. People wish to suppress pornography, as they suppress within themselves impulses that they feel threaten them. Suppression may not be an ideal solution to the problem of anxiety arousing stimuli, external or internal. Ideally we should get rid of anxiety, and of unwelcome stimuli, by confrontation and sublimation. But we are not ideal and we do not live in an ideal world. Real as distinguished from ideal persons must avoid what threatens and upsets them. And real as distinguished from utopian societies must help them to do so.

However, there are stronger grounds for suppressing pornography. Unlike the 18th-century rationalists from whom the ultralibertarians descend, I do not believe that society is but an aggregation of individuals banded together for their mutual convenience. Although society does have utilitarian functions, it is held together by emotional bonds, prior to any rational calculations. Societies survive by feelings of identification and solidarity among the members, which lead them to make sacrifices for one another, to be considerate and to observe rules, even when they individually would gain by not doing so. In animal societies (e.g., among social insects) the members identify one another instinctively, for example, by smell. The identification leads them not to attack or eat one another and it makes possible many manifestations of solidarity. It makes the insect society possible. Human societies, too, would be impossible without such identification and solidarity among the members. Else we would treat one another as we now treat insects or chickens—or as the Nazis treated Jews. It is to preserve and strengthen traditional emotional bonds, and the symbols that stand for them, that the government of Israel prohibits the raising of pigs, that of India the slaughtering of cows.

Solidarity is as indispensable to the United States as it is to Israel. It is cultivated by institutions which help each of us to think of others not merely as means to his own gratification, but as ends in themselves. These institutions cultivate shared customs, expectations, traditions, values, ideals and symbols. The values we cultivate differ from those of an aboriginal tribe; and the range left to individual choice is broader. Social solidarity is less stringent than it is in most primitive tribes. But neither our society nor an aboriginal tribe could survive without shared values which make it possible for us to identify with one another.

One of our shared values is the linkage of sexual to individual affectional relations—to love and stability. As our society has developed, the affectional bonds associated with sexual love have become one of its main values. Indeed with the weakening of religious institutions these bonds have acquired steadily more importance. Love is worshiped in numerous forms. There is, to be sure, a gap between the reality and the ideal, just as there is a gap between the reality of patriotism—or nationalism—and the ideal. But it would be silly to deny that patriotism plays an important role in our society—or that love, affection, and compassion do.

Pornography tends to erode these bonds, indeed, all bonds. By inviting us to reduce others and ourselves to purely physical beings, by inviting each of us to regard the other only as a means to physical gratification, with sensations, but without emotions, with contacts but without relations, pornography not only degrades us (and incidentally reduces sex to a valueless mechanical exercise),[3] but also erodes all human solidarity and tends to destroy all affectional bonds. This is a good enough reason to outlaw it.

There are additional reasons. One is very simply that the majority has a right to protect its tradition. The minority is entitled to argue for change. But not to impose it. Our tradition has been that sexual acts, sexual organs, and excretion are private rather than public. The majority is entitled to preserve this tradition by law where necessary just as the majority in India, offended by the slaughtering of cows which is contrary to Hindu tradition, can (and does) prohibit it.

Nobody is forced to see the dirty movie or to buy the pornographic magazine. Why then should the minority not be allowed to have them? But a public matter—anything for sale—can never be a wholly private matter. And once it is around legally one cannot really avoid the impact of pornography. One cannot avoid the display and the advertising which affect and pollute the atmosphere even if one does not enter or buy. Nor is it enough to prohibit the movie marquee or the display of the magazine. Anything legally for sale is the more profitable the more customers it attracts. Hence the purveyors of pornography have a strong interest in advertising and in spreading it, in persuading and in tempting the public. Prohibitions of advertising will be circumvented as long as the sale of pornography is lawful. Moreover, if the viewer of the pornographic movie is not warned by the marquee that he is about to see a dirty movie, he might very likely complain that he has been trapped into something that upsets him without being warned.

I should not prohibit anyone from reading or seeing whatever he wishes in his own home. He may be ill advised. But interfering with his home habits surely would be more ill advised. Of course if the stuff is not legally available the pornography fan will have difficulty getting it. But society has no obligation to make it easy. On the contrary, we can and should prohibit the marketing, the public sale of what we perceive as harmful to society even if we do not wish to invade homes to punish those who consume it.

## NOTES

1 The First Amendment right to peacefully assemble may protect whatever is part of, or required for, peaceful assembly. It is hard to see that either nudity or swastikas are needed for that purpose.

2 Thus a prurient passage does not make a magazine or a book offensive unless, taken as a whole, the magazine or book dominantly appeals to the prurient interest.
3 As feminists have pointed out, pornography often degrades females more directly than males. But, in reducing themselves to a mere craving for physical gratification males degrade themselves as well.

# Repeating Past Mistakes:
## The Commission on Obscenity and Pornography

**Geoffrey R. Stone**

The Attorney General's Commission on Pornography had a unique opportunity to redirect society's regulation of obscene expression. The current state of the law is marred by overly broad, ineffective, and wasteful regulation. This was an appropriate opportunity to take a fresh look at the problem and to strike a new balance—a balance that more precisely accommodates society's interests in regulation with the individual's often competing interests in privacy, autonomy, and free expression. The commission squandered this opportunity. Instead of taking a fresh look, it blindly performed its appointed task of renewing and reaffirming past mistakes.

The United States Supreme Court has held that federal, state, and local government officials have the power, consonant with the First Amendment, to prohibit all distribution of obscene expression. The mere existence of power, however, does not mean that its exercise is sound. The commission should have recommended that government officials exercise restraint. Specifically, the commission should have recommended the repeal of laws that criminalize the distribution of obscene expression to consenting adults.

The Supreme Court itself is sharply divided over the constitutional power of government officials to prohibit the distribution of obscene expression to consenting adults. In its 1973 decisions in *Miller* v. *California* and *Paris Adult Theatre* v. *Slaton,* the Court divided five-to-four on this issue. Justices Douglas, Brennan, Stewart, and Marshall concluded that the First Amendment strips government officials of any power to deny consenting adults the right to obtain obscene expression.

Even apart from the division of opinion in these cases, the Court's analysis of obscene expression is anomalous in terms of its overall First Amendment jurisprudence. At one time, obscene expression was merely one of several categories of expression held by the Supreme Court to be "of such slight social value as a step to truth that any benefit that may be derived from them is clearly outweighed by the social interest in order and morality." In the past quarter-century, the Court has increasingly recognized that such previously unprotected categories of expression as profanity, commercial advertising, incitement, and libel can no longer be regarded as wholly unprotected by the First Amendment. The Court has held that, although such categories of

Geoffrey R. Stone is Harry Kelman Jr. Professor of Law and Dean, University of Chicago School of Law. From Geoffrey R. Stone, "Repeating Past Mistakes," *Society,* 24 (July/August, 1987), pp. 30–32.

expression have only a "subordinate position in the scale of First Amendment values," they can nonetheless be restricted only if government has at least a substantial justification for the restriction. The Court has thus recognized that even low-value expression may have some First Amendment value, that government efforts to restrict low-value expression will often chill more valuable expression, and that the constitutional and institutional risks of restricting low-value expression are worth taking only if the restriction furthers at least a substantial governmental interest.

Obscene expression now stands alone. No other category of expression is currently regarded as wholly outside the protection of the First Amendment. No other category of expression may be suppressed merely because it has only "slight social value." No other category of expression may be censored without a showing that the restriction serves at least a substantial governmental interest. The current analysis of obscene expression is thus the sole remaining artifact of a now discarded jurisprudence.

The current analysis of obscenity is not necessarily wrong as a matter of constitutional law. Nevertheless, the constitutional authority to act in this context hangs by the slender thread of a single vote and is very much in doubt as a matter of constitutional principle. In such circumstances, government must exercise special care in deciding whether and how to exercise its power. We should not simply assume that because it is constitutional to act it is wise to do so. The very closeness of the constitutional question is itself a compelling reason for caution.

In deciding on the appropriate regulation of obscene expression, we must consider both the costs and benefits of regulation. Laws prohibiting the distribution of obscene expression to consenting adults impose at least three types of costs. First, although the Court has held that such expression has only low First Amendment value, it may nonetheless serve a useful function both for society and the individual. That the demand for sexually explicit expression is as great as it is, suggests that such expression serves an important psychological or emotional function for many individuals. It may satisfy a need for fantasy, escape, entertainment, stimulation, or whatever. Thus, whether or not obscene expression has significant First Amendment value, it may have important value to the individual. Laws prohibiting its distribution to consenting adults may frustrate significant interests in individual privacy, dignity, autonomy, and self-fulfillment.

The suppression of obscene expression may also have a severe chilling effect on more valuable expression. The legal concept of obscenity is vague in the extreme. As a consequence, individuals who wish to purchase or distribute sexually explicit expression will invariably censor themselves in order to avoid being ensnared in the ill-defined net of our obscenity laws. Laws prohibiting the distribution of obscene expression spill over and significantly limit the distribution of constitutionally protected expression as well.

Any serious effort to enforce laws prohibiting the distribution of obscene expression to consenting adults necessarily draws valuable police and prosecutorial resources away from other areas of law enforcement. In a world of limited resources, we must recognize that the decision to criminalize one form of behavior renders more difficult and less effective the enforcement of laws directed at other forms of behavior. It is necessary to set priorities, for the failure to enforce our laws vigorously can serve only to generate disrespect for law enforcement and bring the legal system into disrepute.

Two interests are most commonly asserted in support of laws prohibiting the distribution of obscene expression to consenting adults. First, it is said that government must suppress the distribution of such expression to consenting adults in order to prevent the erosion of moral standards. The moral fabric of a society undoubtedly affects the tone and quality of life. It is thus a legitimate subject of government concern; but as Justice Brennan recognized in his opinion in *Paris Adult Theatre,* "the State's interest in regulating morality by suppressing obscenity, while often asserted, remains essentially ill-focused and ill-defined." It rests ultimately on "unprovable . . . assumptions about human behavior, morality, sex, and religion." Perhaps more importantly, the notion that government may censor expression because it may alter accepted moral standards flies in the face of the guarantee of free expression. A democratic society must be free to determine its own moral standards through robust and wide-open debate and expression. Although government may legitimately inculcate moral values through education and related activities, it may not suppress expression that reflects or encourages an opposing morality. Such paternalism is incompatible with the most basic premises of the First Amendment.

Second, it is said that government must suppress the distribution of obscene expression to consenting adults because exposure to such expression may "cause" individuals to engage in unlawful conduct. The prevention of unlawful conduct is a legitimate governmental interest, but the correlation between exposure to obscene expression and unlawful conduct is doubtful, at best. As the President's Commission on Obscenity and Pornography found in 1970, there is "no evidence to date that exposure to explicit sexual materials plays a significant role in the causation of delinquent or criminal behavior." The Attorney General's Commission's contrary conclusion in 1986 is based more on preconception than on evidence. An issue that has long divided social scientists and other experts in the field can hardly be definitively resolved by a commission of nonexperts, most of whom were appointed because of their preexisting commitment to the suppression of obscene expression. In any event, even those who claim a connection between exposure to obscene expression and unlawful conduct claim no more than an indirect and attenuated "bad tendency." Thus, although some individuals may on some occasions commit some unlawful acts "because of" their exposure to obscene expression, the connection is indirect, speculative, and unpredictable. It is not even remotely comparable to the much more direct harm caused by such products as firearms, alcohol, and automobiles. The suppression of obscene expression is also a stunningly inefficient and overly broad way to deal with this problem, for even a modest change in law enforcement or sentencing practices would have a much more direct and substantial impact on the rate of unlawful conduct than the legalization or criminalization of obscene expression.

Laws prohibiting the distribution of obscene expression to consenting adults impose significant costs on society and frustrate potentially important privacy and autonomy interests of the individual for only marginal benefits. It is time to bring our regulation of such expression into line with our constitutional traditions, our law enforcement priorities, and our own self-interest and common sense.

The course I propose, and which the commission emphatically rejected, would leave government free to direct its enforcement energies at the more important concerns generated by obscene expression. These fall into three related categories: the protection of juveniles, the protection of captive viewers, and the regulation of the secondary effects of obscene expression. The Court has long recognized government's interest in sheltering children from exposure to obscene expression. What I propose does not undermine this interest. Nor does it interfere with society's substantial interest in restricting child pornography, which poses significantly different issues. My proposal would not in any way prevent government from protecting individuals against the shock effect of unwanted exposure to obscene expression. Government would remain free to prohibit children from viewing movies or buying books found ''obscene,'' and it would remain free to prohibit or otherwise regulate the exhibition of obscene expression over the airwaves. Sensible accommodations can also be devised for other media, such as cable television. Also, my proposal would not prevent government from using zoning and other regulatory devices to control the distribution of obscene expression in order to prevent the decay of neighborhoods or other secondary effects associated with the availability of obscene expression.

By leaving consenting adults free to obtain obscene expression at their discretion, and by protecting our important interests through narrowly defined regulations, we can strike a sensible balance, protecting important societal interests while at the same time preserving our traditional respect for free expression and for the privacy and autonomy of the individual.

The commission has opted to do otherwise and repeat past mistakes— with a vengeance. It has recommended, among other things, significant changes in state and federal legislation to enable more vigorous enforcement of antiobscenity laws; creation of a special Obscenity Task Force in the office of the attorney general to coordinate the prosecution of obscenity cases at the national level; allocation of additional resources at the federal, state, and local levels for the prosecution of obscenity cases; ''aggressive'' Internal Revenue Service investigation of the ''producers and distributors of obscene materials''; and imposition of ''substantial periods of incarceration'' for violators of anti-obscenity laws. This draconian approach is wasteful, misguided, and inconsistent with the real concerns of most of our citizens.

# 16

# Civil Rights
## Racial Quotas

*In the case of* Bakke v. Regents of the University of California *(1978), the United States Supreme Court ruled that the special admissions program for minorities at the University of California at Davis Medical School violated the Civil Rights Act of 1964. The Court ordered Davis officials to admit 38-year-old Allan Bakke, a white engineer who had scored higher on the entrance examination than any black applicant and yet was denied entrance because of the university's racial quota system. The ruling of the Court was widely acclaimed by some whites as a victory against "reverse discrimination."*

*In making its ruling, the Supreme Court did not completely disallow the use of racial criteria in university admissions, but it strongly discouraged the use of racial quotas or other such preferential systems for minorities.*

*The Court was not unanimous in its opinion, however, and one of those who dissented was Justice Thurgood Marshall, a former NAACP attorney and longtime civil rights advocate. In Justice Marshall's opinion, a portion of which is presented here, medical schools and other types of professional schools must give preferential treatment to blacks because of the past history of discrimination in the United States. Without such a policy, he argues, blacks will continue to suffer the consequences of that past discrimination.*

*Taking issue with Marshall's position is Thomas Sowell, a professor of economics at Stanford University. Sowell's counterargument is based on three main contentions: first, that the absence of minorities in professional positions is not necessarily due to past discrimination; second, that a policy of racial quotas may actually be unfair to blacks because it places black students at a disadvantage at some colleges and universities; and third, that a majority of blacks are, in fact, opposed to racial quotas. Thus in Sowell's view having racial quotas may well lead to an increase rather than a decrease in racial tensions.*

# The Case for Racial Quotas

## Thurgood Marshall

Mr. Justice MARSHALL.

. . . I do not agree that petitioner's admissions program violates the Constitution. For it must be remembered that, during most of the past two hundred years, the Constitution as interpreted by this Court did not prohibit the most ingenious and pervasive forms of discrimination against the Negro. Now, when a state acts to remedy the effects of that legacy of discrimination, I cannot believe that this same Constitution stands as a barrier. . . .

## I

The status of the Negro as property was officially erased by his emancipation at the end of the Civil War. But the long awaited emancipation, while freeing the Negro from slavery, did not bring him citizenship or equality in any meaningful way. Slavery was replaced by a system of "laws which imposed upon the colored race onerous disabilities and burdens, and curtailed their rights in the pursuit of life, liberty, and property to such an extent that their freedom was of little value." *Slaughter-House Cases,* 16 Wall. 36, 70, 21 L.Ed. 394 (1873). Despite the passage of the Thirteenth, Fourteenth, and Fifteenth Amendments, the Negro was systematically denied the rights those amendments were supposed to secure. The combined actions and inactions of the state and federal government maintained Negroes in a position of legal inferiority for another century after the Civil War.

The southern states took the first steps to reenslave the Negroes. Immediately following the end of the Civil War, many of the provisional legislatures passed Black Codes, similar to the Slave Codes, which, among other things, limited the rights of Negroes to own or rent property and permitted imprisonment for breach of employment contracts. Over the next several decades, the South managed to disenfranchise the Negroes in spite of the Fifteenth Amendment by various techniques, including poll taxes, deliberately complicated balloting processes, property and literacy qualifications, and finally the white primary.

Congress responded to the legal disabilities being imposed in the southern states by passing the Reconstruction Acts and the Civil Rights Acts. Congress also responded to the needs of the Negroes at the end of the Civil War by establishing the Bureau of Refugees, Freedmen, and Abandoned Lands, better

Thurgood Marshall is associate justice of the U.S. Supreme Court. This opinion is excerpted from *Regents of University of California v. Bakke,* 98 S.Ct. 2733 (1978).

known as the Freedmen's Bureau, to supply food, hospitals, land and education to the newly freed slaves. Thus for a time it seemed as if the Negro might be protected from the continued denial of his civil rights and might be relieved of the disabilities that prevented him from taking his place as a free and equal citizen.

This time, however, was short-lived. Reconstruction came to a close, and, with the assistance of this Court, the Negro was rapidly stripped of his new civil rights. . . .

The Court began by interpreting the Civil War Amendments in a manner that sharply curtailed their substantive protections. See, e.g., *Slaughter-House Cases, supra; United States v. Reese,* 92 U.S. 214, 23 L.Ed. 563 (1876); *United States v. Cruikshank,* 92 U.S. 542, 23 L.Ed. 588 (1876). Then in the notorious *Civil Rights Cases,* 109 U.S. 3, 3 S.Ct. 18, 27 L.Ed. 835 (1883), the Court strangled Congress's efforts to use its power to promote racial equality. In those cases the Court invalidated sections of the Civil Rights Act of 1875 that made it a crime to deny equal access to "inns, public conveyances . . . , theatres, and other places of public amusement." According to the Court, the Fourteenth Amendment gave Congress the power to proscribe only discriminatory action by the state. The Court ruled that the Negroes who were excluded from public places suffered only an invasion of their social rights at the hands of private individuals, and Congress had no power to remedy that. *Id.,* at 24–25, 3 S.Ct., at 31. "When a man has emerged from slavery, and by the aid of beneficent legislation has shaken off the inseparable concomitants of that state," the Court concluded, "there must be some stage in the progress of his elevation when he takes the rank of a mere citizen, and ceases to be the special favorite of the laws. . . ." *Id.,* at 25, 3 S. Ct., at 31. As Justice Harlan noted in dissent, however, the Civil War Amendments and Civil Rights Acts did not make the Negroes the "special favorite" of the laws but instead "sought to accomplish in reference to that race . . . —what had already been done in every State of the Union for the White race—to secure and protect rights belonging to them as freemen and citizens; nothing more." *Id.,* at 61, 3 S.Ct., at 57.

The Court's ultimate blow to the Civil War Amendments and to the equality of Negroes came in *Plessy* v. *Ferguson,* 163 U.S. 537, 16 S.Ct. 1138, 41 L.Ed. 256 (1896). In upholding a Louisiana law that required railway companies to provide "equal but separate" accommodations for whites and Negroes, the Court held that the Fourteenth Amendment was not intended "to abolish distinctions based upon color, or to enforce social, as distinguished from political equality, or a commingling of the two races upon terms unsatisfactory to either." *Id.,* at 544, 16 S.Ct., at 1140. Ignoring totally the realities of the positions of the two races, the Court remarked:

> We consider the underlying fallacy of the plaintiff's argument to consist in the assumption that the enforced separation of the two races stamps the colored race with a badge of inferiority. If this be so, it is not by reason of anything found in the act, but solely because the colored race chooses to put that construction upon it. *Id.,* at 511, 16 S.Ct., at 1143.

Mr. Justice Harlan's dissenting opinion recognized the bankruptcy of the Court's reasoning. He noted that the "real meaning" of the legislation was "that colored citizens are so inferior and degraded that they cannot be allowed to sit in public coaches occupied by white citizens." *Id.*, at 560, 16 S.Ct., at 1147. He expressed his fear that if like laws were enacted in other states, "the effect would be in the highest degree mischievous." *Id.*, at 563, 16 S.Ct., at 1148. Although slavery would have disappeared, the state would retain the power "to interfere with the full enjoyment of the blessings of freedom; to regulate civil rights, common to all citizens, upon the basis of race; and to place in a condition of legal inferiority a large body of American citizens. . . ." *Id.*, at 563, 16 S.Ct., at 1148.

The fears of Mr. Justice Harlan were soon to be realized. In the wake of *Plessy,* many states expanded their Jim Crow laws, which had up until that time been limited primarily to passenger trains and schools. The segregation of the races was extended to residential areas, parks, hospitals, theaters, waiting rooms, and bathrooms. There were even statutes and ordinances which authorized separate phone booths for Negroes and whites, which required that textbooks used by children of one race be kept separate from those used by the other, and which required that Negro and white prostitutes be kept in separate districts. . . .

Nor were the laws restricting the rights of Negroes limited solely to the southern states. In many of the northern states, the Negro was denied the right to vote, prevented from serving on juries and excluded from theaters, restaurants, hotels, and inns. Under President Wilson, the federal government began to require segregation in government buildings; desks of Negro employees were curtained off; separate bathrooms and separate tables in the cafeterias were provided; and even the galleries of the Congress were segregated. . . .

The enforced segregation of the races continued into the middle of the twentieth century. In both world wars, Negroes were for the most part confined to separate military units; it was not until 1948 that an end to segregation in the military was ordered by President Truman. And the history of the exclusion of Negro children from white public schools is too well known and recent to require repeating here. That Negroes were deliberately excluded from public graduate and professional schools—and thereby denied the opportunity to become doctors, lawyers, engineers, and the like—is also well established. It is of course true that some of the Jim Crow laws (which the decisions of the Court had helped to foster) were struck down by this Court in a series of decisions leading up to *Brown* v. *Board of Eduction of Topeka,* 347 U.S. 483, 74 S.Ct. 686, 93 L.Ed. 873 (1954). See, e.g., *Morgan* v. *Virginia,* 328 U.S. 373, 66 S.Ct. 1050, 90 L.Ed. 1317 (1946); *Sweatt* v. *Painter,* 339 U.S. 629, 70 S.Ct. 848, 94 L.Ed. 1114 (1950); *McLaurin* v. *Oklahoma State Regents,* 339 U.S. 637, 70 S.Ct. 851, 94 L.Ed. 1149 (1950). Those decisions, however, did not automatically end segregation, nor did they move Negroes from a position of legal inferiority to one of equality. The legacy of years of slavery and of years of second-class citizenship in the wake of emancipation could not be so easily eliminated.

## II

The position of the Negro today in America is the tragic but inevitable consequence of centuries of unequal treatment. Measured by any benchmark of
comfort or achievement, meaningful equality remains a distant dream for the
Negro. . . .

When the Negro child reaches working age, he finds that America offers
him significantly less than it offers his white counterpart. For Negro adults, the
unemployment rate is twice that of whites,[1] and the unemployment rate for
Negro teenagers is nearly three times that of white teenagers.[2] A Negro male
who completes four years of college can expect a median annual income of
merely $110 more than a white male who has only a high school diploma.[3]
Although Negroes represent 11.5 percent of the population,[4] they are only 1.2
percent of the lawyers and judges, 2 percent of the physicians, 2.3 percent of
the dentists, 1.1 percent of the engineers, and 2.6 percent of the college and
university professors.[5]

The relationship between those figures and the history of unequal treatment afforded to the Negro cannot be denied. At every point from birth to
death the impact of the past is reflected in the still disfavored position of the
Negro.

In light of the history of discrimination and its devastating impact on the
lives of Negroes, bringing the Negro into the mainstream of American life
should be a state interest of the highest order. To fail to do so is to ensure that
America will forever remain a divided society.

## III

. . . It is plain that the Fourteenth Amendment was not intended to prohibit
measures designed to remedy the effects of the nation's past treatment of
Negroes. The Congress that passed the Fourteenth Amendment is the same
Congress that passed the 1866 Freedmen's Bureau Act, an act that pro-
vided many of its benefits only to Negroes: Act of July 16, 1866, ch. 200, 14
Stat. 173. . . .

Since the Congress that considered and rejected the objections to the 1866
Freedmen's Bureau Act concerning special relief to Negroes also proposed the
Fourteenth Amendment, it is inconceivable that the Fourteenth Amendment
was intended to prohibit all race-conscious relief measures. It "would be a
distortion of the policy manifested in that amendment, which was adopted to
prevent state legislation designed to perpetuate discrimination on the basis of
race or color." *Railway Mail Association* v. *Corsi,* 326 U.S. 88, 94, 65 S.Ct.
1483, 1487, 89 L.Ed. 2072 (1945), to hold that it barred state action to remedy
the effects of that discrimination. Such a result would pervert the intent of the
framers by substituting abstract equality for the genuine equality the amendment was intended to achieve.

As has been demonstrated in our joint opinion, this Court's past cases establish the constitutionality of race-conscious remedial measures. Beginning with the school desegregation cases, we recognized that, even absent a judicial or legislative finding of constitutional violation, a school board constitutionally could consider the race of students in making school assignment decisions. See *Swann* v. *Charlotte-Mecklenberg Board of Education*, 402 U.S. 1, 16 . . . (1971); *McDaniel* v. *Barresi*, 402 U.S. 39, 41, . . . (1971). . . .

> . . . As we have held in *Swann*, the Constitution does not compel any particular degree of racial balance or mixing, but when past and continuing constitutional violations are found, some ratios are likely to be useful as starting points in shaping a remedy. . . .

As we have observed, "[a]ny other approach would freeze the status quo that is the very target of all desegregation processes." *McDaniel* v. *Barresi, supra,* 402 U.S. at 41, 91 S.Ct. at 1289.

Only last term, in *United Jewish Organization* v. *Carey,* 430 U.S. 144, 97 S.Ct. 996, 61 L.Ed. 229 (1977), we upheld a New York reapportionment plan that was deliberately drawn on the basis of race to enhance the electoral power of Negroes and Puerto Ricans; the plan had the effect of diluting the electoral strength of the Hasidic Jewish community. We were willing in *UJO* to sanction the remedial use of a racial classification even though it disadvantaged otherwise "innocent" individuals. In another case last term, *Califano* v. *Webster,* 430 U.S. 313, 97 S.Ct. 1192, 51 L.Ed.2d 360 (1977), the Court upheld a provision in the Social Security laws that discriminated against men because its purpose was "the permissible one of redressing our society's long standing disparate treatment of women.'" *Id.,* at 317, 97 S.Ct. at 1195, quoting *Califano* v. *Goldfarb,* 430 U.S. 199, 209n. 8, 97 S.Ct. 1021, 1028, 51 L.Ed.2d 270 (1977) (plurality opinion). We thus recognized the permissibility of remedying past societal discrimination through the use of otherwise disfavored classifications.

Nothing in those cases suggests that a university cannot similarly act to remedy past discrimination.[6] It is true that in both *UJO* and *Webster* the use of the disfavored classification was predicated on legislative or administrative action, but in neither case had those bodies made findings that there had been constitutional violations or that the specific individuals to be benefited had actually been the victims of discrimination. Rather, the classification in each of those cases was based on a determination that the group was in need of the remedy because of some type of past discrimination. There is thus ample support for the conclusion that a university can employ race-conscious measures to remedy past societal discrimination, without the need for a finding that those benefited were actually victims of that discrimination.

# IV

While I applaud the judgment of the Court that a university may consider race in its admissions process, it is more than a little ironic that, after several hundred years of class-based discrimination against Negroes, the Court is unwilling to hold that a class-based remedy for that discrimination is permissible. In declining to so hold, today's judgment ignores the fact that for several hundred years Negroes have been discriminated against, not as individuals, but rather solely because of the color of their skins. It is unnecessary in twentieth-century America to have individual Negroes demonstrate that they have been victims of racial discrimination; the racism of our society has been so pervasive that none, regardless of wealth or position, has managed to escape its impact. The experience of Negroes in America has been different in kind, not just in degree, from that of other ethnic groups. It is not merely the history of slavery alone but also that a whole people were marked as inferior by the law. And that mark has endured. The dream of America as the great melting pot has not been realized for the Negro; because of his skin color he never even made it into the pot.

These differences in the experience of the Negro make it difficult for me to accept that Negroes cannot be afforded greater protection under the Fourteenth Amendment where it is necessary to remedy the effects of past discrimination. . . .

It is because of a legacy of unequal treatment that we now must permit the institutions of this society to give consideration to race in making decisions about who will hold the positions of influence, affluence, and prestige in America. For far too long, the doors to those positions have been shut to Negroes. If we are ever to become a fully integrated society, one in which the color of a person's skin will not determine the opportunities available to him or her, we must be willing to take steps to open those doors. I do not believe that anyone can truly look into America's past and still find that a remedy for the effects of that past is impermissible.

It has been said that this case involves only the individual, Bakke, and this university. I doubt, however, that there is a computer capable of determining the number of persons and institutions that may be affected by the decision in this case. For example, we are told by the attorney general of the United States that at least 27 federal agencies have adopted regulations requiring recipients of federal funds to take *"affirmative action* to overcome the effects of conditions which resulted in limiting participation . . . by persons of a particular race, color, or national origin." Supplemental Brief for the United States as *Amicus Curiae* 16 (emphasis added). I cannot even guess the number of state and local governments that have set up affirmative action programs, which may be affected by today's decision.

I fear that we have come full circle. After the Civil War our government started several "affirmative action" programs. This Court in the *Civil Rights Cases* and *Plessy* v. *Ferguson* destroyed the movement toward complete equality. For almost a century no action was taken, and this nonaction was with the tacit approval of the courts. Then we had *Brown* v. *Board of Education* and the Civil Rights Acts of Congress, followed by numerous affirmative action programs. *Now,* we have this Court again stepping in, this time to stop affirmative action programs of the type used by the University of California. . . .

# NOTES

1  U.S. Dept. of Labor, Bureau of Labor Statistics, Employment and Earnings, January 1978, at 170 (table 44).
2  *Ibid.*
3  U.S. Dept. of Commerce, Bureau of the Census, Current Population Reports, Series P-60, No. 105, at 198 (1977) (table 47).
4  U.S. Dept. of Commerce, Bureau of the Census, Statistical Abstract of the United States 25 (table 24).
5  *Id.,* at 407–8 (table 622) (based on 1970 census).
6  Indeed, the action of the university finds support in the regulations promulgated under Title VI by the Department of Health, Education, and Welfare and approved by the President, which authorize a federally funded institution to take affirmative steps to overcome past discrimination against groups even where the institution was not guilty of prior discrimination. 45 CRF sec. 80.3(b)(6)(ii).

# Are Quotas Good for Blacks?

## Thomas Sowell

Race has never been an area noted for rationality of thought or action. Almost every conceivable form of nonsense has been believed about racial or ethnic groups at one time or another. Theologians used to debate whether black people had souls (today's terminology might suggest that *only* black people have souls). As late as the 1920s, a leading authority on mental tests claimed that test results disproved the popular belief that Jews are intelligent. Since then, Jewish IQs have risen above the national average and more than one-fourth of all American Nobel Prize winners have been Jewish.

Today's grand fallacy about race and ethnicity is that the statistical "representation" of a group—in jobs, schools, etc.—shows and measures discrimination. This notion is at the center of such controversial policies as affirmative-action hiring, preferential admissions to college, and public-school busing. But despite the fact that far-reaching judicial rulings, political crusades, and bureaucratic empires owe their existence to that belief, it remains an unexamined assumption. Tons of statistics have been collected, but only to be interpreted in the light of that assumption, never to test the assumption itself. Glaring facts to the contrary are routinely ignored. Questioning the "representation" theory is stigmatized as not only inexpedient but immoral. It is the noble lie of our time.

## AFFIRMATIVE-ACTION HIRING

"Representation" or "underrepresentation" is based on comparisons of a given group's percentage in the population with its percentage in some occupation, institution, or activity. This might make sense if the various ethnic groups were even approximately similar in age distribution, education, and other crucial variables. But they are not.

Some ethnic groups are a whole decade younger than others. Some are two decades younger. The average age of Mexican Americans and Puerto Ricans is under twenty, while the average age of Irish Americans or Italian Americans is over thirty—and the average age of Jewish Americans is over forty. This is because of large differences in the number of children per family from one group to another. Some ethnic groups have more than twice as many children per family as others. Over half of the Mexican American and Puerto Rican population consists of teenagers, children, and infants. These two groups

Thomas Sowell is an economist and Senior Fellow at the Hoover Institution on War, Revolution, and Peace at Stanford University. This article is reprinted from *Commentary* 65 (June 1978), pp. 39–43, by permission; all rights reserved.

are likely to be underrepresented in any adult activity, whether work or recreation, whether controlled by others or entirely by themselves, and whether there is discrimination or not.

Educational contrasts are also great. More than half of all Americans over thirty-five of German, Irish, Jewish, or Oriental ancestry have completed at least four years of high school. Less than 20 percent of all Mexican Americans in the same age bracket have done so. The disparities become even greater when you consider quality of school, field of specialization, postgraduate study, and other factors that are important in the kind of high-level jobs on which special attention is focused by those emphasizing representation. Those groups with the most education—Jews and Orientals—also have the highest quality education, as measured by the rankings of the institutions from which they receive their college degrees and specialize in the more difficult and remunerative fields, such as science and medicine. Orientals in the United States are so heavily concentrated in the scientific area that there are more Oriental scientists than there are black scientists in absolute numbers, even though the black population of the United States is more than twenty times the size of the Oriental population.

Attention has been focused most on high-level positions—the kind of jobs people reach after years of experience or education, or both. There is no way to get the experience or education without also growing older in the process, so when we are talking about top-level jobs, we are talking about the kind of positions people reach in their forties and fifties rather than in their teens and twenties. Representation in such jobs cannot be compared to representation in a population that includes many five-year-olds—yet it is.

The general ethnic differences in age become extreme in some of the older age brackets. Half of the Jewish population of the United States is forty-five years old or older, but only 12 percent of the Puerto Rican population is that old. Even if Jews and Puerto Ricans were identical in every other aspect, and even if no employer ever had a speck of prejudice, there would still be huge disparities between the two groups in top-level positions, just from age differences alone.

Virtually every underrepresented racial or ethnic group in the United States has a lower than average age and consists disproportionately of children and inexperienced young adults. Almost invariably these groups also have less education, both quantitatively and qualitatively. The point here is not that we should "blame the victim" or "blame society." The point is that we should, first of all, *talk sense!* "Representation" talk is cheap, easy, and misleading; discrimination and opportunity are too serious to be discussed in gobbledygook.

The idea that preferential treatment is going to "compensate" people for past wrongs flies in the face of two hard facts:

1. Public opinion polls have repeatedly shown most blacks opposed to preferential treatment either in jobs or college admissions. A Gallup poll in March

1977, for example, found only 27 percent of nonwhites favoring "preferential" over "ability as determined by test scores," while 64 percent preferred the latter and 9 percent were undecided. (The Gallup breakdown of the U.S. population by race, sex, income, education, etc. found that "not a single population group supports affirmative action."[1])

How can you compensate people by giving them something they have explicitly rejected?

2. The income of blacks relative to whites reached its peak *before* affirmative-action hiring and has *declined* since. The median income of blacks reached a peak of 60.9 percent of the median income of whites in 1970—the year before "goals" and "timetables" became part of the affirmative-action concept. "In only one year of the last six years," writes Andrew Brimmer, "has the proportion been as high as 60 percent."[2]

Before something can be a "compensation," it must first be a benefit.

The repudiation of the numerical or preferential approach by the very people it is supposed to benefit points out the large gap between illusion and reality that is characteristic of affirmative action. So does the cold fact that there are few, if any, benefits to offset all the bitterness generated by this heavy-handed program. The bitterness is largely a result of a deeply resented principle, galling bureaucratic processes, and individual horror stories. Overall, the program has changed little for minorities or women. Supporters of the program try to cover up its ineffectiveness by comparing the position of minorities today with their position many years ago. This ignores all the progress that took place under straight equal-treatment laws in the 1960s—progress that has not continued at anywhere near the same pace under affirmative action.

Among the reasons for such disappointing results is that hiring someone to fill a quota gets the government off the employer's back for the moment, but buys more trouble down the road whenever a disgruntled employee chooses to go to an administrative agency or a court with a complaint based on nothing but numbers. Regardless of the merits, or the end result, a very costly process for the employer must be endured, and the threat of this is an incentive *not* to hire from the groups designated as special by the government. The affirmative-action program has meant mutually cancelling incentives to hire and not to hire—and great bitterness and cost from the process, either way.

If blacks are opposed to preferential treatment and whites are opposed to it, who then is in favor of it, and how does it go on? The implications of these questions are even more far-reaching and more disturbing than the policy itself. They show how vulnerable our democratic and constitutional safeguards are to a relative handful of determined people. Some of those people promoting preferential treatment and numerical goals are so convinced of the rightness of what they are doing that they are prepared to sacrifice whatever needs to be sacrificed—whether it be other people, the law, or simply honesty in discussing what they are doing (note "goals," "desegregation," and similar euphemisms).

Other supporters of numerical policies have the powerful drive of self-interest as well as self-righteousness. Bureaucratic empires have grown up to administer these programs, reaching into virtually every business, school, hospital, or other organization. The rules and agents of the empire can order employers around, make college presidents bow and scrape, assign schoolteachers by race, or otherwise gain power, publicity, and career advancement—regardless of whether minorities are benefited or not.

While self-righteousness and self-interest are powerful drives for those who have them, they can succeed only insofar as other people can be persuaded, swept along by feelings, or neutralized. Rhetoric has accomplished this with images of historic wrongs, visions of social atonement, and a horror of being classed with bigots. These tactics have worked best with those most affected by words and least required to pay a price personally: nonelected judges, the media, and the intellectual establishment.

The "color-blind" words of the Civil Rights Act of 1964, or even the protections of the Constitution, mean little when judges can creatively reinterpret them out of existence. It is hard to achieve the goal of an informed public when the mass media show only selective indignation about power grabs and a sense of pious virtue in covering up the failures of school integration. Even civil libertarians—who insist that the Fifth Amendment protection against self-incrimination is a sacred right that cannot be denied Nazis, Communists, or criminals—show no concern when the government routinely forces employers to confess "deficiencies" in their hiring processes, without a speck of evidence other than a numerical pattern different from the government's preconception.

## PREFERENTIAL ADMISSIONS

Preferential admissions to colleges and universities are "justified" by similar rhetoric and the similar assumption that statistical underrepresentation means institutional exclusion. Sometimes this assumption is buttressed by notions of "compensation" and a theory that (1) black communities need more black practitioners in various fields; and (2) black students will ultimately supply that need. The idea that the black community's doctors, lawyers, etc. should be black is an idea held by white liberals, but no such demand has come from the black community, which has rejected preferential admissions in poll after poll. Moreover, the idea that an admissions committee can predict what a youth is going to do with his life years later is even more incredible—even if the youth is one's own son or daughter, much less someone from a wholly different background.

These moral or ideological reasons for special minority programs are by no means the whole story. The public image of a college or university is often its chief financial asset. Bending a few rules here and there to get the right body count of minority students seems a small price to pay for maintaining an image that will keep money coming in from the government and the foundations. When a few thousand dollars in financial aid to students can keep millions of tax dollars rolling in, it is clearly a profitable investment for the institution. For the young people brought in under false pretense, it can turn out to be a disastrous and permanently scarring experience.

The most urgent concern over image and over government subsidies, foundation grants, and other donations is at those institutions which have the most of all these things to maintain—that is, at prestigious colleges and universities at the top of the academic pecking order. The Ivy League schools and the leading state and private institutions have the scholarship money and the brand-name visibility to draw in enough minority youngsters to look good statistically. The extremely high admissions standards of these institutions usually cannot be met by the minority students—just as most students in general cannot meet them. But in order to have a certain minority body count, the schools bend (or disregard) their usual standards. The net result is that thousands of minority students who would normally qualify for good, non-prestigious colleges where they could succeed, are instead enrolled in famous institutions where they fail. For example, at Cornell during the guns-on-campus crisis, fully half of the black students were on academic probation, despite easier grading standards for them in many courses. Yet these students were by no means unqualified. Their average test scores put them in the top quarter of all American college students—but the other Cornell students ranked in the top *1 percent*. In other words, minority students with every prospect of success in a normal college environment were artificially turned into failures by being mismatched with an institution with standards too severe for them.

When the top institutions reach further down to get minority students, then academic institutions at the next level are forced to reach still further down, so that they too will end up with a minority body count high enough to escape criticism and avoid trouble with the government and other donors. Each academic level, therefore, ends up with minority students underqualified for that level, though usually perfectly qualified for some other level. The end result is a systematic mismatching of minority students and the institutions they attend, even though the wide range of American colleges and universities is easily capable of accommodating those same students under their normal standards.

Proponents of "special" (lower) admissions standards argue that without such standards no increase in minority enrollment would have been possible. But this blithely disregards the fact that when more *money* is available to finance college, more low-income people go to college. The GI Bill after World War II caused an even more dramatic increase in the number of people going to college who could never have gone otherwise—and without lowering admissions standards. The growth of special minority programs in recent times has meant both a greater availability of money and lower admissions standards for black and other designated students. It is as ridiculous to ignore the role of money in increasing the numbers of minority students in the system as a whole as it is to ignore the effect of double standards on their maldistribution among institutions. It is the double standards that are the problem, and they can be ended without driving minority students out of the system. Of course, many academic hustlers who administer special programs might lose their jobs, but that would hardly be a loss to anyone else.

As long as admission to colleges and universities is not unlimited, someone's opportunity to attend has to be sacrificed as the price of preferential admission for others. No amount of verbal sleight-of-hand can get around this fact. None of those sacrificed is old enough to have had anything to do with historic injustices that are supposedly being compensated. Moreover, it is not the offspring of the privileged who are likely to pay the price. It is not a Rockefeller or a Kennedy who will be dropped to make room for quotas; it is a De Funis or a Bakke. Even aside from personal influence on admissions decisions, the rich can give their children the kind of private schooling that will virtually assure them test scores far above the cutoff level at which sacrifices are made.

Just as the students who are sacrificed are likely to come from the bottom of the white distribution, so the minority students chosen are likely to be from the top of the minority distribution. In short, it is a forced transfer of benefits from those least able to afford it to those least in need of it. In some cases, the loose term "minority" is used to include individuals who are personally from more fortunate backgrounds than the average American. Sometimes it includes whole groups, such as Chinese or Japanese Americans, who have higher incomes than whites. One-fourth of all employed Chinese in this country are in professional occupations—nearly double the national average. No amount of favoritism to the son or daughter of a Chinese doctor or mathematician today is going to compensate some Chinese of the past who was excluded from virtually every kind of work except washing clothes or washing dishes.

The past is a great unchangeable fact. *Nothing* is going to undo its sufferings and injustices, whatever their magnitude. Statistical categories and historic labels may seem real to those inspired by words, but only living flesh-and-blood people can feel joy or pain. Neither the sins nor the sufferings of those dead are within our power to change. Being honest and honorable with the people living in our own time is more than enough moral challenge, without indulging in illusions about rewriting moral history with numbers and categories. . . .

However futile the various numerical approaches have been in their avowed goal of advancing minorities, their impact has been strongly felt in other ways. The message that comes through loud and clear is that minorities are losers who will never have anything unless someone gives it to them. The destructiveness of this message—on society in general and minority youth in particular—outweighs any trivial gains that may occur here and there. The falseness of the message is shown by the great economic achievements of minorities during the period of equal-rights legislation before numerical goals and timetables muddied the waters. By and large, the numerical approach has achieved nothing, and has achieved it at great cost.

Underlying the attempt to move people around and treat them like chess pieces on a board is a profound contempt for other human beings. To ignore or resent people's resistance—on behalf of their children or their livelihoods—is to deny our common humanity. To persist dogmatically in pursuit of some abstract goal, without regard to how it is reached, is to despise freedom and reduce three-dimensional life to cardboard pictures of numerical results. The false practicality of results-oriented people ignores the fact that the ultimate results are in the minds and hearts of human beings. Once personal choice becomes a mere inconvenience to be brushed aside by bureaucrats or judges, something precious will have been lost by all people from all backgrounds.

A multi-ethnic society like the United States can ill afford continually to build up stores of intergroup resentments about such powerful concerns as one's livelihood and one's children. It is a special madness when tensions are escalated between groups who are basically in accord in their opposition to numbers games, but whose legal establishments and "spokesmen" keep the fires fueled. We must never think that the disintegration and disaster that has hit other multi-ethnic societies "can't happen here." The mass internment of Japanese Americans just a generation ago is a sobering reminder of the tragic idiocy that stress can bring on. We are not made of different clay from the Germans, who were historically more enlightened and humane toward Jews than many other Europeans—until the generation of Hitler and the Holocaust.

The situation in America today is, of course, not like that of the Pearl Harbor period, nor of the Weimar republic. History does not literally repeat, but it can warn us of what people are capable of, when the stage has been set for tragedy. We certainly do not need to let emotionally combustible materials accumulate from ill-conceived social experiments.

## NOTES

1. Gallup Opinion Index, June 1977, Report 143, p. 23.
2. *Black Enterprise,* April 1978, p. 62. A newly released RAND study similarly concludes that very little credit should be given to government affirmative-action programs for any narrowing of the income gap between white and black workers. The RAND researchers write, "Our results suggest that the effect of government on the aggregate black-white wage ratio is quite small and that the popular notion that . . . recent changes are being driven by government pressure has little empirical support" (*New York Times,* May 8, 1978).

# Abortion

*Probably no domestic issue has polarized the nation more during the last twenty years than abortion. It has proven to be a hotly contested subject in state and national elections and has been the occasion for repeated mass demonstrations in our nation's capital. That abortion has aroused such strong feelings is not surprising, for some see the right to privacy at stake even as others insist that the real issue is the taking of human life.*

*In the first selection, Susan Estrich and Kathleen Sullivan argue that if the decision on abortion is taken out of the hands of the mother, then she will necessarily be forced to surrender autonomy over both her body and family decisions. Government intrusion into these spheres would constitute an intolerable infringement on the fundamental right to privacy—a view shared by the Supreme Court when it upheld a woman's right to an abortion in* Roe v. Wade *(1973).*

*In the second essay James Bopp and Richard Coleson contend that the* Roe v. Wade *decision (1973) was a glaring example of judicial power gone wild, with the justices manufacturing a right to privacy in the Constitution where it was nowhere to be found. In doing so, the Court not only violated its own stated criteria for determining what qualifies as a fundamental right, but also arrogated to itself a power which the people alone may exercise. Bopp and Coleson further argue that the right to abortion should be rejected on moral as well as legal grounds, and they also challenge pro-choice claims that the outlawing of abortions would have harmful social consequences for women.*

# Abortion Politics:
## The Case for the Right to Privacy
**Susan R. Estrich and Kathleen M. Sullivan**

## I. THE EXISTENCE OF A LIBERTY INTEREST

. . .

### A. Reproductive Choice Is Essential to Woman's Control of Her Destiny and Family Life

Notwithstanding the abortion controversy, the Supreme Court has long acknowledged an unenumerated right to privacy as a species of "liberty" that the due process clauses protect.[1] The principle is as ancient as *Meyer v. Nebraska*[2] and *Pierce v. Society of Sisters*,[3] which protected parents' freedom to educate their children free of the state's controlling hand. In its modern elaboration, this right continues to protect child rearing and family life from the overly intrusive reach of government.[4] The modern privacy cases have also plainly established that decisions whether to bear children are no less fundamental than decisions about how to raise them. The Court has consistently held since *Griswold v. Connecticut*[5] that the Constitution accords special protection to "matters so fundamentally affecting a person as the decision whether to bear or beget a child," and has therefore strictly scrutinized laws restricting contraception.[6] *Roe* held that these principles extend no less to abortion than to contraception.

The privacy cases rest, as Justice Stevens recognized in *Thornburgh*, centrally on " 'the moral fact that a person belongs to himself [or herself] and not others nor to society as a whole.' "[7] Extending this principle to the abortion decision follows from the fact that "[f]ew decisions are . . . more basic to individual dignity and autonomy" or more appropriate to the "private sphere of individual liberty" than the uniquely personal, intimate, and self-defining decision whether or not to continue a pregnancy.[8]

In two senses, abortion restrictions keep a woman from "belonging to herself." First and most obviously, they deprive her of bodily self-possession. As Chief Justice Rehnquist observed in another context, pregnancy entails "profound physical, emotional, and psychological consequences."[9] To name a few, pregnancy increases a woman's uterine size 500-1000 times, her pulse rate

Susan R. Estrich and Kathleen M. Sullivan are professors of law at Harvard University. This selection is from Susan R. Estrich and Kathleen M. Sullivan, "Abortion Politics: Writing for an Audience of One," *University of Pennsylvania Law Review* 138: 125–132, 150–155 (1989). Notes have been renumbered to correspond with edited text—Editors.

by ten to fifteen beats a minute, and her body weight by 25 pounds or more.[10] Even the healthiest pregnancy can entail nausea, vomiting, more frequent urination, fatigue, back pain, labored breathing, or water retention.[11] There are also numerous medical risks involved in carrying pregnancy to term: of every ten women who experience pregnancy and childbirth, six need treatment for some medical complication, and three need treatment for major complications.[12] In addition, labor and delivery impose extraordinary physical demands, whether over the six-to-twelve hour or longer course of vaginal delivery, or during the highly invasive surgery involved in a cesarean section, which accounts for one out of four deliveries.[13]

By compelling pregnancy to term and delivery even where they are unwanted, abortion restrictions thus exert far more profound intrusions into bodily integrity than the stomach-pumping the Court invalidated in *Rochin v. California*,[14] or the surgical removal of a bullet from a shoulder that the Court invalidated in *Winston v. Lee*.[15] "The integrity of an individual's person is a cherished value of our society"[16] because it is so essential to identity; as former Solicitor General Charles Fried, who argued for the United States in *Webster*, recognized in another context: "[to say] that my body can be used is [to say] that I can be used."[17]

These points would be too obvious to require restatement if the state attempted to compel abortions rather than to restrict them. Indeed, in colloquy with Justice O'Connor during the *Webster* oral argument, former Solicitor General Fried conceded that in such a case, liberty principles, although unenumerated, would compel the strictest review. To be sure, as Mr. Fried suggested, restrictive abortion laws do not literally involve "laying hands on a woman."[18] But this distinction should make no difference: the state would plainly infringe its citizens' bodily integrity whether its agents inflicted knife wounds or its laws forbade surgery or restricted blood transfusions in cases of private knifings.[19]

Apart from this impact on bodily integrity, abortion restrictions infringe a woman's autonomy in a second sense as well; they invade the autonomy in family affairs that the Supreme Court has long deemed central to the right of privacy. Liberty requires independence in making the most important decisions in life.[20] "The decision whether or not to beget or bear a child" lies at "the very heart of this cluster of constitutionally protected choices,"[21] because few decisions can more importantly alter the course of one's life than the decision to bring a child into the world. Bearing a child dramatically affects " 'what a person is, what [s]he wants, the determination of [her] life plan, of [her] concept of the good' " and every other aspect of the " 'self-determination . . . [that] give[s] substance to the concept of liberty.' "[22] Becoming a parent dramatically alters a woman's educational prospects,[23] employment opportunities,[24] and sense of self.[25] In light of these elemental facts, it is no surprise that the freedom to choose one's own family formation is "deeply rooted in this Nation's history and tradition."[26]

Today, virtually no one disputes that these principles require heightened scrutiny of laws restricting access to contraception.[27] But critics of *Roe* sometimes argue that abortion is "different in kind from the decision not to conceive in the first place."[28] Justice White, for example, has asserted that, while the liberty interest is fundamental in the contraception context,[29] that interest falls to minimal after conception.[30]

Such a distinction cannot stand, however, because no bright line can be drawn between contraception and abortion in light of modern scientific and medical advances. Contraception and abortion are points on a continuum. Even "conception" itself is a complex process of which fertilization is simply the first stage. According to contemporary medical authorities, conception begins not with fertilization, but rather six to seven days later when the fertilized egg becomes implanted in the uterine wall, itself a complex process.[31] Many medically accepted contraceptives operate after fertilization. For example, both oral contraceptives and the intra-uterine device (IUD) not only prevent fertilization but in some instances prevent implantation.[32] Moreover, the most significant new developments in contraceptive technology, such as RU486, act by foiling implantation.[33] All such contraceptives blur the line between contraception and abortion.

In the absence of a bright physiological line, there can be no bright constitutional line between the moments before and after conception. A woman's fundamental liberty does not simply evaporate when sperm meets ovum. Indeed, as Justice Stevens has recognized, "if one decision is more 'fundamental' to the individual's freedom than the other, surely it is the postconception decision that is the more serious."[34] Saying this much does not deny that profound evolutionary changes occur between fertilization and birth. Clearly, there is some difference between "the freshly fertilized egg and . . . the 9-month-gestated . . . fetus on the eve of birth."[35] But as *Roe v. Wade* fully recognized, such differences go at most to the weight of the state's justification for interfering with a pregnancy; they do not extinguish the underlying fundamental liberty.

Thus *Roe* is not a mere "thread" that the Court could pull without "unravel[ing]" the now elaborately woven "fabric" of the privacy decisions.[36] Rather, *Roe* is integral to the principle that childbearing decisions come to "th[e] Court with a momentun for respect that is lacking when appeal is made to liberties which derive merely from shifting economic arrangements.[37] The decision to become a mother is too fundamental to be equated with the decision to buy a car, choose optometry over opthalmology, take early retirement, or any other merely economic decision that the government may regulate by showing only a minimally rational basis.

## B. Keeping Reproductive Choice in Private Hands Is Essential to a Free Society

Even if there were any disagreement about the degree of bodily or decisional autonomy that is essential to personhood, there is a separate, alternative rationale for the privacy cases: keeping the state out of the business of reproductive decision-making. Regimentation of reproduction is a hallmark of the totalitarian state, from Plato's Republic to Hitler's Germany, from Huxley's *Brave New World* to Atwood's *Handmaid's Tale*. Whether the state compels reproduction or prevents it, "totalitarian limitation of family size . . . is at complete variance with our constitutional concepts."[38] The state's monopoly of force cautions against *any* official reproductive orthodoxy.

For these reasons, the Supreme Court has long recognized that the privacy right protects not only the individual but also our society. As early as *Meyer*[39] and *Pierce*,[40] the Court acknowledged that "[t]he fundamental theory of liberty" on which a free society rests "excludes any general power of the State to standardize" its citizens.[41] As Justice Powell likewise recognized for the *Moore* plurality, "a free society" is one that avoids the homogenization of family life.[42]

The right of privacy, like freedoms of speech and religion, protects conscience and spirit from the encroachment of overbearing government. "Struggles to coerce uniformity of sentiment," Justice Jackson recognized in *West Virginia State Board of Education v. Barnett*,[43] are the inevitably futile province of "our totalitarian enemies."[44] Preserving a private sphere for child-bearing and childrearing decisions not only liberates the individual; it desirably constrains the state.[45]

Those who would relegate all control over abortion to the state legislatures ignore these fundamental, systematic values. It is a red herring to focus on the question of judicial versus legislative control of reproductive decisions, as so many of *Roe's* critics do. The real distinction is that between private and public control of the decision: the private control that the courts protect through *Griswald* and *Roe*, and the public control that the popular branches could well usurp in a world without those decisions.

Precisely because of the importance of a private sphere for family, spirit, and conscience, the framers never intended to commit all moral disagreements to the political arena. Quite the contrary:

> The very purpose of a Bill of Rights was to withdraw certain subjects from the vicissitudes of politial controversy, to place them beyond the reach of majorities and officials and to establish them as legal principles to be applied by the courts. One's right to life, liberty, and property, to free speech, a free press, freedom of worship and assembly, and other fundamental rights may not be submitted to vote; they depend on the outcome of no elections.[46]

Such "withdrawal" of fundamental liberties from the political arena is basic to constitutional democracy as opposed to rank majoritarianism, and nowhere is such "withdrawal" more important than in controversies where moral convictions and passions run deepest. The inclusion of the free exercise clause attests to this point.[47]

The framers also never intended that toleration on matters of family, conscience, and spirit would vary from state to state. The value of the states and localities as "laborator[ies for] . . . social and economic experiments"[48] has never extended to " 'experiments at the expense of the dignity and personlity of the individual.'"[49] Rather as Madison once warned, " 'it is proper to take alarm at the first experiment on our liberties. We hold this prudent jealousy to be the first duty of citizens, and one of [the] noblest characteristics of the late Revolution.'"[50]

*Roe v. Wade* thus properly withdrew the abortion decision, like other decisions on matters of conscience, "from the vicissitudes of political controversy." It did not withdraw that decision from the vicissitudes of moral argument or social suasion by persuasive rather than coercive means.[51] In withdrawing the abortion decision from the hot lights of politics, *Roe* protected not only persons but the processes of constitutional democracy.

* * *

## II. THE POLITICAL PROCESS: NOT TO BE TRUSTED

On October 13, 1989, *The New York Times* declared that the tide had turned in the political process on abortion.[52] The Florida legislature, in special session, rejected a series of proposals to restrict abortion, and Congress voted to expand abortion funding for poor women to cases of rape and incest. And most stunningly of all, the Attorney General of Illinois on November 2, 1989, settled a pending challenge to Illinois' abortion clinic regulation rather than risk winning his case in the United States Supreme Court. These events have triggered the assessment that the post-*Webster* pro-choice mobilization has succeeded. Which raises the question: why not leave these matters to the political process?

The short answer, of course, is that we don't leave freedom of speech or religion or association to the political process, even on good days when the polls suggest they might stand a chance, at least in some states. The very essence of a fundamental right is that it "depend[s] on the outcome of no elections."[53]

The long answer is, as always, that fundamental liberties are not occasions for the experimentation that federalism invites. The right to abortion should not depend on where you live and how much money you have for travel.[54] And, regardless of our recent, at long-last successes, the reality remains that the political process is to be trusted the least where, as here, it imposes burdens unequally.

The direct impact of abortion restrictions falls exclusively on a class of people that consists entirely of women. Only women get pregnant. Only women have abortions. Only women will endure unwanted pregnancies and adverse health consequences if states restrict abortions. Only women will suffer dangerous, illegal abortions where legal ones are unavailable. And only women will bear children if they cannot obtain abortions.[55] Yet every restrictive abortion law has been passed by a legislature in which men constitute a numerical majority. And every restrictive abortion law, by definition, contains an unwritten clause exempting all men from its strictures.

As Justice Jackson wrote, legislators threaten liberty when they pass laws that exempt themselves or people like them: "The framers of the Constitution knew, and we should not forget today, that there is no more effective practical guaranty against arbitrary and unreasonable government than to require that the principles of law which officials would impose upon a minority must be imposed generally."[56] The Supreme Court has long interpreted the equal protection clause to require even-handedness in legislation, lest the powerful few too casually trade away for others key liberties that they are careful to reserve for themselves.

For example, in striking down a law permitting castration of recidivist chicken thieves but sparing white collar embezzlers the knife, the Court implied that, put to an all-or-nothing choice, legislators would rather sterilize no one than jeopardize a politically potent class.[57] In the words of Justice Jackson: "There are limits to the extent to which a legislatively represented majority may conduct biological experiments at the expense of the dignity and personality and natural powers of a minority—even those who are guilty of what the majority defines as crimes."[58]

At least there should be. Relying on state legislatures, as Chief Justice Rehnquist would, to protect women against "abortion regulation reminiscent of the dark ages,"[59] ignores the fact that the overwhelming majority of "those who serve in such bodies"[60] are biologically exempt from the penalties they are imposing.

The danger is greater still when the subject is abortion. The lessons of history are disquieting. Abortion restrictions, like the most classic restrictions on women seeking to participate in the worlds of work and ideas, have historically rested on archaic stereotypes portraying women as persons whose "paramount destiny and mission . . . [is] to fulfill the noble and benign office of wife and mother."[61] Legislation prohibiting abortion, largely a product of the years between 1860 and 1880, reflected *precisely* the same ideas about women's natural and proper roles as other legislation from the same period, long since discredited, that prohibited women from serving on juries or participating in the professions, including the practice of law.[62] And modern studies have found that support for laws banning abortion continues to be an outgrowth of the same stereotypical notions that women's only appropriate roles are those of mother and housewife. In many cases, abortion laws are a direct reaction to the increasing number of women who work outside of the home.[63] Those involved in anti-abortion activities tend to echo the well-known views of Justice Bradley in *Bradwell:*

> Men and women, as a result of . . . intrinsic differences, have different roles to play. Men are best suited to the public world of work, whereas women are best suited to rearing children, managing homes, and loving and caring for husbands. . . . Mothering, in their view, is itself a full-time job, and any woman who cannot commit herself fully to mothering should eschew it entirely.[64]

But the lessons of history are not limited to the powers of enduring stereotypes. History also makes clear that a world without *Roe* will not be a world without abortion but a world in which abortion is accessible according to one's constitutional case. While affluent women will travel to jurisdictions where safe and legal abortions are available, paying whatever is necessary, restrictive abortion laws and with them, the life-threatening prospect of back-alley abortion, will disproportionately descend upon "those without . . . adequate resources" to avoid them.[65] Those for whom the burdens of an unwanted pregnancy may be the most crushing—the young, the poor, women whose color already renders them victims of discrimination—will be the ones least able to secure a safe abortion.

In the years before *Roe,* "[p]oor and minority women were virtually precluded from obtaining safe, legal procedures, the overwhelming majority of which were obtained by white women in the private hospital services on psychiatric indications."[66] Women without access to safe and legal abortions often had dangerous and illegal ones. According to one study, mishandled criminal abortions were the leading cause of maternal deaths in the 1960s,[67] and mortality rates for African-American women were as much as nine times the rate for white women.[68] To trust the political process to protect these women is to ignore the lessons of history and the realities of power and powerlessness in America today.

In the face of such lessons, those who would have us put our faith in the political process might first want to look a little more closely at the victories which are said to support such a choice. The Florida legislature's rejection of proposed abortion restrictions came days *after* the state's highest court held that the State Constitution protects the right to choose abortion, rendering the entire session, by the press's verdict before it began, symbolic at best. The session was still a triumph, but hardly one in which the courts were beside the point. And while extending funding to cases of rape and incest would have been a step forward, the narrowness of the victory and the veto of the resulting legislation should give pause, at least.[69]

We believe that energizing and mobilizing pro-choice voters, and women in particular, is vitally important on its own terms. We hope, frankly, that with apportionment approaching in 1990, that mobilization will affect issues well beyond abortion. We hope more women will find themselves running for office and winning. We hope pro-choice voters and the legislators they elect will attack a range of issues of particular importance to women, including the attention that children receive after they are born.

But we have no illusions. We will lose some along the way. Young and poor and minority women will pay most dearly when we do. That's the way it is in politics. That's why politics should not dictate constitutional rights. . . .

## NOTES

1 The right of privacy is only one among many instances in which the Court has recognized rights that are not expressly named in the Constitution's text. To name just a few other examples, the Court has recognized unenumerated rights to freedom

of association, see *National Association for the Advancement of Colored People v. Alabama,* 357 U.S. 449, 466 (1958); to equal protection under the Fifth Amendment due process clause, see *Bolling v. Sharpe,* 347 U.S. 497, 500 (1954); to travel between the states, see *Shapiro v. Thompson,* 394 U.S. 618, 638 (1966); to vote, see *Harper v. Virginia Bd. of Elections,* 383 U.S. 663, 665–66 (1966); *Reynolds v. Sims,* 377 U.S. 533, 554 (1964); and to attend criminal trials, see *Richmond Newspapers Inc. v. Virginia,* 448 U.S. 555, 579–80 (1980).

2  262 U.S. 390 (1923).

3  268 U.S. 510 (1925).

4  See, e.g., *Moore v. City of East Cleveland,* 431 U.S. 494, 503–06 (1977) (plurality opinion) (noting a constitutional right to live with one's grandchildren); *Loving v. Virginia,* 388 U.S. 1, 12 (1967) (affirming a right to interracial marriage).

5  381 U.S. 479 (1965).

6  *Eisenstadt v. Baird,* 405 U.S. 438, 453 (1972).

7  *Thornburgh v. American College of Obstetricians & Gynecologists,* 476 U.S. 747, 777 n.5 (1985) (Stevens, J., concurring) (quoting former Solicitor General Fried, "Correspondence," 6 *Phil. & Pub. Aff.* 288–89 (1977)).

8  *Thornburgh,* 476 U.S. at 772.

9  *Michael M. v. Sonoma County Superior Court,* 480 U.S. 464, 471 (1981).

10  See J. Pritchard, P. McDonald & N. Gant, *Williams Obstetrics,* 181–210, 260–63 (17th ed. 1985) [hereinafter *Williams Obstetrics*].

11  See *id.*

12  See R. Gold, A. Kenney & S. Singh, *Blessed Events and the Bottom Line: Financing Maternity Care in the United States,* 10 (1987).

13  See D. Danforth, M. Hughey & A. Wagner, *The Complete Guide to Pregnancy,* 228–31 (1983); S. Romney, M. J. Gray, A. B. Little, J. Merrill, E. J. Quilligan & R. Stander, *Gynecology and Obstetrics: The Health Care of Women,* 626–37 (2d ed. 1981).

14  342 U.S. 165 (1952).

15  470 U.S. 753 (1985).

16  *Id.* at 760.

17  C. Fried, *Right and Wrong,* 121 n.* (1978).

18  "Transcript of Oral Argument in Abortion Case," *N.Y. Times,* Apr. 27, 1989, at B12, col. 5.

19  Likewise, a state would surely infringe reproductive freedom by compelling abortions even if it became technologically possible to do so without "laying hands on a woman."

20  See *Whalen v. Roe,* 429 U.S. 589, 599–600 (1977).

21  *Carey v. Population Serv. Int'l,* 431 U.S. 678, 685 (1977).

22  *Thornburgh v. American College of Obstetricians & Gynecologists,* 476 U.S. 747, 777 n.5 (1985) (Stevens, J., concurring) (quoting C. Fried, *Right and Wrong,* 146–47 (1978)).

23  Teenage mothers have high dropout rates: eight out of ten who become mothers at age seventeen or younger do not finish high school. See Fielding, *Adolescent Pregnancy Revisited,* 299 Mass. Dep't Pub. Health, 893, 894 (1978).

24  Control over the rate of childbirth is a key factor in explaining recent gains in women's wages relative to men's. See Fuchs, "Women's Quest for Economic Equality," 3 *J. Econ. Persp.* 25, 33–37 (1989).

25  This fact is evident even if the biological mother does not raise her child. Relinquish-

ing a child for adoption may alleviate material hardship, but it is psychologically traumatic. See Winkler & VanKeppel, *Relinquishing Mothers in Adoption: Their Long-Term Adjustment,* Monograph No. 3, Institute of Family Studies (1984).

26 *Moore v. City of East Cleveland,* 431 U.S. 494, 503 (1977) (plurality opinion).

27 The United States has conceded before the Supreme Court that the *Griswold* line of cases was correctly decided. See *Brief for the United States as Amicus Curiae Supporting Appellants,* 11–13; *Webster v. Reproductive Health Serv.,* 1109 S. Ct. 3040 (1989) (No. 88–605); "Transcript of Oral Argument in Abortion Case," *N.Y. Times,* Apr. 27, 1989, at B13, col. 1 (Argument of former Solicitor General Fried on behalf of the United States).

28 *Thornburgh,* 476 U.S. at 792 n.2 (White, J., dissenting).

29 See *Eisenstadt v. Baird,* 405 U.S. 438, 463–64 (1972) (White, J., concurring in result); *Griswold v. Connecticut,* 381 U.S. 479, 502–03 (1965) (White, J., concurring in judgment).

30 See *Thornburgh,* 476 U.S. at 792 n.2 (White, J., dissenting) (arguing that the fetus's presence after conception changes not merely the state justification but "the characterization of the liberty interest itself").

31 See *Williams Obstetrics, supra* note 10, at 88–91; Milby, "The New Biology and the Question of Personhood: Implications for Abortion," 9 *Am. J.L. & Med.* 31, 39–41 (1983). Indeed, the American College of Obstetricians & Gynecologists, the preeminent authority on such matters, has adopted the following official definition of conception: conception consists of "the implantation of the blastocyst [fertilized ovum]" in the uterus, and thus is "not synonymous with fertilization." *Obstetric-Gynecologic Terminology* 229, 327 (E. Hughes ed. 1972). Such a definition is not surprising in view of the fact that less than half of fertilized ova ever successfully become implanted. See "Post-Coital Contraception," 1 *The Lancet* 855, 856 (1983).

32 See R. Hatcher, E. Guest, F. Stewart, G. Stewart, J. Trussell, S. Bowen & W. Gates, *Contraceptive Technology,* 252–53, 377 (14th rev. ed. 1988) [hereinafter *Contraceptive Technology*]; *United States Department of Health and Human Services, IUDs: Guidelines for Informed Decision-Making and Use* (1987).

33 See *Contraceptive Technology, supra* note 32, at 378; Nieman, Choate, Chrousas, Healy, Morin, Renquist, Merriam, Spitz, Bardin, Balieu & Loriaux, "The Progesterone Antagonist RU486: A Potential New Contraceptive Agent," 316 *N. Eng. J. Med.* 187 (1987). RU486 is approved for use in France but not in the United States.

34 *Thornburgh,* 476 U.S. at 776 (Stevens, J., concurring).

35 *Id.* at 779.

36 "Transcript of Oral Argument in Abortion Case," *N.Y. Times,* April 27, 1989, at B12, col. 5 (former Solicitor General Fried, arguing on behalf of the United States). Counsel for Appellees gave the following complete reply: "It has always been my personal experience that when I pull a thread, my sleeve falls off." *Id.* at B13, col. 1 (argument of Mr. Susman).

37 *Thornburgh,* 476 U.S. at 775 (Stevens, J., concurring) (citing *Griswold v. Connecticut,* 381 U.S. 479, 502–03 (1965) (White, J., dissenting)).

38 *Griswold,* 381 U.S. at 497 (Goldberg, J., concurring).

39 *Meyer v. Nebraska,* 262 U.S. 390 (1923).

40 *Pierce v. Society of Sisters,* 268 U.S. 510 (1925).

41 *Id.* at 535.

42 See *Moore v. City of East Cleveland,* 431 U.S. 494, 503 n.11 (1977) (quoting from a discussion of *Griswold* in Pollak, "Thomas I. Emerson, Lawyer and Scholar: *Ipse Custodiet Custodes,*" 84 *Yale L.J.* 638, 653 (1975)).

43  319 U.S. 624 (1943).

44  *Id*. at 640–41.

45  See generally Rubenfeld, "The Right of Privacy," 102 *Harv. L. Rev*. 737, 804–07 (1989) (arguing that the constitutional right of privacy protects individuals from being turned into instrumentalities of the regimenting state, or being forced into a state-chosen identity).

46  *Barnette*, 319 U.S. at 638.

47  Justice Douglas wrote:

> The Fathers of the Constitution were not unaware of the varied and extreme views of religious sects, of the violence of disagreement among them, and of the lack of any one religious creed on which all men would agree. They fashioned a charter of government which envisaged the widest possible toleration of conflicting views.

> *United States v. Ballard*, 322 U.S. 78, 87 (1944). See also *Webster*, 109 S. Ct. at 3085 & n.16 (Stevens, J., concurring in part and dissenting in part) (noting that "the intensely divisive character of much of the national debate over the abortion issue reflects the deeply held religious convictions of many participants in the debate").

48  *New State Ice Co. v. Liebmann*, 285 U.S. 262, 311 (1932) (Brandeis, J., dissenting).

49  *Poe v. Ullman*, 367 U.S. 497, 555 (1961) (Harlan, J., dissenting) (quoting *Skinner v. Oklahoma*, 316 U.S. 535, 546 (1942) (Jackson, J., concurring)).

50  *Everson v. Board of Educ.*, 330 U.S. 1, 65 (1947) (Appendix, Rutledge, J., dissenting) (quoting Madison, *Memorial and Remonstrance Against Religious Assessments*).

51  Nor, of course, did it bar political efforts to reduce the abortion rate through non-coercive means, such as funding sex education and contraception, or providing economic security to indigent mothers.

52  See Apple, "An Altered Political Climate Suddenly Surrounds Abortion," *N.Y. Times*, Oct. 13, 1989, at A1, col. 4; see also Berke, "The Abortion-Rights Movement Has Its Day," *N.Y. Times*, Oct. 15, 1989, § 4 at 1, col. 1.

53  *West Virginia Bd. of Educ. v. Barnette*, 319 U.S. 624, 638 (1943).

54  Even if only ten or eleven states were to preclude abortion within their borders, many women would be held hostage there by the combination of geography, poverty, and youth. This situation would be no more tolerable than the enforcement of racial segregation in a "mere" ten or eleven states in the 1950s.

55  See *Michael M. v. Sonoma County Superior Court*, 450 U.S. 464, 473 (1981) ("[V]irtually all of the significant harmful and inescapably identifiable consequences of teenage pregnancy fall on the young female").

56  *Railway Express Agency v. New York*, 336 U.S. 106, 112 (1949) (Jackson, J., concurring).

57  See *Skinner v. Oklahoma*, 316 U.S. 535 (1942). *Cf*. Epstein, "The Supreme Court, 1987 Term: Foreword: Unconstitutional Conditions, State Power, and the Limits of Consent," 102 *Harv. L. Rev*. 4 (1988) (arguing that enforcement of unconstitutional conditions doctrine similarly functions to put legislatures to an all-or-nothing choice).

58  *Skinner*, 316 U.S. at 546 (Jackson, J., concurring).

59  *Webster*, 109 S. Ct. at 3045.

60  *Id*.

61  *Bradwell v. Illinois*, 83 U.S. (16 Wall.) 130, 142 (1873) (Bradley, J., concurring).

62  See J. Mohr, *Abortion in America: The Origins and Evolution of National Policy, 1800–1900*, at 168–72 (1978). To many of the doctors who were largely responsible

for abortion restrictions, "the chief purpose of women was to produce children; anything that interfered with that purpose, or allowed women to 'indulge' themselves in less important activities, threatened . . . the future of society itself." *Id.* at 169. The view of one such nineteenth-century doctor drew the parallel even more explicitly: he complained that "the tendency to force women into men's places" was creating the insidious new idea that a woman's "ministrations . . . as a mother should be abandoned for the sterner rights of voting and law making." *Id.* at 105; see also L. Gordon, *Woman's Body, Woman's Right: A Social History of Birth Control in America* (1976) (chronicling the social and political history of reproductive rights in the United States).

63 See generally K. Luker, *Abortion and the Politics of Motherhood,* 192–215 (1984) (describing how the abortion debate, among women, represents a "war" between the feminist vision of women in society and the homemaker's world view); Luker, "Abortion and the Meaning of Life," in *Abortion: Understanding Differences* 25, 31–33 (S. Callahan & D. Callahan eds. 1984) (concluding that "[b]ecause many prolife people see sex as literally sacred, *and because, for women, procreative sex is a fundamental part of their "career* . . . abortion is, from their [the prolife] point of view, to turn the world upside down").

64 Luker, *supra* note 63, at 31. It is, of course, precisely such stereotypes, as they are reflected in legislation, which have over and over again been the focus of this Court's modern equal protection cases. See, e.g., *Califano v. Goldfarb,* 430 U.S. 199, 206–07 (1977) ("Gender-based differentiation . . . is forbidden by the Constitution, at least when supported by no more substantial justification than 'archaic and overbroad' generalizations."); *Weinberger v. Wiesenfeld,* 420 U.S. 636, 645 (1975) ("Gender-based generalizations" that men are more likely than women to support their families "cannot suffice to justify the denigration of the effects of women who do work. . . ."): *Stanton v. Stanton,* 421 U.S. 7, 14 (1975) ("A child, male or female, is still a child. No longer is the female destined solely for the home and the rearing of the family, and only the male for the marketplace and the world of ideas."); *Frontiero v. Richardson,* 441 U.S. 677, 684 (1973) ("[O]ur Nation has had a long and unfortunate history of sex discrimination . . . which in practical effect put women, not on a pedestal, but in a cage.").

65 *Griswold v. Connecticut,* 318 U.S. 479, 503 (1965) (White, J., concurring).

66 *Polgar & Fried,* "The Bad Old Days: Clandestine Abortions Among the Poor in New York City Before Liberalization of the Abortion Law," 8 *Fam. Plan. Persp.* 125 (1976); see also Gold, "Therapeutic Abortions in New York: A 20-Year Review," 55 *Am. J. Pub. Health* 964, 66 (1965) (noting that the ratio of legal hospital abortions per live birth was five times more for white women than for women of color, and twenty-six times more for white women than for Puerto Rican women in New York City from 1951–62); Pilpel, "The Abortion Crisis," in *The Case for Legalized Abortion Now* 97, 101 (Guttmacher ed. 1967) (noting that 93% of in-hospital abortions in New York State were performed on white women who were able to afford private rooms).

67 See Niswander, "Medical Abortion Practice in the United States," in *Abortion and the Law,* 37, 37 (D. Smith ed. 1967).

68 See Gold, *supra* note 66, at 964–65.

69 Requiring prompt reporting of cases of rape and incest to criminal authorities, measured in terms of days if not hours, as the White House has suggested, is to ignore study after study that has found precisely such cases among the least often

reported to the police. Yet late reporting, which should be encouraged, becomes grounds to deny funding, and excludes altogether those who fear, often with reasons, to report at all. The pain and suffering of brutal victimization and of an unwanted pregnancy are in no way affected by the speed of the initial criminal report. A small victory, indeed.

President Bush vetoed the legislation on October 21, 1989. The House vote to override was 231–191, short of the necessary two-thirds majority. See 135 *Cong. Rec.* H7482-95 (daily ed. Oct. 25, 1989).

# Abortion on Demand Has No Constitutional or Moral Justification

**James Bopp, Jr., and Richard E. Coleson**

## I. THE ABSENCE OF A CONSTITUTIONAL RIGHT TO ABORTION

Abortion is not mentioned in the United States Constitution. Yet, in *Roe v. Wade*,[1] the United States Supreme Court held that there is a constitutional right to abortion.

How could the Court justify such a decision? Actually, it never did. The Court simply *asserted* that the "right of privacy . . . is broad enough to encompass a woman's decision whether or not to terminate her pregnancy."[2] Leading constitutional scholars were outraged at the Court's action in *Roe* and vigorously argued that the Court had no constitutional power to create new constitutional rights in this fashion.[3] And, of course, many people were incensed that a whole class of innocent human beings—those awaiting birth—was stripped of all rights, including the right to life itself.

Why does it matter whether abortion is found in the Constitution? Why shouldn't the United States Supreme Court be free to create new constitutional rights whenever it chooses? The answers lie in the carefully designed structure of our democracy, whose blueprints were drawn over two centuries ago by the framers of the Constitution and ratified by the People. This design is explained below as the foundation for rejecting abortion on demand on a constitutional basis.

But what of abortion on demand as a legislative issue? Even if there is no constitutional right to abortion, how much should state legislatures restrict abortion? The answer lies in the states' compelling interest in protecting innocent human life, born or preborn. This interest is given scant attention by abortion rights advocates. Rather, they envision an extreme abortion-on-demand regime; but their societal vision is overwhelmingly rejected by public opinion. As shown below, the states constitutionally may and morally should limit abortion on demand.

James Bopp, Jr. is partner in the law firm of Brames, McCormick, Bopp & Abel, Terre Haute, Indiana, and General Counsel to the National Right to Life Committee, Inc. Richard E. Coleson is an associate with Brames, McCormick, Bopp & Abel, and General Counsel, Indiana Citizens for Life, Inc. This article was written especially for *Points of View* in 1990.

## A. The People Have Created a Constitutional Democracy With Certain Matters Reserved to Democratic Control and Other Matters Constitutionally Protected

The United States Constitution begins with the words "We the People of the United States . . . do ordain and establish this Constitution for the United States of America."[4] Thus, our Republic is founded on the cornerstone of democratic self governance—all authority to govern is granted by the People.[5] The only legitimate form of government is that authorized by the People; the only rightful authority is that which the People have granted to the institutions of government.[6]

The People have chosen to authorize a regime governed by the rule of law, rather than rule by persons.[7] The supreme law of the land is the Constitution,[8] the charter by which the People conferred authority to govern and created the governing institutions. Thus, the only legitimate form and authority for goverance are found in the Constitution.

The constitutional grant of governing authority was not a general grant but one carefully measured, balanced, and limited. Three fundamental principles underlie the Constitution: (1) the People have removed certain matters from simple majority rule by making them constitutional rights but have retained other matters to be democratically controlled through their elected representatives;[9] (2) the People have distributed governmental powers among three branches of government, with each limited to its own sphere of power;[10] and (3) the People have established a federal system in which the power to regulate certain matters is granted to the national government and all remaining power is retained by the states or by the People themselves.[11]

Because these fundamental principles were violated by the Supreme Court in *Roe v. Wade*,[12] leading constitutional scholars condemned the decision. Law professors and dissenting Supreme Court Justices declared that the Court had seized power not granted to it in the Constitution, because (1) it had created new constitutional rights, which power only the People have,[13] (2) it had acted as a legislature rather than as a court,[14] and (3) it had trespassed into an area governed by the states for over two centuries.[15] The scholarly rejection of *Roe v. Wade* continues to the present.[16]

Although the Court's power grab in *Roe* was a seizure less obvious to the public than tanks in the street, it has nevertheless been rightly characterized as a "limited *coup d'état*."[17] The Court seized from the People a matter they had left to their own democratic governance by declaring a constitutional right to abortion without establishing any connection between the Constitution and a right to abortion. Richard Epstein attacked the Court's *Roe* decision thus, "*Roe* . . . is symptomatic of the analytical poverty possible in constitutional litigation."[18] He concluded: "[W]e must criticize both Mr. Justice Blackmun in *Roe v. Wade* . . . and the entire method of constitutional interpretation that allows the Supreme Court . . . both to 'define' and to 'balance' interests on the major social and political issues of our time."[19]

## B. To Determine Which Matters Are Constitutionally Removed from Democratic Control, the Supreme Court Has Developed Tests to Determine Fundamental Rights

The Court did not violate the Constitution in *Roe* simply because there is no *express* mention of abortion in the Constitution. There are matters which the Constitution does not *expressly* mention which the Supreme Court has legitimately found to be within some express constitutional protection. But where the Court employs such constitutional analysis, it must clearly demonstrate that the newly recognized constitutional right properly falls within the scope of an express right. This requires a careful examination and explanation of what the People intended when they ratified the particular constitutional provision in question. It was the *Roe* Court's failure to provide this logical connection between the Constitution and a claimed right to abortion which elicited scholarly outrage.

Under the Supreme Court's own tests, the Court had to find that the claimed right to abortion was a "fundamental" right in order to extend constitutional protection to it under the Fourteenth Amendment, the constitutional provision in which the Court claimed to have found a right to abortion.[20] The Fourteenth Amendment guarantees that no "State [shall] deprive any person of life, liberty, or property, without due process of law."[21] While the provision on its face seems to guarantee only proper legal proceedings before a state may impose capital punishment, imprisonment, or a fine, the Court has assumed the authority to examine activities asserted as constitutional rights to determine whether—in the Court's opinion—they fall within the concept of "liberty."[22] The notion that the Court may create new constitutional rights at will by reading them into the "liberty" clause of the Fourteenth Amendment could readily lead to a rejection of the foundational constitutional premise of the rule of law, not of persons. If a handful of Justices can place whatever matters they wish under the umbrella of the Constitution—totally bypassing the People and their elected representatives—then these Justices have constituted themselves as Platonic guardians,[23] thereby rejecting the rule of law for the rule of persons. What would prevent a majority of the Supreme Court from declaring that there is a constitutional right to practice, e.g., infanticide or polygamy (matters which the states have historically governed)?

This danger has caused many scholars to reject the sort of analysis which allows five Justices (a majority of the Court) to read new constitutional rights into the "liberty" clause.[24] It led the Court in earlier years to forcefully repudiate the sort of analysis the Court used in *Roe v. Wade*.[25] This danger has caused the current Court to establish more rigorous tests for what constitutes a constitutional right to prevent the Supreme Court from "roaming at large in the constitutional field."[26] These tests had been established at the time of *Roe,* but were ignored in that case.[27]

The Court has developed two tests for determining whether a new constitutional right should be recognized. The first test asks whether an asserted fundamental right is "implicit in the concept of ordered liberty."[28] The second test—a historical test—is whether the right asserted as "fundamental" is "so rooted in the traditions and conscience of our people as to be ranked as fundamental."[29] The historical test is the one now primarily relied upon by the Court.

## C. Applying the Proper Test for Determining Constitutional Rights Reveals That Abortion Is Not a Constitutional Right

In *Roe,* the Court should have determined whether or not there is a constitutional right to abortion by asking whether it has historically been treated as "implicit in the concept of ordered liberty" in this nation or whether it has been "deeply rooted [as a right] in this Nation's history and tradition."

The *Roe* opinion itself recounted how abortion had been regulated by the states by statutory law for over a century and before that it had been regulated by the judge-made common law inherited from England.[30] In fact, the period from 1860 to 1880—the Fourteenth Amendment was ratified in 1868[31]—saw "the most important burst of anti-abortion legislation in the nation's history."[32] Therefore, the framers of the Fourteenth Amendment and the People who ratified it clearly did not intend for the Amendment to protect the right to abortion, which was considered a crime at the time.

Now Chief Justice Rehnquist stated well the case against *Roe*'s right to abortion in his 1973 dissent to that decision:

> To reach its result, the Court necessarily has had to find within the scope of the Fourteenth Amendment a right that was apparently completely unknown to the drafters of the Amendment. As early as 1821, the first state law dealing directly with abortion was enacted by the Connecticut Legislature. By the time of the adoption of the Fourteenth Amendment in 1868, there were at least 36 laws enacted by state or territorial legislatures limiting abortion. While many states have amended or updated their laws, 21 of the laws on the books in 1968 remain in effect today. Indeed, the Texas statute struck down today was, as the majority notes, first enacted in 1857 and has remained substantially unchanged to the present time.
>
> There apparently was no question concerning the validity of this provision or of any of the other state statutes when the Fourteenth Amendment was adopted. The only conclusion possible from this history is that the drafters did not intend to have the Fourteenth Amendment withdraw from the states the power to legislate with respect to this matter.[33]

Thus, applying the Court's own tests, it is clear that there is no constitutional right to abortion. As a result, the Supreme Court has simply arbitrarily declared one by saying that the right of privacy—previously found by the Court in the "liberty" clause—"is broad enough to encompass a woman's decision whether or not to terminate her pregnancy."[34] In so doing, the Court brushed aside the restraints placed on it by the Constitution, seized power from the

People, and placed within the protections of the Constitution an abortion right that does not properly belong there.

One thing is clear from this nation's abortion debate: abortion advocates do not trust the People to decide how abortion should be regulated.[35] However, in rejecting the voice of the People, abortion partisans also reject the very foundation of our democratic Republic and seek to install an oligarchy—with the Court governing the nation—a system of government rejected by our Constitution.

## II. THE INTEREST IN PROTECTING INNOCENT HUMAN LIFE

Abortion rights advocates generally ignore one key fact about abortion: abortion requires the willful taking of innocent human life. Abortion involves not merely the issue of what a woman may do with her body. Rather, abortion also involves the question of what may the woman do with the body of another, the unborn child.

## A. The People Have an Interest in Protecting Preborn Human Life

The fact that human life begins at conception was well known at the time the Fourteenth Amendment was ratified in 1868. In fact it was precisely during the time when this Amendment was adopted that the medical profession was carrying the news of the discovery of cell biology and its implications into the legislatures of the states and territories. Prior to that time, science had followed the view of Aristotle that the unborn child became a human being (i.e., received a human soul) at some point after conception (40 days for males and 80–90 days for females).[36] This flawed scientific view became the basis for the "quickening" (greater legal protection was provided to the unborn from abortion after the mother felt movement in the womb than before) distinction in the common law received from England, which imposed lesser penalties for abortions performed prior to "quickening." With the scientific discovery of cell biology, however, the legislatures acted promptly to alter abortion laws to reflect the newly established scientific fact that individual human life begins at conception.

Victor Rosenblum summarized the history well:

> Only in the second quarter of the nineteenth century did biological research advance to the extent of understanding the actual mechanism of human reproduction and of what truly comprised the onset of gestational development. The nineteenth century saw a gradual but profoundly influential revolution in the scientific understanding of the beginning of individual mammalian life. Although sperm had been discovered in 1677, the mammalian egg was not

identified until 1827. The cell was first recognized as the structural unit of organisms in 1839, and the egg and sperm were recognized as cells in the next two decades. These developments were brought to the attention of the American state legislatures and public by those professionals most familiar with their unfolding import—physicians. It was the new research findings which persuaded doctors that the old "quickening" distinction embodied in the common and some statutory law was unscientific and indefensible.[37]

About 1857, the American Medical Association led the "physicians' crusade," a successful campaign to push the legal protection provided for the unborn by abortion laws from quickening to conception.[38]

What science discovered over a century before *Roe v. Wade* was true in 1973 (when *Roe* was decided) and still holds true today. For example, a recent textbook on human embryology declared:

> It is the penetration of the ovum by a spermatozoon and the resultant mingling of the nuclear material each brings to the union that constitutes the culmination of the process of *fertilization* and *marks the initiation of the life of a new individual.*[39]

However, abortion rights advocates attempt to obscure the scientific evidence that individual human life begins at conception by the claiming that conception is a "complex" process and by confusing contraception with abortion.[40]

The complexity of the process of conception does not change the fact that it marks the certain beginning of individual human life.[41] Moreover, the complex process of conception occurs in a very brief time at the beginning of pregnancy.[42]

Furthermore, the fact that some so-called "contraceptives" actually act after conception and would be more correctly termed "abortifacients" (substances or devices causing abortion, i.e., acting to abort a pregnancy already begun at conception) does nothing to blur the line at which individual human life begins. It only indicates that some so-called "contraceptives" have been mislabelled.[43] Such mislabelling misleads women, who have a right to know whether they are receiving a contraceptive or are having an abortion.

The "spin"[44] which abortion advocates place on the redefinition of "contraception" is deceptive in two respects. First, there is a clear distinction between devices and substances which act before conception and those which act after conception. This was admitted by Planned Parenthood itself (before it became involved in advocating, referring for, and performing abortions) in a 1963 pamphlet entitled *Plan Your Children:* "An abortion kills the life of a baby after it has begun . . . . Birth control merely postpones the beginning of life."[45]

Second, even if there were no "bright physiological line . . . between the moments before and after conception"[46] this does not mean there can be no constitutional line.[47] At *some point* early in pregnancy, scientific truth compels the conclusion that individual human life has begun. If the indistinction is the real problem, then abortion advocates should be joining prolife supporters in protecting unborn life from a time when there is certitude.[48] However, abortion partisans are not really interested in protecting unborn human life from the time when it may be certain that it exists. They are seeking to justify absolute, on-demand abortion throughout pregnancy.

## B. Abortion Rights Advocates Envision an Abortion-on-Demand Regime Unsupported by the People

Abortion rights proponents often argue that our democratic Republic must sanction abortion on demand lest women resort to dangerous "back-alley" abortions. The claims of abortion advocates that thousands of women died each year when abortion was illegal are groundless fabrications created for polemical purposes.[49] In reality, the Surgeon General of the United States has estimated that only a handful of deaths occurred each year in the United States due to illegal abortions.[50] Even since *Roe,* there are still maternal deaths from legal abortions.[51] As tragic as the death of any person is, it must be acknowledged that women who obtain illegal abortions do so by choice and most women will choose to abide by the law. In contrast, preborn human beings are destroyed—without having a choice—at the rate of about 1.5 million per year in the United States alone.[52]

Abortion supporters also resort to the practice of personally attacking prolifers and making false charges about them.[53] A founding member of what is now called the National Abortion Rights Action League (NARAL) chronicles how prolifers were purposely portrayed as Catholics whenever possible, in an attempt to appeal to latent (and sometimes overt) anti-Catholic sentiment in certain communities.[54] It is also routinely claimed that opposition to abortion is really an attempt to "keep women in their place"[55]—to subjugate them—as if requiring fathers to support their children subjugates them. And prolifers are depicted as forcing what are merely their religious views upon society,[56] despite the fact that the United States Supreme Court has held that opposition to abortion "is as much a reflection of 'traditionalist' values towards abortion, as it is an embodiment of the views of any particular religion."[57] Those attempting so to "poison the well," by attacking prolife supporters with untruthful allegations, ignore the fact that polls consistently show that abortion opinion is rather evenly divided in our country within all major demographic groups. For example, women are roughly equally divided on the subject, as are whites, non-whites, Republicans and Democrats.[58] Abortion advocates also ignore the fact that most prolifers simply are opposed to the taking of what they consider (and science demonstrates) to be innocent human life.

Of even greater risk than the risk to a few women who might choose to obtain illegal abortions is the effect of abortion on demand—for any or no reason—on society. Abortion cheapens the value of human life, promotes the idea that it is permissible to solve one's problems at the expense of another, even to the taking of the other's life, legitimizes violence (which abortion is against the unborn) as an appropriate solution for problems, and exposes a whole class of human beings (those preborn) to discrimination on the basis of their age or place of residence (or sometimes their race, gender, or disability).

The regime which abortion-on-demand advocates envision for our society is a radical one. Their ideal society is one where abortions may be obtained for any reason, including simply because the child is the wrong sex; where a husband need not be given any consideration in (or even notice of) an abortion decision involving a child which he fathered; where fathers are shut out even when the child to be aborted might be the only one a man could ever have; where parents could remain ignorant of their daughter's abortion, even when she is persuaded to abort by counselors at an abortion mill whose practitioners care only about financial gain, practice their trade dangerously, and never bother to follow up with their patients; where abortion may be used as a means of birth control; where abortionists do not offer neutral, scientific information about fetal development (and about resources for choosing alternatives to abortion) to women considering abortion; where women are not given adequate time to consider whether they really want an abortion; where abortion is available right up to the time of birth; and where our taxes are used to pay for abortion on demand.[59]

The American People reject such a regime. In fact, polls show that an overwhelming majority would ban well over 90% of all abortions that are performed.[60] For example a *Boston Globe* national poll recently revealed that:

> Most Americans would ban the vast majority of abortions performed in this country . . . .

> While 78 pecent of the nation would keep abortion legal in limited circumstances, according to the poll, those circumstances account for a tiny percentage of the reasons cited by women having abortions.

> When pregnancy results from rape or incest, when the mother's physical health is endangered and when there is likely to be a genetic deformity in the fetus, those queried strongly approve of legal abortion.

> But when pregnancy poses financial or emotional strain, or when the woman is alone or a teen-ager—the reasons given by most women seeking abortions—an overwhelming majority of Americans believes abortion should be illegal, the poll shows.[61]

Yet *Family Planning Perspectives,* a publication of the Alan Guttmacher Institute, which is a research arm of the Planned Parenthood Federation, reveals that these are precisely the reasons why over 90% of abortions are performed.[62]

Thus, it is little wonder that the Supreme Court's effort to settle the abortion question with its decision in *Roe v. Wade* has utterly failed. That there is not an even greater groundswell of public opposition to abortion must be attributed to the fact that many Americans are not aware that *Roe* requires virtual abortion on demand for the full nine months of pregnancy.[63] Many people still believe that abortion is only available in the earliest weeks of pregnancy and that abortions are usually obtained for grave reasons, such as rape and incest, which abortion rights advocates always talk about in abortion debates. Of course, such ''hard'' cases make up only a tiny fraction of all abortions, and many state abortion laws, even before *Roe*, allowed abortions for such grave reasons. It is clear, therefore, that the People reject the radical abortion-on-demand regime promoted by abortion rights advocates.

## III. CONCLUSION: STATES CONSTITUTIONALLY MAY AND MORALLY SHOULD LIMIT ABORTION ON DEMAND

One of the principles underlying our liberal democratic Republic is that we as a People choose to give the maximum freedom possible to members of our society. John Stuart Mill's essay *On Liberty*,[64] a ubiquitous source on the subject, is often cited for the principle that people ought to be granted maximum liberty—almost to the degree of license. Yet, Mill himself set limits on liberty relevant to the abortion debate. Mill wrote his essay *On Liberty* to assert "one very simple principle," namely, "[t]hat the only purpose for which power can be rightfully exercised over any member of a civilized community, against his will, is to prevent harm to others."[65] Thus, under Mill's principles, abortion should go unrestricted only if it does no harm to another. But that, of course, is precisely the core of the abortion debate. If a fetus is not really an individual human being until he or she is born, then the moral issue is reduced to what duty is owed to potential life (which is still a significant moral issue). If however, a fetus is an individual human being from the moment of conception (or at least some time shortly thereafter), then the unborn are entitled to legal protection. Ironically, the United States Supreme Court neglected this key determination—when human life begins—in its *Roe* decision.[66]

Science, of course, has provided the answer to us for well over a hundred years. Indeed, modern science and technologial advances have impressed upon us more fully the humanity and individuality of each unborn person. As Dr. Liley has said:

> Another fallacy that modern obstetrics discards is the idea that the pregnant woman can be treated as a patient alone. No problem in fetal health or disease can any longer be considered in isolation. At the very least two people are involved, the mother and her child.[67]

In fact, since *Roe*, the technology for improving fetal therapy is advancing exponentially.[68] In sum, modern science has shown us that:

> The fetus as patient is becoming more of a reality each year. New medical therapies and surgical technology increasingly offer parents a new choice when a fetus has a particular disorder. Recently, the only choices were abortion, early delivery, vaginal versus a caesarean delivery, or no intervention. We are now able to offer medical and/or surgical intervention as a viable alternative to a number of infants. With advancing technologies, it is clearly evident that many new and exciting therapies lie just ahead for the fetus.[69]

Because all civilized moral codes limit the liberty of individuals where the exercise of liberty would result in the taking of innocent human life, arguments that abortion is necessary to prevent the subjugation of women must also be rejected.[70] It cannot logically be considered the subjugation of anyone to prevent him or her from taking innocent human life; otherwise, society could not prevent infanticide, homicide, or involuntary euthanasia. No civilized society could exist if the unjustified killing of one citizen by another could not be prosecuted.

Nor do abortion restrictions deny women equality by denying them the same freedom which men have. Men do not have the right to kill their children, nor may they force women to do so. Thus, abortion rights advocates are really arguing for a right that men don't have, and, indeed, no one should have—the right to take innocent human life.

Society has recognized that in some situations men and women should be treated differently, because they are biologically different and are, therefore, not similarly situated for constitutional purposes. For example, the Supreme Court decided in 1981 that a statute that permitted only men to be drafted was not unconstitutional because "[m]en and women . . . are simply not similarly situated for purposes of a draft or registration for a draft."[71] The same principle, however, made constitutional a Navy policy which allowed women a longer period of time for promotion prior to mandatory discharge than was allowed for men.[72] The Supreme Court in this case found that "the different treatment of men and women naval officers . . . reflects, not archaic and overbroad generalizations, but, instead, the demonstrable fact that male and female line officers . . . are not similarly situated."[73] Because men and women are not similarly situated—by the dictates of nature rather than by society or the law—with respect to pregnancy, it is neither a denial of equality to women nor the subjugation of women to provide legal protection for unborn human beings.[74]

It is essential to a civilized society to limit liberties where reasonably necessary to protect others. Thus, government has required involuntary vaccination to prevent a plague from decimating the community,[75] military conscription to prevent annihilation of the populace by enemies,[76] and the imposition of child support—for 18 years—upon fathers unwilling to support their children.[77] These and other limits on freedom are not the subjugation of citizens, but are the essence of life in a community.

In sum, the states constitutionally may and morally should limit abortion on demand.

## NOTES

1  410 U.S. 113 (1973).

2  *Id*. at 153.

3  See *infra,* notes 13–19 and accompanying text.

4  U.S. Const., preamble.

5  In the landmark case of *Marbury v. Madison,* 1 Cranch 137, 176 (1803), the United States Supreme Court explained, "That the people have an original right to estab-

lish, for their future government, such principles, as, in their own opinion, shall most conduce to their own happiness is the basis on which the whole American fabric has been erected. See also The Declaration of Independence, para. 2 (U.S. 1776); *The Federalist,* No. 49 (J. Madison).

6 *Marbury,* 1 Cranch at 176 ("The original and supreme will [of the People] organizes the government, and assigns to different departments their respective powers. It may either stop here, or establish certain limits not to be transcended by those departments. The government of the United States is of the latter description.").

7 See, e.g., *id.* at 163 ("The government of the United States has been emphatically termed a government of laws, and not of men."); *Akron v. Akron Center for Reproductive Health,* 462 U.S. 416, 419–20 (1983) (We are a "society governed by the rule of law.").

8 *Marbury,* 1 Cranch at 177 ("Certainly all those who have framed written constitutions contemplate them as forming the fundamental and paramount law of the nation. . . ."); *id.* at 179 ("[T]he constitution of the United States confirms and strengthens the principle, supposed to be essential to all written constitutions, that a law repugnant to the constitution is void; and that courts, as well as other departments, are bound by that instrument.").

9 The Constitution enumerates certain rights; the creation of additional constitutionally protected rights is through amending the Constitution, which depends upon establishing public support for such a right by a supermajority of the People acting through their elected representatives. U.S. Const., art. V. *Cf.* Bork, "Neutral Principles and Some First Amendment Problems," 47 *Ind. L.J.* 1, 3 (1971).

10 U.S. Const., art. I, § 1, art. II, § 1, art. III, § 1.

11 U.S. Const., amend. IX ("The enumeration in the Constitution, of certain rights, shall not be construed to deny or disparage others retained by the people."), amend. X ("The powers not delegated to the United States by the Constitution, nor prohibited by it to the States, are reserved to the States respectively, or to the people.").

12 410 U.S. 113.

13 Ely, "The Wages of Crying Wolf: A Comment on *Roe v. Wade,*" 82 *Yale L.J.* 920, 947 (1973) (*Roe* was "a very bad decision. Not because it [would] perceptibly weaken the Court . . . and not because it conflict[ed] with [his] idea of progress. . . . It [was] bad because it [was] bad constitutional law, or rather because it [was] *not* constitutional law and [gave] almost no sense of an obligation to try to be.") (emphasis in the original). *Doe v. Bolton,* 410 U.S. 179, 222 (1973) (White, J., dissenting in this companion case to *Roe*) (The Court's action is "an exercise of raw judicial power. . . . This issue, for the most part, should be left with the people and to the political processes the people have devised to govern their affairs.").

14 The *Michigan Law Review,* in an edition devoted to abortion jurisprudence, contained two passages which summarize the scholarly critiques well. In the first, Richard Morgan wrote:

Rarely does the Supreme Court invite critical outrage as it did in *Roe* by offering so little explanation for a decision that requires so much. The stark inadequacy of the Court's attempt to justify its conclusions . . . suggests to some scholars that the Court, finding no justification at all in the Constitution, unabashedly usurped the legislative function.

Morgan, "*Roe v.Wade* and the Lesson of the Pre-*Roe* Case Law," 77 *Mich. L. Rev.* 1724, 1724 (1979). The editors of the journal concluded from their survey of the literature on *Roe*, "[T]he consensus among legal academics seems to be that, whatever one thinks of the holding, the opinion is unsatisfying." "Editor's Preface," 77 *Mich. L. Rev.* (no number) (1979).

15  *Roe*, 400 U.S. at 174–77 (Rehnquist, J., dissenting).

16  See, e.g., Wardle, " 'Time Enough': *Webster v. Reproductive Health Services* and the Prudent Pace of Justice," 41 *Fla. L. Rev.* 881, 927–49 (1989); Bopp & Coleson, "The Right to Abortion: Anomalous, Absolute, and Ripe for Reversal," 3 *B.Y.U. J. Pub. L.* 181, 185–92 (1989) (cataloging critiques of *Roe* in yet another critique of *Roe*).

17  Bork, *supra* note 9, at 6.

18  Epstein, "Substantive Due Process by Any Other Name: The Abortion Cases," 1973 *Sup. Ct. Rv.* 159, 184.

19  *Id.* at 185.

20  The Court acknowledged this duty in *Roe* itself, but failed to apply the usual tests for determining what rights are rightfully deemed "fundamental." *Roe*, 410 U.S. at 152.

21  U.S. Const., amend. XIV, § 1, cl. 3.

22  *Roe v. Wade*, 410 U.S. 113, revived this sort of "substantive due process" analysis in recent years.

23  The Greek philosopher Plato advocated rule by a class of philosopher-guardians as the ideal form of government. A. Bloom, *The Republic of Plato*, 376c, lines 4–5, 412b–427d (1968).

24  See, e.g., Ely, *supra* note 13; Bork, *supra* note 9.

25  In repudiating an earlier line of "substantive due process" (i.e., finding new rights in the "liberty" clause of the Fourteenth Amendment) cases symbolized by *Lochner v. New York*, 198 U.S. 45 (1905), the Supreme Court declared that the doctrine "that due process authorizes courts to hold laws unconstitutional when they believe the legislature has acted unwisely, has been discarded." *Ferguson v. Skrupa*, 372 U.S. 726, 730 (1963). The Court concluded in *Ferguson*, "We have returned to the original constitutional proposition that courts do not substitute their social and economic beliefs for the judgment of legislative bodies, who are elected to pass laws." *Id.*

26  *Griswold v. Connecticut*, 381 U.S. 479, 502 (1965) (Harlan, J., concurring.)

27  *Cf. Duncan v. Louisiana*, 391 U.S. 145, 149–50 n.14 (1968), with *Roe v. Wade*, 410 U.S. at 152, and *Moore v. City of East Cleveland*, 431 U.S. 494, 503–04 n.12 (1977). See also Ely, *supra* note 13, at 931 n.79 (The *Palko* test was of "questionable contemporary vitality" when *Roe* was decided).

28  *Roe*, 410 U.S. at 152 (quoting *Palko v. Connecticut*, 302 U.S. 319, 325 (1937)) (quotation marks omitted).

29  *Palko*, 302 U.S., at 325 (quoting *Snyder v. Massachusetts*, 291 U.S. 97, 105 (1934)) (quotation marks omitted).

30  *Roe*, 410 U.S. at 139.

31  *Black's Law Dictionary*, 1500 (5th ed. 1979).

32  J. Mohr, *Abortion in America: The Origins and Evolution of National Policy 1800–1900*, 200 (1978). These laws were clearly aimed at protecting preborn human beings and not just maternal health, *id.* at 35–36, so that medical improvements bringing more maternal safety to abortions do not undercut the foundations of these laws, as *Roe* alleged. *Roe*, 410 U.S. at 151–52.

33 *Roe,* 410 U.S. at 174–77 (Rehnquist, J., dissenting) (citations and quotation marks omitted).

34 *Id.* at 153.

35 *Cf.* Estrich & Sullivan, "Abortion Politics: Writing for an Audience of One," 138 *U. Pa. L. Rev.* 119, 150–55 (1989), with *Webster v. Reproductive Health Services,* 109 S.Ct. 3040, 3058 (1989) (plurality opinion). In *Webster,* the plurality opinion declared:

> The goal of constitutional adjudication is to hold true the balance between that which the Constitution puts beyond the reach of the democratic process and that which it does not. We think we have done that today. The dissent's suggestion that legislative bodies, in a Nation where more than half of our population is women, will treat our decision today as an invitation to enact abortion regulation reminiscent of the dark ages not only misreads our views but does scant justice to those who serve in such bodies and the people who elect them.

*Id.* (citation omitted).

36 *Roe,* 410 U.S. at 133 n.22.

37 *The Human Life Bill: Hearings on S. 158 Before the Subcomm. on Separation of Powers of the Senate Comm. on the Judiciary,* 97th Cong., 1st Sess. 474 (statement of Victor Rosenblum). See also Dellapenna, "The History of Abortion: Technology, Morality, and Law," 40 *U. Pitt. L. Rev.* 359, 402–04 (1979).

38 J. Mohr, *supra* note 32, at 147–70. This nineteenth-century legislation was designed to protect the unborn as stated explicitly by eleven state court decisions interpreting these statutes and implicitly by nine others. Gorby, "The 'Right' to an Abortion, the Scope of Fourteenth Amendment 'Personhood,' and the Supreme Court's Birth Requirement," 1979 *S. Ill. U.L.J.* 1, 16–17. Twenty-six of the thirty-six states had laws against abortion as early as 1865, the end of the Civil War, as did six of the ten territories. Dellapenna, *supra* note 37, at 429.

39 B. Patten, *Human Embryology,* 43 (3rd ed. 1969) (emphasis added). See also L. Arey, *Developmental Anatomy,* 55 (7th ed. 1974); W. Hamilton & H. Mossman, *Human Embryology,* 1, 14 (4th ed. 1972); K. Moore, *The Developing Human: Clinically Oriented Embryology,* 1, 12, 24 (2nd ed. 1977); *Human Reproduction, Conception and Contraception,* 461 (Hafez ed., 2nd ed. 1980); J. Greenhill & E. Friedman, *Biological Principles and Modern Practice of Obstetrics,* 17, 23 (1974); D. Reid, K. Ryan & K. Benirschke, *Principles and Management of Human Reproduction,* 176 (1972).

40 See, e.g., Estrich & Sullivan, *supra* note 35, at 128–29. While a complete discussion of cell biology, genetics and fetology is beyond the scope of this brief writing, the standard reference works cited by Estrich & Sullivan verify the fact that individual human life begins at conception.

41 *Supra,* note 39.

42 *Id.*

43 By its etymology (*contra* + *conception,* i.e., against conception) and traditional and common usage, the term *"contraception"* properly refers to "[t]he prevention of conception or impregnation," *Dorland's Illustrated Medical Dictionary,* 339 (24th ed. 1965) or a "deliberate prevention of conception or impregnation," *Webster's Ninth New Collegiate Dictionary,* 284 (1985).

44 Estrich & Sullivan, *supra* note 35, at 1.

45 Planned Parenthood International, *Plan Your Children* (1963).

46 Estrich & Sullivan, *supra* note 35, at 129.

47 At oral arguments in *Webster v. Reproductive Health Services,* 109 S. Ct. 3040 (1989), Justice Antonin Scalia could see a distinction between contraception and abortion, remarking, "I don't see why a court that can draw that line [between the first, second, and third trimesters of pregnancy] cannot separate abortion from birth control quite readily."

48 For example, the West German Constitutional Court in 1975 set aside a federal abortion statute which was too permissive, for it "did not sufficiently protect unborn life." M. Glendon, *Abortion and Divorce in Western Law,* 33 (1987). The West German court began with the presumption that "at least after the fourteenth day, developing human life is at stake." *Id.* at 34.

49 B. Nathanson, *Aborting America,* 193 (1979). Nathanson, a former abortionist and early, organizing member of the National Association for the Repeal of Abortion Laws (NARAL, now known as the National Abortion Rights Action League), says:

> In N.A.R.A.L. . . . it was always "5,000 to 10,000 deaths a year [from illegal abortion]." I confess that I knew the figures were totally false. . . . In 1967, with moderate A.L.I.-type laws in three states, the federal government listed only 160 deaths from illegal abortion. In the last year before the [*Roe*] era began, 1972, the total was only 39 deaths. Christopher Tietze estimated 1,000 maternal deaths as the outside possibility in an average year before legalization; the actual total was probably closer to 500.

*Id.* at 193. Nathanson adds that even this limited "carnage" argument must now be dismissed "because technology has eliminated it." *Id.* at 194 (referring to the fact that even abortions made illegal by more restrictive abortion laws will generally be performed with modern techniques providing greater safety, and antibiotics now resolve most complications).

50 U.S. Dept. of Health and Human Services, *Centers for Disease Control Abortion Surveillance,* 61 (annual summary 1978, issued Nov. 1980) (finding that there were 39 maternal deaths due to illegal abortion in 1972, the last year before *Roe*).

51 Deaths from legally induced abortions were as follows: 1972 = 24, 1973 = 26, 1974 = 26, 1975 = 31, 1976 = 11, 1977 = 17, 1978 = 11. *Id.* During the same period, deaths from illegal abortions continued as follows: 1972 = 39, 1973 = 19, 1974 = 6, 1975 = 4, 1976 = 2, 1977 = 4, 1978 = 7. *Id.*

52 See, e.g., Henshaw, Forrest & Van Vort, "Abortion Services in the United States, 1984 and 1985," 19 *Fam. Plan. Persps.* 64, table 1 (1987) (at the rate of roughly 1.5 million abortions per year for the 18 years from 1973 to 1990, there have been about 27 million abortions in the U.S.A.).

53 Estrich & Sullivan, *supra* note 35, at 152–54.

54 B. Nathanson, *The Abortion Papers: Inside the Abortion Mentality,* 177–209 (1983).

55 Estrich & Sullivan, *supra* note 35, at 152–54.

56 See, e.g., *id.* at 153 n.132.

57 *Harris v. McRae,* 448 U.S. 297, 319 (1980).

58 See generally R. Adamek, *Abortion and Public Opinion in the United States* (1989).

59 These are some of the radical positions urged by abortion rights partisans in cases such as *Roe v. Wade,* 410 U.S. 113, *Planned Parenthood of Central Missouri v. Danforth,* 428 U.S. 52 (1976), and *Thornburgh v. American College of Obstetricians and Gynecologists,* 476 U.S. 747 (1986).

60 "Most in US favor ban on majority of abortions, poll finds," *Boston Globe,* March 31, 1989, at 1, col. 2–4.

61 *Id.*

62 Torres & Forrest, "Why Do Women Have Abortions?" 20 *Fam. Plan. Persps.,* 169 (1988). Table 1 of this article reveals the following reasons and percentages of women giving their most important reason for choosing abortion: 16% said they were concerned about how having a baby would change their life; 21% said they couldn't afford a baby now; 12% said they had problems with a relationship and wanted to avoid single parenthood; 21% said they were unready for responsibility; 1% said they didn't want others to know they had sex or were pregnant; 11% said they were not mature enough or were too young to have a child; 8% said they had all the children they wanted or had all grown-up children; 1% said their husband, wanted them to have an abortion; 3% said the fetus had possible health problems; 3% said they had a health problem; less than .5% said their parents wanted them to have an abortion; 1% said they were a victim of rape or incest; and 3% gave another, unspecified reason. (Figures total more than 100% due to rounding off of numbers.) It is significant to note, also, that 39% of all abortions are repeat abortions. Henshaw, "Characteristics of U.S. Women Having Abortions, 1982–1983," 19 *Fam. Plan. Persps.* 1, 6 (1987).

63 *Roe* held that a state may prohibit abortion after fetal viability, but that it may not do so where the mother's "life or health" would be at risk. 410 U.S. at 165. In the companion case to *Roe, Doe v. Bolton,* the Supreme Court construed "health" in an extremely broad fashion to include "all factors—physical, emotional, psychological, familial, and the woman's age—relevant to the well-being of the patient." 410 U.S. 179, 195 (1973). The breadth of these factors makes a "health" reason for an abortion extremely easy to establish, so that we have virtual abortion on demand for all nine months of pregnancy in America. Moreover, there are physicians who declare that if a woman simply seeks an abortion she *ipso facto* has a "health" reason and the abortion may be performed. *McRae v. Califano,* No. 76-C-1804 (E.D.N.Y. Transcript, August 3, 1977, pp. 99–101) (Testimony of Dr. Jane Hodgson) (Dr. Hodgson testified that she felt that there was a medical indication to abort a pregnancy if it "is not wanted by the patient.").

64 J. Mill, *On Liberty* (Atlantic Monthly Press edition 1921).

65 *Id.* at 13. It should be noted that Mill's contention that society should never use its power to protect the individual from the actions of himself or herself is hotly disputed. See, e.g., J. Stephen, *Liberty, Equality, Fraternity* (R. White ed. 1967) (the 1873 classic response to Mill); P. Devlin, *The Enforcement of Morals* (1974).

66 *Roe,* 410 U.S. at 159 ("We need not resolve the difficult question of when life begins.").

67 H. Liley, *Modern Motherhood* 207 (1969).

68 "Technology for Improving Fetal Therapy Advancing Exponentially," *Ob. Gyn. News,* Aug. 1–14, 1987, at 31.

69 P. Williams, "Medical and Surgical Treatment for the Unborn Child," in *Human Life and Health Care Ethics,* 77 (J. Bopp ed. 1985).

70 Estrich & Sullivan, *supra* note 35, at 152–54. In legal terms, this argument is an equal protection one. See *id.* at 124 n.10. However, equal protection of the laws is only constitutionally guaranteed to those who are equally situated, and the Supreme Court has held that treating pregnancy differently from other matters does not

constitute gender-based discrimination. *Geduldig v. Aiello,* 417 U.S. 484, 496–97 n.20 (1974). For a further discussion of this point, see Bopp, "Will There Be a Constitutional Right to Abortion After the Reconsideration of *Roe v. Wade?"* 15 J. *Contemp. L.* 131, 136–41 (1989). See also Smolin, "Why Abortion Rights Are Not Justified by Reference to Gender Equality: A Response to Professor Tribe," 23 *John Marshall L. Rev.* 621 (1990).

71 *Rostker v. Goldberg,* 453 U.S. 57 (1981).
72 *Schlesinger v. Ballard,* 419 U.S. 498 (1975).
73 *Id.* at 508.
74 Bopp, "Is Equal Protection a Shelter for the Right to Abortion?" in *Abortion, Medicine and the Law* (4th ed. 1991) (in press).
75 *Jacobson v. Massachusetts,* 197 U.S. 11 (1905).
76 The Selective Service Draft Law Cases, 245 U.S. 366 (1918).
77 See, e.g., *Sistare v. Sistare,* 218 U.S. 1 (1910). All states have recognized this obligation by passage of the Uniform Reciprocal Enforcement of Support Act. See Fox, "The Uniform Reciprocal Enforcement of Support Act," 12 *Fam. L.Q.* 113, 113–14 (1978).